THE BOOK IN AMERICA

The Book
IN AMERICA

*A History
of the Making and Selling
of Books
in the United States*

by

Hellmut Lehmann-Haupt

In Collaboration with Lawrence C. Wroth
and Rollo G. Silver

SECOND EDITION

R. R. Bowker Company: New York

1951

COMPOSED, PRINTED AND BOUND IN THE UNITED STATES OF AMERICA
BY KINGSPORT PRESS, INC., KINGSPORT, TENNESSEE

*This book is dedicated
to all those who
in the two decades
since the work was first begun
have helped to make it
more complete, more authentic, and
more truly representative
of what authors and editor
would like it to be.*

FOREWORD

This book, a history of the book in America, has by now its own little history. Some twenty years ago an encyclopedic dictionary of all matters concerning the book was being prepared by the Hiersemann publishing house of Leipzig. When it came to collecting material on American developments the editors of the *Lexikon des gesamten Buchwesens* realized that there was very little reliable information available in German. They turned to American sources, and were surprised to see how many important questions remained unanswered. There was, to be sure, a voluminous and many-sided literature, but it was uneven in quality and somewhat arbitrary in its emphasis of certain periods and subjects and in the omission of others. The Colonial period, for instance, had been much more carefully studied and recorded than the nineteenth and twentieth centuries; then again, the developments of the early twentieth century had been more eloquently described than the whole of the last century. No comprehensive accounts of printing and the allied crafts and industries, of bookselling and publishing, of book collecting and the growth of libraries could be found, which showed their continuous development from colonial times to the present day.

In 1932 the Leipzig publishing house asked if I would undertake the responsibility for a volume which would fill this gap—at least as far as the needs of European readers were concerned. This I agreed to, because the opportunity to contribute a study in answer to an actual need was tempting. Also, I welcomed the chance to render an account of experiences in the world of American books during my first years in this country. Very soon it became apparent that the responsibility was more than a single person could shoulder. Obviously, the assistance of experienced American authorities was called for. That Ruth Shepard Granniss and Lawrence C. Wroth agreed to collaborate was the best kind of encouragement which the arduous undertaking could receive. Their whole-hearted acceptance of the plan and their generous contribution of time, energy and of a great deal of patience made the book possible.

It should be explained that for the German edition the contributions of my collaborators, which were written in English, had to be translated, while my own section was written in German. For the first edition in English, which appeared in 1939, we went back to the English texts of Miss Granniss and Mr. Wroth which, somewhat revised and amplified, thus appeared for the first time in their original form, while my own section was translated and revised from the original German text.

The volume first appeared in Leipzig in the spring of 1937 and it can be said that it was well received. It was carefully and sympathetically reviewed in the literary and bibliographical magazines of eight countries. Some American reviews, it is true, expressed a measure of surprise that such a volume should have first appeared abroad. To this I would say that at least as far as my own contribution, as editor and co-author, is concerned, I would never have dared at that time to sit down and write about American books for an American audience. To bring forth a somewhat elementary account, taking nothing for granted and building up from the simple foundations in the manner of a primer for the use of foreign readers, was a different matter, particularly when aided by outstanding authorities of American booklore. Somewhat surprisingly, it appeared that the very thing that had made this book possible and had made it suitable for readers abroad—namely, its explanatory character and the condensation of a great mass of information into a comparatively simple formula—made it also desirable for American readers. The reception of the first American edition of 1939 was also a favorable one and the place which the book has made for itself more than justified the effort spent in its preparation.

The present edition faced a number of difficult problems, which we have tried our best to solve. We can only hope that the solutions decided upon will be considered adequate by most of the readers of the present volume. One of the most startling developments which has taken place in the last ten years has been the rapid and extensive growth of serious research in nineteenth century American bibliography and book trade history. It is no longer true that this period is a neglected field. The American Imprints Survey, initiated by the late Douglas Mc-Murtrie, the work of the Bibliographical Society of America, especially through its committee on the study of nineteenth century publishing, various projects initiated by the Bibliographical Society of the University of Virginia, and, last but not least, the efforts of a number of enterprising and well-trained specialists, have contributed much towards a more intimate knowledge of the American book in the last century.

Authors and editor of the earlier editions of this book used bold strokes in an attempt to draw essential, elementary outlines for an originally uninformed audience. This meant the constant necessity of condensation and selection. For the sake of unity of style and editorial consistency we have retained these methods in the present edition, even though the large amount of fresh information and of new projects has made this more difficult to achieve. For this reason it was fortunate that Rollo Silver, one of the leading authorities in nineteenth century American bibliography, agreed to assist Mr. Wroth in the revision of the chapters covering the years of the young republic up to the Civil War, which form Part II of the present edition. We are grateful to the trustees of the Peabody Institute Library in Baltimore, Maryland, for having made it possible for Mr. Silver to devote time to this project.

The problem of space was a serious one. Not only did we have to find room for the necessary extensive revision and expansion of the text of the earlier editions, but also for the many new developments of the last decade. In order to prevent the growth of the volume to a size which would make the price prohibitive, especially for students, publisher and editor regretfully decided to omit Miss Granniss' section on the history of book collecting and the growth of libraries from the present edition. These chapters had formed Part III in the earlier editions. For the present volume the chapters on the history of printing, publishing and bookselling since the Civil War, previously designated as Part II, have become Part III. The chapter on book auctions, originally part of Miss Granniss' contribution, is included in Part III of this edition.

The number of men and women who have rendered valuable assistance to editor and authors of this volume in the nearly twenty years since the work began is a very large one. A printed list of the names would be so long as to be unreadable and it would thus defeat its own purpose. We have therefore decided instead to dedicate this book to the innumerable experts and students, old and young, who have generously contributed time and effort to the preparation of this volume.

H. L-H.

February 11, 1951

TABLE OF CONTENTS

PART I

BOOK PRODUCTION AND DISTRIBUTION FROM THE BEGINNING TO THE AMERICAN REVOLUTION

By Lawrence C. Wroth

PART II

BOOK PRODUCTION AND DISTRIBUTION FROM THE AMERICAN REVOLUTION TO THE WAR BETWEEN THE STATES

By Lawrence C. Wroth and Rollo G. Silver

PART III

BOOK PRODUCTION AND DISTRIBUTION FROM 1860 TO THE PRESENT DAY

By Hellmut Lehmann-Haupt

APPENDIX

THE BOOK IN AMERICA

PART I

BOOK PRODUCTION AND DISTRIBUTION FROM THE
BEGINNING TO THE AMERICAN REVOLUTION

by

Lawrence C. Wroth

INTRODUCTION

In MOST ESSENTIALS of political constitution and governmental administration the English colonies of North America differed fundamentally from the establishments of France and Spain which lay contiguous to them. Whether proprietary colonies, philanthropic enterprises, or the establishments of chartered companies, each of the English colonies was a separate state, governed by an elective assembly sitting in its provincial capital. These representative bodies possessed the privilege of initiating local legislation, and their enactments were subject, in theory, to no external restraint save the veto of king or proprietor. The French and Spanish colonies, on the other hand, were governed in local affairs by royal officers advised by appointed councils, while in matters of larger policy they were administered directly by edict of their kings from Fontainebleau or Versailles, from Seville or Madrid. The French and Spanish establishments nearest the English settlements—those in Canada, Louisiana, and Florida—displayed the characteristics of semi-military colonies of the Roman pattern, garrisons set down at strategic points of empire and nourished as a matter of course by the parent countries. The English system of self-governing, economically independent colonies, neither military outpost nor trading station, formed a congeries of individual states, weak and unwieldy in federation, but each self-contained and proudly conscious of its entity. It is this picture of the English colonies that the reader of the ensuing pages must keep before him, visualizing always a group of small, mutually independent states held together by common material interests, a common culture, and a common loyalty to the crown of England. In the knowledge of these facts and their implications lies the beginning of understanding so far as concerns the cultural history of the English in colonial America.

The establishment of the English colonies was a process conducted by many men urged by many motives throughout a century and a quarter of effort, a period of time extending from the settlement of Jamestown in 1607 to the foundation of Oglethorpe's philanthropic colony of Georgia in 1733. This slow formation of a group of colonies dependent for livelihood upon agriculture, commerce, fisheries, and hunting was accompanied by a persistent opposition from other colonizing nations of Europe. On the Delaware and Hudson Rivers, the Dutch and Swedes for a short time disputed with English settlers the right to the soil; along the shores of the Great Lakes and the St. Lawrence, Lake Champlain and Lake George, the presence of the French set a barrier to northward expansion and actively menaced English security; to the southward, the Spanish military colony in Florida, which was an outpost of the strong Mexican and Cuban states, and the French in West Florida and Louisiana continuously threatened South Carolina and Georgia throughout their formative years; while to the westward, from Canada to Florida, the Indian, of his own volition or encouraged by France or Spain, forced the English American into frequent offense and defense.

However distressing may have been the conditions of environment just described, they yet were rich in factors of ultimate benefit to the English in America. They compelled the colonist of whatever group, section, or creed to remain constantly alert to the dangerous circumstances of his position. They bred in the individual and in the communities a habit of self-awareness, awakening the dissimilar and widely extended groups to the recognition of homogeneity in interests, and intensifying in them a sense of geographical unity and of racial identity that became apparent in their actions long years before their separation from the mother country. One result of the self-realization thus enforced upon the English American, was the development in him of the habit of political thinking, of speculation as to the place of citizen and state in the economy of the larger world. Though isolated geographically from European affairs, he lived spiritually in the thick of them, aware of himself as an important piece in the game of world diplomacy and politics. When, therefore, we observe him developing a press and an intellectual habit more active than seemed essential to the needs of his pioneer life, we shall find in the external influences just spoken of a cogent explanation of the phenomenon.

Other influences than those of European thought and politics were effective in bringing into being an active and important press. Questions of religious doctrine and church polity, for example, compelled, of their very nature, public discussion, and demanded dissemination of their premises. The unremitting struggle in several of the colonies between the liberal lower houses of assembly and the conservative governors and councils required the services of the press for statement and refutation of argument. The several governments of the decentralized empire constituted by the colonies had need of it, moreover, for recording their statutes, their assembly proceedings, and their administrative instruments. And, finally, the business interests of the communities gradually awoke to the effectiveness of the printed word in the advancement of their projects. United in defense and offense against the external forces of man and nature, divided among themselves on questions of religion, of the constitution, and of politics, vigorous in trade on land and sea, the English colonies of North America present to one looking back a picture of life intensely and shrewdly lived. It would, indeed, have been an extraordinary condition if, in that ferment of men and ideas, the press had shown itself anything but important in the life of the community.

It was inevitable that in a new land, faced with the immediate necessity of building a state and drawing a living from farm, forest, and sea, of adapting old traditions and theories to fresh conditions, the thinking of these people should have been at first utilitarian in character, and that in consequence their writing and publishing should have been of the same nature. Religious speculation and affirmation formed the only exception to this generalization until the eighteenth century brought greater ease of body and release of mind. But the early English Americans brought with them a great tradition in the form of a literature already distinguished and a language set in its final shape. During their period of hewing wood and drawing water, their brothers in England were expanding the realms of this common heritage of literature and philosophy. Though the Americans could not share that work, they remembered the racial culture left behind them and trained their children as befitted its inheritors.

Because of conditions of climate and natural resources the social and economic structure of the English colonies presented different faces in different sections of the country. These conditions so operated as to bring the New Englanders together in towns and to insure for them in consequence a more closely-knit social and intellectual organization than existed at first in the middle and southern colonies, where, from the beginning, agriculture had predominated as the basis of living. South of New England the farm or the plantation early became the economic unit, and the county rather than the town, the focus of political organization. It was inevitable under these circumstances that the chief intellectual manifestations should proceed from those urban communities of the North where the daily fret of mind upon mind in commercial life, in the town meeting, and in the church, produced tangible results in several forms of expression. It is natural, therefore, that we should look to New England for the earliest establishment of the press and for its greatest activity during the first century of its existence.

The Establishment of the Presses in New England

IT WAS THE RECENT foundation of a college in Cambridge, and the existence of plans for the conversion of the Indians among the London friends of the colony that encouraged the Rev. Jose Glover to purchase a printing press and carry it with him when he embarked for Massachusetts in the summer of 1638. With Mr. Glover went also Stephen Daye who, although a locksmith by trade, became, in contracting for the operation of the press, the prototypographer of the English colonies. Because of the death of Mr. Glover on the voyage to Massachusetts, his press and appurtenances came into the country in the hands of his widow. As the property of Mrs. Glover and her children, this first English-American press was set up in Cambridge, the seat of the College, late in 1638. Early in 1639, or to be exact in 1638/1639, it began its long career of service, utilitarian and cultural, to the life of the community. The earliest issues seem to have been *The Oath of a Free-man*, a formulary used by the citizen in affirming allegiance to the government, and *An Almanack for the Year 1639*, compiled by William Peirce, Mariner. Neither of these is known to exist in an actual copy. In 1640 *The Whole Booke of Psalmes* came from this press in the form of a volume in quarto of 148 leaves. The "Bay Psalm Book," to use the familiar designation of later years, was edited by Richard Mather, progenitor of the celebrated family of writing men of that name. Its significance was something more than religious in that it comprised a new metrical translation of the Psalms from the Hebrew into English and a preliminary discourse on the Psalms in public worship by its learned editor. This earliest printed book of the English colonies, therefore, was a work of literature expressive of the intellectual and spiritual interests of the community which produced it.

The Cambridge press issued in ensuing years a series of works that bespeaks the quality of its service to the community—a book of capital laws, it is believed, in 1643; small pieces relating to the scholastic activities of the college; annual almanacs; a second edition of the "Bay Psalm Book"; catechisms; a document relating to the troubles with the Narragansett Indians; a platform of the prevailing Congregational faith; and numerous sermons and doctrinal treatises. It reached the highest point of its activity with the publication in 1663 of John Eliot's translation of the whole Bible into the Indian tongue; a work remarkable in the physical sense as an issue of a small press in a pioneer country and supremely creditable, in its conception and execution, to its pious translator and to his supporters in England. One conceives the Cambridge press as having met fully in the course of its half century of existence certain routine demands of the surrounding community, and of having nourished perceptibly its intellectual activity. No other press of the whole colonial period partook to the same degree of the qualities of the learned presses of Europe, or maintained so successfully the great traditions of the craft as an intellectual force in the midst of a new and rude environment. Its inability to show the production of any work of imaginative secular literature was not an item in its discredit. In New England, and elsewhere in a country of laborious living, that particular flower of the spirit came to blossom only in the relative leisure of the next century. Nor did that press concern itself to any extent with the material affairs of the people, with the farming, fishing, buying, selling, and building by which they lived. It had been established, Edward Johnson wrote in 1654, to advance the work of church and commonwealth. Within that limitation it was a successful concern, surpassing, it may be, the expectations of its founder.

After the first decade of its operation under Stephen Daye and his son Matthew, the work of the Cambridge press from the year 1649 until its dissolution in 1692 was carried on by Samuel Green. This printer is singled out for mention here because he was the founder of a dynasty of American printers. In Massachusetts, Connecticut, Maryland, and Virginia, descendants of Samuel Green were to be found for nearly two centuries continuously engaged in the activities of printing and publishing.

It was not to be expected that the flourishing city of Boston should permit the business of printing to remain forever the monopoly of its neighbor across the Charles River. In 1674 Marmaduke Johnson, an associate of Green's in the Cambridge press, secured official permission to establish an independent press in Boston. Johnson died before he was able to put his establishment into operation, but his press was carried on from the year 1675 by John Foster, a graduate of the college at Cambridge. Foster was a successful printer and a versatile craftsman who practiced occasionally the art of engraving on wood. The rude but effective cuts with which he embellished some of his books, notably the "Mapp of New England" in Hubbard's *Narrative of the Troubles with the Indians in New-England* (Boston, 1677), and his separately issued portrait of Richard Mather, dating from an earlier year, constitute the beginnings of the woodcut and, in the case of the map, of book illustration in English America.

It was in Boston, too, that the earliest newspapers had their origin. An abortive newspaper, suppressed immediately by governor and council, appeared from the press of Richard Pierce and Benjamin Harris in September, 1690, but it was not until fifteen years later that the *Boston News-Letter*, printed by Bartholomew Green, made its initial appearance on April 24, 1704.

The press of Boston was able to take care of the work of the colonies contiguous to Massachusetts until well after the turn of the century, but as New England grew in population and extent of occupied area, the several inconveniences of that procedure became too great for effectiveness. Urged by officials of Connecticut, Thomas Short of Boston settled in New London in 1709 as the resident printer of that colony. Because of its proximity to the well-established and aggressive printing-houses of Boston, the Connecticut press was slow in attaining importance. It was not until 1755 that James Parker established in New Haven, capital of the colony and seat of Yale College, the first newspaper of Connecticut under the title *The Connecticut Gazette*.

Resentful of his treatment by the Massachusetts authorities on the occasion of some indiscreet publications, James Franklin, elder brother of Benjamin, in 1727 carried his press from Boston to Newport, Rhode Island, making that colony, too, independent of the Boston printers. Five years later James Franklin began at Newport the publication of a newspaper, *The Rhode Island Gazette*. This journal lived only a few months, but in 1758 Ann Franklin, his widow, in partnership with

James Franklin, Jr., brought out the first issue of *The Newport Mercury*, a newspaper that as weekly or daily has continued publication to the present time. The first press of Providence, soon to become the chief city of Rhode Island, was established by William Goddard with the support and active participation of his mother, Sarah Updike Goddard. Later, in New York, Philadelphia, and Baltimore, William Goddard attained fame as a skilled printer, as a newspaper publisher of extraordinary effectiveness, and as the founder, single-handed, of a private system of post offices and riders which, in 1775, the Continental Congress declared to be the official postal system of the country, and which continues in operation today as the Post Office Department of the United States. His sister, Mary Katherine Goddard, as printer and as editor of *The Maryland Journal* in the period of the Revolution, became the most distinguished of the several women who have been prominent in the history of typography and journalism in the United States.

It was again resentment against the undue severity of the Massachusetts authorities that led Daniel Fowle to take his press in 1756 to Portsmouth, New Hampshire, where he began almost at once the *New Hampshire Gazette*. After a history of publication for 195 years, this journal is still in existence as a weekly supplement to the *Portsmouth Herald*. With such qualifications as are implied in the foregoing description of its status, it may still fairly claim to be the oldest newspaper continuously published in the United States.

The Vermont press was established by Alden Spooner in 1778, though the town in which he printed, Hanover (then called Dresden) lay in a strip of debatable land claimed also by New Hampshire, and which afterwards reverted to that state. The geographical area known as Vermont, therefore, has no claim upon this press, though the political entity of that name may rightly call Spooner her first printer and Dresden, New Hampshire, the seat of her earliest press.

Few first presses have issued in their very beginnings work of so great consequence to their supporters as the pioneer press at Dresden. The long-standing quarrel between New Hampshire and New York over the territory lying, roughly, between the Connecticut River and the north-south line established by Lake Champlain, known from the circumstances of its first settlement as the "New Hampshire Grants," was brought to an end when, in 1777, the settlers of the debatable lands took matters into their own hands and formed the independent government of Vermont. The Dresden press began at once the publication of documents and pamphlets essential to the very life of the newly born commonwealth.

The first press on the soil of Vermont, as now constituted, was that which Judah Padock Spooner and Timothy Green established at Westminster in 1780.

The Maine press owes its inception to a partnership formed in 1785 at Falmouth, now Portland, between Benjamin Titcomb, Jr., a printer, and Thomas B. Wait, a bookseller. The most important work of this firm seems to have been its publication of the *Falmouth Gazette*. The chief interest in early Maine typographical history, however, centers about the printing office set up at Augusta by Peter Edes in 1795.

The Middle Colonies

The presses which have been mentioned in the foregoing section were the first printing establishments of the New England colonies. Boston has continuously maintained its supremacy as the chief city in that section, and its press has always been the most active and the most important of any in New England. It was, indeed, the most prolific press of the entire country until Philadelphia assumed the lead in publication soon after the middle of the eighteenth century. From the beginning of its operations, the press of the Pennsylvania city was the chief of those of the Middle Colonies. It was established late in the year 1685 by William Bradford, a son-in-law of the Quaker printer Andrew Sowle of London. The issues of the Pennsylvania press show a greater variety in matter than those of any other colonial establishment. In that Quaker commonwealth, with its later immigration from Scotland, England, and Germany, the conflict of races, creeds, and politics was at its sharpest. Throughout the eighteenth century the presses of the Bradfords; of Benjamin Franklin; of the German Sauers, father and son; of the German Seventh Day Baptist Brotherhood at Ephrata; of Goddard; Bell; and the Dunlaps expressed in book, pamphlet, and newspaper the active intelligence of a community rendered complex by the racial factors and varying creeds of which we have spoken.

The first paper mill of the country was built in 1690, near Germantown, by William Bradford in partnership with Samuel Carpenter and William Rittenhouse. By this action Pennsylvania at once acquired a pre-eminence in the papermaking industry which it retained throughout the colonial period. The German printer, Christopher Sauer the younger, imported type matrices and molds about the year 1770, and after 1772 diligently cast German letter for his own use for many years, training in his foundry Justus Fox and Jacob Bay, one of whom cast on his own account a roman letter first used commercially in 1775. Fox went on with his newly learned trade, and soon after the close of the Revolution, type founders from England and Scotland made their way to Philadelphia. Pennsylvania had no serious rivalry in the early stages of the American type founding industry. The geographical position of Philadelphia brought to it in 1774 the Continental Congress, whereupon that city became politically, as it had long been commercially, the center of a group of colonies now confederated for purposes of mutual defense. All these things combined to give special importance to the press of the Quaker colony and to make its issues numerically greater than those of any American city until its eclipse in the nineteenth century by that of New York. One of Bradford's successors in Philadelphia was his son Andrew, who, in 1719, began the publication of *The American Weekly Mercury*, the first newspaper to be established south of Boston.

The origin of the press in the little town on Manhattan Island which was destined to become the metropolis of the country and one of the greatest cities of the modern world traces to the disagreement between William Bradford, the first printer of Philadelphia, and the Quaker rulers of his community. Charged in the course of a local quarrel with printing seditious matter, Bradford was brought to trial and against him was cited by his accusers one of the clauses of the Parliamentary press restriction act of 1662, the only occasion upon which that statute, so rigorous in its application in England, was cited in the regulation of the American press. Through the influence of Governor Fletcher of New York, temporarily in jurisdiction over Pennsylvania, Bradford was released from his Philadelphia prison. In the late spring of 1693, he removed his press to New York, carrying thither an appointment from the Governor as public printer of that colony. In this year he issued, among a number of official documents, a small group of controversial pamphlets having to do with the cause he had championed in Pennsylvania, the first fruits of the vast publishing business which has since been a notable feature of the intellectual and commercial activities of his city of refuge. The first New York newspaper, Bradford's *New York Gazette*, did not begin publication until the year 1725.

Two sets of New Jersey Assembly publications were brought out in 1723 and 1728, at Perth Amboy and Burlington respectively, by neighboring New York and Pennsylvania printers, but the first permanent printing establishment of the colony was that of James Parker, an accomplished printer and publisher of New York who, in 1754, set up a press in his native town of Woodbridge. It was not until December, 1777, that Isaac Collins began at Burlington the publication of *The New Jersey Gazette*, the first newspaper of the colony named in its title.

In 1761, James Adams, until then a journeyman in the office of Franklin & Hall of Philadelphia, opened a printing establishment in Wilmington, Delaware. *The Delaware Gazette*, the earliest journal of the state, was begun by Jacob A. Killen, of Wilmington, in 1785.

The Southern Colonies

The first establishment of a press in one of the southern group of colonies occurred when in the year 1682 a printer named William Nuthead came to Jamestown, Virginia, under the protection of John Buckner, a wealthy merchant and landowner of the neighborhood. Before the press was well under way, the indiscretion of Nuthead in printing certain Assembly papers without permission of the Governor and Council was punished in February, 1683, by the temporary inhibition of his press. Ten months later this action of the local authorities was approved by a royal order prohibiting further printing in Virginia. It was not until 1730 that the press was permanently established in Williamsburg, then become the capital of Virginia, by William Parks, who at that time had been successfully operating a press in Maryland for four years. Parks's newspaper, *The Virginia Gazette*, was begun in 1736.

William Nuthead found greater encouragement for the practice of his craft in the neighboring colony of Maryland than had been offered him in Virginia. It is likely that he had removed his press to the Maryland town of St. Mary's City, the capital of Lord Baltimore's Province, soon after the coming to Virginia, early in 1684, of a new governor bearing the King's order prohibiting all printing in that colony "upon any occasion whatsoever." It has not been possible until lately to name any product of Nuthead's Maryland press of earlier date than the year 1689, when two important political documents are known to have issued from it. About the year 1935, however, there were discovered in the Land Office at Annapolis a number of printed blank forms of early date, among them several bonds bearing an unmistakable typographical resemblance to the only remaining unquestioned production of Nuthead's press, the *Address of the Representatives*, printed in St. Mary's City in 1689. One of these forms is filled in by hand with the date [31 August] 168[5]. There seems no reason to doubt, therefore, that Nuthead was in Maryland operating his press by or before the month of August, 1685, several months, indeed, before William Bradford on December 28, 1685, announced in his *Kalendarium Pennsilvaniense* that he had established in Pennsylvania by this publication the "great Art and Mystery of Printing." The widow of William Nuthead, Dinah, removed the press in 1695 to Annapolis, the new capital, and in 1696 received from Governor and Council a license to print in succession to her husband. Dinah Nuthead was the first of a long succession of women to operate a press in colonial America. The earliest newspaper of Maryland was *The Maryland Gazette*, begun by William Parks at Annapolis in 1727. After the middle of the eighteenth century, the chief center of life in the colony became the relatively new city of Baltimore. The first individual to operate a press in that town was the German printer, Nicholas Hasselbach, who went there from Philadelphia in 1765. The earliest newspaper of the city was *The Maryland Journal*, begun in 1773 by William Goddard, a printer mentioned in several connections in this brief review of the beginnings of the American press.

The press in South Carolina was begun in 1731 by three printers acting independently of one another—Eleazer Phillips, Jr., Thomas Whitemarsh, and George Webb. None of these was able to establish himself firmly in Charleston, the capital city, though Thomas Whitemarsh remained there at work until his death in 1733. As we learn from the researches of Douglas C. McMurtrie, George Webb began well and, according to the evidence of the remaining imprints, was probably the first of the three to get his press into operation. Nothing is heard of Webb in Charleston, however, after his first month of residence, and Phillips died in his first year of operation with little accomplished. In 1733 Lewis Timothy went to that city from Philadelphia under a partnership agreement with Franklin, his former employer, and began there the operation of a press which remained in the Timothy family for nearly seventy-five years, passing successively into the control of his widow, his son, his daughter-in-law, and his grandson. Lewis Timothy re-established in 1734 *The South Carolina Gazette*, a journal begun by Thomas Whitemarsh in 1732 and carried on by that printer until his death in September, 1733.

The first printer of North Carolina was James Davis, who went from Virginia to New Bern in 1749. Two years later he began the publication of *The North Carolina Gazette*, the first newspaper of the colony.

James Johnston, a printer from England, initiated the Georgia press, to the best of our knowledge, with the publication at Savannah in 1763 of *The Georgia Gazette*. His first duty as public printer seems to have been to catch up with the recent activities of the Assembly, and in 1763 we find him publishing a series of separate acts of which the passage extended as far back as the year 1759.

Denis Braud, the first printer of Louisiana, began his press by the issue of a document of tragic import in the history of his people. The *Extrait de la Lettre du Roi*, New Orleans, 1764, announced to the French *habitants* of Louisiana the cession of their colony to Spain. The first newspaper of the colony was the *Moniteur de la Louisiane*, which began publication in 1794 in the establishment of another French printer, Louis Duclot.

Early in the year 1783, Dr. William Charles Wells, a loyalist refugee from Charleston, South Carolina, established a press in St. Augustine, Florida. He was soon joined in its operation by his brother John Wells, Jr., who in Charleston had been associated with his father, Robert Wells, in conducting the *Royal Gazette*. William Charles Wells began, probably with the issue of February 1, 1783, the publication of the *East-Florida Gazette*, a newspaper which enjoyed an existence of about one year when, the Spanish having taken over Florida, Dr. Wells returned to England. John Wells went to Nassau in the Bahamas, where for the remainder of his life he continued in the business of printing and newspaper publishing. One of the early issues of the *East-Florida Gazette* contained in its imprint the statement that it had been printed "by Charles Wright for John Wells, jun." Charles Wright, evidently the practical printer of the establishment, is not heard of afterwards in American typographical history. In addition to the newspaper only two imprints of this press are known to exist, both of them, for different reasons, of importance. Their titles are: *Essay II, On the Nature and Principles of Public Credit*, an economic tract by Samuel Gale; and *The Case of the Inhabitants of East-Florida*, a document containing claims to compensation presented by the East Florida loyalists for the property loss they would suffer through the cession of their country to Spain.

In organizing the foregoing statement of the facts and circumstances attending the dissemination of the press in the colonial period of the United States, we have kept in mind cultural groups coterminous with the natural geographical divisions of the country. An abstract of this information also appears in chronological order in the chart of the first presses of each of the United States (p. 69-70).

The Colonial Press in Operation: 1638-1783

The dissemination of printing throughout the British colonies in America and its spread into provincial centers of England were, in point of time, almost exactly parallel movements. Because of successive parliamentary restriction acts, it was not until 1695 that any of the cities of England except London, York, and the two great university towns possessed permanent presses. Actually when the last inhibitory act expired in England in 1695 there were already in operation in the colonies the printing houses of Cambridge, Boston, St. Mary's City, Philadelphia, and New York, establishments which preceded by varying terms of years the first presses of such English cities, now important, as Liverpool, Birmingham, and Leeds. So much of a statement of circumstances is needed to place the infant American press in perspective in relation to the status of printing in the English world.

With the exception of the Massachusetts press, established in the interests of church and state, and enlarged through the missionary zeal of the New England Corporation, the first presses of English America were utilitarian in motive and practice. They were set up upon assurance of government patronage and without that patronage they could not have existed. The private employment of the press in those communities would have been insufficient in amount to keep their printers alive, and it was only as the commercial life of the country slowly developed that the government work became merely an incidental source of income to a printer who might be engaged in the publication of a newspaper, an annual almanac, legal manuals, business guides, separately printed advertisements, sermons, and finally, original and reprinted works of a literary character. The partnership of Franklin & Hall, for example, drew from the *Pennsylvania Gazette* a gross income about three times as great as that which it received from the government work. Indeed the newspaper income amounted to half the total receipts of the shop during the seventeen years of the partnership.

Employment by the government not only provided the early printer with a living, it gave him a distinction not ordinarily possessed by the proprietor of a provincial press. As public printer of New York, of Massachusetts, or of South Carolina, or of any other colony, he handled the business of a separate political division, of a commonwealth proud of its entity, proud of its comparative independence of Parliament or of any restraint upon its actions save the will of the sovereign and their legality in the opinion of the attorney general of the realm. The English provincial printer, his counterpart in most other respects, knew no such relationship. William Parks, printer of Ludlow, England, lived under a government centralized at London and served by the King's Printer, resident in that city. Parks's relation to the English government was that of any other citizen in his position in life, but William Parks, public printer of Maryland and Virginia, by printing the laws, assembly proceedings, and minor utterances of two self-governing commonwealths maintained a position of dignity not commonly the possession of a provincial printer in a small way of business. That the responsibilities of his office stimulated him to exercise care and thoughtfulness in typographical performance is granted by everyone familiar with the volumes of laws and other public documents that came from the presses of any American government printer of the colonial period. Furthermore, the quality attained in the government work set a standard of excellence that influenced for good the whole body of colonial printing.

The Nature of the Printer's Equipment: The Printing Press

In the English colonies, as elsewhere throughout the world in the seventeenth and eighteenth centuries, the actual equipment of the printing-houses was very little different in its mechanical features from that used by the European typographers of the closing years of the fifteenth century. It might even be said that in all essential principles the equipment of the colonial American printer was even less elaborate than that with which Gutenberg of Mainz initiated the art of typography, for this printer of the seventeenth and eighteenth centuries had long ago given up the practice of casting his own type and, except in one instance later to be specified, did not even possess the tools and materials essential to that operation. Though the press had undergone minor mechanical improvements in certain places—in the Low Countries, for example—these were improvements in details of construction and in fixtures rather than in principles of operation. But the improved Dutch press, loosely described as the "Blaeu" press, was never generally adopted in England, where a press of an older type seems to have formed the reliance of the printer until the invention of the iron press about the year 1800. The American printing-house was a replica in its equipment of the English establishment of the corresponding period, and the specimens that remain of early American printing machines are all of the variety which Moxon, in describing the Blaeu press, spoke of in 1683 as the "old-fashioned English press." With this machine the English and American printer worked happily enough until the early years of the nineteenth century. During the greater part of the colonial period the American printer was compelled to buy his presses from England, though there is evidence that an occasional printer, notably Christopher Sauer the elder, of Germantown, was sufficiently skilled in mechanics to build presses for use in his own establishment. But the industry of commercial press building was of relatively late development. The earliest instance of its operation on record is the construction in 1769 of an especially fine press by Isaac Doolittle of New Haven for William Goddard, then printing in Philadelphia. Only six years after this we find two Philadelphia craftsmen advertising their ability to build good presses and to make other articles of printing-house equipment until then generally imported from England. Soon thereafter, in many places, the building of presses became in America a commonplace of manufacturing industry.

The Type

The types used by the American printer were, like his presses, generally of English importation until the early years of the Revolutionary War. In 1744, Franklin purchased a set of "founding tools" from England, but it seems to be a fair assumption that he made no use of this equipment. It has been asserted, indeed, that three years later he sold these materials to the Brotherhood at Ephrata. No type is known to have been made at the Ephrata Monastery, however, either with these tools or any others, but it is a matter of record that as early as 1771, Christopher Sauer the younger began making an excellent German letter with founding equipment imported from Germany. One of the issues of his *Ein Geistliches Magazien* of that year bore at the end the declaration: "Gedruckt mit der ersten Schrift die jemals in America gegossen worden." But though Sauer continued to cast type in quantity, and was possessed of a complete letter founding establishment when his goods were sequestrated by the Americans in the Revolution, his efforts in this direction were not part of the main stream of type founding history in the colonies. The German letter he made was an exotic product and remained an exotic product in a country in which the roman shape of letter was the standard in general use. We shall see in a moment, however, that his activity in type founding indirectly affected the development of that industry in America.

The first roman type designed, cut, and cast in English America was that which Abel Buell of Killingworth, Connecticut, produced in 1769. Aided by a subvention from the Connecticut Assembly, he prepared to manufacture type for sale. Because of personal instability, however, he made no progress in his task until, in 1781, he began to cast type in quantity for certain Connecticut printers, who, because of the war with England, were not able to replenish their worn supplies of letter by new fonts from abroad. In the intervening years type founding had become an active business in other hands in another part of the country.

It is uncertain to whom must be allowed the honor of establishing type founding as a commercial enterprise of English America, for contemporary records are anything but clear on that point. But circumstances narrow the field of claimants to two journeymen employed by the younger Sauer to cast German letter for the printing of his great Bible of 1776—that is, to Justus Fox, a German mechanic and to Jacob Bay, or Bey, as sometimes written, a Swiss weaver. Both these men learned in Sauer's foundry the trade of letter casting, and soon proceeded on their own account from making German letter to designing and casting the prevailing roman letter. Both claimed to be the "ingenious artist of Germantown" engaged in type founding, who, in 1775, was referred to in a resolution of the Pennsylvania Assembly which urged local printers to use American-made type rather than that imported from England. The contemporaries of Fox and Bay seem to have been uncertain as to which of them was meant by the terms of that resolution, and since their time no documents have been discovered which aid in resolving the doubt. The earliest use of the American-made type in question that has yet been identified was the printing of the first number, on April 7, 1775, of the *Pennsylvania Mercury* a newspaper published by Story & Humphreys, of Philadelphia. It seems likely that this founder's work was slow in affecting the problems of his contemporaries among the printers. A letter of December, 1782, in the William L. Clements Library, from George Lux of Baltimore to General Nathanael Greene, then in command at Charleston, South Carolina, requested that there be purchased for William Goddard the fonts of type left behind by any loyalist printers who might have fled the city because of its occupation by the Americans. The Wells brothers—William Charles and John—were probably in the mind of the alert Baltimore printer, but it is known that in leaving Charleston for St. Augustine those printers, or printing-house proprietors, had taken with them their types, so that Goddard did not find relief through their misfortune from a prevailing type shortage not yet relieved by the activities of the Philadelphia founders. Other fonts were cast by Fox and by Bay in later years, but responsibility for the development of American type founding did not long remain in their hands. The houses of John Baine and Archibald Binny of Philadelphia soon were carrying the industry far beyond the humble beginnings instituted by Sauer's journeymen.

The Ink

It is probable that the normal practice of the colonial printer in the maintenance of his ink supply was to import the ready-mixed product from English manufacturers. He was, we may be sure, little concerned with the assertion, made by Moxon in his *Mechanick Exercises*, of 1683, that manufactured ink was of inferior quality. Indeed he may have been among those printers who, too busy or too indolent to make their own ink, were, according to Moxon, willing that the product of the manufacturers remain inferior in quality in order that they might continue to have an old and reliable excuse for the poor character of their own printing. Isaiah Thomas records that in his time most of the ink used was of the manufactured variety, imported from England, and we should be willing to let the question rest with his statement if it were not that there is evidence in plenty of a contrary practice prevailing in some parts of the country. In 1723 we find Franklin making ink for the use of his master, Samuel Keimer of Philadelphia. It is probable that the lampblack he used in the operation was locally purchased, for a petition requesting a monopoly of that manufacture was presented to the Pennsylvania Assembly on January 16, 1721/22 by the printer, Andrew Bradford, who alleged that he had "been at great Charge in bringing to Perfection the making of Lamp-Black." In 1733 Franklin purchased on his own account equipment for the manufacture of lampblack. Some years later Jonas Green of Annapolis wrote him ordering both lampblack and "varnish," that is, the linseed oil boiled to the point of viscidity which forms the other ingredient of printers' ink. In 1756 Franklin's lampblack house was rented from him by Anthony Armbruester, a German printer of Philadelphia, and even before this time another German printer, that universal mechanical genius, the elder Christopher Sauer of Germantown, had been engaged in the manufacture of ink for his own use and probably for sale. The inventory of the younger Christopher Sauer, made out in 1778, names a "Lam black house" among his possessions.

It is likely that both the practices in question—importation and home manufacture of ink—prevailed throughout the colonies. In fact the partnership account of Franklin & Hall shows that firm purchasing in the same term of years, ready-made ink from England as well as large quantities of lampblack from local manufacturers. Doubtless the mixing of ink in their own shops was an economy in cash expenditure for the American printer and a means of occupying the spare time of apprentices, but whether moved by these or other considerations it is clear enough that ink-making continued to be one of the practices of the colonial printing shop throughout the eighteenth century. It is not certain when the making of printing ink for sale became a specialty in American manufacturing, but in 1792 and for years thereafter Mathew Carey and other printers of the Middle Colonies were buying supplies of ready-mixed ink from Justus Fox of Germantown, an individual whom we have already encountered as a pioneer in the making of type.

The Paper

In the year 1690 William Bradford, the Philadelphia printer, and Samuel Carpenter built a paper mill near Germantown and put it in charge of William Rittenhouse, German by birth and papermaker by trade. In the course of a few years this concern seems to have passed entirely into the hands of Rittenhouse, whose family continued for generations to manufacture paper in the same mill. This was the origin of a trade in papermaking which in later years became of great importance in Pennsylvania. In 1787 that state claimed forty-eight of the ninety mills then in operation in the United States, and in 1789 it was affirmed in Congress that the annual product of the Pennsylvania mills alone was 70,000 reams of paper. Necessity, as often happens, applied the spur to this industry. During the Revolutionary War, when English importations had been cut off, several other colonies, aided by government subsidies, became self-sufficient in the matter of paper supply. The earliest mill in the South was that which the printer William Parks, with aid and advice from Franklin, established at Williamsburg, Virginia, about the year 1743. Franklin, indeed, was deeply interested in the papermaking industry. In the later years of the century he told the French traveler, Brissot de Warville, that alone he had established or helped establish no fewer than eighteen paper mills. His account books show him to have been a large and, presumably, a successful dealer in papers of all sorts—printing paper, writing paper, and the coarser papers for wrapping—and a dealer on an equal scale in linen rags, the raw material of paper manufacture.

It is not to be assumed that the establishment of these American mills rendered the local printers entirely independent of importation. The quality of the paper produced in them was not of the highest. It served admirably for newspapers, current broadsides, pamphlets, almanacs, primers, and ephemeral works generally, but almost invariably when one examines an American work intended for something more than current usefulness, its paper is seen to bear the signs of English or Dutch manufacture. The paper made in the colonial period was always "laid" paper. It was only in 1757 that Baskerville perfected in England the process of making "wove" paper, and it was not until 1795 that Isaiah Thomas printed a small book of poems upon a locally-made "wove" paper, the first American specimen of that variety which has come to the notice of the historians of papermaking.

Bookbinding

Before the invention of printing in Europe, bookbinding had already developed into a full, seasoned profession which offered to members of the craft their principal means of livelihood. In English America, too, the first bookbinder preceded the first printer. The earliest was John Sanders, "a bookebynder," who took the Freeman's Oath in 1636 and purchased a shop in Boston in 1637. Nothing is known of him after that year. One of the unanswered questions of the time relates to the degree of his activity as a binder, whether indeed he actually practiced his craft in Boston or was engaged there in other pursuits. If he was living in 1640 and active in bookbinding, it is likely that he was responsible for the sound and workmanlike bindings in calf that appeared on the first real book from the press in what is now the United States, that is, the *Whole Booke of Psalmes*, of Cambridge, 1640. But whoever may have been the binder of that book, there is no question that some twenty years later, the trade of bookbinding, as a craft practiced independently of the printing office, was in operation in Boston. The opportunity of binding the Eliot Indian Bible had brought to Massachusetts in 1663, as a permanent resident, one John Ratcliff. His emolu-

ment in this work was small, but after its completion he continued to
follow his trade in Boston for many ensuing years. During a large part
of this time he engaged also in the business of bookselling and publishing, and we find that his rival and successor, Edmund Ranger, also
combined in his business these two functions of the book trade. Yet
it was not until the following century that binderies independent of
printing offices appeared in other colonial cities. William Davies and
John Hyndshaw set up shops in Philadelphia in 1730, and in 1734
Joseph Johnson established his business in New York. Thus, by the
middle of the eighteenth century the printers of these cities could, if
they wished, relinquish the binding of books to specialists.

But in the smaller towns like Annapolis, Williamsburg, and Baltimore, where existing conditions made the division of labor uneconomi-
cal, the printer had perforce to become also the binder. Inadequate
patronage was not the only reason for linking the two crafts; we must
not forget the nature of the printer's role in the community. He frequently ran the general store, was postmaster, and sometimes held town
office, as well as being printer and publisher. In the turn of events he
mastered whatever came to hand, and in the case of binding, so closely
allied to his main purpose, it was many years before he discontinued this
activity. He overcame the lack of skilled binders by employing one or
two printers familiar with the processes of folding, gathering, sewing,
lacing, covering, and decorating. Often the women of the household,
accustomed to delicate needlework, participated in this department of
the firm. The necessary materials, wooden board or pasteboard, leather
or parchment, glue, paste, pack thread for bands, and linen thread for
sewing, were obtained without difficulty. In New England, for instance, where wood was easily procured, the books frequently had
covers of thin boards of birch, maple, or oak—the same material used
by the binders of early European books. In Pennsylvania, the site of
many paper mills, pasteboard covers became more popular. The fertile
fields of the colonies provided flax for linen thread; the verdant
pastures nourished the sheep and cattle from which came leather for
covers. Leather manufacturing, one of the earliest industries, was encouraged by local laws. Therefore, we find books bound in sheep or
calf, rather than imported morocco or levant. These early books bore
little decoration, resembling the typical law-book style of binding, a

resemblance which increased when, in the eighteenth century, gilt-lettered red leather labels appeared on the backs. Occupied as he was in varied activities, the colonial printer-binder lacked the time as well as the skill to produce many handsome ornamental bindings. His printed work, for the most part, comprised laws, pamphlets, and sermons which were issued in blue or marbled paper covers. Occasionally craftsmen like William Parks or Robert Aitken created delightful gold-tooled bindings of artistic excellence. In general, however, the bound books of the period, with their hardy and severe appearance, express the spirit of the growing country where life was rough and uncertain and where pleasant embellishments were not yet demanded by the purchaser.

Labor and Working Conditions

The American printing craft remained in the household stage of economic development throughout the colonial period. The fixed element in the printer's labor supply was the assistance he might demand from members of his own family—his wife, his daughters, and his sons. The printer drew also into his service trained journeymen, who came to the new country either as free agents or under terms of indenture, but of course the chief source of his labor supply was the boy of the neighborhood whom he attached to himself through the apprenticeship system. As everywhere under this system, the boy worked without wages in return for his keep and for instruction from the master in the whole art of printing. His apprenticeship ended, his wages as a journeyman printer were distinctly better than those paid the practitioners of less exacting crafts. The wage scales of Franklin in 1754 and of Isaiah Thomas in 1792 seem to have been about the same, and these corresponded closely to the English scale of the period limited by these dates. The main elements in these scales were, roughly, payment to the compositor at the rate of a shilling a thousand ems, and to pressmen at the rate of a shilling a token. We are entering here into technicalities, but when it is understood that an expert pressman under theoretically perfect conditions might operate his press at the rate of a token an hour, that is, 240 sheets printed on one side, it becomes clear that his compensation for a day's work was moderately high. In this day of the fluctuating value of money, it is difficult to state in terms of

modern currency the colonial journeyman printer's wages, but it seems
reasonable to believe that then, as now, his was a well-paid craft.

There is little recorded evidence of labor troubles in the shops of the
seventeenth and eighteenth centuries, but our ignorance of the relations
in this respect between journeymen and masters does not permit us
to assume that the colonial period was a golden age in the American
printing industry. Labor was just then beginning to organize in England and in continental Europe. So far as it concerned the printing
trade, the earliest impetus of the movement did not reach the colonies
until the year 1776, when the journeyman printers of New York
forced, by means of the strike, an increase of wages from their employers.

The Amount of the Printer's Equipment

The normal printing establishment of the period we are treating
was small indeed in comparison to the shop of the present day. Even
such an excellently run and prosperous establishment as that of Franklin & Hall of Philadelphia boasted only three presses and a supply of
type amounting in weight to about 4000 pounds, comprising eight
fonts of as many sizes of letter. At the time of its sequestration in 1778
the establishment of Christopher Sauer the younger of Germantown,
Pennsylvania, was perhaps the largest in the colonies. In addition to its
four presses, it was, like the early European establishments, equipped
to cast type and to manufacture ink. The normal printing office, represented by such establishments as those of Jonas Green of Annapolis,
John Holt of New York, and William Rind of Williamsburg, contained but two presses and about 2250 pounds of type, comprising four
sizes of roman letter.

The Output of the Press—Amount and Typographical Quality

It was from the relatively ill-equipped printing-houses just described
that there proceeded an output which may reasonably be characterized
as impressive, whether it be regarded from the standpoint of numbers,
of intrinsic importance, or, and this is a matter of opinion, of typographic quality.

The chief burden of any typical printing office of the period was,
of course, its weekly newspaper. In compiling a list of imprints it is

customary to record a whole year's issue of a newspaper as a single entry. This practice is sensible and expedient from the standpoint of the bibliographer, but it does not convey a true understanding of the printer's activities, for obviously, instead of one item to his credit, a weekly newspaper should count fifty-two items, each representing many hours weekly of editorial and typographical labor. In our revaluation of this printer's activities, we must recall, too, that in compiling lists of imprints one necessarily may enter only such pieces as have survived in actual examples or in undisputed records of their printing. It has been estimated on the basis of the manuscript Work-Book of Franklin & Hall in the New York Public Library, that the ratio between imprints of this firm recorded in bibliographies and pieces known to have come from its presses is 1 to 4.7. It is reasonable to believe that the same ratio holds for other establishments, and upon the basis of that ratio we must think of the total output of the American presses from 1639 to 1783 as numbering 86,000 instead of the 18,300 recorded for that period in Charles Evans's *American Bibliography*. Even this respectable figure, for the reason that a year's newspaper issues are recorded by Evans as a single entry, really gives no indication of the degree of the printer's activity. It may be that we shall be able to realize more fully his actual performance by examining in detail the output of the press of a single printer, choosing for the purpose that of William Parks of Annapolis and Williamsburg. In the fourteen year period, 1736 to 1749 inclusive, there are recorded for Parks's Williamsburg press approximately 100 items, excluding the fourteen annual single entries of the *Virginia Gazette*. Multiplied by the 4.7 which we have suggested as the ratio between what has survived and what was actually printed, we have 470 items, exclusive of newspapers, as the probable production of his press in this period. His newspaper output in the same term numbered fifty-two annual separate issues multiplied by fourteen years, that is, 728 productions of his press in addition to those usually counted. Each of these newspaper issues must have comprised at least 1000 copies, for we know that in this period Jonas Green, in the very much smaller neighboring province of Maryland, was distributing weekly between five and six hundred issues of his *Maryland Gazette*.

It could be said that the ratio of one known production to 4.7 actually printed, derived from a special knowledge of the Franklin & Hall press of Philadephia in the period 1760-1765, is not necessarily correct for the earlier press of William Parks of Williamsburg. The Virginia town was much smaller than Philadelphia, and its surrounding community was industrialized hardly at all. But perhaps it may be permitted to employ that ratio as an approximation. The 470 imprints resulting from its use would indeed have seemed an improbable total in 1904 when Mr. Evans entered only thirty Parks imprints for the period 1736-1749, but today when there have been recorded nearly one hundred issues, exclusive of newspapers, it begins to seem that the Parks establishment, like that of Franklin & Hall, had been more active than previously supposed. The probability is that a similar ratio exists in connection with the production of most active American establishments.

The cold statistics just presented give body to the picture we are trying to obtain of the activities of a normal colonial printing house at work with equipment inferior to that of a small job printer of today. In the year 1737, for example, Parks is credited with nine titles exclusive of his newspaper. If his output in this year really was 4.7 times greater than this, still excluding the newspaper, he would have issued an average of three items a month ranging in size from a single leaf advertisement, or government proclamation, to the closely printed octavo of 476 pages which came from his press in July of that year. In addition to this rate of a separate piece produced every ten days, there is to be counted the newspaper number issued concurrently every seven days. The various issues of this year would range in size of editions from about 100 copies of a local advertisement, through 500 copies of the large book mentioned, to the 1000 copies of each weekly number of the *Gazette*. One would say that this amount of production meant a steady day of labor for the printer and his two journeymen, for we must suppose that with himself engaged in gathering material for the newspaper and in correcting the press, he would have found it necessary to employ as assistants at least one compositor and one pressman. All these servants of the press would be fully occupied in the routine business of the establishment, and the compositor would doubtless be at work in all odd moments throughout the week setting the fresh news text of the journal, which occupied three, three-column folio pages, or in setting and revising its pages of advertisements. On the day of issue the pressman would have an extremely full day's work before him in printing his 1000 copies. Even at the theoretical rate of a token an hour with two men at the press; that is 240 sheets an hour printed one side only, there would be consumed in printing the paper, at the very least, eight hours of constant activity one day a week. The rate was doubtless appreciably slower than this because of the inevitable delays of any train of work performed with imperfect machinery operated by human hands. But with his press in good repair and operated by competent workmen, it is likely that Parks would have been able to print in a full working day of ten hours the whole issue of 1000 copies of his four-page folio newspaper. Folding, addressing, and distributing the newspaper are further operations that must be taken into account in a reconstruction of our printer's activities.

We are too condescending, perhaps, in thinking of the old wooden press of the colonial printing-house as an inexact instrument, laboriously and slowly operated. As its finer productions show, it was capable in good hands of producing excellent presswork, of giving clean sharp impression and exact register. And though it was laboriously operated, it does not follow that its operation was slow. Impelled by a sharp pull at the bar, the platen moved quickly through its short descent, and the movements of the pressmen followed a set order and rhythm which, under theoretically perfect conditions, enabled them to print, with two pulls each, one side of 240 sheets every hour; that is, four sheets a minute, or one every fifteen seconds. This press may have been, as Moxon called it, a "makeshift, slovenly contrivance," but in its operation, the orderly method and persistence of the craftsmen triumphed over its imperfections.

The most tedious and difficult task that confronted a colonial printer of this period, or a printer anywhere in a small way of business, was the production of a book of a considerable number of pages. With only a single font of type of any given size available in his cases, he was not able to keep pages of metal standing, but must set a few signatures, print them, and distribute the type before he might proceed with the composition of the next group of signatures. A paper shortage during this process would therefore mean laying aside the job until another shipment of suitable paper had been received. Bacon's *Laws of Mary-*

land, printed by Jonas Green of Annapolis, was something like four years in press, and an appreciable part of the delay in its production was attributed to the failure of a London agent to ship the paper ordered by the printer. A large rush order coming to a busy printer in the midst of a job of book composition, demanding the use of the type with which the book was being printed, would likewise necessitate a postponement of its completion. It is reflection upon such circumstances as these which causes the student to feel a special degree of admiration for the achievement of the colonial printer in producing so many books of notable size, whether measured by inches or by the extensiveness of their texts. On the one hand we find ourselves regarding such productions as the folio books of laws of printers in every colony, Green & Kneeland's edition of Willard's *Compleat Body of Divinity* (1726), and the Ephrata Press edition of *Der Blutige Schau Platz* (1748); on the other hand, there are to be considered the workmanlike, compact octavos in which William Parks set forth in 1737 Mercer's *Exact Abridgement of all the Public Acts of Virginia*, and, ten years later, Stith's *History of the First Discovery and Settlement of Virginia*, or in which Rogers & Fowle published in 1749 Douglass's *Summary of the British Settlements*, and James Parker, in 1765, Smith's *History of the Colony of New-Jersey*.

It is a question as to whether the aesthetic quality of the printing of a place or period should be judged by its normal product or by its best. If we are to judge the American press of the seventeenth and eighteenth centuries by its normal product, we shall be constrained to allow it small distinction either in design or execution. It partook throughout the seventeenth century and the first half of the eighteenth, of the decadence in book design, in letter design, and in mechanical craftsmanship then current throughout the world. In the colonies, as elsewhere, its characteristics were an undistinguished letter, poorly cast; the use, for the sake of economy in paper, of a type often too small for the letterpress area; a tendency to overclose setting of type; a disregard of the niceties of page proportion; hurried press work performed with wretched ink upon paper of which the chief virtue was its toughness. But in America as everywhere there were printers in this period who had not lost touch with the older traditions of their craft, and who, upon that basis, were able to build a typographical style which was an expression of the neo-classical spirit that pervaded the eighteenth century in literature, architecture, painting, and decoration. The balance, simplicity, proportion, and massing that characterized Georgian architecture and furniture found repetition in the designing of printers intent upon the production of works of consequence. The English and American printers of the eighteenth century were assisted also in the production of their finer works through being able to import book papers from Holland, and by the fact that in their time occurred a growth in skill among English papermakers. Above all were their purposes advanced by the improvement in type founding that occurred in England through the agency of William Caslon, whose well-designed and exactly cut letters became available to the printing trade about the year 1734. There exist, however, no small number of American-printed works before that year in which the printer's sense of design, his skill in composition and the conscious dignity of his purpose resulted in the production of books for which no apology is necessary. As the century grew older, we find such printers as Franklin, James Parker, John Green of Boston, Jonas Green of Annapolis, and William Goddard of Providence, Philadelphia, and Baltimore, producing books distinctly fine in typographic quality. The *Charter of the College of William and Mary*, printed in 1736 by William Parks of Williamsburg; almost any one of the thirteen editions of the Indian Treaties printed by Franklin; the *Charter of the College of New-York* (1754), by James Parker of New York; the *Pietas et Gratulatio* (1761), by John Green of Boston; Bacon's *Laws of Maryland* (1765), by Jonas Green of Annapolis, are books of careful proportions, readability, and monumental dignity, displaying the work of the American printer at a best which was very good indeed. The headings of many newspapers were notably well designed, and broadsides printed by such men as William Goddard and Jonas Green often betrayed the quality of charm in the arrangement and display of types. Because of the utilitarian nature of his service, the colonial printer was not normally called upon to produce work in the tradition of what we call today "fine printing," but of his own volition or through circumstances, he engaged in such tasks often enough to convince us that the best practi-

tioners of the craft in his time and place were not entirely outside the
ancient tradition of excellence, that they were indeed neither insensi-
tive to its spirit nor unskilled in the processes which had created it.

Characteristics of the Output

It is not necessary to make further explanation and apology for the
paucity of works of pure literature among the issues of the American
press of the colonial period. There was indeed an appreciable amount
of verse found in its output, a sprinkling of literary essays, and a few
imaginative works of other varieties, but, on the whole, the press of
that pioneer country, as was to be expected, confined itself largely to
the production of works that expressed the everyday concerns of a
people struggling against the forces of nature, preoccupied intellectu-
ally, in some sections, with religious questions, and intent everywhere
upon the maintenance of their freedom against foreign enemies and
the development of a new liberalism in political thought. These problems were given expression in the press. A brief analysis of two years
of the press of William Parks of Annapolis and Williamsburg, to
whom one returns again and again because he typifies in many features
the normal printer of the country, serves to indicate the extent to
which the general and particular problems of the colonies were being
met by him and by printers everywhere. There are recorded from his
Maryland and Virginia presses in the years 1736 and 1737 nineteen
separate items, exclusive of newspapers. These comprise seven official
publications of the Maryland and Virginia governments; one original
work on the treatment of the prevailing pleurisy; an original medical
handbook; an abridgement of the laws of Virginia; a college charter; a
piece of official printing for a neighboring government in which no
press existed; a discussion of a locally engrossing economic question; a
military manual; a book of poems; a reprinted religious treatise; a legal
handbook; and two annual almanacs. To these must be added a newspaper of regular issue. This list is fairly typical of the product of leading printers of other colonies, though it lacks the sermons that would
certainly have found place in the issues of a New England press, and its
volume of original verse was an exceptional rather than a regular feature of publication. Furthermore, not every printer was, like Parks, a
"publick printer," engaged in the issuing of official publications. In

most colonies such an official existed, though in some places the government work was divided among two or more leading printers of the capital.

Through researches of Arthur Benedict Berthold, generously placed at our disposal, it is possible to present figures showing the proportions in which the several departments of knowledge found representation in the output of the press in the period 1639-1763. The figures for the whole country show the following percentages of the total production distributed among these classes of writings:

Theology	37.0	Education	3.5
Law	19.5	Science	1.5
Literature	19.5	Economics	1.5
Political sciences	6.5	Applied science and arts	1.0
Social sciences	4.5	Philosophy	.5
History	4.5	Bibliography	.5

The characteristics cultures of the three geographical sections of the country are suggested when we examine further Mr. Berthold's summaries and discover certain outstanding differences in their relative production in some of the categories named in the foregoing table. In philosophy, science, applied science, history, and bibliography, small categories in every section, there is hardly enough difference in percentages to be remarked upon, but in the other subjects, as displayed in the following table, a wider variance exists:

	New England	*Middle Colonies*	*Southern Colonies*
Theology	46.0	24.0	11.5
Education	4.0	4.0	1.0
Social Science	5.5	3.0	1.5
Economics	1.0	1.0	4.0
Political Science	3.5	11.0	9.0
Law (Statutes, Assembly Proceedings, Executive Utterances)	17.0	21.0	52.0
Literature	15.5	27.5	13.5

These figures have meaning only along the lines of the broadest generalization. In the case of publications in the field of law, certainly, it is misleading to cite them as indicative of sectional characteristics. Legal and governmental publications show a percentage larger than one half the output of the southern presses because the total of that output was small, while the number of governmental publications—

statutes, assembly proceedings, proclamations—of their very nature, was relatively the same in the South as in New England and the Middle Colonies. Their preponderance in this table may not be taken, therefore, as supporting the assertion, frequently made and probably true, that the chief intellectual concern of the South was in law and politics. That preponderance is, however, an indication that the interest of the South in theology, social science, and literature was less active or less widely permeative of its society than was the case in the northern sections of the country. In recording the high percentage of theological works issuing from the New England press, moreover, our table makes implications which stand the test of analysis. And it seems to be, furthermore, a reliable guide to the cultural life of the Middle Colonies when it asserts through its figures the wholesome balance in interests that marked the output of the press in that section, where theology, law, and literature show almost the same percentages. Read with critical reservations, this table presents a reliable picture of the intellectual interests of the three main divisions of the country.

Staple Productions

In the colonial period, as at the present time, there existed certain species of publications that we may regard as staples of the press. Thus, because of the frequency of their mention by many printers in many generations, we are brought to realize the importance in their business of the sale of legal and commercial blank forms. Almanacs and primers also were universally relied upon as regular sources of profit. We may take these forms for granted as staple productions and go on to speak of other kinds less well known in this association.

The legal handbook was important among the staple issues of the American press. *The Constables Pocket-Book* of Boston, 1710, the *Conductor Generalis* of [New York, 1711], and the well-known edition of this title of Philadelphia, 1722, were the earliest of the kind to find publication. A new version of the second of these appeared in Williamsburg, in 1736, with the title, *The Office and Authority of a Justice of Peace*. A bibliography by Eldon R. James lists under their various titles some forty editions between 1710 and 1800 of legal handbooks of the two varieties represented by *The Constables Pocket-Book* and the *Conductor Generalis*. Legal handbooks of other sorts, *Every*

Man His own Lawyer, The Englishman's Right, An Essay on Crimes and Punishments, The Young Clerk's Vade Mecum are works issued chiefly for laymen in communities where any man, regardless of his lack of special training, might be called upon to serve as justice of the peace, town officer, sheriff, or clerk of court.

Other kinds of books of a utilitarian character are found issuing from the various presses of the colonies with such frequency as to justify the description of them as staple productions. Following the publication by William Bradford in 1705 (some writers mention an edition of 1698) of *The Secretary's Guide, or, Young Man's Companion,* there were issued in numerous editions many handbooks of a similar character designed to give instruction to young men entering mercantile life. *The Dealer's Pocket Companion* and *The Merchant's and Trader's Security* were specimens of commercial handbooks of the ready-reckoner variety which found frequent republication in a country in which education was not necessarily a possession of the shopkeeper's assistant. Household guides in the form of cook books began with the publication of *The Compleat Housewife* by William Parks of Williamsburg, in 1742. *The American Instructor,* first brought out by Franklin in 1748, was a compendium in which were to be found sections treating most of the practical sciences already mentioned here as the subjects of separate works. The annual almanac, the New England Primer, and primers of other sorts, the book of hymn and psalm tunes, the moralized tale in chapbook form for children, the broadside ballad, the separately printed advertisement are all staples of the colonial American press which, taken with the other types mentioned and studied in their perspective, aid in building up a livelier picture of colonial social life than may be attained from any other single source known to the historian.

In New England and to a less degree in the Middle Colonies, but to a very small degree in the South, the printed sermon was a staple of the press. It is customary by way of generalization for the critics of the modern age to speak in terms of mocking reprobation of the New England sermon as dry, as intolerant, and as breathing the message of a vindictive Jehovah. But not all these sermons, in truth, nor even the greater part of them, were of that description. The pulpit took the place in those serious communities of the newspaper, the magazine, and the public lecture of a later day. Through it ideas were conveyed to a people intensely interested in ideas, and though the underlying theology of the preachers might be harsh, the practical aspects of their teaching, as it emerged from their sermons, revealed usually gentleness of character, respect for human personality, a desire to elevate men beyond their material concerns, and a sympathetic appreciation of certain central facts of life which made it a creditable expression of the spiritual, as opposed to the material, life of the community.

Our attention should be drawn to the fact that by an odd and little remarked circumstance the English Bible, that most stable of all productions, was not printed by the colonists until their declaration of freedom from the mother country. The primary reason for this was that the English Bible could legally be printed only by a patent from the Crown or *cum privilegio*. There were, of course, editions of the Bible printed in foreign languages: the first, John Eliot's translation for the Indians, appeared in 1663, and Christopher Sauer's edition of Luther's translation—the earliest American edition in a European tongue—was issued for the Pennsylvania Germans in 1743. But when William Bradford of Philadelphia proposed the publication of an English Bible in 1688 and John Fleming of Boston announced a similar venture in 1770, both were obstructed by public apathy. We may summarize the causes for their failure to attract a sufficient number of subscribers: the vigorous import trade, the smuggling of Bibles into America from Holland, and the power of an interdiction from the throne. Yet about 1752, according to Isaiah Thomas, Kneeland & Green of Boston attempted to avoid prosecution by printing a quarto edition with a London imprint, but competent scholars have vainly exerted intense efforts to verify and identify such an issue. All in all, it is quite evident that there existed no special need of an American-printed Bible until importation ceased at the beginning of the Revolution. Soon afterwards, the Congress received a petition to promote the printing of Bibles, and the Congressional committee, aware that the book trade was already burdened with shortages of type and paper, recommended that Congress either advance money for publication or import Bibles from Holland and other countries. Accordingly, by the vote of seven states against six states, Congress directed its committee to import 20,000 copies. No further action was taken as the committee undoubtedly found itself occupied with more important events. But as the war continued, the demand for Bibles naturally increased, and it took one printer, Robert Aitken of Philadelphia, little time to recognize the commercial potentialities of the situation. Between 1777 and 1781, he published five editions of the New Testament. Encouraged by this success, he planned the publication of a complete Bible which would have the official endorsement of Congress. His petition for support, submitted in 1781, received serious consideration, coming as it did from the Congress's own printer. After the text had been examined by the two chaplains, Congress recommended "this edition of the Bible to the inhabitants of the United States," a recommendation for which the Congress of 1782 has often been called the "Bible Congress." With this accolade, Aitken's Bible, published in September of the same year, became the precursor of many American editions of the English Bible.

Newspapers and Periodicals

Discussion of the staple publications of the colonial press is incomplete without special reference to the newspaper and to the periodical in the later years of the eighteenth century. Attention to the main purposes of the newspaper, the conveyance of news of the outside world and the dissemination of local information through the medium of advertisements, told upon its development in the colonies to such an extent that an English writer of 1789 commented in these words upon the quality it already displayed at that time. "The newspapers of Massachusetts, Connecticut, Rhode Island, Pennsylvania, and Maryland," he wrote "are unequalled, whether considered with respect to wit and humour, entertainment or instruction. Every capital town on the continent prints a weekly paper, and several of them have one or more daily papers." It is interesting to observe that the American newspaper assumed distinctive characteristics in editorial and typographical form in the early period of its development.

Between the years 1690 and 1820, there were published in thirty colonies and states a total number of 2120 newspapers. More than one-fourth of these journals failed to continue publication for a single year, and more than one-half expired before the end of the second year. More than 500 of them, however, ran for periods varying between five and nine years in duration, while 461 maintained publication for periods greater than ten years. This was indeed a high mortality rate, but a more interesting reflection upon the figures is that the rate was not higher, even, than here shown in view of the difficulties under which periodical journals must be published in an undeveloped country. The statistics of the distribution of these newspapers illustrate also the distribution of the publishing business of the country over that whole term of years in so far as its three chief cities were concerned. Boston issued in these years 73 journals, Philadelphia 107, and New York 138. The great number of journals published in the western states in that period indicates the extraordinarily alert character of the newer communities; Ohio, between 1793 and 1820, published 99 journals, while Kentucky, beginning six years earlier could show a total of 88 publications of a similar character. With his country in the stage of a great experiment in political and social theory, the American felt the need of keeping himself informed on public matters both for his own protection and in order that he might have his part in guiding that experiment to the point of success. Clarence S. Brigham's monumental *History and Bibliography of American Newspapers, 1690-1820* supplies a detailed record of this, the earliest period of American journalism.

It is not to be understood that the colonial newspaper pretended, through editorial utterance, to be the maker of public opinion. It conveyed news and information, leaving discussion and judgment largely to the reader. Its correspondence columns, however, in some degree took the place of the modern editorial page, for the publisher himself, or some other public-minded person, writing under a pseudonym, contributed letters inimical or friendly to movements, persons, or administrations. By closing his columns to opponents upon one excuse or another, the publisher could control the political policy of his paper. It often happened that the too-free expression of sentiments in news or correspondence columns brought the publisher into conflict with local authority or with public opinion. Such respectively were the cases of John Peter Zenger of New York, in 1734, and of William Goddard of Baltimore, in 1777 and 1779. In the celebrated Zenger trial for libel the action brought by the government was defeated through the decision of a court which affirmed that "in prosecution for libel the jury were the judges of both the law and the facts," thus establishing the germ in the English-speaking world of the idea of the freedom of the press within the limitations of truthful statement. When William Goddard found himself the object of indignity at the hands of his neighbors because of his publication in the *Maryland Journal* of matter offensive to them, the Maryland Assembly gave him protection and brought his persecutors to the bar of the House for reproof, thus making an active principle of the phrase, written in the Maryland Declaration of Rights, "that the liberty of the press ought to be inviolably preserved." These two events, respectively considered, established in principle the right of the newspaper to express opinion in the face of administrative disapproval and of popular dissent, and, taken together, formed the basis in this country of the acceptance of the newspaper press as the Fourth Estate.

It is only of late years that scholars, by investigation of their content, have evaluated the early American magazine as a factor in social and cultural development, and in the development of a class of professional men of letters. Beginning in 1740-41 with the publication in Philadelphia, three days apart, of *The American Magazine* of Andrew Bradford and *The General Magazine* of Benjamin Franklin, and carrying through the year 1800, one finds that a total of ninety-eight magazines and periodicals other than newspapers were published in the country. Principally the output of Philadelphia, New York, and Boston, these publications were for the most part vigorous in tone, hospitable to local writers, and of the first importance in developing literary tastes and pursuits throughout the nation. By far the greater number of them, about sixty, were general and literary in character, while the remainder were either religious or political, or else devoted to the interests of farm and household.

The Size of Editions

It is difficult to reach general conclusions as to the size of editions brought out by the colonial printer. The subscription book, of course, was issued in an approximation to the number of subscriptions received in advance of publication. A staple product like an almanac or a primer would reach into editions of some thousands of copies to be disposed of by the printer himself, by associated printers in nearby towns, and by hawkers and shopkeepers. In 1766 Franklin & Hall printed and sold 9,771 copies of *Poor Richard's Almanack*. In that year and the year before the same firm issued a primer in an edition of 2000 copies, and an edition of Dilworth's spelling book of an equal size. Works of original creation such as Colden's *History of the Five Indian Nations* (New York, 1727) would generally come out modestly in an edition of 500 copies. It was better business, the printer felt, to be forced to reprint a successful book than to carry on his shelves a large "remainder" of a volume that had failed to make its way. In the Franklin & Hall Work Book for 1764 and 1765, and in the firm's partnership account of 1766, we find numerous entries specifying sizes of editions that probably were normal throughout the country in the classes of publication represented.

Title	Form	Edition
Catalogue of the Library Company of Philadelphia	Book	400
Governor Franklin's Answer to the Charges	Broadside	1000
Dickinson's Address to the Inhabitants of Pennsylvania	Broadside?	2000
Remarks upon a Message	Book	500
Advertisements relating to keeping streets clean	Broadside	2500
Galloway's Vindication	Broadside	400
Meditations	Book	500

Such figures as these indicate a wide range in the size of editions in the colonial period, and confirm the obvious reflection that then as now the number of copies printed in any case was determined by the nature of the work and the probable market for it. If there needs to be stated an average figure for editions of books and pamphlets of a literary or political character in the early and middle years of the eighteenth century, it would not be far out of the way to suggest 300 to 500 copies as probable. Such a figure does not apply to the exceptional books, long awaited and of known general interest. The first book from the press in the United States, for example, *The Whole Booke of Psalmes* (Cambridge, 1640), appeared in an edition of 1700 copies; the Eliot Indian New Testament (Cambridge, 1661), in 1000 or 1500 copies; the Mennonite Martyr Book, *Der Blutige Schau Platz*, printed by the Ephrata Press in 1748, the largest book of the colonial period, was issued in an edition of 1300 copies. These were extraordinary undertakings, reflecting the confidence of the publishing agencies in the value of their productions. It is to be doubted whether similar works produced today would be issued in larger or even in equal numbers.

Costs and Charges

The cost of the normal book to printer and to purchaser in the colonial period is ascertainable in enough instances to make possible general conclusions. It has been estimated that the cost to the customer of the *Remarks upon a Message*, a small book in octavo of 72 pages, mentioned above, was about 8½ pence for each of the 500 copies printed, and the printer's net profit upon the whole job about £6. Franklin & Hall charged the customer for this octavo at the rate of 50 shillings Pennsylvania currency (or 30 shillings sterling) a sheet for composition and press work; 14 shillings currency a ream for its five reams of paper; and 40 shillings currency for folding and stitching the edition. Twenty years later, in the years immediately after the Revolution, one finds a slight increase in printing charges. Franklin's 30 shillings sterling for a sheet of octavo with its much greater amount of composition and more tedious imposition, has become, in the bill of a Connecticut printer in 1748, 28 shillings sterling for a sheet in folio. This Connecticut printer paid a local engraver about 28 shillings sterling for engraving a copperplate of the state seal to decorate the title page of the book. The cost of the paper was approximately 14 shillings sterling a ream as opposed to the 10 shillings sterling charged by Franklin. Examination of the printing charges prevailing in London in the second half of the century indicates that the American charges were appreciably higher than those of the English printer. Journeymen's wages in London in the period specified were equal to or slightly greater than in America, but the American printer must import his type, his press, a portion of his ink, and a portion of his paper. His overhead, therefore, was larger than that of his English contemporary, and living in a land in which printing houses were relatively few, his selling price did not suffer greatly from the downward pressure of competition. Throughout the period of his partnership with David Hall, including many years in which he was merely a silent partner, Franklin received from the firm annually about £467 sterling as his half of the profits arising from an establishment in which the equipment was worth only £184 in the same money. One hesitates to attempt the statement of these sums in terms of modern money, but it is obvious that a successful printing establishment of the Franklin & Hall class might be regarded as an uncommonly well-paying business.

The selling price of books, one concludes by means of extremely rough estimates, was about the same as that which prevails in our own time in the United States. William Parks issued a small book of poems —*Poems on Several Occasions*—in Williamsburg in 1736 at 15 pence hard money a copy. This sum, stated in United States money, would probably be equal today, or in this general period, to about $1.50, a normal price for the current small book of original verse. Tennent's *Essay on the Pleurisy* of the same place and year, a small octavo of 46 pages, sold at 10½ pence a copy, or about $1.05 today at the somewhat arbitrarily chosen ratio of money values in the mid-eighteenth and mid-twentieth centuries; that is as 1 is to 5. The huge Mennonite Martyr Book, comprising 1512 pages in folio, was sold in 1748 at £1 a copy. Such a volume in our period would be fairly priced at $25 or more. Bacon's *Laws of Maryland* (Annapolis, 1765), a folio of 736 pages, on an imported paper, was intended by its promoters to be sold at £1 a copy. Today a book of similar utilitarian purpose and of relative quality would sell for a sum five times as great. Innumerable examples might be set forth without greatly altering the conclusion that the cost of books to the eighteenth-century American reader was not greatly different, relative money values considered, than to his descendant of the present day.

The Censorship of the Press

The operation of the Press Restriction Acts of the English Parliament did not extend to the American colonies. Before the expiration of the last of these in 1695, presses had been established without hindrance in Massachusetts, Maryland, Pennsylvania, and New York. The interdict upon the Nuthead press of Jamestown in 1682 was the result of action by the Governor and Council of Virginia, reinforced by specific royal order. A Parliamentary restriction act was cited for the only time against an American printer, and then ineffectually, when in 1693 the Quaker magistrates of Philadelphia charged William Bradford with the violation of one of its provisions. But this does not mean that the printer operated his press free of all restraint. He recognized at least five restrictive influences upon his actions. The existence of the press in the several colonies was recognized and the machinery for its control set up by those royal instructions to governors which said "you are to provide by all necessary Orders that noe person have any press for printing, nor that any book, pamphlet or other matters whatsoever be printed without your especial leave & license first obtained." The Lower Houses of Assembly which voted the printer his salary also claimed the right to hold him to the strictest account for his actions. His position between Governor and Council on the one hand and Lower House on the other frequently drew upon him the resentment of both parties. Groups of individuals strongly entrenched in privilege occasionally were able to prevent the publication of matter affecting their policies; now and then the mob took upon itself the summary punishment of the printer who went against its current opinion; and, finally, the plea of libel in the courts provided an effective deterrent to indiscreet utterance through the press.

The censorship thus constituted, exercised now on religious or social grounds, now on political, continued to manifest itself occasionally throughout the colonial period. The regulatory power of the government came early into operation. In 1662 a law of Massachusetts required copy to be approved by a board of licensers before publication, and though there exists little evidence that this supervision often resulted in the suppression of books, it was probably at the instigation of these censors that books were occasionally prohibited publication by the General Court. *The Isle of Pines,* an amusing hoax, widely published in Europe, expressed in language and dealing with incidents of a sort not regarded as edifying by the stricter element in Massachusetts, was prohibited publication on moral grounds in 1668. An edition of the *Imitation of Christ* was refused publication in 1669 until its papistical tendencies should be subjected to revisal. The earliest newspaper of the colonies, the *Publick Occurences* of 1690, was suppressed in Boston by Governor and Council after its first issue.

A special set of circumstances brought it about that certain governors of Massachusetts exercised with marked seriousness their prerogative of licensing the printing of books within their jurisdiction, so that we can point to a few instances in which American eighteenth-century books actually display an official "leave to print." On the verso of the title leaf of John Williams's *Redeemed Captive* (Boston, 1707) is a bold "Imprimatur, || J. Dudley," and, more specifically, in the same position in [John Colman's] *Some Reasons for the Setting up of Markets in Boston,* printed by James Franklin in 1719, appears: "Boston, Feb. 29.1719. || Imprimatur, || Samuel Shute." It was as the result of action against them by the Massachusetts Assembly that James Franklin and Daniel Fowle, in 1727 and 1756 respectively, removed from Massachusetts to other colonies. We have already spoken of the conflicts with authority of William Nuthead in Virginia and of William Bradford in Pennsylvania, as the result of which these two printers removed, respectively, to Maryland and New York. The provost of the College of Philadelphia, the Rev. William Smith, for some weeks conducted classes in the Philadelphia jail, where he had been imprisoned for being concerned in the publication of matter regarded by the Lower House of Assembly as reflecting upon its dignity.

Class or group dominance often was as effective in preventing publication as government prohibition. The Mather influence in Boston weighed so heavily upon the local printers that Thomas Maule was compelled to apply to William Bradford of New York for the publication of one of his works; the Rev. Jacob Henderson of Maryland found it expedient in 1732 to fight the battle of the Maryland clergy through the medium of the Philadelphia press; and the clerical defender of the Two-Penny Act in Virginia, the Rev. John Camm, found the Williamsburg press so greatly in awe of his influential opponents that he was compelled in 1763 to send one of his pamphlets to Annapolis for publication.

The best remembered of the instances in which the offended populace, or organized minorities within it, took action against the press were those in which, in 1775, the Connecticut Sons of Liberty sacked the New York establishment of James Rivington, and, in 1777 and 1779, the Whig Club of Baltimore mistreated William Goddard and attemped to force his exile from the city.

But there was another side to the picture made by these acts of persecution. As early as 1696 a courageous Salem jury, though instructed by hostile and angry judges, pronounced Thomas Maule not guilty of libel against government, church, and ministry in the publication of his *Truth held Forth,* and vindicated his right to print fact, however disagreeable to those whom it might concern. The Maule decision, how-ever, failed to establish a precedent in English and American law. The battle for the right of the press to print the facts even when these were unwelcome to authority or the populace had to be fought over again, as told on an earlier page, by John Peter Zenger in 1734 and by Wil-liam Goddard in the early days of the Revolution. In 1774, the Conti-nental Congress in its *Letter to the Inhabitants of the Province of Quebec* had named the freedom of the press as one of the five invalu-able rights enjoyed by the English colonies of North America. The Goddard incidents of 1777 and 1779 made it clear that this assertion was more than political propaganda, that the freedom of the press had become indeed an accepted principle in American thought and action.

Despite the examples of press censorship that may be cited between 1639 and 1783, official action against the printer was the exception rather than the rule. Though the Governor's power over him was ab-solute in theory, it was in practice a power lightly and infrequently ad-ministered. Within very wide limitations of speech his press was free also from interference by the Assembly, and thanks to those circum-stances it was possible that there should occur throughout the colonial period in America, in the fields of politics and religion, a steady pro-gression towards liberalism in theory and practice. In the chapters of this section which treat the developments of the years 1784-1860, this discussion of the censorship of the press is resumed and carried into the period of the young Republic.

THE BOOK TRADE ORGANIZATION
IN THE COLONIAL PERIOD

A DISTINCTION BETWEEN the functions of printer and publisher has been recognized everywhere from the early days of the trade in printed books. We conceive of the one as the technical producer, the manufacturer of the book; of the other, as the promoter who finds the money for its printing, and directly, or through agencies of various kinds, distributes the book to the public. This broad division of function still underlies normal book trade organization in most countries of the world. It had an early beginning in the American colonies, where all its elements showed themselves fully developed in Boston in the second half of the seventeenth century.

By way of elaboration of this statement it is important to observe that in Boston, side by side with the dual organization just described, there existed an organization of a more primitive sort in which the functions of printer, binder, and publisher were united in the single person of the printer. And it must be emphasized that this more primitive system, in which a single establishment combined all the operations of manufacture and distribution, was the form of organization normal to the book trade throughout the country virtually to the end of the colonial period. In Boston, throughout the late years of the seventeenth century, we observe such men as Bartholomew Green and Benjamin Harris printing books for others, or printing and selling them at their own risk, in the normal fashion of printers everywhere in the colonies. At the same time John Usher and several others of the town were acting strictly as bookseller-publishers, and Edmund Ranger was conducting a business in which he performed the functions of bookseller-publisher and binder. Neither in New York nor in Philadelphia, in that period or for many years afterwards, did any such complexity enter the trade. William Bradford, the prototypographer of Philadelphia and New York, was, in his own person or in the persons of his immediate employees, printer, publisher, binder, and bookseller, and Benjamin Franklin throughout his business career united all these functions in the persons of himself and his staff of workmen.

The first bookseller of the colonies was Hezekiah Usher, of Boston, who, about the year 1647, added the selling of books to the general merchandise business in which he was then engaged. His relatively small dealings in books were greatly enlarged by his son John, who made bookselling his principal occupation. At the time of John Usher's greatest prosperity, there existed in Boston several competitors in his business. Neither Usher nor his rivals were mere retail booksellers; they were truly publishers whose names appeared in imprints preceded by the distinguishing words "Printed for." Though the term does not seem to have been regularly employed in the colonies, it was the function of the London "stationer" which at the turn of the century was being performed in Boston by John Usher and the other important booksellers of the town. These men initiated projects of publication, financed them, and sold the product at both wholesale and retail.

The good fortune that attended the Ushers in the business of bookselling is accounted for by the combination of political, social, and intellectual factors which existed in the thriving town of Boston and the collegiate community of Cambridge, the seat of Harvard College, but no explanation of their success would be valid that omitted emphasis upon their own intelligence and fitness for the work in hand. Basing his career upon the foundation laid down by his father, John Usher carried the business far beyond its mid-century beginnings. He began publishing on his own account in 1669, in which year his father seems to have given over to him the bookselling and publishing departments of his business of general merchandising. In addition to his selling of large importations of English books and, doubtless, of large stocks of pamphlets and books from the local presses of Boston and Cambridge, John Usher was responsible in the next thirty years for the publication of several important New England writings and a large number of local works of lesser importance. Nathaniel Morton's *New-Englands Memoriall*, a book of definite importance as an historical source, bore the imprint "Cambridge: Printed by S. G. and M. J. for John Usher of Boston, 1669." A similar imprint appeared on the title page of the *General Laws and Liberties of the Massachusetts Colony* (1672), the first

American book to be issued under an official privilege for exclusive sale. In 1675, a reissue of the sheets of this book appeared in London with an imprint bearing the names of Usher as publisher and Richard Chiswell as bookseller. Chiswell was a London stationer with whom over a period of many years Usher had dealings considerable in size for a colonial merchant of that day or even of a century later. John Usher was described by a contemporary who encountered him in 1686 as "very Rich, adventures much to sea; but has got his Estate by Bookselling." But active though the Boston book trade was in this period, it is probable that most of its votaries were forced to be satisfied with a moderate living. Usher was a man of inherited means who was bookseller, merchant, and politician at the same time. His prosperity is, accordingly, easily accounted for, but, after all, the importance of his life for us is not what the book trade of Boston did for him, but what he did for the book trade. There is no doubt that he established the tradition of aggressive vigor in method coupled with dignity in the character of production that gave individuality to the Boston book trade throughout the colonial period.

It has already been indicated that the Boston book trade organization was rendered complete by the presence in that city of independent bookbinders not directly connected with a printing house. We have seen, then, that almost every feature of the complex book trade organization of the present day existed either in fact or in germ in seventeenth-century Boston. That city was neighbor to Cambridge with its vigorous young college; it was a prosperous port, the center of an economic life based upon agriculture, commerce, and fisheries; and finally, circumstances earlier spoken of brought it about that its people were readers and students to a degree unknown elsewhere in the colonies. Generations were to pass before a system of book production and distribution approximating in extent or in fineness of organization the system in operation in seventeenth-century Boston was to be found in any other American town. And in the other towns in the meantime—in New London, in Annapolis, in Williamsburg, even in New York and Philadelphia—the twin functions of the book trade, production and distribution, were normally united in the person of the community printer, though at different times and places this duality of function seemed in the way of disappearing before the intrusion of the more complex form of organization. Such an instance occurred when a sermon by Thomas Bray appeared in Annapolis in 1700 with the statement in the imprint that it had been printed "By Thomas Reading . . . for Evan Jones Bookseller." This seems to have been the first appearance of an individual describing himself as bookseller and acting as a bookseller-publisher in any American town except Boston, but though Evan Jones appears in one capacity or another in connection with later Maryland publications, he seems never again to have described himself specifically as bookseller. Almost a century passed after his death in 1722 before the publisher, as a functionary distinct from the printer, appeared again in the book trade of Annapolis or Baltimore.

It is obvious that many of these printing establishments had attached to them bookshops in which the printer disposed not only of his own publications but, in addition, sold books imported from London. The function of the American bookseller, indeed, whether simple bookseller, publisher-bookseller, or printer-bookseller, was very largely the sale of the imported book, for the literary standard of the educated colonial American was higher than that exemplified by the product of his local press, which, it may be worth while to assert once more, was primarily utilitarian in its purpose. But on the booksellers' shelves of Boston, New York, and Philadelphia, and in the printing offices of these and the smaller cities were to be found, newly imported from London, the Greek and Roman classics and the favorite standard English works in history, theology, philosophy, and letters, together with current publications of English writers. In the *Boston Book Market*, Worthington C. Ford printed and analyzed a number of lists of books imported in the seventeenth century by John Usher, and others, with results that are confirmatory in a high degree of the accepted tradition as to the cultural status of that city in its early days. The examination in 1920 of numerous lists of private libraries by Thomas Goddard Wright for the purposes of his study, entitled *Literary Culture in Early New England*, again emphasized the high quality of the New Englander's literary interests. Later analyses of books imported by dealers in New York, Philadelphia, Annapolis, and Williamsburg, and examinations of the libraries of the gentry, merchants, and professional men of those cities and the country surrounding are leading students to conclusions not greatly different from those arrived at in regard to New England, certainly so far as the reading habits of the more prosperous and better educated groups are concerned. It is hardly necessary to develop this thesis by illustration, nor is it necessary to catalog here the contents of the colonial American bookshops, for in all essentials, except that of size, they must have been replicas of the London establishments of the period.

Bookselling Methods in the Colonies

The printing shop of the colonial small town became from its very nature a center of community life. To begin with, it was the clearing house of local information and the receiving station of news from the outside world. Its normal functions of newspaper publication and book and job printing brought to it many persons in the course of a day of business. And finally, because its proprietor was the chief local patron of the post office system, he very frequently held the office of postmaster of his town, thus adding another to the causes which made his shop a place of public assemblage. The presence of the townspeople in and about his establishment for such reasons as these encouraged him often to conduct in connection with his printing business a shop for the sale of articles of merchandise not definitely enough classified to find their way into the regular mercantile establishments, the small wares which a later period knew as "notions." On his shelves, if we may generalize from advertisements in the newspapers of all sections, might be found commodities as varied as cough medicine, sealing wax, chocolate, lemons, writing paper, pens, and fiddle strings. It would have been extraordinary if a shop with so diversified a stock had not also contained for sale books printed by its proprietor or taken on consignment from outside publishers, both of England and America. And again from advertisements, from imprints, and from other contemporary sources we learn that this was the case, that the progressive printer regarded his importation and sale of books as a service to the community almost as important as his printing. The bookselling department of the printer's business therefore formed an important addition to the agencies for book distribution provided by the separately maintained bookshop, the auction house, and the wagon of the chapman. One need mention specifically only the better known of such establishments—the bookselling departments of the printing houses of Franklin & Hall in

Philadelphia, of Hugh Gaine in New York, and of Isaiah Thomas in Worcester.

In addition to the sale of books over the counter by printer or retail bookseller, we recognize in the colonies three other modes of distribution familiar in the European practice of the time—sale by subscription, by traveling booksellers, by auction. Let us give a few moments to studying the American adaptation of these methods of bookselling.

The Subscription Method

The publication and sale of books by subscription is a development of, or, rather, a cleavage from the ancient system of individual patronage of authors. It is in effect the exchange of the single patron for the many; the single patron, with his indefinite assurance of aid, for the many, with their pledges to purchase upon publication, at a fixed price, one or more copies of a proposed book. Instead of the dedication to the single patron, the book contains under the subscription system a list of the many patrons who have made its publication possible. The older system of the single patron does not seem to have rooted itself in the colonies firmly enough to make necessary a consideration of it as a factor in the publication of books. Doubtless there were innumerable instances in which aid was given an author or publisher by individuals, groups, or public officials and public bodies, but there were few in which monetary assistance from an individual was acknowledged by the European method of printing a more or less flattering dedication at the beginning of the book. A notable exception to this general statement is found in the publication of Thomas Bacon's *Laws of Maryland*, printed by Jonas Green of Annapolis in 1765. Failing for political reasons to obtain the support of the Assembly for his project, Bacon procured subscriptions from Lord Baltimore and some twenty gentlemen and merchants of the Province. Before publication, Lord Baltimore withdrew his subscription of £100 sterling from the general fund and gave that sum outright to Bacon in consideration of the proposed dedication to himself of the great book of laws. It is believed that his Lordship's honorarium was the sole emolument received by the compiler for his labors of seven arduous years.

The first use of the subscription system in English book publication occurred in the year 1617, when John Minsheu, tiring of the uncertain ways of the individual patron, asked subscriptions of the public toward the printing of his book, *The Guide into Tongues.* The new method of underwriting expenses ran side by side with the old for two more centuries, when the finer organization of the trade and the dissemination of education made possible the general practice of the present day by which the publisher risks his own funds and recoups himself through direct sale to the public. The subscription system is still an important factor in certain special departments of the book trade, but the ancient method of dependence upon the individual patron is all but unknown in modern publishing.

The normal subscription procedure familiar to us today—the agreement of a group of individuals to take upon publication, at a prescribed rate, one or more copies of a proposed book—is that which in the eighteenth century began to show itself in the colonies as a feature of extraordinary importance in the marketing of books. Certain books which in England would have been published in the regular course of trade must be assured a reasonable sale in advance of publication in an American community containing a relatively small number of cultivated people. Samuel Willard's *Compleat Body of Divinity* (Boston, 1726), with about 650 copies taken by 450 subscribers; Prince's *Chronological History of New England* (Boston, 1736), with about 1450 copies subscribed for; *A Collection of all the Acts of Virginia* (Williamsburg, 1733), with an uncompleted list showing only some 250 books subscribed for; and Thomas Cradock's *New Version of the Psalms of David* (Annapolis, 1756), with 501 copies subscribed for, are representative of the books in prose and verse which found their way into print through vigorous canvassing for subscriptions. The subscription lists printed in some of the earlier books of this character, in the Willard and Prince works for example, are local or, at the least, sectional in the distribution of the names which compose them, but occasionally in other books of the time, and generally in later years, the character of the lists became sensibly different. When William Parks published his collection of Virginia laws, a work of widespread practical usefulness, he was able to obtain subscriptions, in addition to those received from local purchasers, from officials and lawyers throughout the middle and southern colonies, from many ship captains of London and Bristol, and from merchants and gentlemen in various parts of England. According to an advertisement in the *New York Mercury* for November 21, 1768, James Rivington, the enterprising and anonymous publisher of Churchill's *Poems* (1768), brought together a list of 2200 subscribers. The lists published in the book are evidence that his canvassers had been busy in almost all the English-American colonies, including some of those located in the islands of the West Indies.

A case of book publication by subscription that possesses many interesting features was an outright piracy in 1774 by James Rivington of New York, of John Hawkesworth's *A New Voyage Round the World performed by Captain James Cook*. This publisher, recently come from the London booksellers' world, had already gone into the business of importing and selling wholesale (we learn from a letter to Henry Knox of Boston) Irish piracies of contemporary English books. It was only one further step to entering upon the pursuit of piracy on his own account. His proposals regarding Cook's *New Voyage* read in part: "Whosoever would purchase the English Edition of the late Voyage round the World, must give Three Guineas for it; which excessive price has engaged James Rivington's Proposing to the public, a complete edition of that work, . . . in two volumes . . . excellent copperplate cuts . . . a new letter . . . a paper manufactured in this country . . . trifling price viz. one dollar and a half . . ." The publisher named in his prospectus, as prepared to accept subscriptions to the book on his behalf, representative booksellers in New York, Philadelphia, Boston, New Haven, Annapolis, Charleston, and the islands of Dominica, Antigua, St. Christopher, and St. Croix. He concluded his prospectus with a patriotic appeal of a sort not uncommon in the advertisements of printers in those years when the impending separation from England was in every man's mind. "The publication of the most esteemed modern books, at very low prices," he wrote, "will afford encouragement to infant manufactories of paper established in this province, tend to check the remittance of large sums annually, for European editions of authors, and will employ a great number of American Families, so that Mr. Rivington flatters himself a very general support will be afforded by the public to this undertaking, and the list of subscribers amply enlarged." An appeal from Rivington based upon the new American economic nationalism seems somewhat ironic when a few months later we see its writer mobbed and maltreated by his American neighbors for loyalist sympathies and expressions.

If Rivington had relied for his profit in the sale of this book solely upon advance subscriptions he would hardly have been encouraged to carry on the series of similar publications announced in his prospectus. His list shows subscriptions for only about 750 copies. At one dollar and a half each there could hardly have been much profit for him in the publication. One must assume that he expected a large post-publication sale of the book and that he counted upon his subscriptions merely as insurance against possible loss and as a means of advertising his project. From his letters to Henry Knox of Boston, and from other indications, it is clear that this was the case, clear indeed that he planned a wide distribution of the book through the booksellers of other cities. It is probable that he offered each of them, as he did Henry Knox, the privilege of having his own name in the imprint as publisher, but so far as is known from existing copies of the book only one bookseller fell in with this feature of his plan. The American Antiquarian Society possesses a copy of the book which is made up of Rivington's sheets, supplied with a cancel title leaf, bearing the imprint: "New-York: Printed for William Aikman, Bookseller and Stationer, at Annapolis, 1774." Except for the new matter in the imprint after the place of publication, this title page bears the appearance of having been printed by Rivington from the same setting of type as that used for the issue bearing his own name. Clearly Mr. Aikman's only responsibility in connection with the Annapolis issue of the book was to sell it. He advertised it in the *Maryland Gazette* for December 1, 1774, without reference to Rivington's part in the work, as "This day is published, by William Aikman . . . price 16s. currency . . ."

The Book Pedlar

A picturesque mode of bookselling that prevailed in rural America of the colonial days, and still prevails there to some extent, was the hawking of books by chapman, pedlar, and specialist "travelling bookseller." The antiquity of this practice in the colonies is evidenced by an entry in the *Diary* of Cotton Mather, who as early as 1683 (I.65) wrote, "There is an old Hawker, who will fill this Countrey with devout and useful Books, if I will direct him; I will therefore direct Him, and assist him, as far as I can, in doing so." And when in 1713 the Massachusetts Assembly passed an act against "Hawkers, Pedlars, and Petty Chapmen," he recorded in the *Diary* (II.283): "I must also assist the Booksellers, in addressing the Assembly, that their late Act against Pedlars, may not hinder their Hawkers from carrying Books of Piety about the Countrey." One concludes from this passage that the hawkers, at least in the time and place concerned, were employed as distributing agents by the larger booksellers of the city, forming another unit in the complex book trade organization of Boston in their period. A similar condition existed elsewhere in the country at a later time. Another inference to be made from Mather's words is that a doubt existed in his mind as to the application of the law to the activities of the traveling booksellers, but it does not seem that he and the established booksellers were successful in persuading the Assembly to leniency towards that group. It is true that after its term of three years had expired, the law was allowed to lapse for a period of ten years, but in 1726 it was re-enacted without a time limitation. A curious reflection upon the state of the peddling trade of that time is found in the preamble of the act of 1713 in which it is recited that complaint had been made of the injury to regular trade occasioned by hawkers, pedlars, and petty chapmen passing through the country to sell merchandise obtained by theft at the time of the late desolation of Boston by fire, and by frequent robberies and thefts since committed, and further, that with such a source of supply open to them, many dishonest handicraftsmen had given up their trades and turned pedlar.

The pedlar seems about this period to have been an unpopular adjunct to the social and commercial life of the times, for in 1729 the Pennsylvania Assembly, with the Massachusetts law of 1726 as a guide, enacted a licensing law for "Hawkers or Pedlars," and placed in it a restriction upon sale by auction except when conducted by the regularly commissioned Vendue Master of the City of Philadelphia. We shall speak at some length of this Pennsylvania act in a later section. Enactments against hawkers and pedlars are found on the books of most of the colonies north of Maryland, though it seems to have been only Massachusets that sought to eradicate them by an absolute prohibition of their activities. In most of the colonies the payment of a license fee was regarded as a sufficient indication of responsibility and a pledge of good behavior.

If one may judge from the practice of the professional traveling booksellers of a later period, notably of Mathew Carey's celebrated agent, Parson Weems, it is likely that this type of salesman carried with him a stock of well-known, standard works as well as large numbers of titles of that less weighty sort which took its name from the manner of its distribution. The "chapbook," that is, the popular tale, ballad, or pious tract, published to be sold by the chapman, or hawker, formed a considerable part of the output of the American press. From a relatively early period certain printing establishments existed almost entirely for the production of books of this character, small books and pamphlets intended to instruct or amuse the children or the less well-educated members of the rural American communities. Isaiah Thomas tells us that the business of his first master, Zechariah Fowle, was principally the printing of ballads and small pamphlets. An interesting study could be made of the nature, extent, and chief centers of this trade through the centuries. Rich material for such a study would be found in Evans' *American Bibliography*, and in such special bibliographies as Worthington C. Ford's *Broadsides, Ballads, etc., Printed in Massachusetts;* his *Isaiah Thomas Collection of Ballads;* and the *Early American Children's Books* of A. S. W. Rosenbach. The special nature of the chapbook business appears in the following imprints of two editions of a pietistic tale known as *The Prodigal Daughters.* The first reads: "Boston: Printed and Sold by E. Russell . . . 1794; (Price Six Pence)—Where Town and Country Shop-keepers, Travelling-traders, &c. may be supplied with sundry Books, &c." In a later edition, the imprint reads, even more specifically: "New York: Printed for the Travelling Booksellers. 1799."

The Book Auction

A third important means of book distribution in the American colonies is found in the auction, or as it was called in colonial days and is still called in certain rural districts of the United States, the "vendue." The sale of books by auction, long in vogue on the continent of Europe, seems to have been initiated in this country in 1713, some thirty-seven years after the first employment of that method in England, that is, the sale by auction in October, 1676, of the library of Dr. Lazarus Seaman. It was on May 28, 1713, that "a good Collection of Books" was sold in Boston at "Publick Vendue." This earliest American auction to be held solely for the disposal of books was advertised by a printed catalog of the titles, as were indeed ten of the thirteen book auctions which were held in Boston in the three-year period 1716-1718. From this time to the end of the eighteenth century, advertisements in the journals of Boston, New York, and Philadelphia are sufficiently numerous to convince one that the sale of books by the auction method was a widely accepted practice, though in fact a practice called into use with relative infrequency. There are recorded by George L. McKay, for this period of almost ninety years, 865 auctions held in Boston, Cambridge, Salem, Providence, Elizabethtown, Philadelphia, New York, Baltimore, as well as other cities or towns. Representing about ten sales a year for the whole country, this number is indicative of the acceptability to colonial bookseller and public of the auction method of book distribution.

In most of its principles, the early American book auction followed the lines familiar to us today. One observes in its practice, however, one or two variations from the normal that seem to call for particular comment. We encounter an unusual sort of book sale, for example, in reading an advertisement of April 11, 1744, in which Benjamin Franklin announced a sale by auction of choice books with the minimum price marked in each, and added that the sessions would be held daily at specified hours for a period of three weeks. That form of sale does not seem to have become general. The chief difference to be observed in practice between then and now is the employment of the auction as a means for the disposal of new books as well as of old. Of the 865 book auctions recorded by Mr. McKay for the period 1713-1800, no fewer than fifty were held for the purpose of dispersing new books or mixed lots of new books and old. Robert Bell of Philadelphia and Joseph Russell of Boston were the princpal auctioneers making a feature of the sale of new books. It is probable that such sales were a means of disposing of publishers' remainders or of slow-moving stock, but it does not seem that they were the "trade sales" of the next century in which remainders were auctioned to retail booksellers. These new-book auctions were sales open to the public in which the stock was sold a book at a time to the highest bidder. Bell, at least, seems to have had an effective method for stimulating the sale of new books by auction. In the advertisement of a sale of 1770, he announces that the retail prices of the new books are printed in the catalog and that each of them would be set up by the auctioneer at one half that amount. Though he concluded by saying that with the retail figures before them "gentlemen may see the advantage of buying by auction," it has been recorded by a contemporary that at Bell's sales the advantage did not always lie with the buyer. His skill in salesmanship was so great and his personality so engaging that he often succeeded in selling books "higher at auction than in store." It was his custom to hold auctions as far north as Boston and as far south as Charleston, South Carolina, transporting to those places collections of books, new and old, made by him in Philadelphia. A tradition preserves the memory of his dispersal in Philadelphia of forty wagon loads of books which had formerly been part of the library of William Byrd II of Westover, Virginia, though the actual details of this sale, in the absence of a catalog, have never been clearly determined.

It has already been told that in 1729 Pennsylvania passed an act licensing pedlars which included provisions against the unrestricted selling of merchandise by auction. The situation created by this act seems to have gone without effective opposition until the courageous and enterprising Robert Bell found that his business as an auctioneer of books was adversely affected by it. In January, 1773, appeared a broadside, clearly attributable to him, which called for the revision or repeal of a law which, the writer maintained, restricted the dissemination of literature. This *Observations relative to the Manufactures of Paper and Printed Books in the Province of Pennsylvania* seems to have been a successful protest. In the year 1774 a new law was enacted which rescinded the provisions of the act of 1729 in so far as they referred to books, removing "the Sale of Books, by Auction," says *Bell's Memorial* [*to the Assembly*], of 1784, "from every Restraint whatsoever." But during the Revolution, in 1777 and 1779, after profiteers had seen in the auction a method of enhancing the prices of commodities, other acts were passed placing all public vendues, not excepting those held for the sale of books, in the hands of the public auctioneer of Philadelphia. In 1783, this temporary act, made for the wartime emergency, was replaced by a permanent law of the same tenor. Bell protested most strongly to the next session of Assembly against an enactment that might result in "a Monopoly of the Book Trade," and alleged that his own efforts as a private auctioneer had added to the development of the arts, sciences, and manufactures in Pennsylvania. Bell declared, furthermore, that during the war, when the restrictions prevented him selling by auction in Philadelphia, he had "carried over-land at a very great expence several Tons of Books Manufactured in Pennsylvania, and sold them by Auction in the State of Massachusetts . . ." His protest, however, was without avail. The act remained upon the books even though its provisions with reference to book auctions do not seem to have been rigidly enforced. There was evidently some loophole in it which enabled the book auctioneers to continue their business for the time being. Throughout the months of 1784, preceding his death in September, Bell continued to hold book auctions in Philadelphia, and in that year also there were several sales by Alexander Boyd, one of the public auctioneers appointed in 1783. Eleven sales were held in 1785, and from 1786 to 1792 William Prichard, a bookseller, held numerous auctions, probably under public appointment. After that year, however, comparatively few sales were held in Philadelphia until the beginning of the new century. It may have been the continuance of this law upon the Pennsylvania statute books that was responsible for the eventual loss to Philadelphia of the chief book auction business of the country, though the truth is that in the closing decade of the century the book auction business dwindled to small volume everywhere. When it began to flourish once more after the War of 1812, its chief activity was found to be centered in the cities of Boston and New York.

In a later section (Pages 119-121), under the heading "The Expansion of the Book Trade," will be found a discussion of the greatly increased bookselling trade of the period 1784-1860.

PART II

BOOK PRODUCTION AND DISTRIBUTION FROM THE
AMERICAN REVOLUTION TO THE WAR
BETWEEN THE STATES

by

Lawrence C. Wroth and Rollo G. Silver

PRINTING AND BOOKMAKING, 1784-1860

The Background of the Period

THE CITIZEN of the United States whose term of life covered the years from the close of the Revolution in 1783 to the eve of the Civil War in 1860 witnessed a series of significant historical events affecting the fortunes of his own country, and took part in the great economic change which gradually in that period altered the face of the world. In his youth and young manhood occurred the quasi-war of the United States with France, the war with Great Britain, and those with the pirates of Tripoli and Algiers—all of them waged in defense of the commercial rights and the dignity of the youthful nation. In his age he saw his country enter upon what many considered a war of aggression against Mexico, a war which resulted in the straightening of boundaries and the accession of territory desired by imperialistic groups since the Louisiana Purchase of 1803. When in the last year of this hypothetical citizen's life the South seceded from the Union, putting to the test a constitutional privilege long in question, it detached itself temporarily from a country of which the boundaries were then Canada, the Lakes, and the St. Lawrence on the north, the Atlantic on the east, the Gulf and the Rio Grande on the south, and the Pacific on the west. The small stream of pioneers which began making its way across the Appalachian ridge about 1750 had become by this time a great river with many branches, drawn to Oregon by furs, to California by gold, to the inland west and southwest by cattle and grain. The steamboat, the railroad, and the electric telegraph had come into being, and, in the factories and mills, steam was supplanting water power and the human arm as the source of effective energy. In that citizen's life of less than eighty years the territory forming the United States changed in size from the limitations of a narrow coastal plain to the vast area of half a continent; in population from something like three million inhabitants to more than thirty-one million; and in economic development from

63

the agricultural stage to the industrial. In that period, also, the center of population had shifted from twenty-three miles east of Baltimore to a point some twenty miles south of Chillicothe, Ohio.

In other fields than the material the country shared the great changes which took place everywhere in this period. Political liberalism invaded the chief countries of Europe, humanitarianism affected every walk of life, and the rationalism which had been gathering force throughout the eighteenth century became the dominant factor in human thought. Physical science was pointing the direction of philosophical thought and forming the basis of a new industrialism.

The year 1790 forms a starting point in the modern annals of the United States, which then still consisted of the original thirteen states and Vermont. The new Constitution had gone into effect only the year before, establishing by its provisions an integrated union of states with a centralized government in place of the loose federation of separate commonwealths under which the country had won its freedom. The government under the new order was still in the hands of the fathers of the country, of Washington, Adams, Hamilton, and Jefferson, a conservative group, though the spirit of French Jacobinism, working through the democratic philosophy of Jefferson, was soon to become a powerful element and to bring about disunion of thought and policy. Even in the first year of the operation of the Constitution, problems of interpretation arose, party lines began to form, and the slavery question to raise its head. The monetary system of the country was in the way of being placed upon a firm basis by Alexander Hamilton. The decimal ratio, with the dollar as its unit, had been adopted by the Continental Congress in 1785, though the British pound and the Spanish milled dollar, the "piece of eight," were still in frequent use as currency or as the basis of commercial calculations. Though the Indian disputed with some effectiveness much of the country between the Appalachian range and the Mississippi, the celebrated "Ordinance for the Government of the Northwest Territory" had been passed without regard to his physical occupation of forest, prairie, and river. Nine out of every ten breadwinners of the country were still engaged in some form of agriculture, but the manufacturing industries and mercantile pursuits were becoming important factors in various parts of the nation. Shipbuilding, fisheries, and maritime trade in New England, iron manufacturing in almost all sections, and papermaking in Pennsylvania were the first of those industries, which, in increasingly great numbers, were soon to begin drawing men from the cultivation of the soil.

In the New England states in 1790 laws existed requiring compulsory rudimentary education. The country as a whole was able to count fourteen colleges within its borders, claiming an enrollment among them of 1200 students. In that year the total periodical publication of the nation numbered 103 titles, of which eight were daily newspapers, seven were magazines, and the remainder were weekly or semi-weekly newspapers. The total population numbered 3,893,635 persons, of whom 694,280 were negro slaves.

Such a brief statement of conditions as has been given here must necessarily fail to mention many social and economic factors that affect the history of printing and bookselling, but it would be a serious omission from any such summary to say nothing about the huge accretions to the population by immigration that occurred in the first half of the nineteenth century. Irish, Scotch-Irish, and Germans came in great numbers to work the new farming lands and to provide man power for the industries of the growing cities. Though retaining in some respects their native characteristics and cultures, the components of these groups were sufficiently like the original stock to be readily assimilated in the racial and social constitution of the land.

The Expansion of the Press

The expansion of the press kept pace with the physical expansion of the country; in the period between the Revolution and the Civil War it displayed the characteristics of the pioneer movement of which it formed a part. Over the Laurel Hills from eastern Pennsylvania to Pittsburgh and the Ohio Country; along the Potomac Route from Maryland and Virginia to the same frontier lands; through the Cumberland Gap from Virginia and the Carolinas to Kentucky; along the Great Lakes from New England and New York to the Northwest went by foot and wagon train thousands of hopeful men and women in search of farm lands and town sites. Now accompanying, now on the heels of this great folk movement, partaking of its physical hardships and its bright expectations, went ambitious and aggressive young men with printing presses and small supplies of type, packed in wagons, on mules and horses, or in the bateaux which floated down the almost virgin rivers of the new country. The genius of this race of northern men, educated, or, in any case, coming from communities in which the school, the church, and the press were the outstanding social forces, seemed to demand the services of the printer for the expression of local needs and for keeping the communities in touch with the outside world. Elsewhere it has been said that the temerity of the Americans in separating from England and in setting up their own and different scheme of government had been an impetus towards stimulation of the national mentality. They felt that their experiment was on trial in the eyes of the world and that it behooved them to conduct it to a successful issue. These Americans of the West desired, therefore, to keep themselves informed of the affairs of their world and of the world beyond the mountains, believing that such knowledge was an essential step in the maintenance of their position. Wherefore to every forest-surrounded hamlet and to the isolated farms of the river bottoms came soon after their settlement the newspaper, the pamphlet, and the book of laws from some nearby press that had followed their inhabitants into the wilderness.

In 1786, Pittsburgh, or Fort Pitt, formerly Fort Duquesne, was a frontier river port of Pennsylvania, numbering some 300 souls. To this outpost of the new nation came, in the year named, two young men, John Scull and Joseph Hall, who at once upon their arrival set up the first trans-Allegheny press. On July 29, 1786, they began the publication of the *Pittsburgh Gazette*, a journal now known as the *Commercial Gazette*, which has been published continuously ever since.

In 1786, also, John Bradford, then active in Kentucky as a land surveyor, was chosen to establish a printing-house by a convention assembled at Danville to discuss and plan the separation of the country from Virginia. Almost at once the citizens of Lexington made over to him without charge a site within their town for the erection of his establishment. The transportation of the Bradford press and appurtenances from Philadelphia to Lexington by wagon, boat, and pack horse is one of the notable episodes in the history of the press in America. While he awaited the arrival of his equipment, John Bradford sent his brother, Fielding, to Pittsburgh to learn printing in the newly established office of John Scull. When at last on August 11, 1787, the first number of the *Kentucky Gazette* appeared in Lexington, its imprint announced that it had been published by John and Fielding Bradford. In the earliest known number of this journal, August 18, 1787, John Bradford informed his readers, in effect, that Kentucky had a future even though for the moment it was "in an infant state, harassed by the most savage enemies, having no profitable trade and being drained of money by its present intercourse with the Eastern parts of America." Under the unpropitious circumstances and amid the dangers of a genuine frontier, Bradford won slowly to the success he deserved, as, in the words of his address previously cited, "the *first adventurer* in a business which has been chiefly instrumental in bringing mankind from a state of blindness and slavery to their present advancement in knowledge and freedom."

In November, 1791, George Roulstone and Robert Ferguson established in Tennessee at Hawkins Court House the *Knoxville Gazette*. In November, 1793, William Maxwell began at Cincinnati, Ohio, the publication of *The Centinel of the North-Western Territory*. Another great natural barrier was passed by the expanding press when, in 1808, Joseph Charless crossed the Mississippi and set up a printing establishment in St. Louis. In July of that year he issued a newspaper entitled the *Missouri Gazette*, and a few months later published a book of more than four hundred pages entitled *The Laws of the Territory of Louisiana*. The earliest Texas press was conducted under local Mexican auspices, as an aid to the revolutionary movement against Spain, by Samuel Bangs, a printer from Baltimore, who in 1817 at Galveston and elsewhere printed proclamations and broadsides of a political nature. In 1834, Ramón Abreu established a press, conducted by Jesús María Baca, in Santa Fé, New Mexico. In the same year the "farthest west" of the press of the United States was reached when Agustín Vicente Zamorano, who had come some years previously from Florida by way of Mexico City, set up at Monterey, California, a regular printing press, having until that time used a method of hand stamping for the production of blank forms. The San Francisco press was established in 1846, in good time to assume the responsibility thrust upon it by the "gold rush" of 1849. It was not until August, 1846, that *The Californian*, the first California newspaper, in English and Spanish, was begun in Monterey by the Rev. Walter Colton and Robert Semple, using for the purpose the old Zamorano press. One of the most romantic episodes in this western dissemination was the coming to Idaho in 1839 of Edwin O. Hall, a missionary-printer, who was sent at the expense of native Christian women of Hawaii to aid in the conversion of the Indians of the Pacific Northwest, particularly of the Nez Percé tribes. He brought with him from Honolulu a small press which he put immediately into operation, and in May, 1839, issued 400 copies of an eight-page book called the *Nez-Perces First Book: designed for Children and new Beginners.* This interesting production bore the imprint: "Clear Water: Mission Press, 1839." In February, 1846, John Fleming issued at Oregon City, Oregon, *The Spectator,* and in the next year an edition of Webster's *Elementary Spelling Book.*

Occasionally the first product of these early presses deviated from the norm of newspaper, broadside, or book. In 1849, for example, Brigham H. Young and Thomas Bullock, as compositors, set type for the first printing in Utah—a fifty-cent bill of paper currency. It is also interesting to note that some printers were fully aware of the symbolic significance of these pioneer presses. When the first copy of the *Du Buque Visitor* was printed on the first press in what is now Iowa, there occurred a pleasant little ceremony in which William Carey Jones, the printer, put the first sheet in the press, Andrew Keesecker, the compositor, pulled the lever, and the sister of Judge King, the owner, removed the sheet. And in his effort to become the first printer in the area now Colorado, John L. Merrick succeeded in issuing his *Cherry Creek Pioneer* on April 23, 1859, approximately 30 minutes before William N. Byers issued his *Rocky Mountain News.* The foregoing record of establishment of presses names the significant stations in the geographical expansion of the printing art throughout the country and supplements the data appearing in the table on page 69.

These editor-printers who lugged their cumbersome appliances into the wilderness attended to the day-by-day printing needs of the community. Newspapers, pamphlets, laws of local interest, commercial announcements, bills, and legal forms comprised their output. Occasionally they produced a book, but when they did so, it was a time-consuming project, usually conducted at odd moments during slack periods and without sufficient equipment. Thus, as Ellison has noted, the text of the first Alabama novel, *The Lost Virgin of the South* (1833), was printed in two sizes of type. Since these infrequent books were really by-products, the editor-printers should not be regarded as book publishers, nor the early printing presses throughout the country as instruments of book production in any general sense. The book publishing industry, as we shall see, was gradually centralized in a few cities during the first half of the nineteenth century.

CHRONOLOGICAL TABLE OF THE FIRST PRESSES IN EACH OF THE UNITED STATES

State	Town	Year	Printer
Massachusetts	Cambridge	1639	Stephen Daye
Virginia[1]	Jamestown	1682	William Nuthead
Maryland	St. Mary's City	1685 (Aug.)	William Nuthead
Pennsylvania	Philadelphia	1685 (Dec.)	William Bradford
New York	New York City	1693	William Bradford
Connecticut	New London	1709	Thomas Short
New Jersey[2]	Perth Amboy	1723	William Bradford
Rhode Island	Newport	1727	James Franklin
South Carolina	Charleston	1731	George Webb Eleazer Phillips, Jr. Thomas Whitmarsh
North Carolina	New Bern	1749	James Davis
New Hampshire	Portsmouth	1756	Daniel Fowle
Delaware	Wilmington	1761	James Adams
Georgia	Savannah	1762	James Johnston
	(First imprint, 1763)		
Louisiana	New Orleans	1764	Denis Braud
Vermont	Dresden (now Hanover, N. H.)	1778	Alden Spooner
Florida	St. Augustine	1783	William Charles Wells John Wells, Jr. Charles Wright
Maine	Falmouth (now Portland)	1785	Benjamin Titcomb, Jr. Thomas B. Wait
Kentucky	Lexington	1787	John Bradford Fielding Bradford
District of Columbia	Georgetown	1789	Charles Fierer
West Virginia	Shepherdstown	1790	Nathaniel Willis
Tennessee	Hawkins Court House (now Rogersville)	1791	George Roulstone Robert Ferguson

[1] The Virginia Press of William Nuthead was inhibited, so far as we know, before it completed a single job. In 1730 a press was permanently established in Williamsburg by William Parks.

[2] William Bradford went to Perth Amboy in 1723 for a special job only. It was in 1754 that James Parker really established a press in New Jersey.

CHRONOLOGICAL TABLE OF THE FIRST PRESSES IN EACH OF THE UNITED STATES (*Cont.*)

State	Town	Year	Printer
Ohio	Cincinnati	1793	William Maxwell
Michigan	Detroit	1796	John McCall
Mississippi	Walnut Hills (now Vicksburg)	c. 1798	Andrew Marschalk
Indiana	Vincennes	1804	Elihu Stout
Alabama	Wakefield	1807	?
Missouri	St. Louis	1808	Joseph Charless
Illinois	Kaskaskia	1814	Matthew Duncan
Texas	Galveston	1817	Samuel Bangs
Arkansas	Arkansas Post	1819	William E. Woodruff
Wisconsin	Navarino (now Green Bay)	1833	Albert G. Ellis John V. Suydam
Kansas	Shawnee Baptist Mission	1834 (Mar.)	Jotham Meeker
California	Monterey	1834 (c. June)	Agustin V. Zamorano
New Mexico	Santa Fé	1834 (Aug. or Sept.)	Jesús María Baca
Oklahoma	Union Mission	1835	John F. Wheeler
Iowa	Dubuque	1836	William C. Jones Andrew Keesecker
Idaho	Clearwater	1839	Edwin O. Hall
Oregon	Oregon City	1846	John Fleming
Nebraska	Winter Quarters (now Florence)	1847	?
Utah	Salt Lake City	1849 (Jan.)	Brigham H. Young Thomas Bullock
Minnesota	St. Paul	1849 (April)	James M. Goodhue
Washington	Olympia	1852	James W. Wiley Thornton F. McElroy
South Dakota	Sioux Falls	1858 (before Oct. 4)	Samuel J. Albright
Nevada	Genoa	1858 (Dec.)	Alfred James William L. Jernegan
Arizona	Tubac	1859 (Mar.)	Jack Sims George Smithson
Colorado	Denver	1859 (April)	John L. Merrick
Wyoming	Fort Bridger	1863 (June)	Hiram Brundage
Montana	Virginia City	1863 (after Oct. 19)	Daniel W. Tilton Benjamin R. Dittes
North Dakota	Fort Rice	1864	Robert Winegar [?] Ira F. Goodwin [?]

The Beginnings of Industrialization

There have been two great periods in the development of typography as a mechanical art—the last half of the fifteenth century and the first half of the nineteenth. The essential factor in the establishment of the art was the invention of the type mold, the instrument by means of which any required number of individual letters could be cast at will. The other implements, materials, and processes of the craft as at first practiced were old and well understood—the designing and cutting of the type punches and the making of matrices were processes taken over from the engraver and die maker; the setting of types in the proper order to impress words and sentences upon a sheet of paper, a substance well known to Europe in Gutenberg's time, was but an extension of the scrivener's task; the press was an implement known to the printer of woodcuts and but little different in mechanical essentials from the familiar wine press of every village. The type mold drew together all these constituents and created a new art upon the foundation they provided. At first laboriously practiced, this art, sometime in the decade 1470-1480, made a surprising advance in mechanical operation with the invention of the chase, the device for locking in a rigid form two, four, eight, or a greater multiple of pages of type in such arrangement that when impressed upon the sheet and folded according to plan, the printed pages would run in consecutive order. There was no further fundamental improvement in the art of printing for a period of more than three hundred years, when, in the first half of the nineteenth century, were evolved new principles in type-casting and setting, in papermaking, and in press building which changed printing from an art to an industry, removing it from the household to the factory stage of development. The part taken in this second birth of the craft by American printers and mechanics, while less notable than that of their English, German, and French contemporaries, is none the less worth the attention of later generations.

As we shall see later, the major American contributions to the mechanical side of the printing industry began to appear after the Civil War. But at least a decade earlier, the large firms had begun to adopt systems of planning and management which resulted in production less costly in time and material than before. When the new machines were invented, the engineering operations were thus easily geared to accommodate them. The Harpers of New York, as early as 1855, manufactured books in an efficient assembly line, remarkably similar to the so-called modern methods of the twentieth century. Their establishment of sixteen buildings had been destroyed by fire on December 10, 1853, and a decision was made to build immediately, at whatever expense, the best equipped printing plant in the United States. The new plant, completed within two years, comprised two seven-floor buildings, each covering about a quarter of an acre. One building, facing Franklin Square, contained the counting room, supplies, paper, and book stock; the other, fronting on Cliff Street, was devoted to manufacturing. Here, in the basement, the paper was pressed in standing presses, and then dampened to receive printing ink. From this room the paper was hoisted to the press room on the first floor. There, twenty-eight Adams bed-and-platen presses were power driven from the steam engine below. Each press was fed by a girl who stood on a raised platform at the side. After printing, the paper went to the drying room on the second floor to remain about twenty-four hours before being placed in the hydraulic pump presses in the next room. Dried and pressed, the sheets were hoisted to the third floor for folding and gathering, then to the fourth floor for pressing, sawing, and sewing. Finally, in the bindery on the fifth floor, the process of bookmaking was completed. The top floor of the building, being light and airy, provided an excellent location for composition and electrotyping. Other advantages accrued from this well-designed plant: by reducing the movement of material to the minimum, the firm was able to use female help for many operations. Approximately 300 girls worked in the building—150 in the gathering and folding room, 100 in the sewing room, 30 in the press room and 12 in the gilding room. In the Harper plant of 1855, we see a microcosm of nineteenth century American industry.

The Development of the Printing Machine

The first change of moment in the improvement of the press after its taking form under Gutenberg and his immediate successors occurred with the development of the iron press by Earl Stanhope in the last year of the eighteenth century. The Stanhope Iron Press was not indeed the first of the modern presses but rather the highest development of the old-style machine. It looked backward to the perfection of old principles rather than forward to the creation of new. Its structural material made possible two things, the application of compound power to its impressing mechanism, whereby a stronger pressure could be exerted with less effort, and the fashioning of an absolutely true flat surface of any reasonable dimension, thus making it possible to create platens large enough to print one side of a whole sheet by a single pull of the bar, an improvement instituted in French presses by Annisson in 1783. Before that time even the smaller sheets had required two pulls of the bar and a movement of the carriage between each pull. The Stanhope press, therefore, and certain later machines, such as the Columbian, soon to be described, present themselves to us as marking the apogee of the Gutenberg press. The modern press was to have its origin in the application of an entirely different set of mechanical principles to the problem of impressing inked type faces upon white paper. It discarded vertically applied force for rotary motion, substituting, in both inking and impressing operations, the cylinder for the plane. We shall return to the consideration of this fundamental change in process after we have discussed briefly the last phases of the ancient method. In a volume of the character of this it is not practical to include pictorial illustrations of the many sorts of printing presses to be described in the following paragraphs. In the classified list of references at the end of this book are given under *Printing Manuals* and *Printing Presses* a number of books and articles in which are displayed photographs and drawings of many presses, old and new, with discussion of the details of their mechanism.

The press in use in the United States throughout the colonial period was the common wooden press of the English printers. Despite the praise of the Dutch or so-called Blaeu press by English and Scottish typographical experts, convinced of its stronger and more exact construction and its superiority in minor features of operation, it came into general use neither in England nor in the colonies. The only suggestion we have found in either country for the improvement of the common press came in the instructions which Benjamin Franklin sent to his press builder in England in 1753, in which in discussing the structure of the "ribs" or tracks upon which the carriage traveled back and forth beneath the platen, he wrote, ". . . I would have the ribs made not with the face rounding outwards, as usual, but a little hollow or rounding inwards . . . ; and the cramps made of hard cast brass, fixed not across the ribs, but longways, so as to slide in the hollow face of the ribs. The reason is, that brass and iron work better together than iron and iron. Such a press never gravels; the hollow face of the ribs keeps the oil better, and the cramps, bearing on a large surface, do not wear, as in the common method . . ." Even this sensible suggestion does not seem to have been generally adopted by the press builders of either country.

The American part in the development of the modern press was notable chiefly for the skill with which American press builders adapted and improved fundamental ideas imported from England. We hear frequently of the Ramage press as an American improvement, but it seems difficult to point to a fundamental contribution to structure or operation by Adam Ramage. This individual was nevertheless an accomplished press builder whose establishment in Philadelphia in the first quarter of the nineteenth century supplied numbers of American printers with excellent presses of the old sort, and one who kept his product abreast of current development by the addition to its mechanism of such devices as screws of larger diameter to increase impressing power, spiral springs to support the platen, and the use of iron instead of wood for beds and platens.

The most notable contribution of an American inventor to the improvement of the old flat-bed press occcurred when about the year 1807, George Clymer, of Philadelphia, began the construction of his celebrated Columbian Iron Press. The early stages of invention and use remain obscure, although the research of Ralph Green has recently revealed that the press in its final form appeared in 1813. However, when in 1815 William McCullough, a printer of Philadelphia, addressed to Isaiah Thomas a series of communications intended to aid in a revision and enlargement of the *History of Printing in America*, he was unable to give a description of the invention of his fellow townsman, affirming that he had never seen one of the new presses. But three years later, in Van Winkle's *Printers' Guide* of New York, 1818, testimonials to the value of the Columbian Press are found signed by some nineteen New York printers, and by two well-known printers of London. For the first available technical description of the Columbian Press, it is necessary to turn to the English printers' manuals of the years 1824 and 1825. Because the high price of his press limited the domestic market, Clymer sailed for England in 1817 to arrange for production there. He patented the press in the same year and its advertisement in that country, we learn, had been accompanied by a great deal of what the present-day American describes as "ballyhoo." But despite this fact, wrote Hansard with his customary fairness: "the testimonials published in favour of this press are certainly of the most respectable character, and the private information which has been given me by clever workmen, . . . impresses upon my mind very favourable ideas of its capacity to produce fine and good work . . ." The year before, in 1824, Johnson had given a full account of the Columbian Press in his *Typographia* and had described a technical test in which it had come out victor over the Stanhope and other improved iron presses of the period. The factor of chief significance in the construction of the Columbian Press was that it did away with the screw as the agency for the transmission of the impressing power, substituting the principle of the fulcrum with the power applied by a series of levers set in action by a bar. The Columbian Press had many rivals in England.

When, as late as 1866, Thomas Mackellar brought out a second edition of his *American Printer* he thought it worth while to include a picture of the recently popular Columbian Press. In connection with his account of it he wrote that "Hand presses are now restricted to country papers of small circulation, and to book-offices devoted to extra fine printing." The Columbian continued until recently to be listed in English supply lists; it had, therefore, a length of life well deserved by the first effective and successful hand-worked, iron, flat-bed press to do away with the screw as the impressing power in favor of the principle of the fulcrum and lever.

In America, Ramage and other builders produced machines of greater simplicity but of similar principles which gradually displaced the invention of Clymer. Early in 1819, John I. Wells of Hartford patented a press completely constructed of iron and which, for the first time, employed a simple toggle joint instead of the screw. This press, as Green states, was the form of hand press which established the pattern followed by the successors of Wells. One of the most popular of these later presses, named for Peter Smith, a partner of Robert Hoe, remained in production from 1823 to 1880. Its solid construction and good design, rather than any technical innovations, were, as we shall see, also characteristic of other presses made by the firm of Robert Hoe. But it was Samuel Rust of New York who, by improving the toggle joint (1821) and substituting a beam frame for the heavy cast iron frame (1829), produced a much lighter albeit much stronger mechanism in his Washington Press. The Hoe firm, recognizing its superiority, repeatedly attempted to purchase the patent, finally managing to obtain it about 1834. Thereafter, the firm produced Washington as well as Smith Presses, with both possessing the beam frame devised by Samuel Rust.

Another American hand press must be described here because of the position occupied by its inventor in the general history of typographical development. In speaking of the early typesetting machines, we shall emphasize the contribution of Dr. William Church to modern printing practice. For the present we are concerned only with the printing machine of his invention displayed in England about the year 1821. In Hansard's *Typographia* the press of Church is given three pages of description in connection with the other inventions which were to work in conjunction with it, the press being, in Hansard's opinion, the only practicable feature of the threefold invention. Church's press, though an iron hand press of the old flat-bed type with the impressing power applied vertically, brought into use the new method of ink distribution by rollers, "without which," Hansard wrote, "no machine-printing would ever have succeeded." The following sentences from this same historian of printing methods briefly summarize the chief features of the Church press: "It may be as well," he wrote, ". . . to state, that the object of this press, as to the saving of labour, is that one pressman alone shall perform the whole; he has only to lay the sheet on the tympan, and immediately apply his hand to the rounce, by the turning of which the forme is inked, the frisket and tympan turned down, the press run in, and the impression given: a reverse of motion reverses the process, and prepares for the next sheet. This press certainly turns out very excellent work, at somewhat less expense than a Stanhope, . . . but in its first cost is about double; and I do not find it possible to execute more than one fourth or, at most, one third more than those other presses worked by a man and a boy; . . ." Here, if properly developed and simplified, was undoubtedly a definite improvement in press building, but the fact is, the flat-bed hand press with vertically applied power was never to undergo a much higher development than it represented.

During this time, the early 1820's, manifestations of the industrial revolution began to appear in the American printing industry. With the science of mechanics providing new means for the transfer of energy, it became possible to convert the bed-and-platen hand press to a power-driven machine. About 1822 Daniel Treadwell of Boston started building horsepower presses for which the power was actually supplied by a horse walking on a circular track. Several such presses were put into operation, but it was soon apparent that steam would be a better source of power. And so, in 1823, Jonas Booth of New York used it for printing an *Abridgment of Murray's English Grammar* which, at the time of publication, was said to be the first book printed on a steam power press in the United States. The most successful American press of this type was invented by Isaac Adams in 1830 and improved by him in 1836. It soon captured the American market, and from that time until after the Civil War this power-driven bed-and-platen press was extremely popular for book work and good printing. Our most competent authority in this field, Ralph Green, has estimated that close to 90 per cent of the good book and magazine printing was turned out on Adams presses. But while this was going on, the new era of the cylinder press had already begun.

The broad difference of principle between the cylinder press and the manual press with its vertical application of power both in the inking of forms and in their impression was based, in Hansard's words: upon "the substitution of two cylinders, or of one cylinder and a plane, for producing the impression, instead of the two plane surfaces of the ordinary, or Stanhope press; and secondly, the use of cylinders covered with . . . adhesive and elastic composition, for applying the ink to the surface of the forme of type, . . . which, in the old process, was laid on with large balls, or dabbers." The first appearance of the application of the cylinder to the mechanics of the press is found in the patent taken out in England by William Nicholson in 1790, the terms of which, Hansard affirms, "show that all subsequent attempts at machine-printing are but so many modifications of the same principle, . . ." The discovery of an elastic composition for covering the inking cylinder, instead of the skins proposed by Nicholson, and the refinement of the machinery by mechanics more practical than that inventor established the cylinder press in its various forms as the leading element of the new age in printing. The application to it of steam, and later of electricity, as the source of its motive force was an incident in its progress not connected with its basic principles.

It was on the flat-bed, steam-powered cylinder press of Friedrich König that an edition of the London *Times* of November 28, 1814, was run off in thousands of copies, the first large-scale demonstration of the new principle operated by the new power. There is no need to call the roll of those English inventors who thereafter proceeded to perfect the cylinder press along the lines laid down by Nicholson and König. We are interested in the American contribution to this development and to the revolution it worked in the printing offices of the United States.

The activities of the house of Hoe have formed one of the chief contributions of the United States to the development of modern typography and have placed that name on the honor roll of the great printers and type founders. The striking thing is that this has occurred despite the fact that the Hoe inventions have not been fundamental in the sense that the Nicholson patent for the introduction of the cylinder in impressing and inking was fundamental and subversive of earlier methods. But by a century of persistence in the further application of fundamental principles, the successive generations of that house have done more for the improvement of machine printing than any other agency of their times.

The Hoe firm was established in the United States by Robert Hoe of Leicestershire, England, in the year 1805. In association with Matthew and Peter Smith, Hoe formed a firm for carpentry and machine work which began soon to take up in New York the construction of printing presses of the old flat-bed and platen type. Their chief productions in this field were the Peter Smith Press and, after acquiring the patent, the Washington Press. It should be remembered that these finely constructed hand presses of iron—the Columbian, the Peter Smith, the Ramage presses, the Washington Press—with their application of the principle of the toggle joint, or of the spindle and lever instead of the screw for making the impression, remained in regular use for certain kinds of book and pamphlet work for a great many years after the steam-operated, cylinder machines had been perfected for newspaper and other large edition work.

The Hoes took over also at least two presses that stood halfway between the old form of press and the new. The Daniel Treadwell press of 1822 was a power press of the flat-bed and platen principle, and another and better of the same sort was that which Isaac Adams of Boston sold to the Hoe establishment in 1859.

The real contribution of the Hoes began when the first Napier cylinder presses reached the United States. This machine had been described by Hansard in 1825, punning pleasantly, as the "Nay-peer," and so for its time it seems to have been. In 1830 the firm of Robert Hoe began to study the Napier press and to build others along the lines of its construction. These were flat-bed and cylinder presses with the beds moving back and forth beneath the revolving cylinders, and with improved devices for automatic handling of the paper by "grippers" or fingers. The Hoes made various improvements in operation, and began to acquire an international reputation as press builders. But their great and individual contribution was the development of a press which dispensed with the flat bed and carried the type forms upon the cylinder itself, with supplementary cylinders giving the impression. In 1847 the first specimen of the "Hoe Type Revolving Machine," developed by Richard March Hoe, was put in operation in Philadelphia at the office of the *Public Ledger*. Let us quote from the description of the features of this press given in 1902 by Robert Hoe, the inventor's grandson. "The basis of these inventions," wrote Mr. Hoe, "consisted in an apparatus for securely fastening the forms of type on a central cylinder placed in a *horizontal* position. This was accomplished by the construction of cast-iron beds, one for each page of the newspaper. The column rules were made 'V' shaped; i.e., tapering toward the feet of the type. It was found that, with proper arrangement for locking up or securing the type upon these beds, it could be held firmly in position, the surface form a true circle, and the cylinder revolved at any speed required without danger of the type falling out. Around this central cylinder from four to ten impression cylinders, according to the output required, were grouped. The sheets were fed in by boys, and taken from the feed board by automatic grippers, or fingers, operated by cams in the impression cylinders, and which conveyed them around against the revolving form of the central cylinder." The first of these presses was a Four Cylinder machine. Tended by four boys to feed the paper, it was capable of running off 8000 sheets an hour, printed on one side. A revolution in newspaper printing was the result of the introduction of this Hoe Type Revolving Machine into the publishing houses of the world. As early as 1848 a press of this style was set up in the office of *La Patrie* in Paris, and in 1856 another of six cylinders was made for *Lloyd's Weekly Newspaper* in London. Almost as soon as Lloyd's press was in operation the *Times* ordered two Ten Cylinder presses of this sort, and the Hoe Type Revolving Machine became the world's chief newspaper press. Another important factor in the development of this machine was the eventual application to its need of a method devised about 1820 of casting stereotype plates on a curve, thus doing away with the necessity of types of special shape as suggested by Nicholson and used in the early days of the Hoe Type Revolving Machine. At this point we must leave the story of modern printing machinery. The ultimate development in principle occurred in the last half of the century with the invention of the "perfecting" machine, by means of which were printed simultaneously both sides of a continuous roll of paper, automatically fed.

One need only look at the list of American patents for printing machinery granted between 1790 and 1860 to realize that the foregoing review of the subject has touched only upon what have seemed to be the main points of development. Innumerable devices and improvements have not been mentioned for obvious reasons. Color printing machines have been neglected and job presses have not been described, but enough has been said to indicate the beginning of an era, the opening of the industrial age in the printing craft.

Stereotyping and Electrotyping

Stereotyping and electrotyping are two fundamentally different methods of achieving the same end: to produce solid and rigid printing plates, flat or curved, from forms set up of single types or slugs. By the first process a papier-mâché mold is made from the type and metal plates are cast from this mold; by the second process an impression of the type is made in wax, a thin shell of copper or nickel is deposited in this mold by electrolytic process and melted type-metal cast into the back of this shell. Neither of these two processes was invented in America, but they were quickly and universally adopted here. In fact, they were and probably still are used more extensively here than in Europe.

David Bruce has traditionally been credited with the introduction of stereotyping to America in connection with his return from a visit to his British homeland sometime between 1811 and 1813. He established what has been considered the first American stereotyping plant in New York. It seems as though he should share honors with Francis Shield from London, who established himself in New York City as a builder of printing presses and, in October 1811, announced that he possessed "the art of taking stereotype plates." They both (according to Munsell's *Typograph. Miscellany*, p. 114.) found sharp competition at once in New York, then in Philadelphia, and very soon in all important centers of printing. The new process was first used for books which had to be reprinted frequently in large editions with little or no changes, such as catechisms, Bibles and certain textbooks. Then came the literary works of lasting popularity, such as some of the masterpieces of English literature and the most popular books by Washington Irving and James Fenimore Cooper. The development of rotary presses for newspaper and magazine printing provided important new applications for the process. The London *Times* used the first curved stereotype plates in 1856, utilizing the invention of the Frenchman d'Ardennes, followed by the New York *Times*, in 1861. As stereotyping and electrotyping became less and less expensive, printing from plates was more and more extensively adopted, until it practically superseded the printing from type.

Joseph A. Adams, a wood engraver connected with Harper's, was responsible for the early practice of electrotyping in America. The first electrotyped plate was used in 1841 in *Mape's Magazine* in New York, and it very soon got ahead of stereotyping. Electrotyping was generally superior in that it furnished a plate of greater resistance which did not show wear so quickly, but it also had a special advantage which at that time mattered a great deal: it made possible the successful reproduction of the ever-popular wood engravings, which had not come out very clearly in stereotyping.

There were many reasons for the prompt success and the universal adoption of stereotyping and electrotyping in nineteenth century printing. The most important one was the solution of a problem which had puzzled the designers of the new rotary printing presses: how to mount a form of type on the surface of a cylinder. Stereotyping arrived in the nick of time, the simple answer to a very difficult question indeed.

Typesetting Machinery

Though the enormously hastened development of the printing and publishing trade in the United States in recent times traces in the first instance to the invention of the cylinder press in its various forms, yet to an even greater extent, perhaps, has it been effected by the introduction of the typesetting machine. There was no great advantage in being able to run off thousands of sheets an hour if typesetting could keep up with the presses only by the employment of an inordinately large number of compositors. In another section of this book the development of mechanical type-casting and typesetting machines will be traced, but it seems impossible to write of the period before 1860 without making the assertion that that development had its origin in the period in question in the form of an invention patented in England in 1822 by Dr. William Church, an individual who was referred to in scorn by Johnson in his *Typographia*, in 1824, as an "American Theorist" who imagined he could "cram John Bull with anything." It has been said that the invention of the type-casting and composing machine, great step in progress though it was, in reality restored one of the primitive conditions of the printing trade, bringing back the making of type to the printing office itself, whence it had departed when type founding became a separate trade in the early sixteenth century. Furthermore it came back under conditions greatly to the advantage of the printing trade in so far as were concerned the increase in its productiveness and the general level, not the high level, of excellence in its output. Yet for all this the effort to bring it back, difficult in itself, was met by in-difference, disbelief in its possibilities, and downright hostility.

The chief available source for knowledge of the Church invention of a practicable machine for the casting and composing of type is given by Hansard in the course of an article of fifteen pages in his *Typographia* of 1825, headed "The Printing Machines, and other Inventions relative to Printing, of Doctor William Church." Because of the sound mechanical principles and the prophetic character of the Church inventions, this doctor of medicine turned mechanic deserves more space than the present state of our knowledge enables us to give him. Through the co-operation of the staff of the Birmingham Public Libraries, however, it has become possible to assert that William Church was a native of Vermont who gave up the medical profession, moved to England where he lived and worked as a mechanical engineer from about 1820 to 1859 in the industrial city of Birmingham. Descriptions of his many patents are available, and the time of his death in Vermont, October 7, 1863, at the age of eighty-five years, is known, but the personal life, parentage, and the exact place and date of birth of this significant figure in typographical history have so far evaded discovery.

Church's invention, or inventions, comprised a type-casting machine which automatically distributed the finished letters, and fed them into a magazine from which they were drawn and composed by keyboard operation. After their use these types were not distributed by hand or machine, but were returned to the melting pot of the casting machine. The two pieces of apparatus, the casting and composing machines, were patented in England in 1822. A detailed account of both machines and the Church press with its interesting features is found in the pages of Hansard. Illustrations of the casting and composing machines are given in the modern pages of the great work by Legros and Grant entitled *Typographical Printing-Surfaces*. Unquestionably the three mechanisms taken together formed the most elaborate and largely conceived development in the art of printing since the original invention of Gutenberg, and though the system was subsequently developed and greatly varied by other inventors, its experimental operation by Church opened a new way to the printing trade of the world. One turns to several comments upon the Church invention in Legros and

Grant's comprehensive work. In their chapter on composing machines we find these words: "The earliest and simplest form of composing machine, so far as the authors are aware, was that of Church, whose patent is dated 1822. . . . Though somewhat crude in construction, it is surprising how many features its conception embodies which have since become common and are retained in a large number of well-known machines subsequently designed." After quoting Sir Henry Bessemer's account of his own solution of the problem of setting type by machine, and commenting upon the fact that the later inventor was ignorant of the Church device, they continue: ". . . nearly twenty years before the period he alludes to, the problem of composing by machine had been propounded and solved by Church, whose machines were in actual operation when Bessemer was engaged by Young to carry out his ideas." And finally they speak of a fundamental contribution by Church to the new day in printing practice in these words: "In the opinion of the authors, without question the best method of distribution is that proposed by Church . . . a system which has been almost universally adopted in all modern type-casting and composing machines—namely, distribution through the melting pot."

Though there seems to exist little evidence as to the extent to which the Church inventions came into use in American printing offices, it is clear enough that their principles, and the construction by their inventor of an effective practical embodiment of them, influenced profoundly, if indirectly, the history of the printing art in the United States and throughout the world. Its contemporary reception varied from the contemptuous reference to it in the *Typographia* of John Johnson, who was opposed to all mechanization of the art of printing, to a long and friendly account of the triple machine published in the *London Journal of Arts and Sciences,* quoted by Hansard. Somewhere in between lay the careful, critical examination and skepticism of Hansard himself. Perhaps the least to be forgiven by the inventor of all the contemporary references we have heard of was that in the *American Advocate and General Advertiser* for May 17, 1823, where the brief but comprehensive account of the machine is headed "Is This Not a Hoax?"

When one thinks of the complicated mechanism required, it is not surprising to learn that a period of thirty years elapsed before the typesetting machine was developed sufficiently for commercial use. The first successful machines, designed by William H. Mitchell of Brooklyn and patented in 1853, were installed two years later by John F. Trow of New York, whose printing office was said to be the first in which typesetting machinery was regularly used. It is apparent, then, that during the first half of the nineteenth century, the American printer worked with foundry type which he set by hand. Although the names of the founders are familiar to students of printing history, the identities of the type designers of the period remain obscure. We do not know, for example, the name of the designer, probably working for Baker & Grelle, Boston, who in 1827 produced a Cherokee type, based on the alphabet devised by Se-quo-yah. Nor do we know the craftsman who, about the time of the Civil War, put into type the Deseret alphabet of the Mormon Church. It is indeed unfortunate that we cannot pay proper tribute to the men who designed the type and usually also cut the punches for such foundries as the Boston Type Foundry, D. & G. Bruce, Mackellar, Smiths & Jordan, and the Cincinnati Type Foundry.

After the introduction of stereotyping in 1811 and of electrotyping in 1841, mechanical typesetting processes were increasingly used when large editions were required. These methods will be discussed in Part III of this volume, where the reader will also find a description of mechanical bookbinding.

Papermaking Machinery

It is not an unrelated circumstance that the chief modern developments in the processes of the printing art had their origin in the closing years of the eighteenth and the first quarter of the nineteenth century, for in that period all the old handicrafts began simultaneously to feel the effects of the machine in industry, and to envisage a new era as the result of its intrusion. As we have learned from an earlier section, the printing press completely changed its form and the mechanical principles of its operation in the period between 1790 and 1814. In relatively the same term of years occurred important advances in the hand-casting of type by means of automatic hand molds and through the introduction of type-casting machines for the quantity production of foundry type. Almost coincident with these came in 1822 the first patent for a composing machine. It was in this period, too, that the third great change in printing development was effected, that is, the ability to manufacture paper by machine in great quantity and in sheets of any desired size.

The paper mills of Europe and America in the year 1800 hardly differed from those in which was made the paper for the first printed books. The earlist papermakers had found it necessary to macerate their rags by a tedious process of putrefaction and fermentation before placing them in troughs for beating by the stamping machine. But this method gradually disappeared from paper-mill practice after the invention of the "Hollander" about the year 1690. The principle upon which this Dutch machine operated in reducing rags to pulp, without the intervening process of putrefaction, was the rotation, inside a trough, of a cylinder armed with dull metal blades which operated in proximity to a fixed metal plate composed of similar blades. The revolution of the cylinder created a back-wash which kept the rags passing and repassing beneath the blades until they were completely reduced to a fibrous pulp. The pulp was then led into a vat, and, whether stamping mill or Hollander had been employed in its making, its treatment was the same from that stage to the completion of the manufacture. Dipped from the vat by hand into a wire-bottomed, wooden-sided mold, it was formed into sheets by the dexterous handling of the workman, subjected to pressure between felts, dried and bundled into a ream for use in printing or writing, each sheet of the ream having been the subject of a separate and individual manufacture. With the exception of the improvement in the pulping process brought about by the Hollander, therefore, the mill of 1800 was little different in its processes or equipment from the mill of 1600 or earlier centuries, but in the late years of the eighteenth century a notable change was in preparation. In 1799 there was secured in England the first patent for the Fourdrinier papermaking machine, an invention of Nicholas Louis Robert, which in time was to alter completely the papermaking industry of the world and, by consequence, the industry of printing. This machine once more demonstrated the enormous change worked in the printing and allied trades by the application to their processes about this time of the principle of the revolving, horizontal cylinder. In its simplest terms the Fourdrinier is a machine in the operation of which an endless revolving wire band or web passes through a vat of pulp. This wire web takes up a thin layer of the pulp, shakes it laterally in order to cross and interlace its fibers, and delivers it to an endless revolving belt by which it is carried through "couching" cylinders for the removal of its moisture. Other endless belts then carry the newly formed paper through a second series of cylinders to complete its pressing and drying. The paper emerges in a continuous roll which, as in newspaper printing, may be fed directly in to a press or, for book work, cut into sheets of any desired size.

Very soon after the invention of the Fourdrinier, there was devised another papermaking machine, of different principle but of like effect, which was to share with it the revolutionizing of the industry. In 1809 John Dickinson took out a patent in England for a machine in which a cylinder covered with a wire web revolved in the pulp vat and, taking up the pulp in a thin sheet, passed it on to other cylinders for couching, pressing, and drying, ultimately collecting the finished product in the form of a continuous roll. In 1816 Thomas Gilpin, a papermaker of Wilmington, Delaware, with his brother John and another partner, took out an American patent for a machine of this revolving cylinder principle. The Gilpin machine, differing little in essentials from the Dickinson, though it was less effective, was the first in this country to make paper in a continuous roll. It was put into operation in August, 1817, producing paper about 30 inches wide at a speed of 60 feet a minute. The paper was first used in *Poulson's American Daily Advertiser* and then in Mathew Carey's publication of Lavoisne's *A Complete Genealogical, Historical, Chronological, and Geographical Atlas* (1820) which, at present, is considered the first book printed on American machine-made paper.

Infringements upon the Gilpin invention and improvements in its mechanism by other American manufacturers marked the course and direction of papermaking progress in this country for many years, throughout the period, indeed, in which the Fourdrinier machine was undergoing experimentation and extensive improvement in England. The important moment in the history of the cylinder machine was reached when in 1830 the firm of Phelps & Spafford of Windham, Connecticut, constructed a machine of this type which made it possible "for the paper-maker to take in the pulp at one end of his machine, make the paper, dry it, cut it into sheets of the desired size and turn it out ready for finishing or packing at the other end of the machine."

The earliest importation of a Fourdrinier papermaking machine into the United States seems to have been about the year 1827. The first machine of that type to be constructed here was built in South Windham, Connecticut, in 1829. With the gradual improvement of the Fourdriniers, they slowly drew ahead of the cylinder machine, but both types remain in common use in the modern paper mill.

The New Materials of Papermaking

With the development of papermaking machinery arose a problem that taxed the ingenuity of men of scientific mind for generations. Even before the time when the machines, with their great potentiality of output, were beginning to demand raw materials in large quantity, the supply of linen and cotton rags had hardly been enough to enable the paper mills to keep up with the printer's activities. The story of the search for a substitute material, of the experiments with some five hundred substances susceptible of being reduced to a fibrous pulp, is a special chapter in the history of papermaking and printing.

In order to review the earlier steps in the century-old search for a vegetable pulp paper, for that was the essence of the investigation, we may turn to Dard Hunter's brief statement in the *History of the Printed Book* (volume three of *The Dolphin*) where we learn of the early suggestion by René Antoine Ferchault de Réaumur who in 1719, in an entomological study, instanced the nest of the American wasp as an object constructed of a paperlike substance made from wood fiber, and went on to lay down the broad principle of the use of wood pulp paper for printing and other purposes. Jean Etienne Guettard's treatise on the materials of papermaking, first published in London in 1754, was reprinted in Philadelphia by Robert Bell in 1777 in a collection known as *Select Essays Collected from the Dictionary of Arts and Sciences*. It was in 1765 that the first truly effective experiments in the manufacture of wood pulp paper were made public. Between that year and 1771 Jacob Christian Schaeffer, a German scientist, published at Regensburg a treatise of six volumes in which were contained eighty-two specimens of paper made from wood and various vegetable products. This celebrated work, the *Versuche und Muster ohne alle Lumpen oder doch mit einem geringen Zusatze derselben Papier zu machen,* made clear the future direction of investigation into the materials of papermaking.

The question was first prominently brought to the attention of scientific men in the United States when in 1789 the agriculturist, Hector St. John Crèvecoeur, presented a book to the American Philosophical Society of Philadelphia, printed upon paper made of the barks and roots of different trees and plants. Earlier than this Franklin had been interested in the manufacture of an "asbestos" paper, but it is not supposed that this product was intended for use in writing or printing. The experiments of the first sixty years of the new century were world-wide in distribution. In this country Matthew Lyon of Vermont, among others, made usable paper from the bark of the basswood tree, and about 1830 Wooster and Holmes of Pennsylvania took out a patent for making paper pulp from wood. Most of the early experiments were based upon the the making of pulp by mechanical means, that is by grinding and crushing, with an inevitable injury to the fibers. It was after 1860 that a chemical method of reducing the wood to pulp without destroying the fiber was brought to its highest development through what is known as the sulphite process. But before this end was reached, Hugh Burgess and Charles Watt, working for many years in England, succeeded in 1851 in making a good pulp by boiling wood in caustic alkali. Disappointed in the marketing of the product in England, Burgess moved to the United States where in 1854 he secured a patent for his process and soon thereafter built a large mill in Pennsylvania for the manufacture of paper from a wood pulp made by what was soon known as the "soda" process. In its fundamentals at least, the problem was solved. It is not necessary to point to the fact that the seemingly inexhaustible forests of America soon brought it about that the United States became the center of the wood pulp paper industry.

The dissemination of the papermaking industry throughout the country naturally followed the lines previously established in the spread of printing. When the century opened, it has been calculated, there were in existence about one hundred paper mills. The census of 1810 reported a total of 202 mills, producing annually some 425,000 reams of paper. Pennsylvania was still the center of this industry with 64 mills and an annual product of nearly 166,000 reams of paper of every description. The mills had by this time found their way into the new states and territories. In 1793 the first mill beyond the Alleghenies had been established at Georgetown, Kentucky, and in 1795 a second trans-Allegheny mill was set up near Pittsburgh. Sometime before 1810, as appears from an act of assembly of that year, mills had been established in Tennessee. So important did the encouragement of the industry seem to that frontier state that by the act of assembly just mentioned workers in the paper mills were exempted from labor on the highways and from attendance upon military drill. By the year 1840, more than four hundred mills were in operation in twenty states and the District of Columbia, with Pennsylvania still in the lead with eighty-seven mills. By 1850, the lead had shifted to Massachusetts because of the supply of pure water and available water power in the western part of the state. There, in Berkshire county, many papermakers utilized these facilities which also possessed the attraction of being equidistant from the printing centers of Boston and New York. Although, as we have seen, wood pulp paper was known, rags remained the principal raw material. Eighty-eight per cent of the paper produced during 1860 was still made from rags.

Book Illustration

Some part of early American book illustration was very good; much of it was conventionally second rate; but the bulk of it, crude and unsophisticated though it might be, had a rough sincerity and that same directness of translation which give interest to any form of artistic primitivism.

The first book of the United States to carry an illustration, Hubbard's *Narrative of the Indian Wars*, published by John Foster in Boston in 1677, was embellished by "A Map of New-England", a woodcut made by the printer himself, to whose hand are also attributed at least two separate prints in the same medium. A portrait of Increase Mather by Thomas Emmes of Boston, appearing as frontispiece in certain copies of Mather's *Blessed Hope* (1701) and his *Ichabod* (1702) is the earliest copperplate engraving, other than certain issues of paper money, to be accomplished in what is now the United States. Copperplate engraving was not firmly established in the colonies, however, until the coming of Francis Dewing to Boston about the year 1716. His rendering of Cyprian Southack's *New Chart of the English Empire in North America* (Boston, 1717) was the earliest large-scale copper-plate production known to have been designed, engraved, printed, and published in the country. The most notable engravings upon copper of the first half of the eighteenth century were the fifteen portraits, separately engraved in Boston in the period 1727-1751 by the English-born and English-trained mezzotint engraver, Peter Pelham.

Relief cuts, that is, designs engraved on metal in relief with a graver, a procedure in which the craftsman worked from black to white, were used in the illustration of American books at an early date. A group of these productions, including two portraits, which appeared in certain Boston books of the period 1717-1719 are believed to have been the work of James Franklin, elder brother of Benjamin. About the middle of the century the Pennsylvania German printers were employing in their books an occasional locally-made woodcut.

In the second half of the eighteenth century professional competency with the graver is found in the maps, plans, and views of Lawrence Hebert, James Turner, Thomas Johnston, Henry Dawkins, and others whose names are less well remembered. Paul Revere's copies of English cartoons for the *Royal American Magazine* (1774), his print of *The Bloody Massacre* (1770), and several other pieces of record have taken their place in the history of American political caricature and propaganda. These and his numerous book illustrations and portraits of the same period are evidence of industry and versatility rather than of artistic superiority. Amos Doolittle of Connecticut produced admirable work in more than one field. The work of Abel Buell, also of Connecticut, is of continuing interest to antiquarians and historians. Working in Philadelphia in 1775, John Norman copied from English originals the first architectural designs to be engraved in this country. Thereafter in Boston he applied himself industriously and successfully to the production of architectural works, maps, and prints of a more general character. His portraits of the heroes of the Revolution in the Boston, 1781-1784, edition of the *Impartial History of the War* are vigorous, if not always skillful, characterizations. A gradual increase in ease and finish is perceptible in the work of such men of the post-Revolutionary years as James Trenchard, Samuel Hill, Cornelius Tiebout, and Edward Savage. A truly fine work published at the very end of the century was the colored *Views of Philadelphia,* which William and Thomas Birth engraved in the years 1798-1800 and brought together under this title in 1800. The *Country Seats of the United States* by the same artists was published in 1808. In the meantime the folio Bible published by Isaiah Thomas in 1791 had carried a group of fifty plates by Joseph Seymour, Samuel Hill, John Norman, and Amos Doolittle. Dobson's edition of Rees's *Encyclopaedia*, completed in eighteen volumes in Philadelphia in the period 1790-1797, was illustrated with 543 copperplate engravings by such artists as Scot, Thackara, Vallance, Trenchard, Allardice, and Seymour. With this publication American book illustration, it has been said, came of age. There was much inferior work done in the succeeding years, but the presence of crude work in an American book after 1800 meant that the best resources of the time and place had not been utilized by its publisher.

The earliest comprehensive source of information about the artists, engravers, and artist-engravers who contributed to the enrichment of the American book is William Dunlap's *History of the Art of Design in the United States*, published in 1834. Though the later work of David McNeely Stauffer, *American Engravers upon Copper and Steel*, is concerned only incidentally with the engraver upon wood and stone, it is to that admirable work we go for the background of our knowledge of the book illustration of the period between 1800 and 1860, a period in which the significant book illustration was accomplished by wood engravers and lithographers. *American Book Illustrators*, by Theodore Bolton, carries the story from F. O. C. Darley's early productions in 1843 to the year 1938. Frank Weitenkampf's *American Graphic Art* is a rapid survey of a large field with attention to the book illustration aspect of the subject. Perhaps the most comprehensive work is the catalog, *Early American Book Illustrators, 1670-1870*, published in a second edition in 1950 in mimeographed form, which Sinclair Hamilton has made of the collection of illustrated American books which he gave a few years ago to Princeton University.

Amos Doolittle, who died in 1832, carried on the work of illustration and print-making from the period of the Revolution through the first quarter of the nineteenth century. Alexander Anderson illustrated several works on copper in that period, but his contribution to the history of illustration through the wood engraving as contrasted with the woodcut was of such a character that he has been designated "the

Father of Wood Engraving in the United States." Anderson learned the "white-line" technique of Bewick and made it the basis of a notable achievement in book illustration by that process. In 1804 he redrew and engraved 300 of Bewick's own illustrations for the first American edition of the *General History of Quadrupeds*, and as an engraver on wood he continued to illustrate American books until two years before his death in 1870. Two of the finest American books of the nineteenth century from the standpoint both of printing and illustration were Alexander Wilson's *American Ornithology*, which began publication in Philadelphia in 1808, and its successor of the same title by Charles Lucien Bonaparte. In the second of these, printed by William Brown of Philadelphia in the years 1825-1833, the splendid drawings of birds, chiefly by Titian Peale and Alexander Rider, were engraved beautifully on copper by Alexander Lawson and tinted in lively and faithful colors by Rider. John Warner Barber illustrated in wood engraving numerous fine works of his own authorship on the architecture, scenery, history, and antiquities of various parts of the United States. Benson J. Lossing was another author whose historical works, *The Pictorial Field-Book of the Revolution* (1850-1852) for example, found rich embellishment from his own engravings on wood. Typical of the better travel books of the period was John Russell Bartlett's *Personal Narrative of Explorations and Incidents in Texas, New Mexico, California, Sonora, and Chihuahua* (New York, 1854), illustrated in wood engraving by several different craftsmen and in lithography by Sarony & Co. of New York from drawings by the author and his associates. The book of travel and description, the general magazine, and the popular gift book "annual" support the feeling that far from being a negligible period in book illustration the two or three decades before the Civil War came close to realizing the Golden Age of that art in the United States.

The process of steel engraving, introduced about 1810 for the making of bank notes, was adopted in due course for book illustration. It is not highly thought of today as an artistic medium, but in its hour it possessed for the user one invaluable quality: it was possible to make from the steel plate a much greater number of impressions than could be taken from an engraved copperplate, and therefore to enlarge the size of editions and reduce the cost of the individual illustration. Large

editions of "annuals" were illustrated by the new method. Children's
books, influenced by the successful ideas of S. G. Goodrich, for the
first time contained realistic and practical illustrations engraved by
well-known artists. Certainly the normal illustrated book of the first
half of the nineteenth century, regardless of changes in conceptions of
what is art, was a finer publication in the quality and variety of the
mediums employed than the normal illustrated book of the age of photography. William James Bennett in that period was making landscape
and architectural renderings in aquatint, and before him William
Charles had copied in colored aquatint Rowlandson's illustrations to
the *Vicar of Wakefield* and the *Tour of Dr. Syntax.*

It was in this period, too, that lithography as a medium for illustration came to a high point of excellence in American books. The first
occurrence of lithographic plates in an American book seems to have
been Sir James Edward Smith's *Grammar of Botany,* published by
J. V. Seaman of New York in 1822, with the plates executed by Barnet
& Doolittle. The folio edition of McKenney & Hall's *Indian Tribes of
North America* (Philadelphia, 1834) was adorned with a series of Indian portraits by C. B. King, reproduced in color lithography chiefly
at the establishments of Lehman & Du Val and J. T. Bowen of Philadelphia, a magnificent employment of a process at that time still in its in-
fancy.

In this period were working in various mediums John Sartain, William Rollinson, Peter Maverick, Asher B. Durand, and F. O. C. Darley,
the last named an illustrator whose work, usually reproduced by wood
engraving, spans the generations and carries into the period covered by
the next section of the present history.

This cursory treatment of book illustration before 1860 pretends to
do no more than remind the reader that the subject is rich and varied
from the point of view of the biographer, the amateur of art, and the
historian of the book and society.

Labor Conditions

An American employer of the later centuries, it sometimes seems, has
every reason to look back upon the first hundred years or more of
printing in the colonies as a true golden age in which the journeymen
and apprentices were content with their wages and their hours of labor

and knew not the meaning of organization or the efficacy of the strike. It is improbable, however, that the conditions were invariably so ideal as this from the employer's standpoint, for there must have been occasions when temporary organizations of journeymen forced concessions from a master printer even in that period. The first association of the sort known to us, however, was that set up by the action of certain journeymen printers of New York who in 1776, by means of a strike, secured an increase of wages from their employers. Ten years later in Philadelphia when the employing printers attempted to reduce the minimum earning of an individual to $5.83½ a week, a temporary organization was formed by the workmen of the city to resist this action. The local union thus set up forbade its adherents to accept less than a minimum of six dollars a week, and, quite in the familiar manner of our times, agreed to support any journeymen who were thrown out of employment by their refusal to work for a smaller sum. These indications of the growing solidarity of printing-house craftsmen caused a ripple of uneasiness among the employers. In 1792 one of Isaiah Thomas's partners wrote him from Boston regarding the wage question: "the devil seems to have got into the journeymen." At the same time, the English master printers faced a like revolt in their shops. In London, masters and men signed the first known price scale in 1785, and the earliest society of compositors began in 1792. In the United States, the first organization of working printers in the modern sense originated with the formation in 1795 of the Typographical Society of New York. This union, intended to ameliorate general conditions rather than to concern itself with any immediate or distinct grievance, continued in existence for two and a half years, attempting to reform trade practices and succeeding in the improvement of wage rates. It was followed from 1799 to 1804 by the Franklin Society of Journeymen Printers which submitted to employers in 1800 the first detailed wage scale of the printing craft in the United States. The printers demanded and received 25 cents a thousand ems for composition with minimum wages of $7.00 a week in book and job offices and $8.00 in newspaper offices. Soon after the nineteenth century began, local associations appeared here and there throughout the country. In 1802 typographical societies were organized in Philadelphia and Baltimore; by 1815 societies maintained price lists in New York, Washington,

Philadelphia, Baltimore, Boston, Albany, and probably New Orleans. All of these groups were primarily constituted to raise and establish prices, but they also possessed well-defined beneficiary functions. As the aim of increasing wages was accomplished and as the beneficiary funds expanded, the secondary purpose gradually became more important. And when in 1816 the New York Typographical Society sought incorporation in order to secure its funds, the State Senate refused to approve the charter unless the trade regulation provision was omitted. For two years the printers appealed in vain for the preservation of the clause; in 1818, they accepted the charter without it. This emphasis on beneficiary functions, whether legally required or not, prevailed between 1815 and 1830. By 1830 the Columbia Typographical Society of Washington was the only one which retained the function of wage regulation, and the other societies found their membership decreasing. The reason for this deterioration is found in the "free membership" section of their constitutions: a member became paid-up after a certain period of years. This discouraged new members and, as Stewart states, the "societies generally ceased to exist about the time the first list of free members appears."

The printers, however, were influenced by the pervading interest in labor organizations during the 1830's and, within the decade, printers' societies mushroomed in more than twenty cities. At first the local groups discussed their mutual problems by correspondence, but when this method of communication proved unwieldy, advanced to the next logical step, confederation. At a meeting of the Columbia Typographical Society in March, 1834, plans were suggested but no action was taken. The following year, the New York and Cincinnati members heard a similar motion, and a national convention was called, culminating in the establishment in November, 1836, of the National Typographical Society. But with the country heading into a business depression, the workers lacked the independence favorable to the growth of a national union, and it survived for only two years. Ten years later a propitious moment arrived, and after two conventions the National Typographical Union was successfully organized in 1852. With alterations in name and organization, this union still continues to represent the printers in the regulation of wages, hours, and conditions of labor.

Employers' organizations were even more sporadic. There were, of course, occasional groups which met to deal with a particular set of demands, but the border line between employed printer and employing printer was crossed and recrossed so often that it was difficult to keep the occupations separate. In the 18th century, as Cressingham has remarked, a "journeyman one day was an employer the next." Therefore, it is not surprising to find mention of only a few employers' groups. In Philadelphia, the Company of Printers was organized in 1794 to "regulate the prices at which its members shall execute printing work, determine the terms of employing journeymen;" in Boston in 1805 the Society of Printers of Boston and Vicinity, later the Faustus Association, organized for the same purpose, expanded its activities to include lectures and even the formation of a fire society for the mutual protection of its members. But it was not until 1863 that the Typothetae of New York, an association of master printers, was formed, not primarily as a buffer to the labor union, but rather as a means of controlling the unregulated and wasteful competition among the printing houses of the period. None the less, the national organization, the Typothetae of America, which grew out of this local Society, has been vigilant in looking out for the interests of the employer when in conflict with the demands of labor, as well as serving the general interests of the trade in ways hardly understood by the layman.

Since wage scales were established on the basis of piece-work, the early typographical societies made no attempt to regulate working time which, at the beginning of the century, averaged between ten and eleven hours—slightly less than the day of the London printers. During the first decade of the century, the Philadelphia and New York societies suggested but did not press the matter of limiting the working period for those working on time rather than on piece-work. However, the scales established between 1830 and 1840 called for a ten-hour day, with the regular or a higher rate for overtime, for printers on a time rate. The length of day for piece-work was not specified although these printers were protected by an "after hours" rate. By standardizing the working limit, the societies standardized the weekly wage. This and the discouragement of work at unusual hours seem to be the principal purposes of regulation, for there was no movement for a reduction in hours until the end of the Civil War.

As the result of his arduous apprenticeship, the printer became a specialist craftsman and his wages were normally good in comparison to those of other workmen of his time. In the colonial period the customary payment for the compositor was a shilling for a thousand ems; for the pressman a shilling a token, that is, for 240 sheets printed on one side. This rate of payment varied little in the first half of the nineteenth century. In 1815, the New York Typographical Society demanded for its compositors the sum of 27 cents a thousand ems (the precise rate of the scale of 1851) and for its pressman 33 cents a token. Except under unusual circumstances, no pressman on a morning newspaper was permitted to work for less than ten dollars a week. At this time the master printers were charging their customers 56½ cents a thousand ems on book work composition and the same sum per token on press work.

THE BOOK TRADE, 1784-1860

Literary Property, Piracy, and Copyright Laws

THOUGH A PROTECTION for a term of years granted by the General Court of Massachusetts in 1673 is sometimes referred to as the first American copyright, it must be observed that this was protection given the publisher of a book of laws against reprinting and sale by other publishers, the same sort of protection as that provided in England at the time by entry of a work at Stationers' Hall. To put it briefly, this first American copyright was a "booksellers' copyright." It was not the vesting in the author of that qualified ownership of his work (qualified, that is, as to duration) which we think of today as copyright. Moreover, it was an isolated action; the principle underlying it was not consistently pursued in Massachusetts or elsewhere in the colonies in the 110 years that passed before the establishment of the first American copyright law.

That there existed a sense of mutual obligation on the part of the printers in the colonies to refrain from reprinting one another's works seems certain, but there is nothing to show that this obligation took into consideration the author's right, directly or by assignment, to control the sale of his work. This conception, indeed, had not taken firm hold in England at the time of establishment of the earliest American presses. Throughout the colonial period in America, we find a constant reprinting of a popular work by various presses in various colonies, and, though this was undoubtedly controlled in some cases by agreement, there must have been many instances in which the reprinting constituted an outright piracy, an ignoring of moral obligation in the absence of a specific law, in which both publisher and author suffered the loss of potential profits. It is difficult indeed to understand what there was besides innate decency that kept the publishers of different colonies within reasonable bounds in this respect. They were aware that the laws of England gave protection to the members of the Stationers Company against the unauthorized reprinting of their books by competitors, and after 1710 they were familiar with the statute, the celebrated "8 Anne, Chapter 19," which transferred this protection from publisher to author. In the absence, however, of either inter- or intra-colonial laws resembling these, other forces besides the moral concept of fair play must have been at work, for we read few complaints of piracy in the documents that have come down from the period. Perhaps the publishers of the time took such infringements of their rights as a hazard of the trade and kept silent about it, intending to recoup themselves for injuries by retaliatory action. But to prevent these piracies there were, of course, natural restraints always at work, producing agreements between printers of different colonies, between a publisher and several printers, or between an author and several printers by which reprinting occurred under mutually profitable conditions. Strongest among those natural restraints were common decency and enlightened self-interest, or, to put it differently, the operation of the Golden Rule and the recognition by the printers of their reliance upon one another for news exchanges, for certain sorts of advertising, and for tools and materials in emergencies. Furthermore must be counted the fact that each colony was not only a separate political entity, but socially and economically separate as well. The publications of Boston normally offered little temptation to the piratical printer of New York, because for reasons of situation the sermons, the religious controversies, the political disquisitions, even the literary essays of Boston were foreign literature to the people of New York. It was a different story, of course, when in the later period the political controversies became national in character in the face of some crisis that affected the colonies equally. When, in the Stamp Act controversy, Jonas Green of Annapolis published Daniel Dulany's *Considerations on the Propriety of Taxing the Colonies,* and at least three other printers in three other American cities and still another in London straightway each brought out one or more editions of that vigorous statement of the American position, what recourse was open either to author or publisher? Green may have had an agreement with Holt of New York for his republication of Dulany's treatise, but two of the other editions were issued anonymously, and it is probable that the anonymity was as carefully preserved from the Annapolis publisher as from anyone else. In one field of publication, that of the almanac, it is likely that fair dealing was the rule. Timeliness of issue was a feature in the publication of almanacs. The printer who failed to have his almanac for 1760 ready in November or December of 1759 could not expect satisfactory sale. Consequently he would not be able to wait for the appearance of a rival printer's almanac and then steal its contents for his own market. It behooved him, therefore, to employ his own almanac maker, or to retire from that field of publication. It seems clear, too, that the makers of almanacs were protected by this factor and by an even more powerful factor—the degrees of latitude and longitude. Between Boston and Charleston there were differences between the times of sun rising and sun setting and the times of seed time and harvest. There would be, accordingly, variations in astronomical data for the almanacs of those two places or of any two so far apart as these. The almanac maker who supplied printers in each place was likely to be the only person capable of making the necessary corrections, and each printer must pay him as for a separate work. This, at least, is how we interpret certain entries in the Account Books of Benjamin Franklin, in which, in those days when he was still acting as silent partner and agent for printers throughout the middle colonies and the South, we find him in 1744 buying from Theophilus Grew, on behalf of William Parks, of Williamsburg, for £21, seven copies, unquestionably in manuscript, of the almanac of that Philadelphia mathematician. There is no entry to show how he or William Parks disposed of these copies, but a few years later we find Franklin sending a Grew almanac to James Davis, a printer of New Bern, North Carolina, and charging him £3 for it. One assumes that the seven copies of 1744 had been separately calculated for as many different localities. We may conclude on this point that a deal of piracy was prevented also by the practice that existed among printers of selling one another's works on consignment. The Account Books show Franklin sending books of his own printing northward as far as Boston and southward as far as Charleston. In the case of almanacs such consignments ran sometimes into hundreds of copies. The opportunity for a wide sale presented by the printing of an important political document encouraged him, as we know, to special efforts of distribution. The Indian Treaty of 1744 was of such interest and consequence to the home government and to the middle colonies that he consigned 300 copies to England, 131 to Jonas Green of Annapolis, and smaller numbers to the printers of colonies not directly concerned in the results of the conference in question.

This examination of the loose and fortuitous practice of an earlier period has seemed a necessary preliminary to an understanding of the beginnings of copyright legislation in the United States. The new point of view introduced by the earliest copyright law was the most important landmark yet set up in the history of American authorship and book publishing. It was this law which made possible in the United States the existence of the professional author and gave the necessary encouragement to great publishing ventures.

More than once in relating the history of American printing and publishing we have had occasion to give special consideration to the part played in events by the colony of Connecticut, one of the smaller political divisions of the group, founded by separatists dissatisfied with the hierarchical system of the Massachusetts colony. This self-contained community, the seat of a vigorous intellectual life, was given, for some reason we do not pretend to explain, to experimentation and achievement in the mechanical arts and sciences. From this colony in 1769 we saw coming the printing press made by Isaac Doolittle of New Haven for William Goddard of Philadelphia, the earliest press of the colonies made for sale. In the same year, in the person of Abel Buell of New Haven, we recognize the first American to master the art of type founding in all its processes. The earliest United States patent for a cylinder press of any kind is said to have been that which was granted to Apollos Kinsley of Connecticut in 1796. Between these later events there occurred an incident of greater significance than either when in 1781, before the close of the Revolution, the Connecticut Assembly hearkened to the plea of a distressed author and gave him copyright protection for a book.

Andrew Law was a graduate of what is now Brown University, then Rhode Island College, whose talents were early turned to the study of church music. In later years he was to be wondered at and admired, but not imitated, as the inventor of a new scheme of musical notation, but his books of tunes of the earlier period were set in the conventional note forms of his and our own times. In his petition to the Connecticut Assembly of October, 1781, he affirmed that the compiling, engraving, and printing of one of his books, *Collection of the Best Tunes* (New Haven, 1779), had cost him the sum of £500, and that some unscrupulous persons had begun a counterfeiting of his work. He begged, therefore, for the sole right of "imprinting and vending" an edition now in hand "for the Term of five years." Law stated the principle upon which all later American acts of copyright are based in his declaration "that the works of Art ought to be protected in this Country." Both the special and the general pleas of this petition were so far successful as to cause the Assembly to pass soon thereafter a special act to protect him in the publication of his *Collection of the Best Tunes for the Promotion of Psalmody*, presumably of New Haven, 1781. It is likely that the success of the young musician in securing protection for his book of tunes was the incentive behind the application for a similar privilege which resulted soon afterwards in the all-important copyright legislation of the Connecticut Assembly of 1783.

By one of those satisfactory coincidences that sometimes happen, the actual establishment of the Connecticut copyright statute, the first in the United States, had its origin in the petition of a romantic figure asking protection for a romantic book. John Ledyard, known later to Europe and America as an exponent of somewhat grandiose, but at the same time entirely sensible, visions of world exploration, was one of that band that went upon the celebrated Third Voyage in which Captain James Cook consolidated his fame as an explorer and lost his life. Returning to his home in Connecticut after some years of further wanderings, young Ledyard determined to publish an account of the tragic last voyage. It was only two years earlier that Andrew Law had obtained a special protection from the Connecticut Assembly for his book of tunes, and now in January, 1783, Ledyard appealed to the same sympathetic body for a similar right to the exclusive publication of a book which, published in Hartford in 1783, took the title *A Journal of Captain Cook's Last Voyage to the Pacific Ocean*.

The report of the Assembly's committee on Ledyard's petition is a document in the history of American authorship that deserves honor and attention. It reads as follows:

"Jan 1783

"Your Honours committee appointed to take into consideration The Memorial of John Ledyard prefer^d to this Assembly, take leave to report that in their Opinion a publication of the Memorialists Journal in his voyage round the Globe may be beneficial to these United States & to the world, & it appears reasonable & Just that the Memorialist should have an exclusive right to publish the same for a Reasonable Term, and as it appears that several Gentlemen of Genius & reputation are also about to make similar Applications for the exclusive right [to] publish Works of their Respective Compositions, your Committee are of opinion that it is expedient to pass a general bill, for that purpose and thereupon report the Annexed Bill.

"All which is Submitted by your Honours humble Servants
"Signd pr Order
"Sam Huntington
"In the upper House
"The above Report of the Committee is accepted and approved
"Test. George Wyllys, Secrety."

The recommendation of the Committee for the passage of a general law so greatly appealed to the practical intelligence of the Connecticut legislators that in this same session of the Assembly they placed upon the statute books of the State the memorable "Act for the encouragement of Literature and Genius" which became the model of the later copyright legislation of other states and finally of the Federal law of 1790. The preamble of the Connecticut law of 1783 stated in these words the fundamental principle of an author's equity in the product of his intelligent industry:

"Whereas it is perfectly agreeable to the Principles of natural Equity and Justice, that every Author should be secured in receiving the Profits that may arise from the Sale of his Works, and such security may encourage Men of Learning and Genius to publish their Writings; which may do Honor to their Country, and Service to Mankind . . . Be it enacted . . ."

The act gave to any author of a book not previously printed, provided he were a resident of the United States, "the Sole Liberty of printing, publishing, and vending the same within . . . [Connecticut], for the Term of fourteen years, . . ." It then proceeded to provide a severe penalty for reprinting the book in that state, or importing into it copies reprinted elsewhere without the author's written consent. It stated the methods of registration, and provided further the right of the author to a second fourteen years of protection upon the expiration of the first term. The act went beyond its first purpose somewhat and stated that the right granted the author could be withdrawn by the Superior Court if he neglected to "furnish the Public with sufficient Editions" of his book, or offered it for sale at a price that might be judged greater than would provide him a reasonable compensation for his labor, time, expense, and risk of sale. Its closing section gives us a clear view of the state of a country still in the condition of a loose confederation of states, when it affirms that the provisions of the act should not extend to the "inhabitants of any other of the United States, until the State or States in which such Person or Persons reside . . . shall have passed similar laws in favour of the Authors of new publications, and their Heirs and Assigns." It is unnecessary to call attention to the likeness existing between this act of the Connecticut legislature and the "Act for the Encouragement of Learning" of "8 Anne, Chapter 19," of 1710.

In his entry of Charles Henry Wharton's *Letter to the Roman Catholics of the City of Worcester* (Philadelphia, 1784), Hildeburn (*Issues of the Pennsylvania Press*) makes the following observation: "At the end, 'Entered according to Act of Assembly.' This is the earliest example of copyright in America I have met with." With this assertion repeated by Charles Evans, there is some danger that Wharton's book, which may indeed have been the first to contain within it a printed notice of copyright, may come to be regarded as the earliest copyrighted book of the United States under a state or federal law. That distinction belongs, we believe, to the Ledyard book even though it does not contain printed at beginning or end a notice of copyright.

This is a brief analysis of the first general law of any state of the United States for the encouragement of authorship, the act which eventually made possible the growth of a professional author class in the country. One does not find, except in the field of *belles-lettres*, a great difference in intention between the authors of the unprotected and the protected periods. The historians, the controversialists, the publicists have been normally, in the later as in the earlier period, men who wrote with professional skill and purpose while supporting themselves in some gainful occupation—preaching, teaching, the law, medicine, or business.

The copyright law gave comfort of a sort to these individuals, but it did not set them apart as a class. The change that came about was particularly to be observed in the realm of polite literature, for the writing of the poets and essayists of the earlier period was in general the work of amateurs, of occasional writers without incentive to the maintenance of concentrated effort. The possibility of insuring to themselves profit from their labors worked a gradual change in the attitude of men of this group, creating finally the poet, the novelist, or the essayist who, in whole or in part, gained his bread by his pen.

Ledyard's successful effort to secure copyright protection in Connecticut was only one of several contemporaneous endeavors. In March, 1783, Massachusetts passed a similar copyright law, probably at the instigation of Timothy Dwight, who at that time was a member of the House of Representatives. Maryland followed in April. About the same time, Joel Barlow and other literary personages presented a me· morial to the Continental Congress petitioning for a recommendation that the several states enact copyright laws. In May, upon the favorable report of a committee which included James Madison, the Congress passed the desired resolution. Soon, other states also recognized copyright protection and, later in the year 1783, New Jersey, New Hampshire, and Rhode Island placed corresponding laws upon their books. Delaware did not pass a copyright law, and the last of the other states to do so was New York in April, 1786. While these laws did represent an impressive acknowledgment of an author's rights, they were not completely satisfactory. Seven states required that protection must be reciprocal in the other states and that a citizen of another state could not obtain protection until his own state had passed an equivalent law. Pennsylvania and Maryland averred that their laws should not become effective until every state in the Union had passed similar enforcements. In the variations of the conditions of these laws, one sees a typical example of the weaknesses besetting a loose federation of separate commonwealths.

However inadequate was the degree of protection afforded the authors of the period by these divergent laws, it should be observed that many of the states would have been without copyright benefits at all had it not been for Noah Webster. Quite properly called "The Father of American Copyright," the famous lexicographer vigorously sponsored copyright legislation for more than fifty years. As early as 1782, when still completing his speller and grammar, he set forth from Goshen, New York, and rode to Philadelphia "for the purpose of showing my manuscripts to gentlemen of influence, and obtaining a law for securing to authors the copy-right of their publications." Unfortunately, the legislatures of New Jersey and Pennsylvania were not in session, and Webster's efforts were confined to persuasive intimate conferences. But this did not deter him and during the following three years he visited the capitals of Connecticut, New York, South Carolina, and Delaware. In the course of these journeys he met many political leaders who later called upon him to aid in the movement for a strong federal government, a principle which he advocated as a result of his copyright experiences.

In 1787 the Constitution, which brought the separate commonwealths of the Confederation into a permanent federal union with a centralized government, declares in its first Article: "The Congress shall have power: To promote the progress of science and useful arts, by securing, for limited times, to authors and inventors, the exclusive right to their respective writings and discoveries." This power was exercised at the second session of the first Congress held under the Constitution. On May 31, 1790, there was passed "An Act for the encouragement of learning, by securing copies of maps, charts, and books, to the authors and proprietors of such copies, during the times therein mentioned." This act, as well as the previous state acts, followed the English law in naming successive units of fourteen years as the duration of the author's exclusive privilege to his work, denying implicitly the theory of perpetual copyright. This theory was none the less maintained by some individuals, and it was only after an adverse decision of the Supreme Court in 1834 that it ceased to exist as a practical issue. Various later acts of Congress provided copyright protection for prints and musical compositions. In 1831, the term of copyright was extended to 28 years, with renewal for 14 years to author, widow, or children, and in 1856 the right to control public performances of music and plays was granted the proprietors of copyrights.

Between 1828 and 1898, nine private copyright acts were also passed by Congress. These special laws validated, renewed, or extinguished the copyright of five specific works, and, in two instances, those of

Schoolcraft's books on the Indian tribes and Herndon's *Exploration of the Amazon,* Congress gave the widows of the authors the rights to republish books originally issued by the government.

The movement for international copyright in America began in 1836 when a visiting English publisher, Frederick Saunders, started a flow of petitions to Congress, the best known being the British Authors' Petition of 1837. Although a bill was then introduced in the Senate by Henry Clay, it failed to pass. Clay persevered, reintroducing the bill in 1838, 1840, and 1842, but without success. This lack of interest among the legislators resulted largely from the fear of the developing book trade industry at being retarded in its prosperity, and the unwillingness of the public to surrender the privilege of purchasing cheap books. Nevertheless, led by George Palmer Putnam, the campaign for international justice to authors continued, sensationally advertised by the visit of Charles Dickens to America in the early 1840's, and by the organization of the American Copyright Club whose members included Bryant and Poe. Again, Congress received a bombardment of petitions, for and against, but took no action. As Eaton points out in the excellent study from which most of this information is adapted, the failure to establish international copyright at that moment may be attributed to the opposition of the bookmaking interests, to the lack of organization in the movement, to popular and Congressional indifference to a complex subject, and to the preoccupation of Congress with more pressing issues. In the 1850's, the proponents of the bill attempted another approach—international treaty instead of law. In 1853 Edward Everett negotiated one such treaty with England, but the Senate, still avoiding an intensely controversial subject, tabled it. As the Civil War drew near, the attention of legislators and constituents was directed toward more violent quarrels.

Throughout this period the English author could secure no protection in the United States other than by voluntary payment from the American publisher. On the other hand, the American author could take advantage of a difference in the copyright laws of the two nations. Because the American law provided protection only for *American* authors while the English law merely required priority of publication or residence, the American author would retain protection if his book appeared in England before it was published in the United States or if he lived in England. This formula, according to Spiller, "became an important means of support for most of our mid-nineteenth century writers."

The history of copyright legislation in the United States will be resumed in Part III of this volume.

International Piracy

The popularity of the English writers in America too often resulted only indirectly in financial profit to them, for the absence of an international copyright law made it possible for the American publisher to reprint their works without payment either to the English author or the English publisher. Where no law existed to protect an English book in the United States, the author of that book had, in fact, no "rights" in the fruit of its sale in this country. Actually the copyright act of 1790 protected the American publisher in the reprinting of an English book by the clause which limited the benefits of the law to citizens of the United States. The abuses and injustices under this system were innumerable, but the situation was not quite so completely without ameliorating factors as is sometimes believed. American publishers in many cases paid considerable sums for sheets printed in England which they brought out under their own imprints, or purchased proof sheets and manuscripts from which they set their own editions of English works of fiction, biography, and travel. Many of the most popular English writers received fair treatment and considerable financial reward from their authorized American publishers, and under similar terms of use the works of certain American writers in their turn found publication in England. Materials for a study of the whole relationship of American publishers to English authors, and English publishers to American authors, are found in I. R. Brussel's two books, *Anglo-American First Editions, East to West*, and *Anglo-American First Editions, West to East*.

In assuming that the English laws did not protect English books in a country in which those laws did not operate, the American publisher had precedent from the colonial period. We have seen that James Rivington, a publisher with English upbringing and business experience, had no scruples about the reprinting in New York in 1774 of Hawkesworth's *New Voyage*. At about the same time we find him in treaty with Henry Knox of Boston about the sale of English books printed in Ireland. Naturally these were popular in the American trade because, as they were pirated editions brought out in a country in which at that time, before the Act of Union of 1801, the English copyright law did not prevail, they could be sold by their publisher at a cheaper rate. In 1771 Robert Bell of Philadelphia, whose previous training had been in a Dublin bookselling establishment, brought out, dated 1770, Volume III of Robertson's *History of the Reign of Charles the Fifth*. In an *Address to the Subscribers,* Bell defended himself against the charge of piracy in the publication of that book by reference to the Irish trade in the reprinting of English books "without rendering the smallest pecuniary regard either to Authors or to Booksellers." "The reason is obvious," he continues, "because the monopoly doth not reach beyond the limits of Great-Britain, and cannot extend into any country governed by an Assembly of Representatives . . ." Bell then quotes at length from Blackstone's Commentaries to the effect that Ireland, the Channel Isles, and the American colonies were "not bound by any acts of parliament, unless particularly named." The ingenious Bell concludes his address with these two paragraphs:

"Surely, the precedent of the people of Ireland's reprinting every work produced in London, and the great Lawyer Blackstone's authority concerning the internal legislation of colonies, are demonstrations of the rectitude of reprinting any, or every work of excellence in America, without the smallest infringement of the British embargo upon literature.—Is it not enough that their embargo prevents Americans from shipping their manufactures of this kind into Britain.— Would it not be incompatible with all freedom, if an American's mind must be entirely starved and enslaved in the barren regions of fruitless vacuity, because he doth not wallow in immense riches equal to some British Lords, the origin of whose progenitors are lost in the chaos of antiquity?

"The Editor hopeth, that the facts above exhibited are sufficient support for Americans, to persevere in reprinting whatsoever books merit their approbation, without leave or licence from the Bibliopolists or Monopolists of Great-Britain; he is therefore determined, as much as possible, to practise the advice contained in George Fisher's emphatic lines.

"Since to the Pen and Press we mortals owe,
All we believe, and almost all we know,
Go on ye great preservers of these arts,
Which raise our thoughts and cultivate our parts."

Inasmuch as this argument by the Dublin-Philadelphia bookseller, dated April 4, 1771, continued for more than a century to represent American opinion upon the subject of reprinting English books, it seems important to record it here at some length. In the light of it American piracy, encouraged in precept and example by Bell and Rivington, formerly British booksellers, is seen to be legal and almost respectable instead of an evidence of headlong, reckless greed. Though not so bad as this, however, it was bad enough, injurious to good feeling between the nations, and deterrent of American literary expression. Yet the final word must be that the free reprinting of English books in this country was a tremendous service to a people craving cultural enlightenment. Nor is there any question that the dissemination of an English author's works in the United States was, in many cases, productive of great increase to his reputation, and therefore of indirect value to him from the standpoint of financial benefit.

In the first half of the nineteenth century the trade in pirated English books seems to have been a specialty of the Philadelphia publishers, but, as will be shown in the third part of this work, the palm for this activity returned later to New York and the hands of a group which provided cheap and adequate reprints of English books for a tremendous proportion of the country's readers.

Two incidents illustrate the battle waged by the Philadelphia firms against the growing ascendancy of the New York competitors in the reprint market. In 1822, within twenty-eight hours after receiving *Quentin Durward*, Mathew Carey produced 1500 copies for immediate sale; in 1836, Carey & Hart bought all the seats in the mail stage to ship *Rienzi* to New York and thereby beat the Harpers to the New York distribution of the book. This chapter in book trade history, with its tales of cutthroat competition and refusal to pay royalties abroad, seems intolerably brutal to us today, but it must be understood that the profession was in one of the successive stages in its progress towards the ethical conduct of its affairs. It was coming of age in a time when even the concept of international copyright was new. For it was not until 1828 that Denmark made legal provision for international copyright. Other countries followed after—Prussia in 1836, England in 1837, and their laws, too, contained reciprocity clauses. But before they became finally effective with the Berne Convention of 1886, three-quarters of the nineteenth century had passed.

The Emoluments of Authorship

The nineteenth-century American author who tried to earn a living in his profession found himself in competition with a huge and venerated contemporary literature, published largely without payment to even its foremost living masters. This situation for the minor writers was a calamity, but it became of less consequence to some of the personages who adapted themselves to the mysteries of business management as their writings grew in marketable value. Emerson, for example, shrewdly increased the return from his books by the expedient of paying for their manufacture, and gave his publisher only a commission on their sales. Longfellow and Prescott owned the plates of their works, and sold printing rights to the publishers. As Charvat records in one of his series of admirable studies, Longfellow's royalties from eight books whose plates he owned averaged 18¼ per cent return instead of the 8 per cent earned when, as formerly, he had shared the net proceeds of two books of poetry with his publisher, John Owen. This practice of owning and leasing plates increased in ratio to the repute of indigenous literature; the major writer no longer sold his copyright for a flat fee, nor shared profits with the publisher as customary at the beginning of the century. Inevitably the royalty system emerged as a scheme to regulate payment whenever possible, and has continued to the present. It is said that the arrangements of George Palmer Putnam with Elizabeth Barrett and with Carlyle marked the earliest appearance in the publishing business of the "royalty" system for the remuneration of authors. In the case of Carlyle, the royalty for his *Cromwell* offered by Putnam was such as we understand by that term today—a straight percentage on the retail selling price of all copies marketed.

Unfortunately, however, those authors whose income depended on royalties, whether by necessity or personal preference, were quite at the mercy of capricious economic cycles. As the panic of 1837 ended, and times gradually prospered, the 10 per cent average royalty of the 1840's increased, and in a few instances trebled, but thereafter followed the panic of 1857 which lowered the payments to their former standard. On the other hand, if an author sold well he commanded a higher price than the norm, no matter what the medium—book or periodical. To illustrate, Lowell in 1842 received ten dollars per poem, but in 1850 Graham offered him four times his original bid. In an inter-publishing rivalry, as when Graham and Godey contested for a group of spectacular performers, the incomes of literary figures advanced in proportion to their popularity. As in the twentieth century, a few of the prolific household names earned more than men of greater literary ability. In 1840 Longfellow stated that N. P. Willis declared he was earning ten thousand dollars a year by his writings, or ten times as much as Longfellow himself. The career of William Henry Herbert demonstrates how a translator of cheap novels could average three or four thousand dollars annually. In this connection it may be said that novels, on the whole, were not profitable enough for the full time of most writers and so they understandably wrote the short story or essay for periodicals which were more certainly remunerative. To this circumstance we owe the galvanic development of the characteristic American short story form and the sharp rise in popularity of the periodical which momentarily halted the evolution of the novel.

Another dependable way to relieve an author's debts existed in this early day, the immemorial lecture tour—which later became obligatory to the great and small alike. Emerson for forty years trudged over the countryside lecturing to augment his earnings. It follows, accordingly, that while no one principal occupation may have afforded a living wage for a man of letters, yet technically, despite the lack of international copyright, it was possible for him to exist in his combination role of author-contributor-lecturer.

Censorship

In the earlier discussion of censorship in the colonial period we have shown that the idea of the freedom of the press was well understood by government and people, and that, despite inevitable setbacks, there had existed within limitations a free press which made possible a steady progression in liberal thought. The absence of a statement regarding the press in the Constitution was evidence neither of reaction nor indifference, but simply of the deliberate choice of its makers to regard the freedom of the press as a natural right of man outside the province of government to grant or withhold. But the people of the states, less subtle in their comprehension of the philosophy of government, successfully compelled the insertion of the principle in the first of the Ten Amendments of 1791, the American Bill of Rights.

It might have been supposed that so far as the United States was concerned the battle was won by this action of 1791, but the Sedition Law of 1798 brought the whole subject before the country in an unpleasant form. One provision of that law related to the printing of libels against Congress or the President, and it was not long before several editors were prosecuted under its terms. Benjamin Franklin Bache of Philadelphia, grandson of Franklin, published matter in his *Aurora* which caused him to be arrested on the charge of libeling the President. Matthew Lyon, a congressman from Vermont, was found guilty on a similar charge, and Anthony Haswell, the printer and editor of Bennington, defending him in his newspaper, was brutally treated by an official oaf and sentenced under the law to serve a term in jail. Thomas Cooper of Northumberland, Pennsylvania, editor of the *Sunbury and Northumberland Gazette*, was another of those jailed and fined under the same law in 1800.

This persecution of the opposition to the Federalist government did not go without protest in print. One of the most pertinent of the utterances against it was *An Essay on the Liberty of the Press*, published in Philadelphia in 1799, at the office of the *Aurora*, Bache's newspaper, under the pseudonym of Hortensius, which stood for George Hay, the Virginia lawyer who in 1807 conducted the prosecution at the trial of Aaron Burr. *A Dissertation upon the Constitutional Freedom of the Press in the United States of America*, by an Impartial Citizen, was printed in Boston in 1801 by David Carlisle for Joseph Nancrède, the French publisher of Boston, later of Philadelphia, who is remembered as an active expositor of French liberalism in this country. In the absence of any suggestion as to the authorship of the *Dissertation*, it is not improper to suggest Nancrède himself. The Alien and Sedition acts expired in 1800 and 1801, respectively, having done an injury to their Federalist proponents to which, it has been said, the eventual downfall of their party could be traced.

It has been suggested that the pressure of adverse public opinion upon a publication agency (witness the destruction of Rivington's press and property in New York in 1775; the action of the Whig Club against Goddard in Baltimore in 1777; and the annihilation of the plant of Alexander Contee Hanson's *Federal Republican* in the same city in 1812) provided a censorship more effective and more frequently applied in this country than the operation of governmental restriction or persecution. It seems to be true that the history of Mob vs. Press is a fuller and more interesting one than that of the Press in conflict with Government. The people, yesterday and today, are concerned with the freedom of speech only when the utterance expresses, in general, their own views. In time of war and emotional stress of any sort the careful newspaper becomes the voice of the people. In the face of this fact theories regarding the liberty of the press become matter for academic discussion.

The Government and the Book Trade

Popular opinion regards the book trade as far removed from the grinding commercialism of industry. What is implicit in this romantic attitude is the idea that publishing is high adventure, with business accomplished in an unbusinesslike manner by a mysterious sixth sense that discerns literary genius aforetimes and even creates intellectual trends for the public to follow. The federal government, however, has a more realistic approach to publishing; from the beginning it favored books no more nor less than shoes and furniture—as simply a factor in the nation's economy. When the tariff act of 1789 was passed, books were not exempted nor specifically mentioned, but included as part of "all other goods" subject to a duty of 5 per cent. As the economic pattern of the new republic became more complex, Congress diligently guarded business and began to receive reports on its development. Of particular interest to us is this excerpt from the Report on Manufactures submitted to Congress in 1791 by the Secretary of the Treasury, Alexander Hamilton:

PRINTED BOOKS

The great number of presses disseminated throughout the Union, seem to afford an assurance that there is no need of being indebted to foreign countries for the printing of the books which are used in the United States. A duty of ten per cent., instead of five, which is now charged upon the article, would have a tendency to aid the business internally.

It occurs as an objection to this, that it may have an unfavorable aspect toward literature, by raising the price of books in universal use in private families, schools, and other seminaries of learning. But the difference, it is conceived, would be without effect.

As to books which usually fill the libraries of the wealthier classes and of professional men, such an augmentation of price as might be occasioned by an additional duty of five per cent., would be too little felt to be an impediment to the acquisition.

And with regard to books which may be specially imported for the use of particular seminaries of learning, and of public libraries, a total exemption from duty would be advisable, which would go far towards obviating the objection just mentioned. They are now subject to a duty of five per cent.

As to the books in most general family use, the constancy and universality of the demand would insure exertions to furnish them at home, and the means are completely adequate. It may also be expected ultimately, in this as in other cases, that the extension of the domestic manufacture would conduce to the cheapness of the article.

It ought not to pass unremarked, that to encourage the printing of books is to encourage the manufacture of paper.

Hamilton's advice went unheeded; the duty remained at 5 per cent. Thereafter the book trade uncompromisingly expressed its views on the tariff, pro and con, whenever necessary. In 1802 a few owners of type founding equipment attempted to raise the duty on imported printing type from 12½ to 20 per cent and almost immediately the book business, quick to realize that this would raise the price of domestic output, organized local meetings in protest. As a result Congress received seven petitions against the proposal, signed by virtually all the book trade in five cities from Boston to Charleston, and the tariff failed to pass.

An examination of the legislation at the beginning of the century reveals that the Non-Importation Act of 1806 exerted an unintentional restriction on the importation of books. It seems that the wording of the Act was so general and inconclusive that some officials misinterpreted it to mean that books were prohibited from entering America from abroad. When the Act became operative a disruption of imports must have ensued because a supplementary act was passed in 1808 which declared that "nothing in the act to which this is a supplement shall be so construed as to prohibit the importation of the following articles. . . . Printed books, maps, and charts."

As the War of 1812 approached, Albert Gallatin, then Secretary of the Treasury, conducted a survey of manufactures for the Congress. His appraisal of the book industry determined that

> Printing is carried on to an extent commensurate with the demand. Exclusively of the numerous newspapers, which alone form a considerable item in value, all the books for which there is an adequate number of purchasers, are printed in the United States.

This evidence as to the state of bookmaking decided the government against further action, and we may infer on this basis that the health of the industry was vigorous enough to need no artificial stimulus, and would be equal to meeting existing needs and maintaining its cultural mission, even in war.

One of the consequences of war is the multiplication of new industries, and to protect their manufactures Congress passed the Tariff of 1816. The duty on books was increased to 15 per cent and henceforth, to the beginning of the Civil War, the rate wavered between 8 and 15 per cent, with exceptions at times for classics not printed in America, books for libraries, and the like. Undoubtedly the vigilant interest of the book trade insured the continuance of the tariff. For example, in 1842, when Congress debated a new duty, booksellers, printers, paper-makers, and type founders convened in Boston, marshalled statistics to illustrate the importance of books in the national economy, and sent a committee to Congress to present its testimony. The success of the campaign bulwarked the industry during the 1843 depression and the uncertain period of recovery. As a colorful postscript to the story of the book and the tariff, we must note that two of the leading protectionists of the day, Mathew Carey, of Philadelphia, and Hezekiah Niles, of Baltimore, were publishers and booksellers who used all of their facilities for publicity to further the cause of protecting American manufactures.

The Literary Background

The literary production of the period before 1860 is looked back upon affectionately even by those whom modernism has led far away from its concern in matter and form; by still others it is revered as the Golden Age, and well may it be so considered from many standpoints. The country by that time had passed through its period of formation,

physical and political, through its period of poverty and arduous pioneer labor, and through its feeling of inferiority in the things of literature and art. It retained a sense of intellectual discipleship towards England, but so obvious is it that the men of this period were striking out
for themselves as American writers, dealing with American subjects,
that an affirmation of their American nationalism need hardly be made.
Nineteenth-century American literature was not, as one school of critics has told us, "colonial" in matter and purpose even though its makers
attempted to present it in a form and style that might not be disdained
in any appraisal of English literature. Washington Irving was writing
his legends of the New York countryside in *Rip Van Winkle* and the
Legend of Sleepy Hollow; he turned to the study of American history
in Knickerbocker's *History of New York,* and in his biographies of
Columbus and Washington. James Fenimore Cooper was bringing the
American Indian, the scout, the hunter, and the pioneer into American
literature in *The Deerslayer, The Last of the Mohicans,* and in other
stories of the "Leather-Stocking" series. His very first successful work,
The Spy, had made the American Revolution the subject of a novel.
John Pendleton Kennedy, less well remembered than these, was writing
historical novels and sketches of manners with the South as their background. Hawthorne was the recorder of the old New England in his
Scarlet Letter and *House of the Seven Gables.* Thoreau was preaching
a philosophy of wide social implications with Walden Pond as the center of the world of his actual knowledge. Herman Melville in *Moby
Dick, Typee,* and *Omoo* was telling tales of distant oceans seen by a
youth whose New York and New England background could be forgotten neither by himself nor by his readers. In his address of 1837
entitled *The American Scholar,* Ralph Waldo Emerson set forth what
Oliver Wendell Holmes called "our intellectual Declaration of Independence." In his writings generally, universal in philosophical scope
though they were, Emerson was as American as his native Massachusetts. Francis Parkman, William Hickling Prescott, and George Bancroft, historians steeped in the history of the western continent, were
chronicling a varied drama played upon a stage that reached from Quebec in Canada to Lima in Peru. Among the poets Poe was a disem-
bodied spirit so far as locale was concerned, but Walt Whitman as well
as Longfellow, Whittier, and Lowell were American in spirit and mat-

ter. This prolific period achieved its climax in 1855, the year which witnessed the first editions of Whitman's *Leaves of Grass,* Longfellow's *Hiawatha,* Bulfinch's *Age of Fable,* and Bartlett's *Familiar Quotations.* The one book of the period that rivalled and surpassed the sales records of the modern best sellers was a picture of American life of immense propagandist value. Mrs. Harriet Beecher Stowe wrote her celebrated *Uncle Tom's Cabin* with little idea of its effect upon the opinion of her countrymen, but its pathos, its romanticism, its picture of the daily life of slave and master secured for it enormous distribution and brought the issue of slavery before the country in a fashion that all the efforts of Quaker, Abolitionist, and political orator had not been able to do in generations of effort. It was published by the firm of John P. Jewett & Co., of Boston, after her own publishers, Phillips, Sampson & Co., rejected it for fear of losing their Southern trade. The eight presses of George C. Rand, working day and night, turned out the 300,000 copies which were sold in the twelve-month after its first issue in book form in March, 1852. The total sales approached three million.

It is no wonder that one looks back upon this period, teeming with books and periodicals, with the works of novelists, essayists, poets, and propagandists, a surprisingly large number of them of the quality that endures, as one of the most interesting in the cultural history of the nation.

The Expansion of the Book Trade

Probably the best way to convey an idea of the development of the book trade in the United States in the period which we are now discussing is by a series of statistical tables. These tables are based chiefly upon Evans's *American Bibliography* and Roorbach's *Bibliotheca Americana,* sources which could not in the nature of their compilation be regarded as complete. Mr. Evans listed everything that a rigorous and long-continued search brought under his eye, but it has been calculated that there have disappeared roughly four times as many printed pieces of the period covered by him than he recorded as having been issued. Roorbach's list was rigidly selective, and in only a very limited sense can it be taken to represent the total output of the press in his period.

The first of the tables is this which follows:

PERSONS AND FIRMS ENGAGED AS EMPLOYING PRINTERS, PUBLISHERS, AND BOOKSELLERS
IN FIVE AMERICAN CITIES

	Boston	New York	Philadelphia	Baltimore	Charleston, S. C.
1773	30	13	16	1	3
1778	10	8	21	3	4
1792	30	19	47	15	10
1798	41	56	88	19	15

The figures above given portray the gradually increasing decentralization of the book trade in the new country in the first two decades of its separate existence. In 1773 the figure for Boston is nearly twice as large as that for Philadelphia, its closest competitor, and only slightly under the combined totals of the other four cities examined. Five years later the trade in Boston and New York, affected by the War of the Revolution, had shrunk to relatively small proportions, while in Philadelphia, for four years past the seat of the Continental Congress, it had appreciably gone ahead. In 1792 Boston had got back to its numerical position of 1773, but not to its leadership; New York had advanced; Philadelphia, the temporary capital and seat of the recent Constitutional Convention, had made a notable increase; and Baltimore and Charleston for the first time were making a respectable showing. In 1798 as the century was about to close, an increase had occurred in all five cities, but the significant features of that year were the rapid growth of the trade in Philadelphia and New York as compared to Boston, and the first hint that New York was to become in the book world a serious rival to the Pennsylvania city. The figures for a later period will point to the consummation of these tendencies.

The group of figures analyzed in the foregoing paragraph shows the number of individuals engaged as employers in all branches of the book trade in five cities at various times from 1773 until the end of the century. Those now to be presented for the period 1820 to 1852 do not include printers unless they were also publishers, nor do they take account of bookbinders and retail booksellers. In other words, in this table for the later period we are concerned only with the publisher or, as he happened to be in many cases, the printer-publisher.

PUBLISHERS IN SIX CITIES, 1820-1852

Boston	147	Charleston	15
Baltimore	32	Philadelphia	198
New York	345	Cincinnati	25

By this time, as one sees at a glance, the book trade had found its unquestioned center at New York; Philadelphia and Boston, the ancient rivals, were again approaching equality; Baltimore was advancing slowly; Charleston, still more slowly; and the West was beginning to surpass the South and to make itself a national factor with the publications of twenty-five firms in Cincinnati.

For the century and a half period 1639-1791, Mr. Evans recorded some 24,000 titles, including newspapers, almanacs, and assembly laws and proceedings, as the issue of the press of English America. Roorbach records this same number for the short period 1820-1852, omitting from his lists the specific categories just named as forming an important factor in Evans' total, and concentrating on works of literature, history, and the arts. He records the fact, also, that there were being published in 1850 in the United States 486 periodicals, exclusive of daily and semi-weekly newspapers.

The Small-Town Publishers

From what has been said it may seem to the reader that the entire publishing trade of the first half of the century was carried on in the chief cities by the individuals and firms of whom we have been speaking. But that is not the case. These firms, in all essentials, were small-town printers grown big because their towns had grown big. In innumerable small towns throughout the country, which had been distanced in the race for size and importance by Boston, Philadelphia, and New York, active publishing was being carried on, as it had been throughout the colonial period, by the individual who combined in himself the functions of printer, publisher, newspaper editor, book-binder, and bookseller. His product was largely confined to almanacs, schoolbooks, chapbooks, and reprints of favorite works of fiction, travel, and adventure, but first and last it formed a very large part of the reading matter of the residents in the small towns themselves and in the farms surrounding them. Various causes—railroads and a consequent quicker and wider distribution, the cheapening of the product through quantity production, the use of the stereotype process for the reproduction of standard books, which was hardly feasible on a large scale to the small-town printer—slowly brought it about that after the middle of the century this minor but important figure was stripped of his pride as a book publisher, retaining his newspaper and the local job work of his district as his chief means of support.

It would be invidious to name only a few of the individuals in a group of such size and wide geographical distribution. The greatest activity among those who composed it seems to have centered in rural New York and in New England "north of Boston"; that is, in Albany, Poughkeepsie, Ithaca, Canandaigua, and Cooperstown, New York; Walpole, Keene, Exeter, Claremont, and Concord, New Hampshire; Brattleboro, Montpelier, Woodstock, and Bennington, Vermont; Hallowell and Portland, Maine; and in a number of smaller Massachusetts towns. But that the small-town publisher existed throughout the country, though the New York and New England concentration was his strongest manifestation, one learns from a brief examination of the pages of Roorbach, where publishers are found to be located in Frankfort and Maysville, Kentucky; in Athens and Augusta, Georgia; in Milwaukee, Wisconsin; and in so many other places of like size and character that it would be a simple weariness to particularize them. We may hope that the extensive studies undertaken by Barrows Mussey upon this important subject of the small-town publisher will be carried to the point of publication. We owe him thanks for most of the material on this important subject presented in the paragraphs above. In *The Country Printer*, Mr. Milton W. Hamilton has given us a rich study of how, in New York State in 1785-1830, the small-town printer lived and worked and what were his ambitions and his achievements.

Characteristics of the New Publications

In the categories of knowledge represented by the American press at the close of the eighteenth century, differences are found when comparing the output with that of the colonial period. The table below

CLASSES OF PRODUCT

	Total	Litera-ture	Medi-cine	Music	Theol-ogy	Social Science	Political Science
1778	461	17	7	8	37	15	12
1798	1808	203	38	16	244	62	143
Multiple of increase	4	12	5.5	2	6.6	4	12

needs no comment, except the obvious one that instead of an intellectual interest closely confined to theology, a more broadly-based culture, strong in its interest in literature and political science, was making its way in the country, accompanying, if not caused by, a notable physical growth and a striking experiment in political idealism.

For similar information about the publications of the first half of the nineteenth century, we must rely upon the figures prepared by S. G. Goodrich. Although these are admittedly rough approximations, Goodrich was so closely acquainted with the publishing business of the period that these estimates supply the best available knowledge pending a more intensive study of the imprints. In this table, it must be emphasized, the values are in dollars:

ESTIMATES OF BOOK PRODUCTION
(In dollars)

	1820	1830	1840	1850
School Books...................	750,000	1,100,000	2,000,000	5,500,000
Classical Books.................	250,000	350,000	550,000	1,000,000
Theological Books..............	150,000	250,000	300,000	500,000
Law Books.....................	200,000	300,000	400,000	700,000
Medical Books.................	150,000	200,000	250,000	400,000
All others.....................	1,000,000	1,300,000	2,000,000	4,400,000
Total........................	2,500,000	3,500,000	5,500,000	12,500,000

This table indicates that the rapidly expanding educational system of a fast-growing nation was reflected in book production, in general reading matter as well as in textbooks. But, as with most tables, it fails to make manifest the more subtle and more interesting ramifications. For while, prior to 1820, American creative literature was insignificant, books for American life, such as school texts, theological works, and practical handbooks were an important cultural factor. The architectural books of Asher Benjamin and Owen Biddle, for example, exerted a profound influence and remained in circulation for half the nineteenth century. "It was these books," says Talbot Hamlin, "with their exquisite, delicate details, which made possible those chaste wooden houses with slim-columned porticoes and rich cornices in which for the first time the stone details of the original English inspiration have finally evolved into some of the most perfect expressions of wood which architecture has known." The significant meaning of the great increase in reading between 1830 and 1840 should also be suggested. The new interest in primary and secondary education created greatly improved schoolbooks. This, too, was the period of the establishment of the Penny Press and of many major periodicals—all influencing the reading habits of the populace. Finally, the appearance of annuals and gift books provided illustrated anthologies which were sold in remarkably large quantities. Originally appearing in Germany, the idea of annuals as developed by Ackermann in London was quickly appropriated by American publishers. Well-known authors and artists were employed in the production of these elaborate volumes which, in the words of Goodrich, "became messengers of love, tokens of friendship, signs and symbols of affection, and luxury and refinement." The next decade, 1840-1850, witnessed the production of books which were even more elaborate and which, because of the increasing prosperity, could be readily sold. Harpers, Appleton, Butler, and Putnam published expensive volumes copiously illustrated with engravings of wood or steel. The schoolbooks, improved in format and content, sold in almost astronomical quantities—spelling books in the millions, geographies in the hundreds of thousands. In all fields of authorship, American books were supplanting the British works. Goodrich estimates that in 1820 American authors wrote 30 per cent of the books, while British authors wrote 70 per cent, but for 1850 his estimate is reversed. Soon after the middle of the century, the magazines flourished; *Harpers'*, for instance, achieving a monthly circulation of more than 170,000 copies. Yet they alone did not satisfy the desire for new fiction; novels were sold in editions of thirty, forty and fifty thousand. At this time, it is interesting to note, there was also a great popular interest in "Thrilling, Agonizing Literature"—the forerunner of what we now call science fiction. The limitations of space do not permit an adequate tribute to the standard works of history, law, medicine, and science which appeared between 1800 and 1850. Brilliantly and steadily, throughout these years, scholars prepared and the publishers issued books of importance in national and world culture. This is only a rapid view of some of the trends of publishing which preceded the panic of 1857—a financial upheaval which destroyed some firms and which affected the entire book trade.

The Leading Publishers at the Turn of the Century

The New York book trade in the year 1798 already comprised within its organization a number of individuals who were to be among its leading members in the first half of the new century. Among these we must name Evert Duyckinck, remembered today, when the books he published are all but forgotten, as a capable and industrious editor and writer; Philip Freneau, the best-known American poet of the period; Hugh Gaine, an eminent printer of the colonial period, still vigorous after nearly fifty years of printing and publishing; Noah Webster, whose world-wide fame as a lexicographer has obscured his activity as editor and publisher; and Thomas and John Swords, who were to continue their activities well into the new century and help consolidate the position of leadership of their city.

In Boston there were the firms of Thomas & Andrews, of which the head was the well-remembered Isaiah Thomas of Worcester; Benjamin Edes; and the Russells. In Philadelphia, Robert Aitken, who in 1782 had published the first English Bible printed in America, was still conducting a firm that had been active and important for thirty years; Franklin's grandson, Benjamin Franklin Bache, printer, publisher, and type founder, was continuing the family tradition; three descendants of William Bradford, the city's first printer, were carrying on in their persons a still older and more persistent family tradition; Mathew Carey, who shares with Isaiah Thomas preeminence among the printers of the period, was building up a great business in the publishing of books and in the selling of them by subscription; Thomas Dobson had just brought to an end the most ambitious book project until then conceived this side of the Atlantic, that is, the publication in eighteen large quarto volumes of the revised third edition of Rees's *Encyclopaedia*. Duane, Fenno, Folwell, McCulloch, and Poulson were some of those destined to become prominent in the typographical and publishing activities of the new generation; Moreau de St. Méry, politician, writer, and printer, and Pierre Parent were conducting their French presses for the benefit of the large French element in Philadelphia, augmented earlier in the decade by the refugees from Santo Domingo; Charles Cist, of Philadelphia, was carrying on the old tradition of German publication in the colony in which the Sauers, Steiner, and Armbruester had firmly established it in earlier generations.

The Music Publishers

Powerful religious influences were responsible for the circumstance that before the Revolution the production of sacred music far exceeded that of secular music in volume. Nevertheless, both of these types were to be found in the shops of the booksellers and stationers, although publication itself was usually carried out by the composer or compiler, upon the basis of a subscription list. After the Revolution, the output of secular music gradually increased, particularly in New York and Philadelphia, while Boston continued to lead in publishing sacred works.

In all these cities there arose in the post-Revolutionary period a new type of American publisher in the person of one who devoted himself to the publication of sheet music. In New York were Benjamin Carr, George Gilfert, James Hewitt, and John and M. Paff. In Boston was to be found the active house of P. A. von Hagen. Benjamin Carr conducted a "Musical Repository" in Philadelphia as well as in New York, dividing the business of the first-named city with George Willig. From these shops and others like them issued in the period before 1800, notably in the period 1780-1800, a constant production of sheet music, both instrumental and vocal. The Sonneck and Upton bibliography comprises some 2500 titles of secular music for the period ending with the close of the century. These were the moderate beginnings of a trade that became enormous in the early years of the succeeding century.

The Leading Publishers of the Period 1800-1860

At different times in the period before 1860 arose certain bookselling and printing establishments that eventually became publishing houses of national and even wider fame. We have spoken more than once of the activities of Mathew Carey, who, beginning as a printer and bookseller in Philadelphia in the late eighteenth century, carried on into the nineteenth as one of the leading American publishers of books and periodicals. Carey was himself a writer on economic subjects and a citizen of importance who influenced the thinking of his time as well as the business of bookselling and publishing. His sons and his son-in-law and their descendants have carried on his business for the century and a half which has elapsed since its first establishment. Carey & Lea; Carey, Lea & Carey; Carey, Lea & Blanchard; Henry C. Lea; Lea Brothers & Co.; Lea & Febiger are a few of the firm names under which the printing and publishing house set up by the progenitor in 1785 has continued ever since to carry on a solid business in Philadelphia despite the fact that the chief activity of the book world for the greater part of the period has centered in New York and Boston.

In 1836 was founded in Philadelphia the bookselling and publishing house of J. B. Lippincott & Co., which today carries on a century-old tradition of general publishing.

Charles Wiley established in New York in 1807 a bookshop from which grew a publishing house that still exists, though today, after a long period in which it won distinction in the general publishing business of the country, its activities are restricted to the publication of scientific books and journals. John Wiley, the son of Charles, formed a partnership with George Long, and when, in 1840, Long withdrew from the firm, he replaced him with an individual celebrated in the annals of American publishing, George Palmer Putnam. The firm of Wiley & Putnam soon boasted a branch in London, mainly devoted to bookselling, under the charge of the junior partner. There Putnam came into personal relations with English authors and secured at first-hand their works for publication by his firm in New York. Even earlier than this, Putnam had become a leader in the cause of international copyright, a cause which was later championed by his son George Haven Putnam, who, in 1909, could see in a new act of Congress something that approximated the successful consummation of the long struggle. Soon after its establishment of the principle of royalty payments, the firm of Wiley & Putnam dissolved, and the junior member set up the firm of G. P. Putnam that still carries on the business of publishing in New York.

In 1825 or, as some authorities maintain on good evidence, 1827, Daniel Appleton established a general store in New York which soon began specializing in the sale of books. In 1831, Appleton entered the field of publishing. Under the name of D. Appleton & Co. the firm carried on until its merger in 1933 with The Century Co. Today it operates as Appleton-Century-Crofts, Inc. It has maintained throughout that period of more than a hundred years an admirable record in the publication of general literature.

The house of Harper began in 1817 with the printing firm of J. & J. Harper, comprising James Harper and a younger brother, John, which soon began the publication on a large scale of reprints of the works of contemporary and earlier authors. In 1833 the firm, by then enlarged through the addition of two other brothers, took the name of Harper & Brothers by which it is known at the present day. So nearly equal were the shares of the four brothers in the responsibilities of the firm that it was wittily said "Either one is the Harper, the rest are the Brothers." The wide interests of this firm, including the publication of several periodicals bearing its name, are so well known as to make it unnecessary to dwell further upon the story of its activities.

During this period, many of the religious publishing societies were also located in New York, where they conducted publishing operations of enormous magnitude. Few of us are aware of the amount of religious literature turned out by such organizations as the American Bible Society and the American Tract Society. The latter, founded in 1825 as a result of a merger between the New York and New England Tract Societies, printed over six million tracts in the year ending May, 1829. All of these tracts were "for circulation among the friends of evangelical truth of different denominations"—as were the Society's books, magazines, and almanacs—and all books and tracts were sold at cost. Thompson, in his study of the Society, discusses the methods of distribution involving hundreds of branches, circulating libraries, special services for sailors and boatmen, as well as editions for the blind, books and pamphlets in German, Irish, French, Spanish, Welsh, and Indian dialects. He also notes that for many years the Society conducted a "Tract of the Month" program which, even a hundred years ago, included "book dividends." By 1848 it printed about eight million books and pamphlets annually—many of which were illustrated by the best artists and engravers. The story of the Methodist Book Concern, reaching back in its forerunners to 1789, is fully told on pages 240 and 361.

The first half of the nineteenth century saw the revival for a short period of the eminence of Boston as a publishing center. In 1821, Charles Coffin Little entered the bookstore of Carter, Hilliard & Co., an organization which, through its several proprietors, traced to the eighteenth century, and in 1827 he became a member of the firm, then reorganized as Hilliard, Gray & Co. He became senior member and soon thereafter formed an association with James Brown. The firm of Little, Brown & Co., so called since 1837, thus is to be regarded as one of the few which carry back to the eighteenth century. Boston at that time was entering upon a fresh period of literary glory through the activities of that distinguished group of New England men of letters which comprised Hawthorne, Emerson, Thoreau, Whittier, Parkman, and others of a fame that has endured. The Old Corner Book Store, taken over in 1832 by John Allen and William D. Ticknor, became a gathering place for bookmen and men of letters. Two years later, the partners separated and Ticknor continued the firm alone, specializing in the sale of medical books. In 1843, James T. Fields was admitted as a partner and the firm, known also as Ticknor, Reed & Fields (1849-1854), Ticknor & Fields (1854-1868), began to establish itself as the country's most distinguished literary publishing house. This happy combination of Ticknor, typical New England business man, and Fields, literary entrepreneur, published the work of all the outstanding American authors of the period—except Whitman, Melville, and Poe. Fields, by skillful publicity methods as well as by careful nurturing of editors, reviewers, and critics, set patterns for book promotion which have remained to the present day. *The Cost Books of Ticknor and Fields, 1832-1858* by Warren S. Tryon and William Charvat is a full record of a firm and of the practices of a period. As the result of several combinations and changes of partnership, the firm eventually became Houghton Mifflin Co., which, with Little, Brown & Co., continues in Boston a long record of uninterrupted publication of works of literature.

In the West, Cincinnati was the major center of book production and distribution, retaining its lead over Chicago until the panic of 1857. Soon after Winthrop B. Smith founded Truman & Smith in Cincinnati about 1830, the firm became a leading textbook house, issuing approximately 700,000 books during the first ten years of its existence. By publishing McGuffey's *Readers* and other well-known school texts, it developed into the most extensive schoolbook publishing house in the world, eventually merging into the American Book Company.

The Battle of the Weeklies

During the first three decades of the nineteenth century, books were sturdy and well made, requiring considerable expense to manufacture. However, the sudden impact of the new technology destroyed this traditional concept of bookmaking, and before they realized what was happening, orthodox publishers were beset by an unknown hazard to their business, the cheap book. The lowering of prices and debasing of standards which occurred in the forties was due to the new paper-making machines and cylinder presses which could turn out newspapers and paper books in rapid-fire quantities at low cost. As a consequence, when the first shock and confusion were over, the course of publishing was altered, and the principle of cheap books for large numbers of people remained, gaining in momentum to the present day.

It is obvious that such a change would have occurred eventually, as in other industries, but it was accelerated to a marked degree by a dramatic battle between the editors of two weeklies engaged in a cutthroat competition. This "Great Revolution in Publishing," as it has been called, reached a spectacular turning point when, in 1841, the *New World* competed for markets with *Brother Jonathan*. Both were New York weeklies, printed to resemble newspapers in order to secure a cheap postal rate. Of course some news was printed, but most of the space was devoted to serialized novels, pirated from England or written by native authors. Soon the readers complained that the complete story could be read in book form long before they themselves could finish it in the weekly. In answer, the editors issued "supplements" and "extras," each containing a whole novel, printed on newspaper presses and usually unbound. This intensified their rivalry and soon prices were reduced to absurd lows. In 1841, "extras" were hawked for fifty or even twenty-five cents; in 1842, according to White, "Bulwer's *Zanoni* was published almost simultaneously by Harpers, *New World* and *Brother Jonathan*, and sold for as low as six cents a copy." Despite vanishing profit margins, these books appeared at regular intervals the following year.

This merciless conflict did perfom a public service. The cheap books offered much good literature to those who could not afford the respectable volumes, and presumably introduced books to a new class of readers. The reputable publishers, like Harpers, fought this radical departure in bookmaking all the way, price for price, with their tremendous resources. Others merely waited for the cyclone to spend itself. Finally it did, but only with the aid of the federal government. In April, 1843, postal authorities ruled that "supplements" must be mailed under book rate. This blow, combined with growing public distaste for shoddy books, spelled the decline of the weeklies. Nevertheless, a new factor in publishing had been introduced, never to depart; price wars were to be repeated, in an atmosphere of treachery and malice, at various times in the last half of the century. As Mott states, "never again after the 'great revolution' were cheap books out of the picture."

Bookselling Methods

At the turn of the century and during the first twenty-five years thereafter, book publishing was principally local rather than national and most book publishers continued to use their own retail bookstores as primary distribution agencies. Since no single publisher possessed facilities to produce all the books he could retail, he often exchanged his books, sometimes only the sheets, with other firms—a barter system which had existed in the sixteenth century in Europe. It is this system which accounts for some of the lists of firms often found in the imprints of nineteenth-century books. When, in the second quarter of the century, publishing and bookselling became more specialized and developed as separate occupations, the exchange system declined, being replaced by straight purchase from the publisher and by trade sales. These, plus import channels, were the major sources of supply for the bookseller of the period.

The modes of distribution of books in the years between the Revolution and 1860 show little change from those elsewhere employed in that period—that is, distribution through the retail bookshop, the subscription agent, the pedlar, and the auctioneer. Mathew Carey and Caleb P. Wayne, of Philadelphia, were prolific publishers of books to be sold by subscription. For both these men, but principally for Mathew Carey, worked the celebrated Mason Locke Weems, prince of American traveling book agents from 1794 until 1825. He is familiarly remembered as "Parson Weems," creator of the story of the boy George Washington and the Cherry Tree, and the author of biographies of Washington, Marion, Franklin, and Penn. With horse and wagon, Weems covered the eastern seaboard between Pennsylvania and Georgia. For Wayne he sold nearly 4000 copies of Marshall's *Life of Washington*, collecting for him for that book alone the sum of $40,000; for Carey, unnumbered copies of a long succession of books, including an estimated 3000 copies of Carey's Family Bible.

The auction business, which almost disappeared in 1801 with the record of a single sale, began to raise its head about 1814, when there were held ten sales (eight in Boston, two in New York) of sufficient importance to require printed catalogs. For the year 1860 some sixty sales of a similar character are recorded, more than one half of them held by the New York auction houses of Bangs, Merwin & Co. and George A. Leavitt & Co., the remainder almost equally divided between M. Thomas & Sons of Philadelphia and Leonard & Co. of Boston. Publishers disposed of job lots as well as plates of books in the trade sales which usually occurred annually or semi-annually, beginning in 1824. These auctions, held in Philadelphia, Boston, and New York, were intended for the trade only and also served as a meeting place for the booksellers and publishers. They continued to flourish until after the Civil War.

The more enterprising of the booksellers in the period before the Revolution had customarily issued in the weekly newspaper lists of their importations from the London publishers, and occasionally there were issued separately special lists of books of other sorts for sale. The earliest of these known to us was that well-remembered catalog in which Duncan Campbell of Boston, in 1693, offered to the public by retail sale the library of the Rev. Samuel Lee. We have already seen that in the ensuing years there were frequent issues of catalogs of book auctions, but it was not until after the middle of the century that the booksellers' catalog with lists of importations or of locally printed books for retail disposal began to assume importance as a means of selling books. After the Revolution this form of advertising booksellers' wares became a regular feature of the trade. An octavo of thirty-two pages issued about the year 1790 by Benjamin Guild of Boston offered nearly a thousand titles of books of English, French and classical origin; some forty pieces of music, principally instrumental; and seventeen charts of Nova Scotia and New England waters from the *Atlantic Neptune* of J. F. W. Des Barres. A finer analysis of the contents of this catalog would show the numerical ratios of the several categories of knowledge represented among the books offered for sale. There would be, of course, a striking difference between the reading lists of that day and this, but the growth in popularity of the fictional form which has been chiefly responsible for this difference is so much a matter of commonplace knowledge that it need not be emphasized by further reference. Of more immediate interest in this sense is the number of works found in this catalog on the practical sciences; on a single page appear Glasse's *Art of Cookery*, Gordon's *Geographical Grammar*, Guthrie's *Geographical Grammar*, Hale's *Complete System of Husbandry*, Halley's *Astronomical Tables*, Haselden's *Seaman's Daily Assistant*, Harris's *On the Globes*, the *Art of Hatching Fowls*, Hauxley's *System of Navigation*—all works necessary to a people of whom 90 per cent were still engaged in some form of agricultural pursuit, while many of the remainder gained their living from the sea.

John Dabney's catalog of books for sale or circulation (in the manner of the modern lending library), of Salem, 1791, is larger than Guild's in size, but much the same in content. The catalog of William Blake of Boston offered a similar assortment and, like that of Dabney, contained a section headed "Bibles, Dictionaries, Classical and School Books, Navigation Books, &c." This dealer also offered to form libraries for private gentlemen, schools, or societies. Mathew Carey issued in Philadelphia in 1795 a catalog of his own publications which comprised seventy-six book titles and fifty-eight maps and prints. An examination of Carey's list shows as its first ten numbers: a work of political reference, an anthology of verse, two romances, a miscellany for ladies, two works on the French Revolution, Plowden's *History of the British Empire*, a work of sentimental reflection, and an edition of Gay's *Fables*. It was stock of this varied character that Parson Weems, Carey's famous traveling bookseller, for thirty years carried through the Middle States and the South and disposed of with a curious mingling of the normal desire for gain and the conviction that he was acceptably serving God by distributing good books, whatever their origin or subject.

In 1797 John West of Boston issued *A Catalogue of Books published in America*, the earliest American book trade bibliography we have yet encountered. It contains thirty-six small octavo pages and offers more than 600 titles of current works of United States publication. The student has before him in small compass in such a catalog material for a rich study of social and literary tendencies.

Some of the foregoing catalogs were unpriced. West's list of American books, however, has prices affixed to each title as does Carey's catalog of his own publications. In 1802[?] Joseph Nancrède, the

French bookseller of Boston, issued a "Fixed-Price Catalogue" of his stock, comprising, it seems, a larger proportion of learned works than is to be found in the others mentioned and, in general, a greater variety of topics. About the same time this bookseller issued his *Centinel Extra, Joseph Nancrede's fixed-Priced Catalogue,* a list of recent importations from London, forming a book in oblong quarto, comprising sixteen pages of three columns each, and showing a total number of something like 2000 titles. These Nancrède catalogs are noteworthy as marking the intrusion of bibliographical description into American bookselling, for after each title is a size notation, date, place of publication, and description of binding when that feature was sufficiently notable to deserve remark.

The publication of these catalogs, and of the auction catalogs already described, seems to indicate the existence of a state of vigor in the American trade in the closing years of the eighteenth century and opening years of the nineteenth. That this indication is not misleading seems to be the conclusion from the further particulars of that trade now to be related.

Bookselling and Publishing Organizations

One feature of the early nineteenth-century book trade to be commented upon was the effort made by the booksellers everywhere in the country to form themselves into trade associations for mutual benefit, protection, and establishment of standards. As early as 1801 fourteen Boston firms established the Association of the Boston Booksellers, later called the Boston Association of Booksellers. Throughout its existence, the members exerted a sincere and united effort to maintain an honorable price structure—an effort which was only discontinued when, in 1820, the Association was dissolved because "from the present dullness of Business . . . there seems to exist a necessity for each member to be at liberty to act for himself in transacting his Business, unshackled by existing Rules & Regulations." In 1802 the Philadelphia Company of Booksellers announced that its chief object "shall be to unite in the risque of publishing such books as they may agree upon." These Philadelphia booksellers soon must have realized the value of co-operation, for in two years they were issuing a trade journal comprising lists of books for sale by members of the company, entitled *The Library, or Philadelphia Literary Reporter.* When economic conditions were seriously disturbed by the War of 1812, the company issued an *Address to the Booksellers of the United States* (1813), appealing for smaller editions as a means of reducing losses as well as invested capital. The similar organization in New York, founded about 1802, adopted a constitution which attempted to regulate the book trade in that city in the minutest details. A manuscript sheet appended to a copy of the *Constitution of the New York Association of Booksellers* (1809) shows a membership of twenty firms and individuals. Even as far west as Lexington, Kentucky, a meeting of Kentucky and Ohio printers and booksellers in 1805 attempted to organize a similar group on the frontier.

An incident of great interest in the bookselling trade occurred in 1801 when Mathew Carey issued circulars suggesting that the scattered printers and booksellers unite in the presentation of an annual book fair after the model of the Leipzig and Frankfurt fairs. The effort was successful as far as it went, bringing together for the first time large numbers of American booksellers and publishers and resulting in the temporary stimulation of their sales. Beginning in 1802, the fairs continued for four years, and probably ceased to exist with the fair of June, 1806. By that time, according to Mathew Carey,

it produced an evil that had not been foreseen, and that outweighed all its advantages. Country booksellers published large editions of popular books with half-worn types and on inferior paper, with which, by means of exchanges, they deluged the country—and in many cases the city booksellers had on their hands good editions of the books thus republished. This unexpected result rendered the city booksellers dissatisfied, and they by degrees withdrew.

Out of this attempt to introduce the successful German system came, however, the earliest national booksellers' organization the country was to know, for at that first meeting of June, 1802, was formed what came to be called the American Company of Booksellers. The principles upon which the organization was based were: improvement in the physical quality of books for the sake of the reputation of the trade; avoidance of interference with one another's publications; discontinuance of importations of books already published in this country in good editions; approval of the Literary Fair; and the formation of local booksellers' associations. The organization was in the hands of sensible and intelligent men—Carey, Gaine, Andrews, Swords, and others of their type. Its program widened somewhat two years later when it offered gold medals as rewards for the best American-made ink and paper, the best American binding executed in American leather, and the best American printing with American paper and American ink. Although the association dissolved when the fairs ceased, the organization of the American bookselling trade was well begun with high motives and distinguished members.

Conclusion

In the foregoing condensed statement of the history of printing and bookselling in the United States from 1639 until 1860, the authors have been compelled to use their own judgment as to what names, events, and tendencies were of the greatest significance in that history. It is their earnest hope that their readers will agree with their choice of essential factors and forgive the omission of many things that might have been brought into a more highly elaborated work.

The trade which has been reviewed in these pages has been in the United States an even more important factor in national development, if that is possible, than in other countries, for in most places in the colonies the conditions of life at first obviated the possibility of any but rudimentary intellectual development. After that early period of primitive living and thinking, the cultural spirit had to be recaptured in a few short generations of conscious effort. Church and school and press labored to restore the lost background. Not the least effective of these valiant agencies was the press.

PART III

BOOK PRODUCTION AND DISTRIBUTION
FROM 1860 TO THE PRESENT DAY

by

Hellmut Lehmann-Haupt

INTRODUCTION

The Civil War, ostensibly the conflict between a liberal, progressive North and a feudal, traditional South, had far-reaching social and economic consequences. It brought about the victory of the new industrialism of the Northeastern states and of the large agrarian Western states over the older slavery economy of Southern plantations.

Already in the course of the War those powers were gaining momentum which, after the close of the conflict, found unprecedented opportunities awaiting them. Their successful realization brought boundless prosperity. It can be said that in European countries, too, for instance in Great Britain, and in Germany after the War of 1870, the fruits of industrialization were ripening. But we must not forget that in the United States these developments coincided with another and quite unique unfolding of energies. I mean those powers which arose from the completed colonization and settlement of an entire continent. To grasp and to exploit for the first time the huge western territories, to conquer finally the aboriginal Indian population, to embrace the vast natural resources and to attempt a first economic consolidation of the country—those were the big important tasks of the reunited nation. A symbol of completed conquest, the Union Pacific railroad joining East and West, was finished in 1869, and soon a network of railroad communication spanned the entire continent.

In the new symphony of triumphant material achievement the quieter voices of the scholar, the poet and the philosopher appear to have been drowned. It takes a fine ear, and an intimate knowledge of the older literary traditions, to perceive that these voices were not altogether silenced. The late Vernon Louis Parrington, one of the keenest critics of the American mind, has drawn for us a convincing picture of the older American idealism and romantcism, of the stunned retirement of its surviving leaders in New England, and of the first timid attempts at a spiritual revolution. He has pointed out the ever

139

growing importance of the new American literature in combating the powers of rank commercialism, particularly towards the end of the century. The American novelist, especially, more than the theologian, the scholar or the political philosopher, begins to raise his voice against purely materialistic ideals.

It would, however, be a great mistake to conceive of this period as having relegated its cultural concern to a few conscience-stricken individuals. On the contrary, the decades following the Civil War are in many regards highly productive from the point of view of intellectual achievement. Not only the amount of space, but also the effort and thought bestowed upon this period by Robert E. Spiller and his associates in the *Literary History of the United States* show this clearly. When Abraham Lincoln became President of the United States in 1861, the number of public schools in existence was very small; but by 1880 there were about 800 and at the turn of the century there were over 6,000 schools in the country.[1] In 1876 the merchant Johns Hopkins in Baltimore founded a university bearing his name which became at once an educational power of the first magnitude. Land grant colleges came into being; the higher education for women began. At the same time the older colleges and universities, through generous endowments from the hands of private donors, experienced very decided encouragement and increase of their effectiveness. The activities of collectors in many fields broadened and deepened, and museums and libraries with their very liberal support grew almost over night from modest beginnings into substantial institutions. Public libraries developed on a scale which left far behind them any of the similar European efforts. The critical beholder of nineteenth-century American civilization will find, then, that this age of materialism certainly did not neglect culture, but that it approached it in its own materialistic manner.

It is from this situation that we can take our clue for an understanding of the development of the book in that period. To really appreciate the achievements of those decades one must look primarily at the amazing technical and industrial developments in printing. When the spadework for this book was begun in the 1930's, this was no easy matter. "With the middle of the nineteenth century," to quote from

[1] According to Charles and Mary Beard, *The Rise of American Civilization*, 1930.

the introduction to this section in the first American edition of 1939, "we reach a particularly critical point. By and large, the interests and energies of bibliographers and other students of these matters have centered upon the Colonial period, both in collecting material and in interpreting the assembled facts. Later on, consistent and comprehensive attempts have been made only to describe the modern period beginning with the nineties. For the intervening decades, one has to turn mainly to practical printing manuals and to two encyclopedias of printing published in that period. Then there are miscellaneous sources, such as biographies of prominent printers and publishers, histories of firms issued upon an anniversary occasion, sales catalogs of printing press manufactures, of type founders and binders, the U. S. patent lists, and early numbers of the trade periodicals which began to appear during those years.

"This means that we have to reconstruct the picture of an unusually lively and active period of development from innumerable small pieces which lie before us in no order whatsoever."

It is obvious that this is no longer true to such an extent. The last decade has seen a very considerable increase in individual and cooperative studies in nineteenth-century American printing, bookmaking and publishing. These trends have already been mentioned in the Foreword. One can see now promising beginnings of systematic and, one hopes, sustained effort by competent scholars and students in the field. The authors of the present edition have made every possible effort to include the results of these studies, in so far as they are available and of sufficient general significance to justify their consideration.

One other thing I should like to explain about the pages which follow this introduction. I have said in the Foreword that they were first written for a German audience, more familiar with conditions in the European countries than with American traditions. For that reason I had attempted to emphasize those aspects that differ characteristically from conditions abroad. I think it would be a mistake altogether to give up this element of comparison in the present edition. Many things on the following pages must be familiar, and more than familiar, to many of those who will read them. Some of the very fundamental things in our lives are after all familiar to us, too familiar, in fact, to be easily recognized. Yet, there is a certain definitive value in recognizing them. If I can convey, then, a sense of what is characteristic of this country in its way of dealing with books, I shall be satisfied that I have not altogether failed.

The differences which a European observer will notice first seem to be small and not very significant details. Yet I think they have a definite meaning, and can be taken as the outward symptoms of certain deep-rooted traditions. Once these are recognized, those first disconnected observations reveal themselves as parts of what can safely be demonstrated to constitute a basic condition of broad significance.

Twenty years ago, when I came to the United States to live, and began to explore the world of books, I found myself frequently misled by captions in the newspapers which read something like this—"Publishers Convention to Open on Monday," or "Society of Illustrators holds its Spring Show." I expected news of book publishers and book illustrators, and what I found, of course, were stories about newspaper publishers and magazine illustrators. In Europe a "publisher" was always a book publisher. You had to say "newspaper publisher" if that was what you meant. Then on my first visits to the printing plants here I was amazed to find that most books were printed from plates and only a few from type. In Europe only newspapers and some magazines were printed from plates. Also, I marvelled at the dominating position of the linotype in book production. Linotype machines as I had known them were used for newspapers, rarely for books. Also, I was told about the strength and importance of the typographical unions, and I wondered how and why they had come to be so powerful.

When I visited some of my new friends in their houses in the suburbs I noticed on the train that everybody was buried in his favorite newspaper or magazine, and at the house there were many magazines in the living room and everybody could help himself. There were some books too, on the living room shelf. But I saw that very few people had a room set aside as a library or study, with the walls lined with books, and the doors closed, such as those I had known. I met authors and literary agents and was surprised at how important, financially speaking, the short story and the magazine market was to them.

The publishers, too, seemed to watch very carefully the serial rights of books which they contracted for. Books to be reprinted in a periodical? In Europe, it had always been the other way round. And why did they think that newspaper publicity for their books was so important? At home, I had learned that it did not pay to advertise a book in a daily paper. It was the bookseller's job to sell the book to the public. All you could do was to sell your book to the bookstores. Thus I learned, again with amazement, that there were many cities, large and small, in America, which seemed to get along without a regular bookstore, without a place exclusively or even primarily devoted to the selling of books, and, incidentally, a social center for all people with literary and bookish interests. In this I saw one of the reasons why public library service in this country has come to play such an important part in many communities and why it has developed so amazingly in the last eighty years. I had heard about that, but nobody had explained that the library was really doing many of the things in an American town which in Europe the local bookstore was doing.

The conclusion was inescapable. Obviously, in America, the newspaper and the magazine were more important, from almost every point of view, than the book. Of course it would be absurd to say that the periodical press in Europe was not of immense importance too. But the world of the book had its own independent traditions there, which were older and more substantial than the world of periodicals. Here, the book seems to live in a sort of dependence—not quite on its own, a somewhat patronized appendix to its more powerful brother, the periodical press. Today I still believe that there is a great deal in this, and what I have learned of the history of printing in North America has confirmed this belief. It has shown me what I think are good reasons for this basically different attitude towards the book in Europe and in America. One need only consider under what different conditions, for what different purposes, printing was introduced and was spread in the two continents! In Europe, printing was started in settled communities that were centuries old, and as a mechanical means of duplicating from the accumulated wealth of manuscript collections the literary heritage of the Classical and the Medieval World. In America, printing almost immediately became an important factor of colonization and soon an instrument of active westward expansion of the nation. The fact that printing started in Colonial America under academic auspices is no contradiction of this, because the Cambridge Press was exceptional rather than typical in nature. The European press primarily nourished thought; the American, action. In Europe printing from the very beginning meant "books," in America almost from the start, "newspapers."

In his *History of American Magazines*, Frank Luther Mott has quoted certain utterances by distinguished men which show very clearly that American intellectual leaders have been well aware of the superior importance of the periodical press in the New World. On June 25, 1788, George Washington wrote to Mathew Carey: "I consider such easy vehicles of knowledge as more highly calculated than any other to preserve the liberty, stimulate the industry, and meliorate the morals of an enlightened and free people." Nearly a hundred years later Dr. Holland, editor of *Scribner's Monthly*, wrote in March, 1873, of the magazine: "It stands in the very front rank of the agents of civilisation." The fact has not been sufficiently recognized that this is a characteristic expression of American democracy in the making, distinctly different from European opinion, and of basic influence on the life history and role of the book in American society.

THE INDUSTRIALIZATION OF PRINTING

The Spread of the Printing Press

In THE FIRST PART of this book it has been described how closely the printing press followed in the footsteps of the early settlers on their adventurous and often dangerous migration to the West. It is no mere chance that by the middle of the nineteenth century when the first great wave of settlement had spent itself, the establishment of first printing presses in the new states and territories was practically an accomplished fact. We learn from the chronological table on pages 69-70 that there were only three states left in the Northwest which by 1860 were still without a printing press. Printing started in Montana in 1863; in Wyoming in 1863; and in North Dakota in 1864. We know, of course, that presses continued to be established in new places and that printing offices already established in a given locality moved to some other place. To some extent these movements may be interpreted as a bringing up, so to speak, of the rear guard of the western advance. But it also means that the normal process of change is now taking place in the new territories which at all times and in all places ties men to a locality for a while and then releases them again.

The spreading of the printing press in North America, it is safe to say, was completed before the Civil War. Quite another process of evolution is now coming to the fore and is entering into its most significant phase: the gradual replacement of craftsmanship by machinery and the thorough industrialization of printing and its allied branches of the graphic arts. The eventual consequences of this movement were impossible to foresee. Nor can it be said that these forces have spent themselves. We are still in the midst of the technological revolution of printing.

The Industrial Revolution

The mechanization of the nineteenth century is by no means the first thoroughgoing revolution in bookmaking. The very form of the book today, a series of pages between covers, is the result of a radical change which took place toward the beginning of the Middle Ages and replaced the classical book-roll in favor of the medieval codex. Compared with that first important change, the fifteenth-century invention of printing seems to have much less affected the actual form of the book. It is more a change of production method and it does not really alter physical appearances until about a hundred years later. Comparably, the mechanization of book production in the nineteenth century did not produce an immediately noticeable change in the physical appearance of books. Only gradually did the new production methods make themselves felt in the style of book designing. There can be no doubt that in the three centuries between 1500 and 1800 not nearly as many technical changes took place as in the decades between 1800 and 1890. Nor was the process completed by that time. It has continued right to the present. The analogy with earlier revolutions in the history of bookmaking might tempt one to believe that the mighty change which by now has lasted a century and a half must just about have reached the limit. However, there is no assurance that the production of books might not yet witness some new and radical innovations of far-reaching consequence. There has been some wishful thinking in these directions, especially on the part of those who in recent years have been worried by the seemingly everlasting process of mounting production costs. It is a shrewd observer who remarked that any important technological changes still to be expected in the printing industry would benefit newspapers, magazines and perhaps the cheap reprints more directly than those books which are not a part of the stream of mass communication.

America's share in the history of industrialization becomes increasingly important as the nineteenth century progresses. In the beginning American printers and inventors, with very few exceptions, showed little initiative, relying on the British and on the continental European example to start the ball rolling. By the middle of the century, however, America had caught up with European developments. The printing industry began to emancipate itself from the European precedent, adapting the new inventions to suit conditions in this country. More independent improvements and original inventions followed and by the second half of the century we see America advanced into a position of industrial leadership, contributing processes and machinery developed in this country, and destined to affect the printing industries all over the world.

Two things should always be remembered by any student of the technological revolution of the graphic arts. No invention is ever an isolated achievement nor is it usually the result of the exclusive efforts of an individual genius. The need is there and the opportunity, and there are almost always several minds at work on the solution of a given problem. To assign the credit for a single invention, to interpret the patent lists and to weigh the evidence of priority claims belongs among the most difficult tasks in typographic research. The path is strewn with broken hearts and frustrations. Accounts of illness and ignominious death in the garret or the insane asylum are all too frequent—the inevitable results of complete concentration on a single goal which does not offer any alternative or compensation to failure.

There is no invention in the field of printing and bookmaking which is not the result of a keenly felt need, which is not based on an already existing process and which in its turn does not cause and make necessary further new inventions. The entire nineteenth century history can be seen as a continuous struggle against bottlenecks, many of them caused by the sudden speeding up of a single operation previously performed by hand in a more or less leisurely manner. Thus, the invention of the papermaking machine, which produces a continuous web of paper, calls for the rotary press into which this web can be fed; then there was need for the stereotyping process which allows the production of curved printing plates; and last but not least, composing machines which can produce a sufficient amount of set type to feed the hungry presses. And of what good to anyone would have been the accumulation of printed paper if there had not been machines developed which would cut, fold, sew and bind the sheets?

The industrialization of bookbinding, a craft well over 1500 years old and developed as a succession of a large number of closely interwoven steps, is a particularly interesting achievement and a field in which the American contribution is outstanding.

Book binding

The industrialization of bookbinding in the United States has been the subject of a careful study by Joseph W. Rogers.[1] He distinguishes four important phases in this development. "In the first phase," he says, "we find bookbinders performing all their processes with hand-manipulated tools. Next we find bookbinders, under the pressure exerted by the increased speed of printing machines, seeking methods of simplifying and speeding up their processes while still being forced to work largely with tools. Our third stage is that in which machines are progressively introduced to handle certain of the manipulations, while the balance of the processes are still done by hand. The last phase is that in which the great majority of the bookbinding processes are performed by machine, a phase which marks the complete breaking away of the great modern industry of edition binding from the parent craft of hand bookbinding."

It was in England, early in the nineteenth century, that the first step towards the mechanization of binding was taken. Cloth was introduced as a practical and inexpensive new covering material soon after 1820 and was readily accepted everywhere. When, exactly, American binders adopted the new material is hard to say. Leaving aside a few isolated examples of its use before 1800, there is evidence that the general adoption of the new material followed closely in the wake of the first English experiments. Mr. Rogers has found a copy of *Rome in the Nineteenth Century*, published by J. and J. Harper in 1827, and bound in half purple cloth with paper-covered boards, which, so far, is the earliest known example of the general use of cloth in American bookbinding.

English book cloth dominated the American market throughout most of the nineteenth century. Compared with achievements in other fields, the domestic manufacture of book cloth was slow in getting started. The establishment of the Interlaken Mills in Rhode Island in 1883 was the first lastingly significant step towards independence, followed among others by the founding of the firm of Joseph

---

[1] Mr. Rogers submitted the results of his investigation, which he started at my suggestion, as a master's thesis to the Faculty of the School of Library Service, Columbia University, in February, 1937. His study was published under the title, "The Rise of American Edition Binding," as Part II of *Bookbinding in America*, Portland, Maine, Southworth-Anthoensen Press, 1941.

Bancroft & Sons in Wilmington, Delaware; the Holliston Mills, started in Massachusetts in 1893 by Herbert M. Plimpton; the "Fabrikoid" Company of Newburgh, New York, later owned by E. I. Du Pont de Nemours & Co., which first produced waterproof cloth in 1895; its rival, the Keratol Company of Newark, New Jersey; and several other enterprises.

Although the use of cloth in bookbinding constituted a major departure from century-old traditions, another innovation proved of even greater importance in the development of mechanical binding and in the rise of the American bookbinding industry. It was the casing-in process, which took the place of the older and more complex process known as boarding, and constitutes the chief structural difference between edition binding and hand binding. In hand binding the signatures of the book are sewn over bands or cords and these in turn are attached to single cut boards and the whole is then covered and lettering and decoration applied. In casing-in, the book is sewn separately and the case made separately, and then both are joined by first pasting to a hinge and then by pasting down the end papers. It is important to note that casing-in did not originate as a machine process, but had a preliminary period of manufacture by hand, preceded in its turn by certain simplifications of the traditional hand-binding process. On the basis of books examined, it can be said that casing-in by hand started in America sometime between 1825 and 1835, that is to say, during the same decade which brought cloth as a binding material to America. Logically enough, binding establishments concentrating upon edition work began to be organized towards the end of that same decade. For instance, in 1832 Benjamin Bradley started his shop in Boston.

The first invention of a machine actually designed to take the place of a hand process was made in England in 1823, very close to the date of the other innovations mentioned. It was a rolling press, designed to supplant the hand process of "beating." "Timperley estimated that the rolling press would compress in one day as many books as could be beaten by two bookbinders in a week's time with the beating hammer" (Rogers, p. 146). It is probable that this machine was made in America in the early thirties at the latest. Rolling presses were certainly made by 1840 in the machine shop of James Maxwell in New York.

Hydraulic presses, replacing the older standing presses, were manufactured in England before 1835 and were used in America by 1857 at the latest.

Other important inventions solved the problem of stamping design and lettering onto bookbinding cloth, felt to be urgent as a means to conceal the texture of cloth from the eyes of the public unaccustomed to the new material. In 1832 an embossing press (also called "arming" or "stamping" press) was invented in England, the principle of which was the same as the one underlying the modern machine of today. In America embossing presses were made as early as 1838, and by the same firm which still manufactures them, the T. W. and C. B. Sheridan Company. They, too, were the first firm to apply power to a bookbinding machine, producing a steampower stamping press about 1845. Many of these presses, soon manufactured by various firms, were also used as smashing machines, to compress the pages before casing so that the books would be firm and compact. In the eighties W. D. Hickok began to market his practical "hydraulic dry-pressing machines," still in common use.

In 1845 the first patent was granted for a hand-operated backing machine. Numerous attempts were made to design a machine which would supersede the rounding and backing of books by hand, and it is probable that production on some of these started soon after the granting of the first patent. The first concrete evidence appears in Hickok's catalog for 1870. Crawley took out his first patent for a rounding and backing machine in 1876, others in 1877 and 1892, the probable year of the introduction of the machine to the trade by the E. C. Fuller Company.

Practically all our modern folding machines, which can fold a sheet of paper in any way desired with incredible speed, are based on the invention of Cyrus Chambers, Jr., of Philadelphia. This was the first bookbinding machine which owed its origin to the availability of steam power. Chambers took out his first patent in 1856, and followed this up with many changes and improvements. Other groups, too, were interested in developing this important machine, and sufficiently different solutions were found to justify the founding in 1880 of a rival concern, the well-known Dexter Folder Company in Des Moines, Iowa.

One of the most important hand operations that sooner or later would have to be turned over to the machine was the sewing of the folded signatures of the book. That undesirable short cut known as "stabbing," already practiced in the seventeenth century, found its mechanical application in a machine marketed by Hickok as early as 1860. The rather vicious practice was superseded to a large extent by the invention in America of a binders' sewing machine, which was eagerly accepted by edition binders in America and all over Europe. In 1856 David McConnell Smyth of Hartford, Connecticut, invented the first thread sewing machine for bookbinding, and manufactured machines for the exclusive use of the Appleton firm of publishers in New York. Curiously enough, the patent lists contain no record of this first and most important invention, although they do reveal a series of further improvements, for instance, the curved needle book-sewing machine of 1879. In 1880 the Smyth Manufacturing Company was formed for the purpose of producing and distributing commercially the various types of sewing machines gradually developed.

These various sewing machines allowed, and they still allow, the sewing over bands or cords, although the trend has been decidedly in favor of sewing directly from signature to signature on the "all-along" principle. The use of cords or bands, basic principle of all good hand binding, was of course not at once eliminated. In fact a machine was invented to perform at least one of the operations then customary in sewing over cords, namely the cutting or rather the sawing in of grooves into the back of the book, in which to "sink" the cords, thus allowing for a flat back appearance. By 1856 a sawing machine, made up of a series of small circular saws, was in common use with the bookbinders of that time, and although the Smyth sewing machine with its elimination of cords and bands soon made this process obsolete, it persisted nevertheless for many years. The first patent for a wire stitcher was granted in Philadelphia in 1872 to a man named Brehmer, a native of Lübeck, Germany.

One of the most ingenious American inventions was the case-making machine. As mentioned before, edition binders in the 1830's had started to make separate cases by hand. Not, however, until the last decade of the century were machines invented which would automatically cut the boards for the sides and the back of the book, cut the cloth, paste it onto the boards and neatly fold it over the edges. One of the first machines produced to facilitate this process was the case-smoothing machine introduced by George H. Sanborn & Sons in New York prior to 1891, followed by the successful machine of the T. W. & C. B. Sheridan Company in 1893, and a similar one by the Smyth Manufacturing Company in 1896. Although we do not now know into which machines his inventions were incorporated, A. Bredenberg deserves to go on record for his four patents taken out between 1892 and 1893. In 1901 the Smyth Company brought out a cloth-cutting machine for use in case making.

The logical sequence to this invention was the casing-in machine, which took the completely "forwarded" book and the completed case and joined them together into the finished product. The first successful machine was the Smyth casing-in machine introduced in 1903.

One other major invention perfected before the turn of the century was the automatic gathering machine, introduced by the Sheridan Company between 1900 and 1903 on the basis of earlier patents. This machine solved mechanically the assembling into book form of the loose folded signatures, which had certainly been a most tedious routine. "Factory girls," says Mr. Rogers, "walked miles every day around the sides of a long table picking up one signature after another . . . until a complete book had been assembled, only to repeat the process *ad infinitum*."

If one rehearses in one's mind the traditional sequence of operations in hand binding, one realizes with amazement that there is not one left, of major importance, which could not now be done by machine. Soon after the beginning of the twentieth century a completely mechanized production schedule was practicable. There were, of course, further inventions and improvements, such as the automatic fixing of end papers to the first and last signatures, and the combining of certain separate operations into one new one. Further improvements and further adjustments are still under consideration and will be considered by the engineers of the future. The complete replacement of sewing by new types of adhesives, developed in the mass production of the various inexpensive reprint series, is one of them. Otherwise, the bulk of the job of mechanizing bookbinding seems to have been completed.

The reorganization of the traditional hand binderies into industrialized establishments followed closely in the wake of the invention and construction of the new machines. Publishers who had their own manufacturing plants, such as Harpers and Appleton in New York, Lippincott and Altemus in Philadelphia, found little difficulty in adapting them to edition binding. The same was true of printing firms who went in for book production on a large scale. Notable among the firms organized primarily as edition binderies were Benjamin Bradley in Boston, joined in 1856 by Thomas Y. Crowell, later to found his own publishing firm; Colton & Jenkins and E. Walker & Sons, both in New York; the still existing J. F. Tapley Company, which moved to New York in 1881 from Springfield, Massachusetts; the Becktold Company, founded in 1872, still functioning at its original address in St. Louis; George McKibbin & Son, Braunworth & Company, H. Wolff Book Manufacturing Company, and the American Book Bindery, all established in New York in the 1890's.

That a country which has contributed so enormously to the solution of industrial bookbinding problems should not have found much time to cultivate artistic hand binding, is not astonishing. As a matter of fact, there have been a number of attempts and experiments in that direction, many of them quite recent, which will be discussed later on.

Typesetting and Type Founding

The most significant American contribution to the development of printing was made in the field of mechanical type-casting and typesetting. It is true that that elusive Yankee, Dr. William Church (see page 82), went to England to have his astounding inventions patented, and that, on the other hand, Othmar Mergenthaler was born and trained in Germany. Nevertheless, one can say safely that it was American inventiveness, mechanical skill and persistency which really furnished the final solutions to the pressing problem of mechanical typesetting.

There is no doubt that pressure for the solution of these ever-growing problems was felt all over the civilized world. However, the stimulus must have been felt a little more keenly, must have offered somewhat greater rewards, must have shown opportunities a little more promising, in the United States than elsewhere. By the year 1904 the 1520th patent for a composing machine was granted in Washington! It seems that the reason for greater pressure and greater exertion must be sought in the very territory in which American printing differs most from other countries. The most distinctive characteristic of American printing is the superior role of the periodical press, of newspapers and magazines, over books. In the nineteenth century, especially, newspapers, journals and magazines grew with phenomenal rapidity, aided of course by the growth of commercial enterprise, the rise of advertising and publicity, and by second class postage rates.

Parallel with the progressive experiments in mechanical typesetting, the traditional craft of type founding witnessed for some time after the Civil War a very considerable boom. There seems to have been no end to the establishing of new firms and to expansions among the older ones, at least until the problem of the composing machine was finally settled.

The traditional roots of the industry, the reader will recall, are found in Philadelphia where the two Scotsmen, Archibald Binny and James Ronaldson, established what Carl P. Rollins has called "the first type foundry in the United States to achieve permanency." In 1809 they issued *A Specimen of Metal Ornaments Cast at the Letter Foundry of Binny and Ronaldson*, probably the first American type founders' specimen book ever issued. They followed this in 1812 with the *Specimen of Printing Types, from the Foundry of Binny and Ronaldson*.

Binny and Ronaldson were the first type founders to cast a dollar sign, and it was through their influence that the old-fashioned long *ſ* was driven out of American typography. Their most important achievement was a type face of lasting beauty and distinction. Midway in design between old and modern style, it enjoyed great popularity around the turn of the century. Eventually the matrices of some of the fonts became the property of the American Type Founders Company. Named "Oxford," the type was chosen by the late Mr. Updike for the setting of his famous *Printing Types*, and Bruce Rogers and the Grabhorns have also made good use of it. In connection with the Princeton University Press edition of *The Papers of Thomas Jefferson*, the type was recently adapted by the Mergenthaler Linotype Company, which has named its version "Monticello," to honor the man who had been a friend of the original Binny and Ronaldson foundry.

In 1833 their establishment was in the hands of Lawrence Johnson and George F. Smith. Through further changes of owners and partners the name of the firm towards the middle of the century became Mackellar, Smiths and Jordan, one of the leading, if not the leading concern of the sixties, the seventies and eighties. Thomas Mackellar was a most energetic personality, full of knowledge, and a good businessman. The firm now consisted not only of the type foundry, but had also its own printing and stereotyping plant, and handled the publication of books on typography. Mackellar himself wrote a very successful practical manual called the *American Printer*, which was first issued in 1866 and lived through a great many editions. This book contains, among other things, much valuable information about the status of type founding in those years. In the tenth edition, of 1876, Mackellar mentioned twenty-four type foundries then in existence in the United States; seven of them in New York, three each in Boston and Philadelphia, two each in Baltimore, Cincinnati and in the state of California, and one each in Buffalo, Chicago, Milwaukee, St. Louis and Richmond. We sympathize, under the circumstances, when we hear him complain about too much competition. He also complained about the unfavorable effect of David Bruce's type-casting machine. As another innovation, he mentions the method of reproducing type faces by electrotyping. As early as 1859 this practice had caused concern among the type founders of Europe. In that year an international association was founded in Paris with the expressed purpose of preventing, apparently without much success, the electrotyping of a competitor's designs. Mackellar in 1876 did not seem to see any danger lurking there. By comparison, what he has to say on this point in a later edition, that of 1885, is very interesting. He mentions there that the number of type foundries in the meantime has gone up to thirty-one. Then he goes on (page 27): "The protection now afforded by the patent laws having checked the piratical production of matrixes by electrotyping (except in plain faces, a practice still pursued by unprincipled type-founders), the leading founders in this country have been encouraged to produce types of new styles which in beauty and ingenuity surpass those of foreign origin."

Those who are familiar with the type production of those years will be inclined to take the statement about the beauty of those types with a grain of salt. But ingenious they certainly were, and especially the advertising type faces of that day deserve attention as important stepping stones in the new art of advertising design, then evolving from the accepted traditions of book and newspaper typography.[2]

An event of international importance was the final establishment in 1886 by American type founders of the American point system. Twelve years later this American point system was adopted by the English type founders.

When the American Type Founders Company was organized in 1892, the new firm absorbed, along with most other hitherto independent type founders, Mackellar, Smiths and Jordan, thus forming a continuous link from Binny and Ronaldson down to the present organization. In 1892 Henry Lewis Bullen was appointed joint manager of the New York branch of the American Type Founders Company. In his *Discussions of a Retired Printer*[3] he has interesting details about the founding of the company. "The American Type Founders Company in a consolidation of twenty typefoundries. On starting business in 1891 it had matrixes for over two thousand series of type. Discarding duplications, it had matrixes for about seven hundred and fifty series of distinctive type faces. In 1900, nine years after starting, it issued a complete general specimen book, containing the salable residuum of its type faces—525 series of job and thirty-seven of body type. Not long after it had to face the lining system proposition.[4] In 1903 it issued a quarto (292 pp.) preliminary specimen book of lining type. It now, in 1906, issues its *American Line Type Book*, and it is a safe assumption that its contents represent every series it finds salable enough to go to the expense of changing to the line system."

In 1908 Mr. Bullen laid the foundation for his famous Typographical Library and Museum, in Jersey City, and since 1936 at Columbia University. I shall always remember my first visit, twenty years ago, with a letter from Gustav Mori of Frankfurt in my pocket. The

[2] We still lack an intelligent study of American nineteenth century type design, a work which could profitably employ some of the methods developed in Nicolette Gray's amusing and enlightening analysis of English typographic trends in the Victorian age, *Nineteenth Century Ornamental Types and Title Pages*, London, Faber & Faber, 1938.

[3] Reprinted in book form by his company from the *Inland Printer*, July, 1906.

[4] A system of standardization which made it possible to align different sizes of type by the use of 1-point leads or their multiples, and to align all faces of a given size, whatever their character, with one another.

crowded subway under the river—the glaring hot streets on the other side—riding through rows of shabby wooden shacks on a screeching trolley car—the humming factory building—and then the perfect seclusion of that library—cool and silent—the light filtering into the room through painted glass windows, shutting off the view over endless tracks and loading platforms. And there, amidst the books and broadsides, the old presses and composing sticks, the shrewd, wise, kind, human face of Henry Lewis Bullen, welcoming and at once conducting you to his treasures. He died, over eighty years old, on April 27, 1938.

The real story of American type founding has yet to be written. When in 1937 R. Hunter Middleton brought out a tiny volume entitled *Chicago Letter Founding* many students of typography must have wondered why they had never thought of Chicago as a center of type founding and why they had never heard of Robert Wiebking. This man came to America with his father, Herman Wiebking, in 1881, bringing along from Germany a matrix engraving machine. Robert decided to make his living by cutting punches and matrices. But he also found opportunities to design type, and the list of his designs, as communicated by Mr. Middleton, is impressive. More interesting even is his association with Frederic W. Goudy, for whom he engraved many of his early designs, and whose own method of type production he undoubtedly influenced very decidedly. Wiebking also engraved the matrices for Bruce Rogers's famous Centaur type, and later in his life he was associated with the Ludlow Company.

If a man of such achievements has for long remained unacclaimed, are there not many others, little or not at all known, who have made important contributions to the cause of the graphic arts in America?

There is general acknowledgment throughout the civilized world of what America has contributed to the development of type-setting and type-casting machinery, but perhaps it is not sufficiently recognized how early men in this country (and of this country) directed their attention to these problems. The modern composing and casting machines are ingenious combinations of the best technical solutions of a number of single problems. Chronologically first comes the invention of type-casting machines. The Englishman William Nicholson's comprehensive patents of 1790 already contained type-casting by machine. Among the immediate successors of Nicholson one finds an American,

William Wing, with an invention of 1807. Another important solution was contributed by the younger David Bruce in New York, whose type-casting machine of 1838 was taken up in many countries, for instance in Germany, and was successful enough to threaten the traditional trade of type founding. This David Bruce is the son of George Bruce, who, together with his brother, the elder David Bruce, started the first type founding establishment in New York. The firm was originally a printing-house and among other distinctions has to its credit the introduction of stereotyping into America. Further inventions and improvements of type-casting machinery were made throughout the nineteenth century, in America and abroad. The Englishman, John Robert Johnson, for instance, built a machine in 1853 in which he incorporated ideas of the great Henry Bessemer and which he improved upon in 1862.

The first important invention in the field of composing machines was that of Dr. William Church, who went to England from America and by 1822 had invented a machine which was already combined with a casting arrangement! His patent has been carefully dealt with in the second part of this book. Between 1840 and 1850 further inventions and improvements took place, including a patent granted to Giuseppe Mazzini, the Italian revolutionary, in 1843, and a patent for an "electrotype" system of several machines to be operated simultaneously by one compositor with the use of electric wires, granted to the Englishman, H. Clark. Christian Sörensen's machine, for which he was given a privilege in 1849 in his native Denmark, included a distributing machine.

In 1853 W. H. Mitchell in Brooklyn invented a machine which was the first real commercial success in this country. In Boston, Charles Wilson Felt's machine of 1860 attempted mechanical spacing. The sixties and seventies, too, saw efforts by many individuals in many countries,[5] including Alexander Fraser in Edinburgh (1862), Owen L. Brown in Boston, Ernst Werner Siemens, the great electro-engineering genius who in 1863 built a composing and distributing machine which anticipated the perforated paper ribbon, also incorporated in Alexander

---

[5] Konrad F. Bauer's *Aventur und Kunst*, a year by year chronology of the history of printing and the graphic arts, published by the Bauer Type Foundry in Frankfurt on the 500th anniversary of Gutenberg's invention, is a rich and fascinating source of information for these and many other matters.

Mackie's machine (Great Britain, 1867), Charles Kastenbein's machine (1869) used at the London *Times* up to the year 1908, and many others.

Lynn Boyd Benton, for many years associated with the American Type Founders Company, has been acclaimed as one of the great typographic inventors of the century for his matrix boring machine, patented in 1885. Benton's Pantograph, as it is briefly called in the industry, is an automatic borer attached to a pantograph. With this machine the original design is cut first into a large metal stencil, and from there engraved directly and in the desired size into the matrix or into the steel punch. The machine eliminates not only the traditional punch-cutting by hand, but it also makes it possible to engrave various sizes of types from the same design. From an artistic point of view both these elements are sources of danger. On the other hand, the pantograph is an accurate tool of reproduction, and the speed with which it has made it possible to produce matrices has been of fundamental importance in the development of modern type-casting and composing machinery. It is only fair to say that in recent years the users of the Benton Pantograph have taken great pains to overcome the artistic limitations of this machine.

A similar machine was developed independently from Mr. Benton's invention by Robert Wiebking in Chicago, using a model which was brought to America from Germany by his father in 1881, and became the basis of the Ludlow Company's matrix engraving method.

Anyone who wishes to study these developments in greater detail should look at J. S. Thompson's *History of Composing Machines*. There he will find descriptions and illustrations, for instance, of the Empire Composing Machine with its Empire Distributor, and particularly the Paige Compositor, an interesting but much too complicated predecessor of the Linotype. In 1872 James W. Paige had worked out his invention, but not until 1894, when the Chicago *Herald* for a brief period tried out the new machine, was it finally tested and abandoned. The patents, granted in 1895, were so complicated that two of the men examining them are reported to have lost their minds.[6] It was this machine that Mark Twain was so interested in and which, incidentally, cost him such a great deal of money! The Linotype Company took

[6] Bauer, *op. cit.*

over the patents and the machinery. An unassembled Paige composing machine is at Columbia University.

Like all other great inventions, the Linotype has a somewhat involved origin. The urgent need for a simplification of the printer's daily burden dictated the brilliant invention of Othmar Mergenthaler. The printer's task had rapidly grown into gigantic responsibilities, and he badly needed help. During the seventies the pressure in the composing room increased rapidly, and a number of experiments were started which did not at once yield material results. A group of men had combined to cope with these problems, and they had drawn into their confidence a mechanical expert in Baltimore. This man in turn drew in an employee, Othmar Mergenthaler, the watchmaker and mechanical genius who emigrated as a youth from Germany. Mergenthaler collaborated with the Virginian, Charles T. Moore, who had already participated to a considerable extent in the previous experiments. Step by step the many obstacles were removed, the many problems solved, and in 1884 Ottmar Mergenthaler's famous invention had reached a stage where it could be practically employed. First use of the machine was made by the New York *Tribune* and a number of other newspapers from 1886 on. The first book known to have been set up in linotype composition was *The Open Air Book of Sports*, published by the *Tribune* as a premium book for subscribers.

The Monotype machine, today the favorite instrument of the British quality printer and equally popular for book work on the European continent, is also an American invention. A number of single patents, and a final patent for the Monotype Composing Machine and the separately operated Casting Machine were taken out by Tolbert Lanston of Washington in 1887. He was aided in the technical execution by William S. Bancroft. Further improvements were made during the following decade. In 1893 a Monotype was shown at the Chicago World's Fair, and towards the end of the nineties the machine came into general use.

It is undoubtedly significant that of the two major mechanical solutions of the typesetting problem the Linotype, most excellently suited for newspaper work, has become also the most popular instrument for book composition in the United States, while the Monotype, especially suited for good book composition, has become more popular for that type of work on the European continent and in England. The book faces originated by the English Monotype Company are generally superior to those originated and available in this country, while some of the best book faces designed for the Linotype are of American origin.

The momentum created by the many energetic attacks upon the problem of mechanical composition did not come to an abrupt halt with its successful solution. There were further inventions, some of them theoretically excellent but nevertheless unsuccessful, for instance Alexander Dow's machine of 1896. More successful was the Typograph, also developed during the nineteenth century. This machine was invented by John R. Rogers, a former collaborator of Mergenthaler, and its construction was started in 1888 in the workshops of Fred E. Brights in Cleveland. In 1890 the Typograph made its debut. The Ludlow, a machine which casts large size type for display purposes on single lines, was invented by Washington J. Ludlow in 1906, and developed by a company headed by William A. Reade. The Intertype, perfected under the guidance of Hermann Ridder, appeared on the American market in 1913, and has been accepted in other countries as well, for instance in Germany, where it was introduced in 1925.

As in the field of bookbinding, the twentieth century seemingly dawned upon the completed mechanization of type-casting and type composition. However, at the Leipzig Fair in 1936 there was shown the Hungarian Edmund Uher's "Uhertype," the first photographic composing machine developed in Europe and a pioneer on a completely new road to composition. A word about the current American status of photo-composition will be said in a later chapter.

With a short glance at the construction of new types of printing presses, at the development of the paper industry and the introduction of photomechanical processes of reproduction, the most important phases of the graphic arts industrialization will have been reviewed.

Printing Presses

The American contribution to the development of printing presses up to the time of the Civil War has been dealt with earlier in this book. The account there culminates in a description of Richard M. Hoe's famous Type Revolving Machine. For its time that press performed marvels, yet it left many urgent problems unsolved. Important improvements and additions were soon to follow. It is illuminating to hear the voice of a nineteenth century observer, who in 1888 wrote thus:[7] "The development of the fast newspaper press, with its numerous excellencies, has been the work of the Hoe firm. The eight and ten-cylinder press looked like a finality, but it was not, and was comparatively shortlived. The web perfecting press, which prints both sides at once from stereotype plates that can be duplicated to any extent desired, thus making it possible to set several, and even many, presses at work at once on the same edition, and on a continuous roll (or web) of paper requiring no feeders, cutting the paper so that it will open like a book, pasting the loose parts, printing from two to twelve pages, as desired, or from four to sixteen, and inserting and pasting the supplements, and finally folding and counting the papers—that is the King of printing machines."

The making of this machine, of course, came about gradually. We owe to Henry Lewis Bullen an interesting account[8] of these developments. "When our Civil War began, the circulation of many newspapers outran their printing facilities. In 1861 the New York *Tribune* had the highest circulation and the largest press-room equipment. Thomas Rooker, superintendent of printing for Horace Greeley and his partners, had been investigating the new *papier-mâché* process of stereotyping which had been used by the London *Times* since 1856. Richard March Hoe was consulted. He advocated the continuation of the use of one form, and proposed to build for the *Tribune* a twenty-feeder type-revolving press, with an output of 50,000 impressions an hour. This press would have been 36 feet high, and would have necessitated a new building. Rooker finally had his way, which was to duplicate the form by stereotyping, so that two or more might be printed simultaneously. This new method was the beginning of the end of type-revolving presses. On August 31, 1861, the New York *Tribune* was printed from curved stereotyped plates, the first used in America. The type-revolving presses printed from curved plates as easily as from type forms, and their sale went merrily on."

[7] In an article in *The Paper World*, February, 1888, entitled: "Evolution of the Printing Press. Progress of Invention and Mechanical Achievement that reads like a Story of the Fancy."

[8] "Richard March Hoe and the Evolution of Fast Printing Presses," in: *The Inland Printer*, September, 1922.

It was not until 1876 that the Hoe firm abandoned the manufacture of these type-revolving presses, having turned their attention, since 1871, to the construction of their own web-perfecting machines. The idea of printing a newspaper from a continuous roll of paper was first patented in 1858 for Alois Auer in Vienna. In the United States William Bullock was the pioneer in developing this important process. Bullock, an ingenious inventor, born in 1813 in Greeneville, Greene County, New York, at one time in his varied career was a patent attorney in Philadelphia, and in that capacity secured a patent for Arsene Legat's invention of a platen machine for printing wallpaper from rolls or webs of paper. He started a series of experiments, in which he utilized curved stereotype plates, and by 1865 he had successfully completed, from plans patented in 1863, the construction of his web-perfecting cylinder press which would print from a continuous roll on both sides of paper.[9] He died in 1867, while testing one of his machines. In that same year in Paris Hippolyte Marinoni completed his first high-speed rotary press, which would also print on both sides of the paper. An important improvement of Bullock's press was the addition, in 1868, of a folding apparatus. Nevertheless the firm had a difficult time with its patents. In 1873, for instance, they sued the New York *Times*, because it had bought an English Walker Press, which the Bullock people believed infringed on their patents, and in 1878 the Bullock Company won their case.[10] Eventually, they were absorbed by the Hoe firm.

The role which that firm played throughout the nineteenth century has been a very remarkable one. The firm had been founded, the reader will recall, by Robert Hoe (I, 1784-1833), whose son Richard M. Hoe (1812-1886) had developed the Type Revolving Machine. Richard's brother, Robert Hoe (II), was also a member of the firm, and so was the second Robert's son, Robert Hoe (III, 1839-1909), the bibliophile, who printed and published, in 1902, *A Short History of the Printing Press and of the Improvements in Printing Machinery from the Time of Gutenberg up to the Present Day*. The firm enjoyed

[9] In 1862 the Niagara Falls Paper Mill Company received orders "from New York" to run paper on reels in quantities equal to about 2,000 sheets, according to Joel Munsell's *Chronology of the Origin and Progress of Paper and Papermaking*, which would save the labor of eight men.

[10] According to a clipping from the *New York Sun* of 1878, in the Typographic Library at Columbia University.

through a period of many years the active collaboration and advice of Stephen D. Tucker. This man's share in the development of American printing machinery has been considerable.[11]

It would be a very worthwhile undertaking for someone to make a really comprehensive study of American power presses. A great deal has, of course, been written. I do not think though that anyone has succeeded, or even attempted to demonstrate the many successive and competitive endeavors in the several important branches of the industry in a single reasoned account. For instance, the Hoe firm, although conspicuous in its domination of the field, was by no means the only important firm. There was A. B. Taylor's factory, where Andrew Campbell after many reverses and vicissitudes was accepted as collaborator in the fifties. Campbell's Country Press of 1862 has been called "the first low-priced cylinder press giving perfect register and doing good work." It brought him independence and the chance to make other important contributions.

The Cincinnati Type Foundry and Printing Machine Works built successful cylinder presses, for which in the seventies they enjoyed an international reputation. Another important builder of presses was Robert Miehle, whose first difficult steps were taken sometime after 1886, when he vainly offered his invention to the eastern press builders. Today "Miehle Vertical" is a household word in American printing. Also around the year 1886 Henry P. Feister in Philadelphia built a rotary press which in one operation printed, folded and glued pamphlets.

Another development, quite separate from the construction of large cylinder presses principally designed for newspaper printing, was the building of small job presses. There was, in 1830, the Ruggles Card Press of S. P. Ruggles of Boston, followed by small platen presses designed by Seth Adams; there was George Phineas Gordon's Yankee Job Press, patented in 1850; the successful Liberty Job Press of F. Otto Degener, patented in 1851, followed by Merritt Gally's Universal Press;

---

[11] The Typographic Library at Columbia University has two interesting typewritten manuscripts which are worth studying. One is Stephen D. Tucker's *Narrative of His Life Long Connection with R. Hoe & Co., New York*, written in 1913; the other one is a *History of R. Hoe & Company, New York*, also by Stephen D. Tucker, copied accurately from the original manuscript in the possession of Stephen D. Tucker's son, Edwin J. Tucker, and given by him to the library in 1913.

there were in the eighties and nineties the Golding Press and James Colt's Armory Universal Press, Wellington P. Kidder's and Albert Harris's presses, and later on, the Kelly Press, more like a miniature cylinder press than a regular job press.

Yet another development in press building was brought about by the various photomechanical methods of reproduction, which very soon demanded special types of presses for each of the important new processes. When that exhaustive study of American printing presses, which we hope will be attempted by some student of typographic development, is completed, it will be possible to compare American construction with the corresponding developments in Europe and to see more clearly in what presses and processes America made its own original contributions. Then too, it will be easier than it now is to answer another important question: Which of all these many presses developed in America in the nineteenth century were used for book printing? One would perhaps find that a great variety of presses were used. There is no reason to believe that all book printers abandoned their older presses, if they still filled their needs. Particularly in the case of fine printing, older types of presses continued to give excellent service. R. R. Bowker, in an article on bookmaking, which was published in *Harper's New Monthly Magazine* in July, 1887, particularly mentioned "The Adams Steam-press, invented by Isaac Adams, of Boston, 1830-36, and still much used for fine work. . . ." On the other hand, the responsible book printers were keenly aware of the changes which they themselves witnessed during their lifetimes. John Wilson, for instance, the son of the famous Cambridge printer, in an address to the Master Printers' Association of Boston,[12] said this: "It was on a Stanhope press, in 1840, that I first tried my hand as an apprentice, 2,000 copies being considered a good day's work. On that same press, about 1843, I assisted in printing a sixteen-page octavo tract of 100,000 copies on the 'Corn Law or Free Trade Question,' by Richard Cobden, whose memoir we lately printed in our office in Cambridge. This was a formidable number to print on a hand press, for it took fifty days to print the edition. To-day, on a two-revolution press, we could print the edition in a little over five days, and on a Hoe perfecting machine in five hours!

[12] Reprinted in *The Paper World*, 1888.

De Vinne of New York prints, cuts and folds 32 pages, 8vo., of the
Century Magazine, on Hoe's new perfecting machine, at the rate of
3,000 copies an hour. . . ."

Papermaking

It is futile to try to imagine what would have been the development
of high power cylinder presses, or, for that matter, of the entire graphic
arts industry, if the papermakers had not been ready to supply paper in
the shape of continuous rolls and in the quantites that were now needed.
Earlier in this book it has been shown how the new papermaking machines were speedily brought to the American continent, how they
were put to prompt use and how American papermakers took their
share in the search for new raw materials and in finding effective ways
to turn them into usable pulp. Their search for new materials, as a
matter of fact, continued well into the second half of the nineteenth
century.[13]

In addition to wood, experiments were made with such heterogeneous materials as cane, reed, various straws, grass, plantain, stalks of
the hop plant, ferns, thistles, horseradish, bleached remnants of manure,
peat, bark, refuse leather scrappings, beet roots, moss, ivory shavings,
corn cobs, bamboo, fishes, and even the wrappings of Egyptian mum-
mies.[14]

Of the four great staples, rags, straw, jute and wood, surviving in
varying degrees the rigid tests of practicability, wood proved the most
important. Mechanical methods of decomposing its fibers into pulp
were fully developed by the end of the Civil War. The first American
mill to make paper from ground wood was founded by Albrecht
Pagenstecher in 1867. It was located at Curtisville (now Interlaken)
near Stockbridge, Massachusetts, and worked for the Smith Paper
Company of Lee, Massachusetts, where experiments had been carried
on ten years earlier. Pagenstecher collaborated with Frederick Wuertz-
bach, who came over from Germany with the first Voelter wood-

[13] Much valuable information on this and other points is found in Lyman Horace
Week's *History of Paper-Manufacturing in the United States, 1690-1916.* Joel
Munsell's *Chronology of the Origin and Progress of Paper and Paper-Making,*
5th ed., Albany, 1876, is also a useful source of information.
[14] Dard Hunter has given a fascinating account of this particular subject in his
Papermaking, the History and Technique of an Ancient Craft, 2nd ed., New York,
Alfred A. Knopf, 1947, pp. 382-385.

grinder.[15] Paper consumers were well aware of the shortcomings of a process which so badly affected the length and strength of the individual fibers. Instead, chemical decomposition was resorted to, and during the sixties America saw the perfection of these methods. The soda process had been first developed and patented in England by Charles Watt and Hugh Burgess. Their first American patent was granted in 1854, and became the basis of Burgess's forty years of successful managership in the United States papermaking industry.

The important invention of the sulphide process, patented in 1867, goes to the credit of the American, Benjamin C. Tilghman, who began his experiments in Paris in 1857. It is true that he was not at once successful in this country. His invention was recognized, however, in Sweden, in England and in Germany, where it became the basis of Mitcherlich's patents. Curiously enough, it was only through the introduction of the Mitcherlich patents into America that Tilghman's experiments were first recognized in his own country. Other methods of chemical decomposition were developed later on, such as the sulphate processes of 1884, invented by Carl F. Dahl.

The next important question is how this new kind of paper was received and how it was introduced into use. Konrad F. Bauer tells us that the first newspaper to use a mixture of rag and wood pulp was the *Kreisblatt* of Frankenberg in Saxony in 1845. In the United States a paper made principally of straw was used by the Philadelphia *Ledger* in 1854. Dr. Harry M. Lydenberg has given us details on the early use of wood pulp in newsprint production. In a study on the early history of paper,[16] André Blum tells how paper was introduced into Spain in the eleventh and twelfth centuries, but was not used at once for an entire book. Rather, it was used intermittently with the conventional parchment. On this point Dr. Lydenberg, who translated the book into English, comments as follows: "This cautious and experimental use of old and new was repeated more than eight centuries later when American newspapers began in the late nineteenth century to substitute wood-pulp paper for the regulation rag stock used hitherto. As parchment and paper were used in alternate sheets in Spain in the eleventh and twelfth centuries, so in America in 1868-78 the news-

[15] See Dard Hunter, *op. cit.*, pp. 377-379.
[16] *On the Origin of Paper*, New York, R. R. Bowker Co., 1934.

papers began with wood pulp by alternating rag and wood stock, sometimes sheets of each in the paper issued for one day, sometimes using wood stock for a week or ten days, going back to rag for a while, sometimes using a mixture of rag and wood, with numerous variations." Dard Hunter[17] gives a somewhat earlier date, mentioning the January 14, 1863 issue of the Boston *Weekly Journal* as the first instance "about which we may be certain."

It is reasonable to assume that wood pulp paper began to be used for books at about the same time that it made its appearance in newspaper printing. Also around this time the printers of fine books began to show a preference for even smoother papers. One of the reasons for this was undoubtedly the fact that wood engravings by that time were cut with remarkably fine and numerous lines. The practice of printing from moistened sheets was gradually discontinued. The introduction of photomechanical line engraving, and particularly of halftone engraving, soon after that, further emphasized the trend towards smooth and shiny papers, culminating in the production of special coated papers made specifically for the printing from halftone plates. Other special papers for various new printing processes were developed in the twentieth century.

One spectacular aspect of nineteenth-century papermaking was the rapid growth of the industry. It has already been shown in the second part of this book that in 1840 somewhat over 400 mills were being operated in 20 states, and by 1860 this number had increased to 555 mills, recorded in the census in 24 states. By that year the annual production of paper in the United States seems to have exceeded the amount produced either in Great Britain or France, and the annual consumption was computed to exceed that of both those countries together.[18] The next two decades saw further steady expansion, 677 mills in 31 states and in the District of Columbia being recorded by 1870.[19] In 1874 the United States out-ranked every other country of the world in the number of mills producing machine-made papers. In 1880, 742 mills operated in 29 states and the District of Columbia. By 1890 the number of mills had dropped, but it has been proved by L. H.

[17] *Op. cit.,* pp. 380, 381.
[18] Munsell, *op. cit.,* p. 164.
[19] These are conservative figures compared with those quoted in Munsell, *op. cit.,* who reports 812 mills in 1872 owned by 705 firms and producing 317,387 tons.

Weeks that at that time in a lesser number of mills than in 1870, more capital was invested, more people employed, and the value of products was larger. The outstanding development in the nineties and for a decade thereafter was the concentration of capital and the consolidation of many individual firms into a few very large concerns. This movement extended well over into the twentieth century before it settled down fixedly into a permanent condition.

As the process of industrialization advanced, the old methods of papermaking by hand went into decline. By the middle of the century, according to Weeks, "nearly all the mills, particularly those that were newly built, had been equipped with Hollanders, Fourdriniers or cylinders and other machinery. Even the old single-vat mills had come into line and there remained few of importance that any longer made pretence of manufacturing paper by hand." Before 1880 handmade paper had nearly disappeared as an American product. In 1897 the mill of the L. L. Brown Paper Company in Adams, Massachusetts, was the only one left to make paper by hand, and even that kind of work ceased there in 1906.

Surprisingly enough, the outlook for handmade paper does not look as hopeless today as it must have looked in 1906. William Morris' valiant attempts to rescue from oblivion various hand processes still precariously existing somewhere have done much to arrest their total extinction. Papermaking by hand today is still a living branch of the industry in several countries. In America, Dard Hunter has done a great deal to promote the interest in handmade paper, especially through his eagerly collected books.[20] In normal times handmade paper from all over the world can be bought in America.

Of great interest is the fact that America's share in the development of new processes and machinery for papermaking, and the place of its industry in the world trade is an exact parallel of its history in other branches of the graphic arts.

Before the middle of the century this country had shown little originality in the invention and construction of machines. For instance, wires for the Fourdrinier machines continued to be imported from England for twenty years after the first Fourdrinier machine was set

[20] Chapter IV of the book cited above is an impressive survey of present day papermaking by hand.

up in the United States. Not until 1847 was the first wire woven on an American loom. In that same year the first dandyroll was made in this country. In 1855 Henry Glynn of Baltimore, Maryland, and in 1856 Joseph Kingsland, Jr. of Franklin, New Jersey, and Vespasian O. Balcom of Bedford, Massachusetts, each obtained patents for improvements in the process of making pulp. They were followed by others working on the same problems.

The first American felts for paper machines were made in 1864. Just as in the other branches of the graphic arts, the middle of the century marks a state of approximate equilibrium between Europe and America, preparing the way for America's forging ahead after the Civil War.

Paper export, for instance, before that time had been negligible in quantity and in value. But soon a slow and steady rise set in. In 1870 about half a million dollars' worth of paper was exported, rising to a million and a half in 1881, to five million and a half in 1900, and seven million and a half in 1910.

Armin Renker, noted German authority on papermaking, and the son of an old family of paper craftsmen, gladly acknowledges America's leading position in the industry. "If the Americans," he writes, "double the width of their seven meter machines, if their paper travels over the screen with the speed of a Pullman train, there will be nothing left for us, but to follow."

Photomechanical Reproduction

It is obvious to everyone today what a tremendous influence the camera has had upon the printing press and upon the book. Within a hundred years photography has completely revolutionized pictorial reproduction. The changes brought about in this field are perhaps more radical than in any other branch of the graphic arts. At the same time the future seems less predictable and more mysterious here than anywhere else. In papermaking, in printing presses, in typesetting and casting and in bookbinding, one can say, the traditional old methods have been mechanized, the human element greatly reduced, the speed of production increased, its cost decreased. In pictorial reproduction, photography has done all this and something more besides. It has eliminated manual labor in transferring onto the printing plate the artist's drawing or painting, and has made speedy and inexpensive reproduction of pictures possible. But the camera and the lens do more than that; they make the pictures themselves, directly from nature, and they then transfer them onto a printing plate.

Within little more than fifty years photomechanical methods have been introduced into all fundamental processes of reproduction. In relief printing, for instance, photomechanical line engraving and half-tone engraving have been added to the traditional woodcut and wood engraving methods. In intaglio, copper engraving, steel engraving and the various types of etching have been developed into the modern photogravure and rotogravure processes. In planographic printing, lithography, the youngest of all "traditional" processes, has been adopted as the basis of photolithography and of offset printing, while collotype is the planographic process most intimately connected with "pure" photography. The most spectacular results have been achieved in photomechancal color printing.

The definitive history of all these amazing developments has not been written. Already it is difficult, if not impossible, fully to disentangle the amazingly intricate pattern of overlapping inventions and experiments. Certain processes are clearly visible as the contribution of a single distinguished personality, others have been solved by several men within a very short period of time in widely separated places. For that reason it is very difficult to say just what the American contribution has been, both in regard to priority and in value. To answer this accurately, technical details would have to be discussed which lie far beyond the scope of this volume. If one wishes to make a general statement about the share of this country, one should emphasize the skill and promptness in adapting newly found principles to practical use, in the designing, production and distribution of useful, time-saving machinery and equipment and in the training of experienced workers in certain of the new processes.

One need only recall America's share in the general development of photography to realize that there is a firm basis for contributions in any specialized application of photography. Robert Taft's volume, *Photography and the American Scene*,[21] is a splendid monument of American achievements in photography.

The publication of Daguerre's original manual in 1839 threw open

[21] Published by Macmillan in 1938. Beaumont Newhall's *History of Photography from 1839 to the present day*, Museum of Modern Art, 1949, also contains valuable material. Chapter 10, on the adaptation of photography to the printed page, is of particular interest to the student of bookmaking.

the gates to what had been a temple of secret magic. The manual appeared in August and by November a translation was published in the *Journal of the Franklin Institute* in Philadelphia. That city immediately became a center of photographic interests and it has retained a leading position throughout the years. But also in New York and Boston invention and practice immediately set in. The first great contribution of international importance was the amazing series of photographs of the Civil War taken by Alexander Gardner and others for Mathew Brady. News photography since those days has remained an American specialty. This country also saw the first reproduction of a photograph in a newspaper, a picture entitled "Shanty-Town," published in 1880 in the March 4th issue of the New York *Daily Graphic* by a halftone process developed by Stephen Horgan. After vainly trying to persuade James Gordon Bennett to develop the process in the *Herald,* he succeeded at the *Tribune,* where the first halftones were printed on power presses in 1897. Edward Muybridge's fundamental work in the photography of animal locomotion was started in California and carried on in Philadelphia under the auspices of the University of Pennsylvania. Edison and his associates and rivals made very important inventions in the field of motion picture photography. Another inventor in the field of photography was a New Jersey minister, Hannibal Goodwin, who was granted a patent for a celluloid film in 1887.

The contribution of the Eastman Kodak Company, both in their scientific research and in the development of amateur photography, lately concentrated upon still and motion color photography, need only be mentioned to be appreciated. Since the turn of the century American photographers are found among the leading exponents of artistic photography and they have done much to remove traditional prejudices, and secure recognition for their field as a legitimate form of art.

In the development of photomechanical processes Americans took an early share. In his book Taft mentions particularly the early experiments in photolithography of Joseph Dixon, and, somewhat later, of Cutting and L. H. Bradford of Boston, who actually patented a process of photolithography in 1858. Probably the most important contribution of American inventors in photomechanical reproduction centers around the development of the halftone process. I have already mentioned Stephen Horgan's success in printing a photograph in a newspaper of 1880. This achievement was of course not brought about over night; rather it was the result of many years of experimentation. Overlapping both in time and scope with Horgan's work were the experiments of Frederic Eugene Ives.[22] At Cornell in 1877 Ives had perfected a relief process of line engraving based upon a swelled gelatine relief from which a plaster cast was made, which in turn was transferred by stereotyping onto the printing plate. This process, while a feasible solution, did not prove as important as his invention in the following year of his "halftone" photoengraving process. He first solved the necessary breaking-up of the halftones of his copy into single, printable units by a series of V-shaped lines, adapting a basic principle of wood engraving to photomechanical reproduction. He later resorted to the use of a crossline screen, whereby the halftone negatives were made directly in the camera. By 1886 he had perfected his method to such a degree that he could introduce it as the regular process of reproduction at the printing firm with which he was connected. In that form it became the basis of the system still in universal use. Also in 1886 he made an important contribution to the etching of the printing plates by working out his "baked enamel copper-etching method."

In 1881 he had turned his attention to the production of three-color halftone plates—a most important attempt to link color photography to the printing press, which he followed up in 1890 by patenting his process of composite heliochromy.

Max Levy of Philadelphia made further improvements in the field of halftone printing. Around 1890 he perfected an etched sealed glass screen for use in the camera, and later he introduced his acid-blast etching machine. These devices were universally acclaimed by makers of halftone plates as substantial aids in securing better results. In 1892 the first satisfactory three-color halftones were printed by Ernst Vogel and W. Kurtz in New York.

After the turn of the century American contributions were made particularly in the field of offset printing. In several countries experiments with that process had been carried on, particularly in printing upon metal surfaces. A rubber blanket had been used in the United

[22] A brief but careful account of his career by Edward Epstean and John A. Tennant appeared in the *Journal of Applied Physics*, vol. 9, no. 4, April, 1938.

States as early as 1852. W. Rubel applied the offset principle to paper, and around 1904 he built the first offset press at the Potter Printing Press Company in Jersey City. Simultaneously and independently Caspar Hermann, a lithographer from Germany, built his first offset press at Niles, Ohio.

The main efforts of American pioneers in the field of photomechanical reproduction, as in typesetting, were directed at the problems facing the periodical press and commercial printing. In these fields spectacular solutions were found. In high-quality reproduction, however, the American position has not been one of pioneer leadership so much as of adaptation and utilization.

The story of collotype printing in America shows this.[23] Collotype, a swelled gelatine process which is the only known means of printing continuous tone pictures on a press without the use of a halftone screen, was developed by 1855 through the efforts of Alphonse Poitevin. In 1870 Joseph Albert produced collotype printing in color by his "Albertype" method. Parallel efforts were carried out by Husnik of Prague, Löwy of Vienna, Obernetter of Munich and Léon Vidal in Paris. It should be explained that the process has been known in England and America under a variety of names, including the designations Albertype, Phototype, Photocollotype, Photogelatine, and Heliochrome.

The first collotypes to appear in America, according to Mr. Kainen, were made in France by du Motay and Marechal in 1865 and 1866. Work by Albert reached this country in 1869 and the "Albertype" was patented here November 30th of that year. In August, 1870, Edward Bierstadt published a letter in *Anthony's Photographic Bulletin*, inviting those interested in the production of "Photographs in Printing-Ink" under the patent of Joseph Albert, to examine specimens of this process and to observe its practical operation in New York City. Bierstadt was responsible for the earliest collotype to appear in a publication, namely in *The City, An Illustrated Magazine* of January, 1872. Ernest Edwards in Boston was a pioneer in the field, and the process

[23] The following information is based on letters received in 1949 from E. H. Hugo of the Meriden Gravure Company, from Arthur Jaffé of the Arthur Jaffé Heliochrome Company, and from Frank A. Taylor, Head Curator, Department of Engineering and Industries at the Smithsonian Institution. His letter contains information supplied by Jacob Kainen, Curator of the Division of Graphic Arts.

which he patented in December, 1872, was used in publications of James R. Osgood & Company of Boston.

Three-color collotypes, it seems, were made in this country around 1890, also by Bierstadt; the Ullman Manufacturing Company in Brooklyn and the Illinois Gravure Company in Chicago used the process in the nineties.

On September 8, 1890, the Meriden Gravure Company purchased its first collotype presses, importing them from Germany. Their first use was for commercial purposes, but soon art books and medical books formed the backbone of the work, spreading to a variety of scientific illustrations. This company is still in the front rank of the small number of concerns responding to the exacting demands of art and science. The use of the process for high-grade reproductions of works of art was greatly furthered by Henry Watson Kent, late secretary of the Metropolitan Museum of Art, who from 1926 on, worked in close cooperation with Max Jaffé in Vienna. His son, Arthur Jaffé, established a branch in New York and produced color-separations from which prints were made in Vienna for the Metropolitan Museum and other institutions and publishing firms. In 1938 Arthur Jaffé established his own presses in New York.

Organization of the Industry

The organization of working men in the printing industry started very early in America. In many regards this development is considered as epoch-making in the history of labor organizations. Some of the most important steps in the consolidation of workingmen took place before the process of mechanization had really begun to set in. Industrialization, of course, has encouraged the movement, but already in the last decade of the eighteenth century we find some definite evidence of the future trend, described in Part II of this volume. One need only consider the fundamental influence of the periodical press in this country to understand what a powerful weapon lay in the hands of the men who were directly responsible for the functioning of this vital, complicated organism.

The most important steps in organizing first the journeymen printers of the various cities, then in consolidating the various local units into a "National Typographical Union," had been taken several years before the Civil War. In the period after 1860, as the result of including the local Canadian unions, this "National Typographical Union" became the "International Typographical Union." After 1870 a change in the structure of the organization took place, whereby a division by types of activities rather than by geographical districts was favored. This led, in 1894, to the establishment of mutually independent unions of compositors, pressmen and bookbinders.

A very detailed study of these developments was published by Professor George E. Barnett in October, 1909, under the title, "The Printers. A Study in American Trade Unionism," in the *American Economic Association Quarterly*. Nearly 400 pages long, this article is not exactly a model of concentration, but it is an immensely valuable source of information. It has been used hardly, if at all, by students of American printing. To attempt even the most condensed summing up of this study would be quite impossible. Instead, a brief report on one particularly picturesque aspect will furnish the reader another proof of the extent to which conditions in newspaper and magazine printing dominated the entire situation of the graphic arts.

The early societies and the later unions shared the anxious concern that none of their members should work for less than established rates. This made it necessary to formulate or adopt a measure for the labor which was to be sold, and to fix a price for it. Piece rate and time rate were used alongside of each other. With time rate as the basis of measurement, the differing capacities of various workmen created problems. The piece rate called for a definition and classification of the various types of printing to be set up. The usual measurement was a square surface known as an em. It was obvious that not all kinds of matter could be set up with equal speed, and an elaborate system of exceptions and adjustments was developed.

However, one very important exception was not taken into consideration. No differentiation was made between straight matter, both in books and magazines, on the one side, and display advertising in newspapers and the front matter in books, on the other. It proved impossible to compensate subsequently for the original failure to distinguish between these two classes of work—with astonishing results. Display work and title pages, etc., measured on the basis of ems, were of course vastly more profitable than straight composition, since all white space and all large letters were counted. "Fat" was the name for all this easy money. The unions showed great reluctance to have any part of the "fat" taken away from the compositors, and they opposed the attempts of employers to give these portions to those employees who were working on a time basis.

The tremendous rise of commercial printing after the Civil War made advertising "fat" into a major item in the earnings of a newspaper compositor. Obviously, the "fat" had to be fairly distributed. "The common method . . . was to require that all copy as it came to the composing room should be placed on a 'hook' or file, and that each compositor should take from it in order." Eventually, "it became the practice to sell at auction to the highest bidder the right to set the advertisements," and he was obliged to turn over a percentage of his extra earnings to the other compositors. It was obvious that the difficulties and complications of such methods would gradually increase. The employers were eventually given a share of the "fat" and the permission to transfer more and more to time work. The period 1830 to 1890 saw a gradual increase in time work, until the introduction of the linotype brought piece work to an end.

The employers organized much later than their employees. It was Theodore Low De Vinne, America's foremost printer of the nineteenth century, who took the initiative. Soon after 1860, while a young man of little more than thirty years, he undertook to bring together the New York owners of printing houses and to create the Typothetae of New York. Other cities followed their example, and from the various "Typothetae" and "Employing Printers" groups, there formed itself, in 1887, the powerful "United Typothetae" organization with De Vinne as the first president.

THEODORE LOW DE VINNE, whom we have just referred to as the most significant American printer of the nineteenth century, was a man of unusual effectiveness and foresight. We may think of him as a characteristic representative of the best and most substantial typographic tradition of this country, which in the field of book printing has often shown a decidedly academic character. Printing started in this country under academic auspices, and one is tempted to look upon that first press in Cambridge as a descendant of those scholarly presses which humanism and renaissance brought forth in the countries of the old world. But not only these first printers were members of a republic of letters; Isaiah Thomas, the foremost printer of his period and founder of the American Antiquarian Society, and, in our own time, Daniel Berkeley Updike, were scholars and antiquarians as much as they were printers.

John Wilson and Joel Munsell

Before we turn to De Vinne and to his contemporaries and successors, two men who preceded him, in the best tradition of American scholar-printers, deserve attention as capable and cultivated craftsmen, full of enthusiasm for their chosen profession and forever in search of new means of improving their work. They were John Wilson (1802-1868), who emigrated from Scotland, and Joel Munsell (1808-1880) of Albany.

John Wilson was born in Glasgow, on April 16, 1802, and in that city was apprenticed to a printing firm, where after some years he became foreman. In 1823 he accepted a position as foreman of a large printing and publishing firm in Belfast, Ireland. During his time there he published his famous book on punctuation, and he wrote on other subjects. By 1840 he owned his own printing plant, where his son, John, joined him. In 1846 they decided to go to America, and landed in

Boston on October 6, 1846. For a time father and son worked in the Dickinson Printing Office, but in 1847 they started out on their own. Steadily their confidence and competence grew, and their activities soon expanded. Twenty-four gentlemen of Boston raised money for the purchase of their first Adams Power Press. In 1865, at the close of the war, Welch and Bigelow in Cambridge were moving to bigger quarters and offered to John Wilson & Son their former premises. So they settled in Cambridge and there enjoyed the confidence of President Eliot of Harvard, and did much of the University's printing. But not only official University printing and jobs for the faculty made father and son feel proud of their work. From the very beginning in Boston they had enjoyed the patronage of famous members of the Boston literary group, the poets, scholars and ministers. They printed for Charles Francis Adams, senior and junior, for Josiah Quincy, Edward Everett, for George Ticknor, James F. Hunnewell, and it was in their shop that Mary Baker Eddy's *Science and Health* was first printed. In 1866 the elder John Wilson was given a Harvard M.A., and two years later on August 3, 1868, he died. His son continued for some ten years, and in 1879, after Mr. Welch's death, he and Charles E. Wentworth bought the University Press, continuing under the firm of John Wilson & Son.

For some reason or other, Joel Munsell, that interesting and versatile printer, was almost forgotten until quite recently.[1] His work as a printer, as much as his literary activities, shows very clearly the active part which he took in the typographic world of his day, and his interest in the traditions of the craft.

In the typographic style of Munsell's printing one can sense the growing aversion to modern face types and the kind of book design based upon their use. First in England, in the collaboration of the Pickering publishing house with the Chiswick Press, then in all English-speaking countries as well as on the European continent, this reaction against classicist typography set in. The modern face types of Bodoni and Didot, and especially their mechanical, hackneyed descendants became the two object of criticism. The original Caslon types and other

---

[1] At the suggestion of the author, his former student David S. Edelstein has completed a full length biographical study entitled *Joel Munsell: Printer and Antiquarian*, which was accepted as a doctoral thesis in Columbia University's History Department and was published by the Columbia University Press in 1950.

old style designs were taken up again and put to good use. In 1856 Joel Munsell printed *Papers relating to the Island of Nantucket* from Caslon types imported by him from the original English foundry. It was the first nineteenth-century book in old style type to appear in the United States. In his printing Munsell reveals an intimate knowledge of the good English printing of his day. There is the same decoration reminiscent of the sixteenth century, there is the red and black on title pages, together with the Aldine dolphin and anchor surrounded by the motto, "Aldi Discipulus Albaniensis." In these efforts, as well as in his careful presswork and discriminating choice of paper, Munsell stands far above the level of the ordinary printer of his time.

This is all the more remarkable, because Munsell did not think of himself at all as a "fine printer" in our sense of the word. He did, to be sure, issue limited editions of historical works on special paper. But he was really a very busy trade printer who produced a considerable volume of book printing, including such varied items as popular tales and chapbooks, textbooks and law reports, directories, almanacs, guide books, and book catalogs for libraries, collectors and dealers. In these jobs he was satisfied with the ordinary book types of the day, and the conventional composition. But his work is usually careful, and here and there one finds a touch of red or a little ornament, betraying his true inclinations.

Munsell was also active as publisher and bookseller. He brought out many works on American history and some works on the history of the graphic arts, which he printed in his own shop. He was his own bookseller, and in 1856 and 1868 he issued catalogs of distinct bibliographic and typographic interest.

Munsell's books about printing are interesting fragments. His *Typographic Miscellany* came out in 1850. It contained short essays on all conceivable aspects of the graphic arts. His main interest was in American books and printing. In 1874 he printed an annotated edition of Thomas' *History of Printing in America*. His *Bibliotheca Munselliana*, listing some 2,000 titles printed by him between 1828 and 1870, is one of the most complete imprint lists of a single press ever issued. On papermaking he published a separate study, *Chronology of Paper and Papermaking*, first printed in 1856, and reissued five times with slightly varying titles and contents.

Both Munsell and Wilson had completed the larger portion of their work before the Civil War. The typographic style of both men's books are in some regards quite similar; they reflect in each case certain features of English book designing of that period. When one considers the success and the influence which John Wilson has had in this country, it is important to note that he emigrated from Great Britain not as a young beginner, but as a mature craftsman with much experience back of him. He was no doubt an important living link between British and American typographic taste in the middle of the nineteenth century.

Theodore Low De Vinne

De Vinne (1828-1912) was one of those fortunate human beings whose every enterprise was apparently crowned by success. In the more than eighty years of his active life he was privileged to participate in all the significant developments in his field, and often to determine the course of events. As early as 1850 he entered the printing firm of Francis H. Hart, and soon he was made a partner; after Hart's premature death he became his sole successor. Thus he found himself early in a position of responsibility, at a time when the old order of work had broken down everywhere, and the mechanization movement was rapidly gaining momentum. Fortunately, he brought and maintained towards these amazing developments an attitude not of critical antagonism, but of intelligent evaluation. Equipped with rich technical experience and a deep understanding of the traditions of the printing craft, he carried the right standards in himself. Thus he became a most valuable link between the old and the new. He was not exactly talented in an artistic way, but throughout the years of his activity he maintained a fine standard of taste in all the products of his press. This was, as a matter of fact, as much as anyone could have done during those revolutionary decades. In the matter of style, he threw his weight against the degenerate modern face types which were then dominating the field. He favored old style type designs and "transitional faces." Although he was not himself a type designer, his advice was listened to, and certain type faces were produced under his direct influence. He observed closely the effects of new methods and materials upon the old standards of composition and press work. When he, like everyone else, was forced to abandon the moistening of paper before printing, he took great pains to compensate for the loss of quality by other means of impression control.

The part which he took in the economic organization of the industry has been described earlier. Another of his activities, that of book collector and pillar of the Grolier Club, has secured him a permanent place in the annals of American bibliophily. A word remains to be said about his contributions to the literature of typography. Perhaps the most important work from his pen is his *Invention of Printing*, published in 1876, the result of very careful reading and thinking. Coming from one so intimately acquainted with all technical details of the craft, his words were as illuminating in their day as the later publications of German scholar-printers such as Heinrich Wallau and of Otto Hupp. De Vinne's book is still read, at home as well as abroad. His typographical manuals, except where later developments have made parts of them obsolete, are full of useful and valuable advice for the practical student of the graphic arts.

Much has been written and published about De Vinne. An intimate picture of the workings of his famous press, of the people that were part of it, the books that were made and those who visited there, was published some years ago. In 1936 the Columbiad Club brought out a chapter from the autobiography of Frank E. Hopkins, born March 30, 1863, in New York City, who joined the De Vinne Press in the fall of 1888, first as proofreader for the *Century Magazine*, then in a responsible position in the office. Years later, in 1896, in the attic of his house at Jamaica, Long Island, Mr. Hopkins started a small private press which he named the Marion Press.[2] There was no other thought in his mind than the pursuit of a hobby and the entertainment of himself and a few friends. But success was so immediate and conspicuous, that it led to a friendly parting from the De Vinne Press. Without any conscious ambition in that direction, and certainly with no desire to emulate William Morris, the Marion Press thus became a forerunner of the

---

[2] This enterprise has become the subject of an unusually thoroughgoing study, a memorial volume written by Thomas A. Larremore and Mrs. Amy Hopkins Larremore, daughter of the late Mr. Hopkins. The book was set by hand and published by the Queens Borough Public Library as *The Marion Press* in 1943, with the active support of Joseph W. Rogers, then on its staff.

many private presses that sprang up in America in the early 1900's in the wake of the Kelmscott Press.

Walter Gilliss

An outstanding younger contemporary of De Vinne was Walter Gilliss (1855-1925), the able founder and director of the Gilliss Press. In his bibliophile inclinations, in the typographic style of the books he printed, and in his choice of technique and material, he closely resembles De Vinne. He, too, wrote on the subject of printing, but without quite the historical and scientific penetration of De Vinne. In his memoirs, however, he has contributed an important record of American fine printing of the late nineteenth and early twentieth centuries. The Gilliss Press enjoyed a high reputation for the quality and taste of its printing, and publishers turned there when they wanted a particularly handsome and distinguished looking volume. For many years Mr. Gilliss printed the catalogs of the Metropolitan Museum of Art, and he enjoyed the lasting friendship of William Loring Andrews, the bibliophile. Some of his best work was done in the printing of illustrations, where he continued to use handmade paper. But he did not despise innovations. He took up halftone printing at an early stage, paying particular attention to the selection of the most suitable papers for the purpose.

However, he was a conservative in matters of typographic taste. When William Morris set the printing world on fire with bold realizations of his dreams of medieval craftsmanship, he ignored the trend. Gilliss was over forty when the new school made itself felt here, and he saw no need to change then. So he carried over into the new century ideas and ideals of another period.

Other Printers

It is no easy matter to add to our account of the most distinguished printers of the period an adequate description of the other men and the presses who deserve to be remembered for their activities in book printing. Obviously, something should be said about the share of the various communities throughout the country and about the heads of the most important establishments, at least. The existing literature is still elusive. True enough, the efforts of a great many bibliographers in recent years to add to our knowledge of nineteenth-century American printing have rescued hundreds of names and firms from oblivion. Yet it is not easy to decide which of those printers were sufficiently interested in the production of books to have made a lasting contribution. In wide sections of the country the emphasis was simply not on book printing but on newspapers and magazines. To be sure, the typical newspaper printer did issue a volume of state laws, or print an occasional book for a local society or church, or even a volume of poetry. But that is a very different thing from active and regular work for a publishing house. We must also consider the fact that although the printing profession attracted men of considerable ability, it did not always hold them. There is an impressive list made by Mr. Bullen, in the Typographic Library at Columbia University, of famous American printers. It is to be noted, however, that they have become famous not as printers, but as editors and legislators, as soldiers and merchants. In fact, the story of the boy with a printing press in attic or cellar who becomes successively the compositor, editor and proprietor of the local newspaper, who studies law on the side, and rises from local politician to legislator and statesman, is one of the great sagas of nineteenth-century American life. In the seventies San Francisco is reported to have harbored no less than a hundred boys who ran small job presses.

In continuation of the pattern developed in the colonial period and during the years of the young republic, the centers of book printing remained, with a few notable exceptions, in the cities along the Atlantic seaboard. In New England, Boston and Cambridge led, but there were a number of smaller centers in Massachusetts, in Rhode Island and in Connecticut, where respectable book printing was still done after the Civil War. New York had come to the fore, and it was on its way to becoming the center of the entire book and printing trade of the country. Philadelphia and Baltimore had noticeably receded. Beyond the Atlantic seaboard centers of importance were few and far between. Ohio, Illinois and Missouri stood out in the Middle West and California on the Pacific Coast.

In Cambridge and Boston a number of excellent book printers should be mentioned. One steady factor was the presence of Harvard University, always an important customer for any ambitious printer of that region. Early in the nineteenth century William Hilliard printed for the college, and his firm with its traditions passed through many hands. It would be a mistake, I believe, to think of the successive owners of this firm as nothing but university printers. They took a good share of work for other customers, particularly for the important book publishers. On the other hand, the university was under no obligation to have all their printing done with them.

This condition is well illustrated in the case of the firm of Welch, Bigelow, & Co., who in 1859 acquired the University Press, but retained the identity of their own organization. A very considerable portion of the literary production of those fruitful years saw the light of day in that printing office, and the modest little line "Printed by Welch, Bigelow, & Co." is found in many important works of the period. In 1865 they moved to larger quarters and it was then that they invited John Wilson & Son to take over their former premises at Cambridge and to buy some of their equipment. We have already told how John Wilson & Son were brought within the orbit of the University. In 1879, John Wilson, Junior, joined forces with Charles E. Wentworth to buy the University Press from Welch, Bigelow, & Co.

Some years before that date, apparently in 1871, the university established a small printing office of its own for the printing of examination papers, circulars, posters and other ephemeral pieces. It was from these modest beginnings that the present Harvard University Press took its origin.

In the same year, 1871, a printer from Germany set up his business in Boston. Carl H. Heintzemann is fondly remembered today by C. P. Rollins, who worked as a young man at the case in the old Heintzemann printing plant, as did D. B. Updike. Like Munsell, he was a practical printer who handled a large volume of work but who never denied himself the satisfaction of printing a volume with special love and care when an opportunity presented itself.

Another important press was the Riverside Press in Cambridge, created in 1852 by Henry Oscar Houghton (1823-1895). Like the Harper brothers, young Houghton built his future on the foundation of a printing press when, in 1849, he entered into a partnership with Bolles, under the name of Bolles & Houghton. Printing and publishing was their aim and the establishment of the Riverside Press marks an important step in the successful development of one branch of the firm's activities, which has been a steady influence for quality and dignity in book production. To Henry Oscar Houghton goes the credit for the rediscovery, in 1864, of the famous roman type of the Englishman, John Bell.[3] Other Boston and Cambridge firms of that time were Rockwell & Churchill, headed by Horace Tyler Rockwell, and the Mudge printing firm. Then there were offshoots from these presses. Josiah Stearns Cushing (1854-1913) had been apprenticed to Welch, Bigelow & Co.; he started on his own in 1878, specializing in the production of school and textbooks, and undertaking an occasional limited edition.

William M. Cubery, born 1836, had been apprenticed to the Riverside Press, and in his memoirs he tells with pride of his personal acquaintanceship with some of the great literary figures of the Boston of that day and of the careful work done at the press. In 1860 he went to California, where in 1866 he opened his own printing press. Full of indignation he speaks of the hasty, superficial and low-grade work performed by the printers of California, which he compares very unfavorably with the solid standards of New England.

A good example of the smaller New England printing centers is Andover, Massachusetts, with its Andover Press. Even before the Civil War this press had specialized in the careful execution of theological works, including the printing of books in exotic type faces. In Amherst the college attracted printers; by 1868 four presses were competing to serve town and gown. In the state of Connecticut, Newton Case (1870-1890) should be mentioned, who lived and worked in Hartford, traditionally a center of school and textbook printing. In New Haven the firm of Tuttle, Morehouse & Taylor, founded in 1859, undertook to print for Yale University. Wilson H. Lee came to New Haven in 1875 and specialized in the printing of directories, starting with local communities, but soon attracting orders from many places in the East.

The most significant printers of the City and State of New York have already been mentioned. The presence of important publishers in the city accounts, of course, for quite a number of other firms there.

---

[3] He brought back from England the fonts which in the Riverside Specimen Book of 1887 are noted as "English Copperface" and which were used for printing some books and pamphlets for Martin Brimmer of Boston, causing Bruce Rogers to name the type "Brimmer," while Updike called the fonts which he acquired "Mountjoye."

The Trow Press, particularly, founded by John Fowler Trow (1809-1886), an enterprising and progressive man, was a large and well-equipped plant, which had been started by Mr. Trow and his partners before the Civil War. Here was printed the great Washington Irving edition of the sixties, published by Putnam. The press owned a good selection of Greek and of Near Eastern types, partly German importations, which secured for the press a share in the production of important scholarly works. Trow's foreman, Peter Carpenter Baker (1822-1889) started out for himself under the firm of Baker, Godwin & Co., who in 1866 purchased the law publishing business of John S. Voorhis, and continued under the name of Baker, Voorhis & Co. Then there were Corydon A. Alvord (1813-1874), who specialized in de luxe editions and in careful printing of illustrations, Edward O. Jenkins (1817-1884), John Johnson Hallenbeck (1820-1891), Joseph J. Little (1841-1913), the founder of the J. J. Little and Ives Company, and Howard Lockwood (born 1846). Some of the firms founded by these men have survived to the present day, partly under altered names or in connection with later partners.

In Albany, the seat of Joel Munsell's activities, there was also John Davis Parsons, whose firm of Weed & Parsons belongs among the most substantial printing plants outside of the great cities. In Troy, too, there were busy printers, and in Rochester Ezra R. Andrews (born 1828) made a name for himself. Even in those days the big publishers began to realize that they could get their printing done at cheaper prices by employing provincial printers.

Further south, in the famous old printing center of Philadelphia, we find the printer Conger Sherman (1793-1874), and particularly the Collins firm, headed by Tillinghast King Collins (1802-1870) and his brother, P. G. Collins. This printing press produced for the Federal Government some lavishly illustrated works, which at the time attracted much attention. In Baltimore there was William Kent Boyles (1816-1884). In Washington the Government Printing Office was started in 1861, with the appointment of the first "Superintendent of Public Printing." A more comprehensive printing act was passed in 1895.

To the printers of the South the War between the States had brought special problems and challenges. They "did not escape their share of the ruin. But they carried on as well as they could with a determination and courage that today seem almost sublime. When approaching armies threatened their lives and their presses they packed up and moved to safe spots in the deep South. When the tide of battle overtook them, again they packed up a second or third time and still moved on, bringing out their papers, turning out such pamphlets and books as were in demand as they moved along . . . until finally overtaken and destroyed. . . . When peace came they started off again and continued to build up the editing and publishing of the state. . . . In the tragic periods like those of the reconstruction days, printed matter became as necessary as food and raiment." (Joseph H. Sears, *Tennessee Printers.*)

There was a temporary halt to the growing centralization of book publishing and, with it, of book printing, in the great seaboard cities of the North. Textbook production saw a regional survival in the South, and there was a certain amount of reprinting of Victorian novels, "when the Federal blockade made it impossible for them any longer to receive 'elegant English books by steamer.'" But the newspaper remained the principal vehicle for fiction, essays and poetry. The newspaper editor-printer "perhaps even more than the itinerant schoolmaster, was the enlightener of the backwoods, bringing the settlers their chief contact with the outside world, its political events and literary tastes . . ." (Rhoda C. Ellison, *Early Alabama Publications.*)

The books, pamphlets and broadsides, produced alongside of the newspapers, were all regional in character. Every imprint list after the war shows the same pattern. Government, legislative and other legal publications form the most important group, closely rivaled in number and importance by religious tracts and sermons, the pamphlets of various sects, especially the Baptists, and by local history, topography and descriptions of natural resources and opportunities, with a small number of natural science publications of a local character. Education is represented chiefly in academic programs and addresses; personal memoirs and biographies play a certain part. Also represented are public health, the railroads, Freemasonry, some city directories and almanacs, but only a stray volume of poetry and fiction.

To isolate the names of Southern printers and firms who showed any degree of specialization in bookmaking is a difficult task indeed. In antebellum Fredericksburg, Virginia, there was a printer by the name of

James S. Magrath who had a Ruggles' machine job press and who boasted of more than fifty varieties of new printing types. But he was dead by 1858 and it is difficult to discern who, if anyone, took his place after the war. In North Carolina, where the Census report of 1850 showed a percentage of illiteracy "about twice as great as that of any of her sister states" (George W. Paschal, *A History of Printing in North Carolina*), textbook production was undertaken during the war by Branson & Farrar in Raleigh and by others in Greensboro, until closed by the Federal troops. In 1871 Cornelius Bryant Edwards and Needham Bryant Broughton established a printing firm in Raleigh, designed to keep all the best of printing in their state. The firm of Edwards & Broughton has survived to the present day. Mobile, Alabama, harbored in the late fifties and the early sixties such a publishing house as the firm of Goetzel's, and there must have been corresponding production facilities. But there seems to be no evidence of survival or revival of specific book printing skills and facilities. "The people of the South," said Judge Crofton,[4] have heretofore cared more for eminence in statesmanship than for eminence in general literature—more for speech-making than for book-making."

Going west one finds that, in these years particularly, St. Louis seems to have developed into a center of considerable interest. There we find Richard Ennis (born 1833), George D. Barnard (born 1846) and William L. Becker (born 1847). The city, however, was overshadowed in importance by Cincinnati, "The Queen City of the inland waterways," and alternately remembered as "the literary emporium" or "The Athens" of the West. It is not surprising that the city which in the nineteenth century was the center of American book trade west of the Alleghenies should have harbored important printers.

Along with the firm of Charles J. Krehbiel (born 1849), there was particularly Oscar H. Harpel, who deserves to be remembered. He issued a specimen book which, in its very decorative and colorful manner, is a quaint document of both book typography and job printing of that day. Five years later, in 1875, he published his *Poets and Poetry of Printerdom: A Collection of Original, Selected, and Fugitive Lyrics, written by Persons connected with Printing*. The little volume is of

[4] In S. S. Scott, *The Mobilians, or Tales about the South*, Montgomery, Alabama, 1898, as quoted by Rhoda C. Ellison, *Early Alabama Publications*.

great interest and value, because it contains a short biographical sketch of each printer-poet fortunate enough to have been included. It makes one realize how much forgotten material about interesting men and their work is still waiting to be resurrected.

Chicago, in the decades following the Civil War, was busily growing into an industrial center of first magnitude. It was during these years that the foundation was laid for some of the large plants that form the backbone of the printing industry of that city today. It is important to note that at one of the most substantial of these firms, namely at the Lakeside Press, distinctive efforts were made and are still made, towards good book production and fine printing. The Lakeside Press was organized by Richard Robert Donnelley (born 1836), who came to Chicago in 1864, where he associated himself with a firm that in 1870 was made into the Lakeside Printing and Publishing Company, later to be known as the Lakeside Press. Among the other printers, Philo Foster Pettibone (born 1841) seems to have been particularly interested in book printing.

During this period the position and the products of printers in the western frontier territories were not too different from those in the South. The only variation in the Dakotas, for instance, lies in an added emphasis on the needs and problems of new settlers, on such occupations as mining and agriculture, and in some missionary tracts in the Dakota language (Albert H. Allen, *Dakota Imprints 1858-1889*). All of the known books, pamphlets and broadsides were produced at newspaper offices, but it seems that many printers "engaged so exclusively in the production of their local newspapers that they printed nothing else. . . . For the wide range of books required to serve their cultural needs . . . the people of Dakota drew upon the resources of publishers elsewhere and depended not at all upon local presses for that kind of material." Oklahoma saw some fairly active book printing before the Civil War, some educational titles and a number of translations of religious works into the Indian languages. In Oregon eight out of the nine books printed by the pioneer press were missionary works translated for the Indians.

In California something very interesting happened. As elsewhere on the frontier, printing had started to serve the immediate, practical needs of the settlers. But there was something in the soil and in the air, some-

thing also in the make-up of the people who came, that allowed literature and authorship to grow early roots, and it made it possible for
some of the printers to make real books. A notable example is "The
Excelsior Book and Job Office, Whitton, Towne Company, Projec-
tors," organized in San Francisco in 1852, and the name changed in
1858 to Towne & Bacon. They produced a large number of books and
pamphlets of historic significance and bibliographic importance. Their
imprint is found on many cherished California items, for instance on
Bret Harte's *Lost Galleon*, of which they made an attractive duodecimo
in 1867. Earlier, they produced Stratton's *Life among the Indians*, and
Theodore H. Hittell's *Adventures of James Capon Adams, Mountaineer
and Grizzly Bear Hunter of California*, illustrated with wood engravings after Nahl's designs.

Another San Francisco printing office was established by Francis
Blake in 1853, and changed in 1855 to Blake & Moffitt. They brought
paper, ink and other equipment from the East, and in 1868 they joined
forces with Towne & Bacon to form a paper supply house which,
under the name of Blake, Moffitt and Towne, is still active on the Coast.
We have already mentioned William M. Cubery, former Riverside
Press apprentice, who came and opened his own press in 1866. A versatile printer was Canadian-born Edward Bosqui. From 1862 to 1906 he
operated a printing firm which included a bindery and equipment for
chromo-lithographic work.

It was a logical development that some of the important printing
presses of the nineteenth century should gradually grow into publishing firms, and some instances of this are mentioned elsewhere in this
volume. On the other hand, it happened that certain firms originally
founded and developed as publishing houses added their own printing
presses to the plants. The establishment of the Knickerbocker Press in
New Rochelle, N. Y., for instance, is due to the initiative of the Putnam
publishing firm, which expanded in 1891 and keenly felt the need for
a larger production department.

American Book Design in the Nineteenth Century

Before going on to an account of publishing and bookselling activities after the Civil War, it might be useful to recall the chief physical
characteristics of the book of that period.

By and large, the aspect in the nineteenth century is fairly stable up to the seventies. The style of bookmaking is simple and somewhat uniform. Typographic design is dominated by the use of modern face types. This meant that the printers could count upon a somewhat mechanical looking, but, on the whole, consistent and clear typographic system which allowed quite a range of variety and differentiation within one main type family. Add to that the fact that the ever-present wood engraving practically monopolized pictorial reproduction. Its tone could be deliberately controlled to fit color and tenor of the numerous modern face types employed, and which demanded a very similar treatment in presswork and paper selection. This style of typography, which we may call "late classicist" and "early romantic," had replaced the Colonial mood in American typography at about the same time that it made its appearance in England, towards the end of the eighteenth century. It lasted until late in the nineteenth century. Between 1830 and 1880 it was the universal manner favored for average, everyday book printing. It was among the men described above as the American scholar-printers that there began to show itself a different trend, particularly in the cases where a book was planned as a specially fine and careful work. One can almost go so far as to say that the rejection of modern face types in favor of old style typography is the symbol of the struggle for the preservation of individual, personal taste in printing against mechanization and standardization. There enters also an element of national tradition into this struggle. In their mathematical precision of structure and of detail, these modern face types are essentially Latin in character, even if they have been used, and are still used, very effectively in England and Germany as well as in America.

The "Modernized Old Styles" which came into vogue in the early seventies attempt to reconcile the two diverging tendencies, by combining elements of both into one. De Vinne, for instance, favored these tendencies and used these types quite frequently.

But other aspects of the book changed, too, around 1870. De Vinne has pointed out that it was then that printers ceased gradually to moisten their paper for printing, because it did not seem to them worth the time and effort. To counterbalance the loss in quality of presswork, they began to favor calendered papers. This was also practical in getting the most out of the wood engravings which were still going strong, and were cut to display an amazingly delicate play of the finest lines. When around 1880 halftones made their appearance, the days of the wood engraving were, of course, numbered, but the smooth papers remained in favor; soon, the coated papers, essential in the successful printing from halftone plates, were generally accepted.

The wealth of new processes and of new materials which besieged the judgment of the ordinary printer brought about a confusion of standards in America very similar to the European decadence of typographic taste. There had to come a general reform of craftmanship and the active protest of a group of progressive young American publishers to bring about a clarification of these conditions.

Literature and Reading after the Civil War

IT CANNOT BE SAID that the decades following the Civil War were particularly productive of outstanding new literary personalities. It was important that the American authors whose works were published in magazines and books were making very real efforts at intellectual and artistic independence, and that the American scene was at last coming into its own as a worthy subject. But the many adventurous tales and sentimental short stories, the local color and the dialect literature of those days show little indication of the singular power and brilliance which was soon to distinguish the modern American novel. On the other hand, one must not forget that in the previous generation this country, for the first time in its history, had produced a literary school of world-wide importance. The powerful effects of the New England Romanticists and Transcendentalists were not spent, their spirit lingered on. The old works and new of Emerson, of Poe and Longfellow, of Hawthorne, Thoreau and Melville were still being printed and were still being read. It was now that the first Collected Works of the authors of that group were published in a great variety of editions. But the older masters, too, the books of Cooper and Irving, were still in favor.

Of the outstanding literary figures of the latter nineteenth century, Walt Whitman had been heard even before the Civil War, but the years 1865-1891 saw the rich harvest of his matured talent. They were also his fellow-printer Mark Twain's best years. Perhaps because they were both so deeply rooted in their native continent, and surely because they penetrated beyond superficial appearances, their work has stirred men and women the world over. Emily Dickinson received posthumous publication and acclaim in the nineties. Henry James, Mark Twain's somewhat younger contemporary, seems to us today not so much the exponent of his own times, as the pioneer of a new generation of American novelists. To the publishers of his day he appeared as a literary problem child, not in the quality of his work, but in his limited public appeal. The sales figures of his novels look small indeed when compared with those of Mark Twain, who was a master at meeting the taste of the broad masses of readers.

The reading public was growing considerably during those years. Large portions of the public were using printed matter for the first time, magazines at the start and then an occasional bound volume. The days after the Civil War were the great days of the semi-literary family magazine, and here it was that the new generation of national authors first spread their wings. There were the political poets of the Civil War, then the discoverers of the American scenery and its new experience, of American ethnology—the lore of the Indian and the ballads and folklore of the mountaineers and the Southern Negro, and the local color and dialect authors, who soon arose in every part of the country. Then, too, began the Wild West stories, producing, among many others, a Bret Harte, whose fame has lasted. After 1870, the great masses of immigrants made themselves felt. Their writers, "increasingly conscious of social and economic issues, began to criticize their environment in realistic novels, as the American-born writers of the period were doing." (Spiller, *Literary History of the United States.*)

And then, we must not forget that the works of American authors, whether in magazines or published as books, still form only a fraction of the total reading matter of the American public. It has been estimated that in the year 1820 only about 30 per cent of all books published in this country were written by American authors; in the year 1840 the proportion was about half and half, and in the sixties the share of native authors had risen to about 80 per cent. These figures would indicate an interesting, close relationship to the growing American independence which we have been able to trace in the development of the various graphic arts industries. But it should be pointed out that the above estimate includes the entire production of school and textbooks, which after the turn of the century shows a very considerable increase.

Also, we should remember that the direct importation of English books by English authors still played an enormously important role. Certainly, whether in original editions or in volumes republished in

America, the entire range of English literature was available. There had been Scott, followed by Dickens and Thackeray, then by George Eliot, the Brontës, Mrs. Gaskell, Wilkie Collins, Trollope, Meredith and young Hardy. There were the great later romantic poets, Tennyson and Browning, the Pre-Raphaelites, Swinburne, Rossetti and Morris. There were Ruskin, the philosopher of art, and Carlyle, the philosopher of history, and all of them followed by a host of lesser talents. The situation was unique, with no real parallel in modern times. England and America were bound together by the common bond of language and tradition, although they were at different stages in their historic and cultural evolution. This relationship of the two countries must be constantly remembered if one wishes really to understand the role of the book in nineteenth-century America.

If one were to appraise this role only from the point of view of the traditional historian of literature, solely in terms of belles-lettres, a very incomplete picture would result. What about the dime novels, for instance? Born in the early sixties, as popular with the soldiers in the Civil War as the Armed Services Editions in World War II, and read as avidly by the general public throughout the century as comic books today, they have now become collectors' items and the object of meticulous scrutiny.

Careful investigation of other types of reading matter, too, has added greatly to our understanding of what books contributed to the life of the citizens in these restless days. One gains the general impression that the decades immediately following the Civil War were inferior in their productivity not only of works of literature but also of many other kinds of books. In many fields the important thinking, the significant impetus seems to lie in earlier days. The seventies and eighties excelled in new ways of mass production and in unorthodox and unprecedented means of distribution.

Important insight into the function of books in American society is gained whenever a special type of publication becomes the object of detailed study.[1] The jest books, those quite trivial collections of jokes and funny stories, conveniently attributed to famous and notorious personages, had their first fling in the days of the young republic. But

---

[1] See the listings under *Selected Subject Bibliographies*, page 427, for the sources of much of the following discussion.

they kept going after the Civil War, and during the eighties these comic almanacs saw commercial exploitation as novel advertising media for various firms. This does not mean, of course, that the humorists had lost their place on the American scene. "In their writings are to be found the most distinctively American strains in our literature." (Spiller, *Literary History of the United States*.)

Undoubtedly of great significance is the fact that the nineteenth century saw a sustained interest in certain volumes which helped the citizens in the rapidly expanding communities of the growing nation to plan their "design for living." Books of etiquette, for instance, enjoyed an enormous popularity in the United States. The men, and especially the women, wanted advice on how to behave in polite society, how to live up to the standards of the "best people," how to become a successful leader in Washington diplomatic circles. Florence Hartley's book, published in 1860 by G. W. Cottrell in Boston, has a title worth quoting: *The Ladies' Book of Etiquette, and Manual of Politeness. Complete handbook for the use of the lady in polite society. Containing full directions for correct manners, dress, deportment, and conversation; rules for the duties of both hostess and guest in morning receptions, dinner companies, visiting, evening parties and balls; a complete guide for letter writing and card of compliments; hints on managing servants, on the preservation of health, and on accomplishments. And also useful receipts for the complexion, hair, and with hints and directions for the care of the wardrobe.*

About 200 distinct editions of a great many different etiquette books were published before 1861, about 170 of them in the thirty years since 1830. Just about the same number of 170 appeared in the thirty years between 1861 and 1890, a steady flow of volumes establishing and reinforcing the genteel tradition in the image of the Victorian pattern of life.

The physical construction of the new American home, too, needed continued guidance through books, and it called forth a broad stream of architectural volumes with plans and designs for houses. After the middle of the forties these "house pattern books" had begun to be published in great quantities, superseding almost completely the older type of "builders' guides." We learn from Henry Russel Hitchcock's bibliography that "first in the year 1857 and again in 1868, 1878, 1885 and 1889, as many as a dozen house pattern books appeared, although in the intervening years their numbers dropped to two or three. Thus, the output of the publishers in this field parallels rather closely the curve of building production."

A particularly rapid increase in the number of volumes published after 1870 can be observed in another group of practical volumes, the books on accounting. While between 1830 and 1870 some 20 new titles were published in each decade, the next decade, 1870-1880, saw 59, or three times as many, and the period 1880-1890, about five times as many new titles, namely, 106. This reflects very clearly expanding needs as they developed in this period of industrialization and large-scale manufacturing, with its founding of the big steel and oil companies, its rapid expansion of railroads. The publishing trade was quick to profit from these new demands for practical manuals for the growing profession of accountants, even before the rise of business schools and long before the introduction of income tax in the years preceding World War I.

These are valuable insights into some of the special fields. A good way to gain an impression of the all-over trends which governed the publishing of books during these decades is a brief examination of production statistics as recorded in the table on page 321. It can be seen there that there was not too great a difference in the total number of titles published in 1869 and, again, in 1880. But by 1890 the annual output was about doubled, and tripled by 1900, statistical proof of the enormous increase in volume which American publishing experienced at the turn of the century. Conspicuous changes in the importance of a number of subjects can also be observed. Between 1869 and 1890 the most obvious gains were made by sociology and economics, in the field of law, and by the fine arts. The noticeable rise of interest in art publications has been attributed to the Philadelphia Centennial Exhibition of 1876, where over a thousand American paintings were shown among the various art exhibits at Fairmount Park's Memorial Hall. One would like to believe that other factors beside this "rich exhibition of international mediocrity" account for these new interests, but it is plausible that the Centennial did exercise a considerable influence. In that same period the art of thinking and the art of the word showed substantial losses, as borne out by the declining publication figures in philosophy, in poetry and drama. Losses were also sustained in geography and travel. The decline of medicine and hygiene books, however, should not be attributed to a lessening of interest or importance in these fields, but to the steady growth, in number of titles and in volume, of the scientific periodical, which took over many of the functions traditionally fulfilled by the medical book.

It should not be forgotten that these observations pertain to the number of different titles published annually in each field of human knowledge and interest. They give, of course, no indication of the sizes of editions and are therefore not a wholly reliable guide to what people at large were reading. Undoubtedly the most important recent contribution to the study of the people's book reading habits in nineteenth-century America is Frank Luther Mott's *Golden Multitudes, The story of best sellers in the United States*, which also throws significant new light on the economics of authorship and of American publishing in general. His definition of a best seller includes each book which is believed to have had "a total sale equal to one per cent of the population . . . for the decade in which it was published, which means a required sale of 300,000 copies for 1860-1869, 375,000 copies for 1870-1879, 500,000 copies for 1880-1889, and 625,000 copies for 1890-1899." Mott has also developed a list of "better sellers."

What are the outstanding features of the broad panorama of popular reading which opens up for us? The historical novel ranks high among the popular best sellers of their day, which reached the American public in a bewildering variety of editions, in both paper and cloth and at prices veering from twenty cents to $129.25 per copy. The most important titles were all published before the end of the Civil War, and they all retained their hold on the public for many decades to come.

Among the juveniles such well-remembered favorites as Jacob Abbott's "Rollo" books, S. G. Goodrich's "Peter Parley" books, the ever beloved fairy tales of the brothers Grimm and of Hans Christian Andersen, the *Swiss Family Robinson* of Johann Rudolph Wyss, Louisa May Alcott's *Little Women*, Mary Mapes Dodge's *Hans Brinker; or the Silver Skates*, and Richard Henry Dana's classic *Two Years before the Mast* shared honors with many a forgotten subcription best seller. The subscription method of publishing worked well for Mark Twain, whose *Innocents Abroad* was sold by agents to upward of 4,000 readers a month, and for *The Adventures of Tom Sawyer*, that book for boys of all ages. Among the outright juveniles that were published in the latter part of the century, the famous Horatio Alger books, the books of Harry Castlemon, E. S. Ellis, Oliver Optic, and *Helen's Babies* by John Habberton joined the best seller parade. Johanna Spyri's "Heidi" books, *The Five Little Peppers* of Harriet M. Stone, Frances Hodgson Burnett's *Little Lord Fauntleroy*, Anna Sewell's *Black Beauty*, and the *Uncle Remus* stories of Joel Chandler Harris, still very much alive today—all these popular favorites achieved exceedingly high sales figures. The same was true of Robert Louis Stevenson's *Treasure Island*, his *A Child's Garden of Verse*, and, of course, *Dr. Jekyll and Mr. Hyde*.

In the field of poetry, Thomas Moore's *Lalla Rookh* "came in on the Byronic wave" and it remained popular throughout the century. Tennyson actually achieved greater popularity in America than in his native England, because of the cheap unauthorized editions, while Longfellow's popularity in England, for the same reason, outranked the large following which he enjoyed in his native America. Edgar Allan Poe's poetry was slow in getting started, and reached the broader masses of readers only after his death. Robert Browning's success created "in the Browning Clubs of the eighties one of the most remarkable social phenomena of those times." Whittier's poetry found its largest audiences after the War. Walt Whitman's *Leaves of Grass* had a fascinating and adventurous publishing history all of its own. Fitzgerald's translation of the *Rubáiyát*, towards the end of the century, pointed the way towards a new receptiveness.

Mr. Mott has been careful to explain that there is no such thing as a typical best seller. Various audiences have always existed simultaneously, and books of vastly different caliber have achieved best seller status in their day. It is therefore not surprising that books calculated to appeal to a common denominator of taste at a fairly low level achieved the same spectacular sales figures as books written with deep conviction of the heart and mind in behalf of the betterment of human society.

Much fourth-rate fiction ranked high among popular favorites. *Uncle Tom's Cabin*, on the other hand, also did well for Harriet Beecher Stowe—300,000 by the end of the first year, 40 pirated editions in Great Britain and colonies within a year, and an enormous reception on the European continent. The crusading spirit resulted in other books in the nineteenth century which achieved great popular success: *Parson Brownlow's Book*, the narrative of his personal adventures among the rebels, published in the summer of 1862; Henry George's *Progress and Poverty*, started in 1877, in the fourth year of a great financial depression; Edward Bellamy's *Looking Backward, 2000-1887;* and William Hope Harvey's *Coin's Financial School,* the fanatical championship of silver coinage.

In the eighties two books with a religious theme became spectacularly successful, Ludovic Halévy's *L'Abbé Constantin,* and, of course, Lew Wallace's *Ben Hur.*

Faced with this picture of popular reading, based on a quantitative analysis and including so many works of European authorship, one may well ask: which American books published during these decades were of outstanding importance? An unorthodox and rather ingenuous answer to this question was supplied a few years ago by the Grolier Club in New York when it organized an exhibition of *One Hundred Influential American Books Printed before 1900* (catalog issued in 1947). These are the 1860-1890 books listed: Ann Sophia Stephens, *Malaeska, the Indian Wife of the White Hunter,* the first of the Beadle Dime Novels; John Greenleaf Whittier, *Snow Bound;* Louisa May Alcott, *Little Women;* Horatio Alger, Jr., *Ragged Dick;* the stories of Bret Harte; Montgomery Ward's mail order catalog; Mary Baker Eddy's *Science & Health;* Anna Katherine Green's *The Leavenworth Case,* father of the modern detective story; Henry George, *Progress and Poverty;* Joel Chandler Harris, *Uncle Remus;* also mentioned, *Mrs. Lincoln's Boston Cook Book,* the direct antecedent of Fanny Farmer's classic.

This selection, too, shows quite clearly that the decades after the Civil War were inferior in creative strength to the years that had gone before and, most assuredly, to the decades immediately ahead.

The most important single factor in bringing the American author into his own was the passing of the copyright law of 1891.

International Copyright

The foundations of copyright legislation in Colonial times and the situation in the days of the young republic have been discussed in the earlier parts of this book. The Civil War brought an interesting and little known development. Perhaps not only as a practical step but also for reasons of international diplomacy, the Confederacy decided promptly on a separate course of action. In the first session of its Provisional Congress in Montgomery, a resolution was adopted for the appointment of commissioners "to visit the European Powers, to enter into treaty obligations for the extension of international copyright privileges to all authors, the citizens and subjects of the powers aforesaid." This resolution of March 7, 1861 was followed on May 21, 1861, by "An Act to secure copyrights to authors and composers" which included provisions for the protection of the copyrights of "citizens or subjects of any foreign state or power."

The most important step taken in the United States after the War was the passing of the Copyright Act of 1870. It had been preceded in 1865 by a regulation which extended the existing copyright to photographs and negatives, and by the act of March 3, 1865, which required that one copy of each work was to be deposited in the Library of Congress within one month of the date of publication. The Act of 1870 took the place of all previous regulations. It included various types of works of art, and did away with the local District Court system of registry. The Librarian of Congress in Washington was now appointed to be "Copyright Officer," to receive a printed title page of every book before its publication, and, within ten days after publication date, two copies of the complete work.

The Library of Congress owes to this regulation a unique collection of literary "dreams that never came true." It has in its possession today the deposited title pages for many books which never passed beyond the stage of the author's manuscript, if they went as far as that. There are, of course, a large number of unimportant plans recorded, but also some very interesting ones which are not known except in those deposited title pages. Together with the various other types of copyright records in the Library of Congress, this is bibliographical source material of first-rate importance for the history of American literature, of the book trade and of printing.

It is of distinct importance to note that the first new step in the international field of literary property after the Civil War was the establishment, in 1868, of the International Copyright Association, which probably owes its origin to Charles Dickens' second trip to

America in 1867. Beginning with this date the demands for America's participation in an international arrangement became articulate, and hardly a year passed without the proposal to the Washington legislators of a new scheme or some revised older plan by a member of Congress. Three presidents successively went on record in favor of a regulation which would heal a rather painful wound in international intellectual relations. Sermons were preached by ministers on the subject, appealing to the conscience of the educated classes. In 1883 a new association was formed, the "American (Authors) Copyright League," followed in 1887 by the "American Publishers Copyright League."

In spite of all these sincere efforts the matter was postponed again and again. Not until 1891, over fifty years after the first proposal of 1837, was a measurably adequate law passed. And even then it was not ideal, not free from certain awkward limitations. America did not become signatory to the Berne Convention, which had been developed in 1886 and had become effective in 1887. That agreement provided automatic mutual protection of literary property for the authors of all countries that were members of the Convention. The American law did not provide for "automatic" protection (copyright on creation) and was only effective in regard to countries which specifically agreed, by separate treaties, to protect American authors. Also, it made obligatory three formalities in order to obtain copyright: to print a notice of copyright in the book, to register and deposit, and to observe the "manufacturing clause," that only those works were to be protected which were set up and printed in the United States.

It is hard to understand why a measure so universally desired by public-spirited individuals and by professional associations of undoubted integrity should have been held off for so long. It is difficult to gather clearly from the published accounts of the controversy who really led the opposition to the law so successfully, and by what means the legislative body was kept inactive over such a long period.

Congress did postpone the matter again and again. Quite likely there was not much interest then in a matter of so specialized a nature and of such apparently limited importance—compared, at least, with other more obviously pressing problems. It is possible, too, that the old aversion of American politicians to enter into international commitments may have played a part in their failure to act more promptly.

More important was the fact that the true nature of the issue was not clearly recognized. Apparently the matter of copyright protection was confused in people's minds with the matter of protective tariff.

It should be mentioned in this connection that the three decades after the Civil War saw a bitter and complicated tariff struggle. The British publisher, Alexander Macmillan, wrote to his friend MacLehose back in Scotland, on the outlook for a proposed New York branch of his firm: ". . . Their high tariff is a terrible drawback undoubtedly, and in case of an international copyright taking place, if the high tariff continued, American publishers would reap the benefit." The book tariff had risen from 10 per cent in 1846 to 25 per cent in 1864, according to a recent study by Donald Marquand Dozer, who also showed how it was favored by various branches of the publishing industry and by groups of its employees, and also by some outstanding authors, Aldrich, Holmes, Howells and Whittier among them. Henry Houghton came to be known as the leading protectionist. One of the aims of high tariff as brought out in the tariff commission hearings of 1882, was to keep out "objectionable foreign ideas." Opponents of a high tariff were found chiefly among academic, scientific and foreign language groups. The McKinley Tariff of 1890 finally permitted the free entry of books not written in the English language, and the Underwood Tariff of 1913 reduced the rate from 25 per cent to 15 per cent. Recent trends have favored a low tariff.

In any event, international copyright had a difficult time in the nineteenth century. In certain cases we do know who protested against such legislation. In 1872, for instance, the publishers of Philadelphia went on record against it, claiming that "Thought, when given to the world, is, as light, free to all." This is a very clear-cut repudiation of the basic moral principle upon which all protection of literary property rests. Why the Philadelphia group should have taken such a stand becomes perhaps more evident from their further reasoning. Copyrighting, they felt, was a matter of domestic law. Any foreigner, they said, could get protection of his literary property by becoming an American citizen. "The good of the whole people and the safety of republican institutions would be contravened by putting into the hands of foreign authors and 'the great capitalists on the Atlantic Seaboard' the power to make books high."

In the same year the house of Harper in New York publicly opposed international copyright legislation, mainly for the reason that it would raise the prices of books and would thus interfere with the education of the people. The average English fiction, one must remember, was published in London in three volumes at 30 shillings. But by 1878 the firm had changed its attitude. They themselves now submitted the draft of a bill in which they appeared in favor of the law, stressing at the same time a strong protection of the interests of American publishers.

The compositors' unions and other labor organizations in the printing industry opposed international copyright because they felt its effects would damage the interests of those employed in the book manufacturing industries. It was at their instigation mainly that the manufacturing clause was embodied in the law of 1891.

The International Copyright Act of 1891 remained in force until the Copyright Code of 1909 was passed. This took the place of previous laws and regulations and covered in its scope not only literary works, but also works of art and music. The manufacturing clause of 1891 was not only retained, but reinforced by demanding that foreign books, in order to enjoy legal protection in the United States, had to be not only set and printed, but also bound, in this country. One important exception to this rule, however, was included in the law upon the insistence of R. R. Bowker. Original works of authors in other than the English language were exempted from the manufacturing clause, and could be copyrighted by registration and the deposit of a single copy of the edition of the country of origin. But the Code of 1909 was a disappointment to those who had hoped that America would join the Berne Convention, or at least make fully equivalent arrangements with other nations. The United States still demanded the depositing in Washington of actual copies of any work for which protection was expected, the specific printing into books of any language of a copyright notice in English, and the manufacturing requirements for works in the English language. Professional and trade associations as well as responsible individuals have continued, and are continuing today, their efforts on behalf of a fully automatic copyright and American membership in the Berne Convention. Unfortunately, the situation has become vastly more complicated from the fact that protection of literary property is bound up in law-making with the protection of works of art and of music. Photography and the motion picture, the phonograph and the radio have presented problems of unprecedented complexity, and the arrival of television has not made things easier.

Hardly a year has passed which has not seen some copyright legislation introduced into Congress, but for the most part, the changes have not been major ones. In the early thirties the Vestal Bill for entrance in the Berne Union passed the House but was left on the Senate calendar. Beginning in 1938 the Shotwell Committee labored for nearly two years in an effort to reconcile the various groups and their often conflicting interests, but with no tangible results. In the continuing absence of the United States from the group of nations joined together in the Berne Convention, a series of bilateral agreements has covered our international relations. The wartime difficulties of communication between America and Europe were responsible for an extension of the British-American ad interim privileges mutually agreed on in 1944, which terminated on December 29, 1950, by Presidential proclamation. The Celler Bill, discussed presently, covered ad interim copyright. The growing piracy of United States titles in China led to the conclusion of a copyright treaty with that country in 1946, which subsequent political developments have left without much effectiveness. The next year brought Pan-American discussions in Washington which culminated in the proposal of an Inter-American Copyright Convention on the Rights of the Author in Literary, Scientific and Artistic Works, still to be ratified by most of the countries. The following year, 1948, saw reciprocal copyright legislation established between the United States and the Philippine Republic, granting to authors and copyright owners in each country the benefits of the copyright laws of the other country.

A famous case revolved around the publication of authorized and unauthorized translations of Adolf Hitler's *Mein Kampf*. Here the American courts decided, in November, 1941, that even a Hitler, whose legal status in connection with the original 1925 edition was defined as a "stateless German," should have the same protection under our copyright law as the "national" of any country with which we have a copyright treaty. It has been pointed out that this decision was of particular benefit to the large group of refugee authors, whose rights were thus secured, by a strange coincidence, in connection with the book of a man who had made them refugees. It should also be pointed out that the neat sum of $22,666 in accumulated royalties has not been made over to Mr. Hitler or his heirs, but is held by the Alien Property Custodian.

Two important steps on the road to a better international copyright situation were taken in recent years. On June 3, 1949, the so-called Celler Bill became public law in the United States. The new law extends the time in which interim copyright for a foreign work in the English language may be obtained, from sixty days to any time up to six months after publication; it protects a work so registered and bearing a notice of American copyright for five years from the date of publication, instead of for six months from date of application; also, and this is perhaps the most important improvement, it provides that the United States publisher may import up to 1500 copies of the foreign edition in five years, thus providing ample time to test the book's market here. It would also seem that this provision favors the importation of the very class of books which it is particularly difficult to publish and market in postwar America, namely, serious critical or creative writing neither addressed to a mass audience nor yet to the highly specialized groups.

In 1949 UNESCO took up the question of international copyright as an appropriate part of its functions. An international committee, including three American members, has begun gathering data and developing a program. It hopes not to disturb the important gains made by the Berne Convention and other treaties but, perhaps with simple regulations, to include more countries, since, in addition to the United States, Russia and China, none of the South American countries except Brazil belong to the Berne Convention.

However, let us return to the period 1860-1890. The fact that in spite of many sincere efforts almost the entire century passed before an international copyright agreement became effective was a major factor in the history of the book trade of those years. There was such apparent confusion and casualness in publishing methods that one sometimes wonders how it was possible for the various firms to live through these decades without utter ruin, and, as a matter of fact, with a frequently very favorable balance.

To simplify the complicated picture of conflicting tendencies and counteracting interests, it is perhaps best to consider the effects of these conditions upon the various groups likely to be affected. One might say that there were altogether six different groups to be considered. These are first the authors, second the publishers, and third, the public—these three groups existing in each of the two countries, America and England. The situation in the retail book trade will be taken up later on.

Of these groups, the English public is hardly affected and can therefore be left out of consideration. The groups most unfavorably affected were probably the English authors and the English publishers. For, under the law as it stood, there was nothing to prevent an unscrupulous printer or publisher in the United States from reprinting any work of an English author without any compensation to author or original publisher. Undoubtedly, there was a great temptation here to ruthless and quite safe exploitation with an excellent prospect of profit. However, in actual practice, certain restrictions came to be set up, for not only the English publisher and the English author lacked protection, but also the reputable American publishers had no legal weapon whatsoever against their less scrupulous competitors. This led to bitter price-cutting battles of amazing proportions. Entire novels were printed on the cheapest paper in miserable print, often in the form of serial issues and at ridiculous prices, sometimes as low as twenty or even ten cents for an entire novel.

It was not only a question of competition between publishers of the same city, but also between the publishers of one city and another. Something has been mentioned of the animosity which Philadelphia publishers felt toward their ever more successful New York competitors. In the rivalry to bring out pirated editions of the most popular English novels the New Yorkers often had the advantage, for the reason that the ships bringing first copies of a novel from abroad came to New York first. They exploited their lead with ruthless vigor. As a countermeasure, Philadelphia publishers would sometimes take the English book to pieces, distribute the parts to a number of different printers for composition and presswork, complete their edition within twenty-four hours after the arrival of the first copies from England, and rush copies to New York City where they were put on the market ahead of the editions of their competitors!

There was one way of tempering this disgraceful struggle. The American publisher could arrange to buy from his English colleague advance sheets of a new novel before it even appeared in England, and therefore before his American competitors in his own or any other city could possibly get hold of a copy. The reputable houses welcomed this arrangement, not only for their own protection's sake, but because it made it possible for them even without legal obligation to pay their share to the English publisher and author. As a matter of fact, considerable sums were paid in this manner for advance sheets of important English novels. The Harpers paid £1250 for Dickens's *Great Expectations* and £1700 for a novel by George Eliot. The great American houses realized the advantages of this arrangement. They voluntarily respected each other's arrangements with British publishers and refrained from going after a competitor's British authors. This was the backbone of the so-called "trade courtesy" which over many years took the place of legal arrangements and which served its purpose well enough for a time. It was, of course, no adequate substitute for a real law which would embrace everybody. In his *Memoirs of a Publisher*, George Haven Putnam tells how even publishers of the first rank would occasionally break the rules of trade courtesy, when the temptation proved too great, or when one publisher had had a quarrel with another one and saw an opportunity to even the score. The worst offenders were, of course, the outsiders, the avowed literary pirates, who specialized in reprinting works which showed signs of success on the lists of the reputable American houses. These pirates worked with a small overhead; they never paid royalties or other compensation to the English publisher or author; they printed in the cheapest fashion and, furthermore, they cashed in on the publicity which the reputable publisher had already started and in which he might have had invested considerable sums. Thus the delicately established equilibrium of forces was once again upset. Particularly in the seventies and eighties the unscrupulous reprinting grew to such proportions that even the big houses felt it necessary to enter extensively into the cheap reprint field in order to maintain their markets. The paper-back series of those days, such as the Chicago "Lakeside Library," and the "Seaside Library" and "Franklin Square Library" in New York were landmarks in this struggle.

The lack of legal protection for literary property had also very unfortunate effects upon the American authors. As long as it was possible to print the works of the most famous English writers and poets at ridiculously low costs, hardly a publisher in this country would consider encouraging unknown young American authors. Authorship as a profession, in fact, did not really become possible in America until after 1891, the date of the international copyright agreement. The comparatively indifferent standard of letters between 1860 and 1890 was surely not only due to cultural conditions. The best proof of the damaging effects of the bad conditions prevailing during most of the century was the appearance of vigorous new talent among American writers soon after the law of 1891 had been passed.

In still another way American authors were often victims of these lawless conditions. Occasionally English publishers would reciprocate the bad treatment which they had received from their transatlantic colleagues by pirating in turn those works of American authors which promised success with the English public. In these cases, too, the American author was the party most unfavorably affected. It has not been generally understood how much of this pirating was done in England. For example, Peter Parley and Alcott outsold in pirated editions any English author of the time. Longfellow outsold Tennyson, *The Wide, Wide World* outsold *David Copperfield*.

The last group which remains to be considered is the American public. The prevailing conditions were advantageous to them so far as the prices of books kept getting lower and lower, and the books of even the most distinguished authors could often be had for but a few cents. But these volumes were not particularly desirable as possessions, for not only were they produced without any love or care as to physical appearance, but their texts were anything but authentic in many instances. English books issued as cheap reprints in America during those years were often ruthlessly cut and altered to adapt them to the supposed taste of the public. The English authors had, of course, no say in the matter and saw themselves not only deprived of their royalties, but, on top of that, had to swallow their indignation over mutilation of their work.

There was also from all this a real loss to the American public because of the fact that the American author, as we have just explained, had such a slim chance of success. Under better conditions, much of interest, value and beauty might have been produced during those years in America, by men and women who, as it was, realized that the profession of letters would not offer them a livelihood.

In his *Golden Multitudes* Frank Luther Mott has spoken in favor of "the literary 'free trade' of the pre-copyright years." There is no question about the availability, during those years, of a good many titles at extremely low prices—an impressive early demonstration of the possibilities of mass production and distribution of books. That these advantages, nevertheless, had to be paid for heavily, will be evident to the reader of these pages. It would be unfortunate, indeed, if the precedence in cheap publishing created by the lawless nineteenth-century methods were to be accepted as a model for current and future developments, in spite of the obvious desirability of inexpensive mass editions of worthwhile books.

Another disturbing factor in the complicated play of forces was the nearness of Canada. This important section of the British Empire is bound by innumerable threads of economic, industrial and cultural bonds to the United States. The Canadian book market has frequently been a bone of contention between the publishers of the various countries, and the triangle England—United States—Canada is always carefully watched whenever European and American publishers contract for a book.

General Characteristics of American Publishing

The three decades following the Civil War brought about a marked change in the character of American publishing, noticeable as much in the publishing programs of the important firms and in their choice of media, as in their economic policies and geographic distribution. It was decidedly a period of transition. Most of the important existing firms, one recalls, had been founded in the years before the middle of the century, and they had been organized originally to cater to some special branch of the trade: Little, Brown for law books, Ticknor and

Fields in the medical field, for instance. Immediately after the Civil War there still lived and worked the fine old gentlemen of the "good old days" of American publishing. There were the brothers Harper, George Palmer Putnam, William Henry Appleton, the first Charles Scribner, and the two Lippincotts. They were assisted by their sons and future successors, by the younger generation of Harpers, by George Haven Putnam, William Worthen Appleton, the second Charles Scribner. These men had inherited the traditions of their fathers, they were keenly interested in their profession and were men of taste and culture. They took an active share in the intellectual life of the community, were members of the various literary and academic clubs, trustees of institutions of higher education. Their firms flourished and grew. But they gradually developed away from the older type of specialized, personal family business, approaching a new kind of large scale general publishing organization, which began to dominate the picture. With this development there emerged clearly those characteristics which to a large extent have remained typical of American publishing to the present day.

European publishing, by and large, is still carried on by firms which cultivate a certain well-defined subject or group of subjects, a condition which has grown out of the very roots of tradition. We need only to remember that the fifteenth century printer-publisher, practically without exception, was a specialist, catering to the needs of his own locality and social environment. Markets have, of course, expanded rapidly, but the preference for specialization has continued to the present day. There is, above all, the truly literary publisher, who surrounds himself with a group of authors of definite literary standards, with whom he remains in close contact. The imprint of such a publisher on a book is a guarantee for a certain minimum level of quality. Very few publishers attempt to devote themselves to more than one or two important fields, and a few minor supplementary fields. Alongside of the literary publisher, in the sense just described, there is a large number of scholarly and scientific houses. Not only law, medicine and theology, but also science and natural history, geography, economics, sociology and government, fine arts, the drama, music, and also children's books are cultivated by publishers almost exclusively devoted to one of these fields. Textbooks on the various subjects are published either by the firms who rule in these fields, or by special textbook houses. There are, of course, also "general" publishers in European countries, but they are the exception rather than the rule.

In America, on the contrary, a large proportion of the important firms are general publishers. They have built up their business by publishing in many fields whatever promised success. Expansion brought new departments devoted to various special subjects, and a variety of new experiences. Most of the large nineteenth-century firms in America included on their lists novels, biography, travel and discovery, poetry, popular science, history, politics, economics and business, music, gift books and children's books, and, of course, magazine publishing.

Only certain types of books are traditionally in the hands of specialized publishers. First in volume and importance are the school and textbook publishers, and the religious book houses, which contribute a very considerable portion of the entire output. Then there are the medical publishers and the law book firms, two groups which have witnessed early concentration in a few large organizations; the publishers of technical books, and certain other specialized firms, such as the music publishers and the play publishers who form independent groups. Subscription book publishers might also be mentioned here. Of course, some of these fields are cultivated also by the general publishers in their special departments. In other words, it can be said that in continental Europe most firms have remained special publishers, and only a few follow a policy of general publishing, while in America most firms are traditionally general publishers, and only relatively few devote themselves to specialized interests. The reasons for the predominantly general character of American book publishing are not hard to find. It can be said that in a country where the periodical press dominated the scene in chronological and functional priority, the publication of books was already in itself a form of specialization. Also, the all-over division of interests into definite subjects can be seen as a criterion of settled communities, stable conditions and some degree of cultural maturity. That is exactly the reason why New England publishing before the Civil War could afford to specialize to the degree it did. By the same token it is evident why, after the Civil War, with the mounting effect of industrialization and mass production in a rapidly expanding society, restless with enterprise and economic opportunism, general publishing became the predominant pattern. Another factor was the instability of a list predominantly made up of fiction when price-cutting became so prevalent. Other lines, such as medicine, law, science, reference sets, plays and textbooks could be sold directly to consumers at stabilized prices.

The great increase in the popularity and importance of various kinds of magazines also worked against specialization. In the decades before the war, the number of magazines published had shown a slight decline. Towards the end of the war the trend reversed itself, and a decided and lasting boom set in. In his study of the American magazine, Frank Luther Mott has estimated that during the two decades, 1865 to 1885, the number of periodicals published annually multiplied over four and a half times. The total number of books published annually between 1869 and 1890 was doubled, according to our estimates on page 321. These figures are tentative ones, but even with the allowance of a wide margin for error there seems little doubt that in this spectacular increase of reading matter magazines once again gave a much more lively account of themselves than books. There was hardly a leading firm which could get along without magazines. In the memoirs of the great publishers of those days one finds it explicitly stated as a sound business rule, that books alone do not pay. The retailers, of course, had the same experience.

The importance of the cheap reprint series is another outstanding characteristic of latter nineteenth-century American publishing that should be emphasized. It played a peculiarly significant role. The *Brother Jonathan* enterprises of the forties had demonstrated the possibilities of low-priced publishing based on literary piracy. A second wave struck the country in the seventies. Frank L. Mott has pointed out that the competition in books priced at less than one dollar continued steadily after the forties. At the end of the war, the dime novels published by Beadle & Company and by their competitors acted as pacemakers for the various series of full-length reprint novels. Piracies of English novels retailing at twenty-five cents and the *New York Tribune* reprints, which sold at ten cents a volume and twenty cents for two volumes, containing an entire English three-decked novel, were possible through the lowering of paper prices and various technological advances in production methods. The Lakeside Library of ten-cent quartos, started by Donnelley, Lloyd & Company in 1875, brought sharp new competition which in turn was answered in New York by Beadle & Adams' Fireside Library, George Munro's Seaside Library, and a host of followers. The long-established houses, too, entered the field, notably Harpers with their Franklin Square Library of ten cent quartos. The next step was the publication of cloth-bound reprints in convenient pocket sizes at fifty cents, introduced by John B. Alden in 1879, soon followed by a flood of paper-bound books in the eighties. This was started by John W. Lovell, who was joined in the field by a group of old and new firms which accounted for no less than twenty-six libraries by 1887, all publishing handy-sized volumes in paper and, from the middle eighties on, in cloth.

Increased concentration of publishing activities in an ever diminishing number of national centers also characterizes the latter decades of the nineteenth century.

The Regional Distribution of Publishing

The geographic distribution of American publishing in the second half of the nineteenth century is fairly easy to recognize. New York, without a doubt, now occupied the leading position, with Boston in the second and Philadelphia in the third place. This closes the list of the centers of national importance.

Before the war, the South had had its own centers of literary culture, with Charleston and Richmond prominent as production and distribution points. The adverse effect of the Northeast concentration on the Southern book trade had already started before the outbreak of hostilities. The loss of influence and importance was not arrested in any permanent way by the brief rallying of regional publishing in the Confederacy.

The most important centers beyond the Alleghenies were Cincinnati, Chicago and San Francisco, each important for a while in their general publishing activities, but soon turning towards regionalization and specialization. Indianapolis with the Bowen-Merrill Company (later Bobbs-Merrill) furnishes a solitary example of successfully continued general publishing outside the great centers. Long before the Civil War Cincinnati had risen to prominence in publishing for the West and the Southwest. It was a general booktrade center of considerable importance, with type founding and stereotyping facilities and active jobbing and retailing. It also played a significant role in the organization of trade associations.[2]

The J. A. & U. P. James Company was known to everyone in the Mississippi Valley. They were often referred to as the Harpers of the West. "The major trends of the Western book trade," writes Sutton, "were reflected in U. P. James' fifty-year career. His general publishing and excursion into the schoolbook trade were typical of the trade of the thirties and forties. He continued general publishing into the 1850's when the eastward gravitation of general publishing made it increasingly necessary for western bookmen to rely upon specialties. James adjusted to this situation by specializing in cheap publications beginning in the middle fifties . . . During the latter part of the third quarter of the century, as the age of regional publishing drew to an end, the character of James' business gradually changed until the transition from a regional publishing and jobbing house to a local bookstore was complete."

Chicago, young and quickly expanding, was still gaining ground in general publishing. While known today chiefly for its important special houses, the city harbored in the nineteenth century some fairly diversified publishing activities by such firms as S. C. Griggs and Company, from which Jansen, McClurg & Company branched out, the latter succeeded by A. C. McClurg & Company. These firms all maintained the traditional double function of publishing and retailing under one roof. St. Louis and Milwaukee, while primarily printing centers, still enjoyed a certain importance for their publishing activities.

San Francisco held its own as a regional center well into the second half of the century. This was due, in no small measure, to the activities of the romantic figure of Anton Roman, Bavarian-born miner and book pedlar, who settled down as a San Francisco bookseller, wholesaler and publisher in 1857. His program may be called a really classic example of regional publishing, unfolding step by step as the needs of the new

[2] At the suggestion of William Charvat of Ohio State University, Walter Sutton has completed an exhaustive study of the Cincinnati book trade, aided by the award of the Elizabeth Clay Howard fellowship of the Ohio State University. It is to be hoped that this excellent study, which bears in manuscript the title, *The Western Booktrade; Cincinnati as a nineteenth century publishing and book trade center*, will see publication in the near future.

community developed. He supplied the miners with technical and legal information as well as with recreational reading; he provided for the farmers and homesteaders books about the history and the resources of their chosen lands, together with practical handbooks on agriculture, horticulture and the care of vineyards; he offered books on the culture and literature of the Orient, to further an understanding of the stream of new immigrants from across the Pacific; he brought out schoolbooks and juveniles for the children of the miners and farmers; he branched off into general literature, gave Bret Harte his first chance to appear before the public as editor of a little gift-book-anthology of California verse, and published his *Luck of Roaring Camp* in the second issue of his magazine, "The Overland Monthly." He failed in 1878, in the aftermath of the panic of 1873, made a brief comeback in the eighties, chiefly in the subscription field, but soon retired permanently from the book field.

The new trend towards general publishing on a very large scale was unfavorable to all but the biggest centers. Increased frequency and speed of communication and transportation, making possible a far-flung net of traveling representatives and nationwide publicity campaigns, the availability, in the big centers, of manufacturing facilities, especially of bookbinding machinery which, unlike printing presses, could not be used for other work—these factors all favored gravitation toward a few focusing points, chief among them New York.

The Great Publishing Houses
New York

The largest and most influential New York publishing house in the nineteenth century was also the oldest of the group. As early as 1817, the brothers James and John Harper, compositors and printers, had opened a modest printing establishment in New York which in the course of thirty years witnessed a really fantastic development. When the Civil War broke out, the House of Harper, then in the hands of the four original brothers, James, John, Joseph Wesley, and Fletcher, was actually one of the most successful publishers of the world. Their lists of novels, their standard editions of world literature, their schoolbook series, all embodying forward-looking principles of selection and of marketing, had received a most favorable reception everywhere; the various series were continuously expanded and new groups successfully added.

Harper's Magazine, one of the first monthly periodicals with illustrations, had started in 1850, and *Harper's Weekly,* which appeared since 1857, had become a veritable household institution. In 1853 the firm underwent a devastating fire, but this meant a really welcome opportunity for the erection of a fine new fireproof building, and the purchase of much up-to-date printing equipment. With untiring energy and courage the Harper brothers looked confidently into the future.

During the war the publishing house had kept its own staff of reporters and artists at the front, who in words and pictures furnished a lively and authentic record of events. The illustrations of *Harper's Weekly* during that period are first-class source material. Some of their wood engravings—we are still in the days before halftone printing—were based on Gardner's famous photographs of the war, but the majority of the cuts were made from drawings of the staff illustrators sent in from the front.

The magazines of the Harper firm, as a matter of fact, were the true life nerve of the enterprise. Soon after the war, in 1867, there began to appear *Harper's Bazaar,* the famous literary fashion magazine, which to this day, though under other ownership, enjoys a world-wide reputation. The first number of *Harper's Young People* appeared in 1879. This was the heyday of the Victorian novel, and serialization of two or three different English novels appeared simultaneously in the *Magazine,* the *Weekly* and in the *Bazaar.* Already before the war the Harpers had become the leading publishers of Dickens, paying considerable sums for advance sheets. The close contact with English publishers, and the opportunity continuously to test in these magazines the taste of the reading public, and gradually to influence it, was a very great advantage to the book publishing departments, too. All the successful English novels which had first appeared in one of the magazines were issued later in book form. Also, the contacts of the magazine editors with the new generation of American authors, with the national and regional authors, with the chroniclers of the war, with Wild West story-tellers, with California mining-story writers, and last but not least, with the literary representatives of the conquered South, all these contacts turned out to be of great value to the Harper book publishing interests. Also, the Harper magazines played some part in the political life of New York, city and state, as well as of the nation. The powerful caricatures of Thomas Nast, the famous political cartoonist, have helped to increase the influence of the firm. This, too, brought certain definite advantages for the book publishing end of things, because it helped in securing official adoptions for school and textbooks.

The authentic source book for the history of the firm is the memoirs of J. Henry Harper, a grandson of Fletcher Harper, the youngest of the four original brothers. *The House of Harper*, published in 1912, is an impressive volume of almost 700 pages, illustrated with fine portrait engravings. Written in the form of a chronicle, the book is full of the most interesting information on the literary, social and political history of nineteenth century America. Among many other things, there is a very fair description of the somewhat unfortunate part which the firm played in the question of international copyright. The very detailed account of the matter is written with the understandable desire to vindicate the position of the firm, yet the story is so accurate and impartial that it is of distinct historical value. The author of this monumental volume published, in 1934, a second book entitled *I Remember*, in which he recorded his memories of friendships and contacts with men and women of his own time—with Mark Twain, Woodrow Wilson, Theodore Roosevelt, William Dean Howells, Bret Harte, Henry James, James McNeill Whistler, Ellen Terry. He died in January, 1936, in Paris.

D. Appleton & Co. is another old firm which dates back to 1825 or 1827, and which had developed from a bookstore. In 1848, when the founder retired (he died a year later), Appleton's was one of the great publishing houses of the world. The business was carried forward by the four sons, headed by William H., one of the strong figures in American publishing history. Their *New American Cyclopedia* was brought to successful completion during the Civil War. Here, too, the decades between 1860 and 1890 saw great changes, changes which eventually were to turn the old, personally conducted firm into a large, impersonal business organization, comparable in structure and fields of interest to the other large publishing houses. Appleton, too, developed inexpensive series of English and American fiction, such as their well-known "Town and Country Library." There were also voluminous books on foreign travel and scenery, such as *Picturesque America,* edited by William Cullen Bryant, *Picturesque Europe, Picturesque Palestine.* Particularly important from a scholarly point of view were some of their medical and scientific publications. Sir William Osler's *The Principles and Practice of Medicine* appeared first in 1892, and reached a printing of over 300,000 copies. Under the editorial direction of Edward L. Youmans, the works of the great group of English scientists, Darwin, Spencer, Huxley and Tyndall, were published in America by Appleton, as well as the "International Scientific Series" and notable books in the field of education. Of the famous Webster's *Blue Back Speller,* which the firm had taken over in 1855, no less than 62,000,000 copies were sold by 1889. The part played by Appleton in the publishing of Lewis Carroll's *Alice in Wonderland* is an amusing one. The book was to appear at Macmillan's in London in 1865, illustrated with wood engravings of the Dalziel brothers after brilliant drawings by John Tenniel, which in turn were based upon the author's own charming sketches. But author and illustrator were so disappointed with the printing of the wood engravings that they demanded the cancellation of the entire first press run. Macmillan thereupon printed a new edition which was completed towards the end of 1865 and appeared with the date 1866. A goodly number of the original copies were distributed as a gift to various children's hospitals in London. William Worthen Appleton happened to be in London at the time, and he managed to secure another lot from the rejected first printing. He cancelled the title page and put in a new one for his own firm, dated 1866 like the official and definitive English first edition. Thus the true first edition was really sold here in America! Of the original edition with the original English title page intact, there exist only a very few rare copies.

The important publishing house of Putnam, too, is an old firm. George Palmer Putnam came to New York in 1829 as a bookseller's apprentice. In 1833 he entered the firm of Wiley & Long as a partner, the firm then becoming Wiley & Putnam. During the Civil War Putnam placed himself at the disposal of the government, and only in 1866 returned to his publishing activities. During that same year his son, George Haven Putnam, entered the firm as a junior partner, followed in 1871 by his brother, Bishop, and in 1872 by another brother, Irving.

The firm's name now became G. P. Putnam's Sons. Old Mr. Putnam was particularly interested in reviving *Putnam's Monthly Magazine*, which he had started in 1853. The times seemed favorable for developments in that direction. But other publishers, too, had made the discovery that magazines were important to their business, and much to his disappointment Mr. Putnam had to abandon the magazine after a few years. *Putnam's Magazine* was bought up by Scribner's, who had been more fortunate with their *Scribner's Monthly*. George Palmer Putnam died in 1872 and left the business in the hands of his sons. Under their direction the firm developed very quickly on a broad scale. The firm played an important part in the industrial development of the book manufacturing industry, so characteristic for these decades. Many of the large publishing houses, such as Harper, Appleton, Lippincott, and Houghton, Mifflin had their own manufacturing plants. Upon the initiative of Bishop Putnam the Putnam firm founded the Knickerbocker Press in 1874, which started as a complete manufacturing department for the publishing firm, and developed so successfully that it was made into a separate organization. It was moved, in 1891, to New Rochelle, where the Knickerbocker Press began to accept work for other firms as well.

In one important regard the house of Putnam differed very decidedly from some of the other large publishers. George Palmer Putnam, and after him his son, George Haven, during all of their lives were unreservedly devoted to the cause of international copyright. One after the other, father and son devoted their untiring efforts to the fight for this vital reform, and there was no committee, no proclamation, where the name Putnam did not figure prominently in favor of American participation in an international agreement. It should be added that the firm was ready to face the consequences of this attitude and to refrain from unauthorized reprinting of English authors. This led, on the other hand, to an early and systematic encouragement of American authors. Before the Civil War Putnam's had published a new and complete edition of the works of Washington Irving, which saved that author from the peculiar oblivion which sometimes beclouds the memory of a great master almost immediately after he has reached the pinnacle of success. *Putnam's Magazine* had from the start been intended for the exclusive publication of American literature, which may, of course, have been one of the reasons why it could not survive the competition of other, less idealistic magazines. In the eighties Putnam published a valuable series of the writings of the men spiritually responsible for American independence, men like Alexander Hamilton, Benjamin Franklin and George Washington. They also developed their long and widely read series, "The Stories of the Nations" and "The Heroes of the Nations."

An account of the great publishing firms of the nineteenth century would be incomplete without mentioning the house of Scribner. Its history goes back to the firm of Baker & Scribner, founded from the outset as a publishing house, and first located in the basement of the Old Brick Church at the corner of Nassau Street and Park Row. The original partners were Isaac D. Baker, who died in 1850, and Charles Scribner the elder, who after his partner's death took Andrew C. Armstrong and Edward Seymour as partners into the firm, changing its name to Scribner, Armstrong and Company. A separate organization, Scribner, Welford & Co., developed the handling of English importations. The older Scribner died in 1871, and in 1878 A. C. Armstrong retired from the business. The firm was then called Charles Scribner's Sons, and the direction of the business fell first to J. Blair Scribner, the oldest son, and after his death in 1879 to the second son, Charles Scribner, who expanded the firm's activities and its reputation. He was joined by his younger brother, Arthur H. Scribner. Of particular interest were the magazines of the firm. A special department was organized to cultivate the magazine field, which became a quite independent unit. *Scribner's Monthly* was founded in 1870 by Roswell Smith with the assistance of Dr. John G. Holland and Charles Scribner. The older Scribner magazine, *Hours at Home*, was abandoned in favor of the new enterprise, which was organized for that purpose under the name of Scribner & Co. Ten years after the elder Scribner's death, in 1881, the second Charles Scribner and Dr. Holland retired from the magazine firm, and their share was taken over by Roswell Smith, the original founder of *Scribner's Monthly*. Smith wanted a new name for the magazine and for the firm to run it, and he hired Dr. Holland as chief editor. Thus the famous *Century Illustrated Monthly Magazine* came into being. It was published by the Century Company, and appeared until the year 1930, when it was merged with the Forum.

The Scribner firm, in the meantime, had by no means abandoned the lucrative magazine field, and in 1886 they presented to the public a new periodical called *Scribner's Magazine*, published by the Scribner Publishing Company, which appeared until 1939. It quickly became one of the outstanding American monthlies, due largely to the caliber of such editors as Robert Bridges and Edward L. Burlingame. His son Roger has paid him discerning tribute: [3] "He was committed, first to his own understanding of literature which had set high levels. But he was committed, too, to a business which must live. He knew that art might please even when it failed, in its entirety, to please him but he refused to let it degrade, whatever the pleasure."

Very much an exponent of the new publishing trends of those years, the juvenile magazine *St. Nicholas* made its appearance in 1871. This paper, too, was a child of Roswell Smith's fertile brain, but at the same time it was the continuation of numerous smaller publications in Boston, Chicago and Philadelphia, proving once more and in its own particular field, the leadership of New York.[4] One must not speak of the *St. Nicholas* magazine without mentioning its rivals, *Harper's Young People*, which became *Harper's Round Table*, and from Boston, *The Youth's Companion* and *Wide Awake*.

The Century Company, founded in 1881, was one of the fine substantial imprints. Frank H. Scott, its president for many years, was one of the distinguished leaders of New York publishing. This company published Nicolay's *Life of Lincoln* and *Battles and Leaders of the Civil War*, and such best sellers as Alice Caldwell Hegan's *Mrs. Wiggs of the Cabbage Patch*, well remembered by the trade. Because many of their volumes were planned by De Vinne, their books were distinguished in format. The *Century Dictionary* was also one of their great enterprises. In 1933 the company was merged with Appleton.

The rapid metamorphosis of American publishing from a quite narrow parochialism to enterprising, expansive business operation is typified in the history of Dodd, Mead & Company. The firm was

---

[3] In Scribner's anniversary volume, *Of Making Many Books,* 1946, based on hundred years of correspondence between publisher and author, "this extremely substantial ghost outside the gate."

[4] *The St. Nicholas Anthology*, edited by Henry Steele Commager and published by Random House in 1948, is a nostalgic revival of some of its best stories and pictures.

founded in 1839 by Moses Woodruff Dodd at the Brick Church Chapel house on Park Row, when he bought a share in John S. Taylor's business and, after a brief partnership, ventured forth alone in 1840. He started as a religious publisher with volumes of Gardiner Spring's sermons, religious textbooks and a prospering retail department. The firm soon imported large quantities of Sunday school volumes from England. The literary field was hesitatingly entered with highly respectable fiction for young ladies, and children's poems. In 1867 Martha Finley's *Elsie Dinsmore* started the spectacular run of the Elsie books, which sold around 5,000,000 volumes in some seventy odd years. In 1870, Moses W.'s son, Frank H. Dodd, then aged twenty-six, and a nephew, Edward S. Mead, twenty-seven, took over the firm as Dodd & Mead, into the face of the awful depression of the early seventies. The two were nephews of Richard and Robert Hoe, who "came across handsomely with advice but sparingly with funds," according to Edward H. Dodd, Jr., who published a lively anniversary volume in 1939. Fine editions of standard English literature, carefully printed at De Vinne's, translations of important scholarly volumes on the fine arts, and the ambitious *International Encyclopedia* were important ventures. Spectacular earnings were made with such successful novels as those of E. P. Roe, Amelia Barr and Ian Maclaren.

A distinguished role both as a publisher and as an organizer of the American book trade was played by Frederick Leypoldt. Born in Stuttgart, Germany, in 1835, he came to America in 1854. He began his career by taking a position with F. W. Christern, and five years later he started a bookshop in Philadelphia. During the Civil War he entered the publishing field with translations of foreign books, some of which he had himself put into English; he wrote under the pseudonym of "L. Pylodet," which will be easily unscrambled by the skilled practitioner. In 1864 he opened a publishing house in New York and in 1867 he joined forces with Henry Holt. Their new firm, which was called Leypoldt & Holt, did not last very long, the partners separating in 1868. Mr. Holt carried on the book publishing as Henry Holt & Co. Leypoldt now turned to those fields where he was to make his most important contributions: the publishing of bibliographical magazines and of book trade periodicals. He abandoned his *Literary Bulletin*, when in 1872 he had the opportunity to become editor of a generously conceived and comprehensive organ for the entire American book trade. The *Publishers' Weekly* first appeared in 1872, and it took the place of two older magazines, the *American Literary Gazette* and the *Publishers' Circular*, which had been started as early as 1852. Leypoldt was fortunate in his intimate knowledge of the organization of the German book trade, with its century-old traditions and its well-weathered system of trade relations. The new magazine appeared as the official organ of both the Publishers' Board of Trade and the American Book Trade Association. From its very start the magazine proved its importance and usefulness as the mouthpiece of the entire American book trade.

The office also took an active interest in the public library field, which was just entering upon a most important phase of expansion. After Frederick Leypoldt's death, in 1884, Mrs. Leypoldt carried forward for thirty years the direction of the bibliographical work of the *Publishers' Weekly*. Richard Rogers Bowker, who had been in earlier association with Mr. Leypoldt on his periodicals, became the head of the firm, and he too carried on with unusual vision and enterprise. Mr. Bowker was active in many directions; it was he who with Melvil Dewey in 1876 had founded the *Library Journal*, and a few months later he helped to found the American Library Association. He also took up the fight for international copyright legislation with energy and vigor. His book on the subject has become a standard.

In 1877 Mr. Bowker added to his staff a young man by the name of Adolf Growoll, son of German parents, who had come over in 1848. Growoll was to become managing editor of the *Publishers' Weekly* under R. R. Bowker, and he made a lasting contribution to the development of professional standards in the American book trade. An influential member of the various organizations of his day, he is chiefly remembered for his bibliographical and book trade publications. He left behind him an important collection of source material on the American and British book trade, on trade associations and on paper-making, to which he added until his death in 1909.[5]

[5] This material is preserved in twenty large scrapbooks at the R. R. Bowker Company. Much of the contents have been photostated for the Library of Congress.

Mr. Bowker survived him by almost a quarter century. After his death in 1933[6] Frederic G. Melcher, who for some years had been co-editor of the *Publishers Weekly*, became the head of the R. R. Bowker Company.

Henry Holt, who had been associated with Leypoldt for a while, founded in 1868 the house of Henry Holt and Company and remained its head until his death in 1926. His cultured and well-informed mind was a steady influence toward quality and scholarship; yet the firm reached popular markets with such best sellers as *The Prisoner of Zenda* and *The Honorable Peter Stirling*. Among its projects was the "American Science Series" and notable among the authors was William James. In 1923, Mr. Holt published *The Garrulities of an Octogenarian Editor*, which sheds much light on nineteenth-century publishing.

Another concern founded in those years and active well into this century was the house of Stokes. It was organized by Frederick A. Stokes in 1881, two years after his graduation from Yale and one year after his first introduction to book publishing. Like the Putnam firm, Frederick A. Stokes made very particular efforts to seek out and encourage promising young American authors, which at the time was an exception rather than a rule among New York publishers. The firm also showed an early interest in art with the publication of large and costly collections of etchings by American artists, and it made successful efforts in the publishing of books for young people.

One of the smaller New York publishers was G. W. Carleton, particularly active in the low-price field. He had started his publishing activities shortly before the Civil War. He had *Les Miserables* translated, and it appeared and sold hundreds of thousands of sets. A similar experiment with some of Balzac proved a failure. Characteristic American humor came out under the Carleton imprint: Artemus Ward, Orpheus C. Kerr, Josh Billings and the vastly popular novels of Mary J. Holmes, Augusta J. Evans and Marion Harland. In 1866 he was joined by George W. Dillingham, who later succeeded him.

---

[6] To perpetuate his memory the Richard Rogers Bowker Memorial Lectures have been established, an annual institution at the New York Public Library "as an aid and stimulus to the study of book publishing in the United States and the mutual problems of authors, publishers, librarians, readers, all makers and users of books." The first twelve lectures have been published in book form in three volumes by The Typophiles.

Carleton was the publisher of J. C. Derby's *Fifty Years among Authors, Books and Publishers,* that mammoth source book on the history of the American book trade. A chapter of the 700-page volume is devoted to Carleton's activities as a publisher.[7]

E. P. Dutton & Co. commenced activities in New York in 1869. The firm had been founded in Boston by Edward P. Dutton, as a small bookshop particularly devoted to the sale of the religious books of the Episcopal Church. In 1865 Dutton with Charles A. Clapp purchased the famous Old Corner Book Store in Boston. This interesting old place had been started in 1828 and has passed through many hands. It has been observed that several of the Old Corner's owners afterwards became publishers, and the shop came to be looked upon as a breeding place for American publishers. Among Dutton's successes was the spectacular sale of the sermons of Phillips Brooks, and recently the A. A. Milne books. For long years the firm remained in the hands of old Mr. Dutton, who lived beyond the age of eighty and relinquished the reins only with his death in 1923.

Yet another New York publishing house, the Thomas Y. Crowell Company, had its origin in Boston, where it had developed from the bookbinding establishment of Benjamin Bradley, which in turn had been founded in 1834. It was in this firm that, perhaps for the first time on this continent, cloth was used commercially as a binding material. Thomas Young Crowell embarked upon his career there in 1856 as an assistant, working up to a partnership, and after Bradley's death, to the sole ownership of the firm. Crowell began publishing in New York in 1876, but the Boston bookbindery remained the property of the firm until 1900. It was moved to New York and given up, after a fire, in 1919. The Crowell firm was conspicuously successful in the field of poetry. They managed to sell between a quarter and a half million each of their editions of the poems of Robert Burns, of Byron, Tennyson

[7] The author of this work, J. C. Derby, was himself an active figure in the mid-nineteenth century book trade. He began publishing in Auburn, New York, in 1840, where he had previously worked in the retail trade, under the imprint of J. C. Derby & Co. In 1848 the firm became Derby and Miller. In collaboration with one of his two brothers, both bookmen, he established a San Francisco store in 1852, a plan which he abandoned upon the sudden death of brother George. The year 1853 saw him publishing in New York and from 1855 to 1861 he had Edwin Jackson with him, in the firm of Derby and Jackson. The next year the imprint Derby and Miller reappeared. Derby later became subscription manager of D. Appleton & Co.

and Browning.[8] Their "Red Line Poets," printed on tinted paper with red rules around the columns of type, were famous in their day. In 1885 Crowell's interest and enthusiasm for Russian literature began to show in his publishing program. Tolstoi was translated and brought out, and afterwards Gogol. Thus Crowell became an early sponsor for modern Russian literature in America.

Although the English firms who opened branches in New York will be discussed later, there is an early pioneer in that movement who should be mentioned now. The earliest New York branch of an English publisher was the Macmillan agency. The English mother house, it will be remembered, was founded by Daniel and Alexander Macmillan in 1843. Even before he was independent, Daniel had written to a bookseller friend: "You surely never thought you were merely working for bread! Don't you know that you are cultivating good taste among the natives of Glasgow; helping to unfold a love of the beautiful among those who are slaves to the useful, or what they call useful? I look on you as a great teacher or prophet, doing work just of the kind that God has appointed you to do." In 1867 Alexander Macmillan came to the United States where he saw the necessity for direct representation by an agency. Two years later the branch was opened, with George Edward Brett, an experienced London bookseller, at the head. Toward the end of the eighties, when his health was giving out, old Mr. Brett was able to lean on his energetic son, George Platt Brett, for assistance and support. The year of his father's death in 1890, the Macmillans asked him to take the elder Brett's place as manager of the American branch. He refused, but offered to buy in as a partner if they would organize the business in this country as an American concern, to which they agreed. In 1896 the American branch separated from the English house, and under the name of The Macmillan Company of New York, it became an independent corporation. The story of its development into one of the largest publishing houses in the country is chiefly of the twentieth century.

Boston

Perhaps the most prominent Boston publishing house toward the middle of the century was Ticknor & Fields. Their early history has

[8] See Mott, *op. cit.*

already been told. In 1868 James T. Fields, with a new partner, founded the firm of Fields, Osgood & Co., noted subsequently as the publishers of the *Atlantic Monthly*. Three years later Mr. Fields retired and Benjamin H. Ticknor, second son of William D., joined in forming the firm of James R. Osgood & Co.

In 1864 H. O. Houghton, who had founded the highly successful Riverside Press in Cambridge, had combined with Melanchton M. Hurd, then a partner in the old New York publishing house of Sheldon, in establishing the New York publishing firm of Hurd & Houghton. Other partners were Albert G. Houghton, Horace E. Scudder and George H. Mifflin. The name of H. O. Houghton was retained for the Cambridge business.

It was this firm which was merged in 1878 with Mr. Osgood's firm resulting in the house of Houghton, Osgood and Company. There were thus combined in one organization some of the best New England literary traditions, including the rights to many important books and authors of the Romantic and Transcendentalist movements, as well as the publication of the *Atlantic Monthly*. In 1880 the firm became Houghton, Mifflin & Co., changed in 1908 to Houghton Mifflin Company.

Another active Boston publishing house of today which goes back in its beginning to the earlier nineteenth century is Little, Brown & Company. Like other Boston publishing houses here mentioned they have emphasized quality rather than quantity in their publishing program. They became the publishers of Parkman and developed a law book department. They were, and still are, the publishers of John Bartlett's *Familiar Quotations*. Late in the nineties they absorbed another well-known Boston firm, Roberts Brothers. Under the direction of Thomas Niles, a man of fine taste in books, Roberts Brothers had published Louisa May Alcott, Helen Hunt Jackson, Edward Everett Hale and had launched the famous Wormeley edition of Balzac, the first complete edition in America.

We shall presently hear of the Boston publishers who specialized in texts and schoolbooks. Juvenile literature and books for Sunday School use, too, were published in Boston on a large scale. There were in particular two firms, well remembered today, which should be mentioned here because they were also general publishers.

Lee and Shepard was established under that name in 1862. William Lee had been a junior partner in the old Boston firm of Phillips, Sampson & Co., who had published Emerson's *Essays*, but had turned down *Uncle Tom's Cabin*, because they did not want to hurt their Southern trade connections. Charles Augustus Billings Shepard, too, had grown up in the book world. He had been a senior partner of Shepard, Clark & Brown, which discontinued business in 1859. Lee & Shepard built up an enormous list of children's books and were very successful with Sunday School literature. They published Sophie May and Oliver Optic, also Francis H. Underwood's handbooks of English and American literature and the "Golden Floral" series of popular hymns and ballads, got up as holiday gift books. Their New York firm, Lee, Shepard & Dillingham, had merged into that of Charles T. Dillingham, in 1875, the latter becoming a well-known wholesale bookseller.

D. Lothrop & Co. was established in Boston in 1868 by Daniel Lothrop (1831-1892) to cater to the needs of Sunday Schools and to specialize in juvenile literature. Previously Daniel Lothrop had developed a chain of drug stores where he had been successful with books. In 1850 he had bought a bookstore in Dover, New Hampshire. His publishing venture saw rapid expansion in the seventies and eighties. The popular juvenile periodical, *Wide Awake*, was started in 1875 and became *St. Nicholas*' chief competitor. The second Mrs. Lothrop, who wrote under the pseudonym of Margaret Sidney, was the author of *The Five Little Peppers*. This firm also published about 175 books by "Pansy." At the end of the century D. Lothrop & Co. brought out Irving Bachellor's *Eben Holden*, one of the great best sellers of the last generation. The firm's merger with Lee and Shepard to form Lothrop, Lee and Shepard Company took place in 1904.

Philadelphia

One of the most important publishers in Philadelphia after the Civil War, and still active, is J. B. Lippincott and Co. In 1827 Joshua Ballinger Lippincott had entered the book business in the employ of a bookseller named Clark, whose firm he purchased in 1836. At that time he made a specialty of publishing religious works, some of them issued as finely bound de luxe editions. In 1850, he boldly purchased Grigg & Elliott, an important old firm of retailers and jobbers. The house now expanded its publishing program, and joined the ranks of the big general publishers. Lippincott published books in practically every field of literature, as well as important medical and educational textbooks. *Lippincott's Pronouncing Gazetteer of the World* appeared in 1855, a monumental volume of over 2,000 pages, to be followed in 1870 by *Lippincott's Pronouncing Dictionary of Biography and Mythology*. Dr. Horace Howard Furness's *New Variorum Edition* of 1871 was a decisive stepping stone in Shakespearean scholarship. Successfully the firm weathered the difficult war times and managed even to put up a new building. In 1885 a joint stock company was founded, and when in the following year old Mr. Lippincott died, he was succeeded by his eldest son, Craig, as president, assisted by his brothers, Walter and J. Bertram, the latter active as chairman of the board of directors of the company until his death on January 19, 1940. In 1926 the direction of the business had passed to his son, Joseph Wharton Lippincott. *Lippincott's Magazine* was started in 1868 and continued in the hands of the firm until 1914, when it was sold to McBride-Nast and discontinued. Swinburne, Kipling, Oscar Wilde, Conan Doyle, Turgeniev, Jack London, and Brander Matthews were some of the authors whose writings appeared in the famous Philadelphia magazine. The good relations of the firm with English publishers and authors date back to a trip of J. B. Lippincott to England in 1851, and they were cemented by the establishment of a London branch office in 1875, which is still functioning.

Another Philadelphia firm was that founded in 1882 by David McKay, who had started his career in publishing as an employee of Lippincott. Mr. McKay began his own business by publishing an edition of Walt Whitman's *Leaves of Grass* which the Boston firm of James R. Osgood had abandoned due to threatened action in Massachusetts on the ground of the book's alleged immorality. Over the years David McKay Company absorbed several firms, building up a list of books on popular technical subjects. In 1903 McKay purchased the American branch of George Routledge & Sons and two years later added a line of cloth-bound juveniles from Street and Smith. Mr. McKay died in 1918. The business was carried on by his family until 1950 when it was sold to two young men who had been with Putnam, Quentin Bossi and Kennett L. Rawson. Alexander McKay, and his son,

David McKay III, are still active in publishing, having started a new firm, the Bell Publishing Company in 1949.

The shift of the center of book publishing to New York during the latter half of the nineteenth century has left many once well-known Philadelphia firms without successors. There existed in the seventies a string of flourishing publishing houses, publishers whose names are practically forgotten today. There were, for instance the firms of Kay & Brother, R. F. Cunningham & Son, Sower Potts & Co., and T. B. Peterson & Brother, noted for their cheap editions of the complete novels of Charles Dickens. Porter & Coates became Henry T. Coates & Co., and were the publishers of immensely popular boys' books by Ellis, Castlemon, and Alger. By the end of the century the list was absorbed by the rising house of John C. Winston & Company. Altemus & Co., already mentioned for its possession of a complete edition bindery used in the production of their cheap reprints, was founded by T. S. and Henry Altemus in 1842 and survived as a family business until about 1936.

Important Special Publishers of the Period

While it is perfectly true that the over-all trend favored general rather than special publishing, this does not mean that successful special publishing did not exist in the latter nineteenth century. There are even some instances of withdrawal from the general field in favor of specialization. This was the case with the famous old publishing house of Lea & Febiger in Philadelphia. Founded in 1785 by Mathew Carey, and originally emphasizing periodicals, the venerable firm has seen many changes. The house had been among the leading American publishers of Sir Walter Scott, it had been prominently associated with the development of subscription bookselling, and it had manifested, long before the middle of the century, a warm interest for native American authors. Cooper and Irving had the Carey imprint and Edgar Allan Poe's first collection of short stories, for instance, appeared in 1839 under the imprint of Lea & Blanchard. Mathew Carey was succeeded by his son, Henry Carey, and his son-in-law, Isaac Lea, and they by that fine scholar and citizen Henry C. Lea. Towards the middle of the century, and this is of symptomatic importance, the competition of the

New York publishing trade began to be felt rather keenly. Particularly the rising star of the house of Harper caused so much concern that the old Philadelphia firm decided upon a change of policy. The general publishing activities were gradually reduced and a concentration was aimed at the medical book field. In 1851 the first step was made in this direction and since then the firm has occupied an important place among the leading medical publishing houses of the country. The present firm name of Lea & Febiger was adopted in 1907, when Christian C. Febiger joined the brothers Lea as partner.

Other old publishing houses in the field of medicine and science in Philadelphia which have survived to the twentieth century are the firms of P. Blakiston's Sons & Co., started in 1843 and absorbed by Doubleday in 1944, and the W. B. Saunders Company, who issued their first book in 1888 and occupy an outstanding position in the field.

The Bible publishing house, A. J. Holman Company, begun 1859 in Philadelphia as William W. Harding & Co., with Andrew J. Holman as a partner, is typical of many active religious houses in many localities.

New York was and still is the seat of a number of substantial special publishers in various fields. However, it is very important to note that there has been no particular concentration of special publishing in New York City. In marked contrast to the trends observed in general publishing, many of the houses devoted to a particular field have been founded in various centers throughout the country, where many of them have remained to this day.

Most of the special publishing houses which we find in New York after the Civil War have their roots in establishments founded earlier in the century. One of the oldest scientific book houses in the country is that of John Wiley & Sons. John Wiley was the son of the old New York publisher, Charles Wiley. He had started independently from his father in 1828, had joined with George Long in 1832, and in 1833 with George Palmer Putnam, until 1848 when the partnership was dissolved. In 1865 John Wiley admitted his son, Charles, to the business and in 1875 his son, William H., to form the imprint John Wiley & Sons. It was Major William H. Wiley, an engineer, who was responsible for the development of the firm as a great technical publishing firm. At one time they brought out American editions of John Ruskin, but "scientific textbooks and industrial works" were their main line of development. Science, technology and business are today the fields extensively cultivated by the old firm.

David Van Nostrand started his publishing activities in the field of engineering and science sometime around 1848. He was a vigorous, enterprising personality whose tastes and aptitudes determined the course of his firm for many years to come. Born in 1811, he had been an assistant and after that, a partner of John P. Haven, the New York bookseller and publisher, another early firm with predominantly religious interests. Later, Van Nostrand was active in New Orleans, then a center for military engineering. His friendship with General Barnard brought close association with a group of young Army officers, his later authors and editorial consultants. He returned to New York and to bookselling and publishing on his own. He now specialized in the publication and importation of military science and history, both for professional Army use and for the layman. The firm became known as official publisher for the United States Army and Navy. General Casey's *Infantry Tactics*, published by Van Nostrand in 1862, was immediately adopted as standard training guide for the northern armies, but also reproduced in Richmond for the use of the Confederate Army. Gradually, science and technology assumed their dominating position in the firm's program, with close attention to mining, metallurgy, railway engineering, chemistry and electrical engineering. John A. Roebling, the creator of the Brooklyn Bridge, saw his *Long and Short Span Railway Bridges* published in an imperial folio edition at twenty-five dollars. In 1869 began the publication of *Van Nostrand's Eclectic Engineering Magazine*, later merged with *The American Railroad Journal* to become *The Railroad and Engineering Journal*. The seventies saw the start of famous pocket-size volumes in "Van Nostrand's Science Series." Edward Nichols Crane, nephew of the founder of the house, succeeded him after his death in 1888 as president and, later, principal owner of the D. Van Nostrand Company.

The oldest American medical publishing house, long known as William Wood & Co., grew out of a small bookstore which Samuel Wood (1760-1844) established in New York in 1804. He soon began to publish a series of primers and juveniles, some of which were illustrated by the famous wood engraver, Dr. Alexander Anderson. The medical interests were developed by a son, William Wood, who followed in 1817 two brothers who had previously joined the firm. The store became the resort of noted physicians and the importation of medical works, mostly from England, was gradually supplemented with the firm's own medical publications. William Wood's son, William H. S., joined the firm in 1863 and the name was now William Wood & Co. In 1866 the *Medical Record* started to appear and other journals, including pharmaceutical trade journals, followed. Medical reference works and medical encyclopedias became the specialties of the house. Gilbert C. Wood, grandson of William, died in 1931 and the house became a division of The Williams and Wilkins Company of Baltimore the following year.

Another old New York firm is the Orange Judd Publishing Company, probably the first American publishing house to specialize in books on farming, gardening and kindred subjects. The firm traces its ancestry to the bookselling and publishing business of Charles M. Saxton, founded in 1836. When his firm took over the publication of the *American Agriculturist*, Orange Judd, who had been connected with that magazine since 1853, came along. Upon Saxton's death in 1864, Orange Judd bought out his business and combined the Saxton and Judd lists, including the *American Agriculturist*, into one publishing venture and gave the firm his own name.

The business of P. J. Kenedy & Sons, in New York, designated in 1895 as "Publisher to the Holy See," was taken over by Patrick John Kenedy in 1866 upon his father's death, after he had assisted in the business for six years. The firm devoted itself to Catholic authors whose work did not seem to find a place on the lists of secular publishing houses; they published novels dealing with Catholic life, ascetical and apologetic works, books on Ireland, a complete series of textbooks in the parochial school field, and annual Catholic directories. Benziger Brothers is another important Catholic house. The American firm of Benziger Brothers was founded in 1853, although the original house dates back to 1792 in Switzerland. The firm specializes in Catholic publishing and bookselling, but also sells church goods and religious articles. A leader in the publication of devotional books was John J.

Murphy & Co. of Baltimore, the city of the first American Cardinal. They operated from 1837 to 1943, when P. J. Kenedy took over their Cardinal Gibbons titles.

Another religious book house of New York was established there by Fleming H. Revell. In 1869 he had started to publish in Chicago *Everybody's Paper*, a religious monthly. The fire of 1871 destroyed his entire establishment, but he started afresh and was so successful with sermons, tracts, and other writings by Moody and similar evangelists that in 1887 he established a branch in New York, followed by other branches in Toronto, London and Edinburgh. He moved his family to New York in 1906 and some years later established the headquarters of his business there.

Funk & Wagnalls, best known for their dictionary publishing, also began as a religious book house in New York. In 1876 Isaac Kaufman Funk, a clergyman by profession, started publishing. He was joined in 1878 by Adams Willis Wagnalls. They developed a program of religious and moral books, specializing in inexpensive books for the clergy and in religious reference works. In 1912, their *New Standard Dictionary of the English Language* was published after years of work. Its editors provided many of the reference books for the Funk list.

The well-known law publishing firm of Baker, Voorhis & Co. came into existence under that name when Peter C. Baker, whom we have already met as an old-time New York printer, purchased in 1866 the law publishing business of John S. Voorhis.

The firm of Samuel French, the largest publisher of plays in the country, was founded in 1830 in England. The New York office was opened in 1850. Another well-known publishing house in this field is Walter H. Baker & Company of Boston, founded there in 1889 with an affiliate in New York, The Fitzgerald Publishing Company, successors to the old house of Dick and Fitzgerald.

Alfred Smith Barnes was the founder of the schoolbook concern of A. S. Barnes & Co., which succeeded in establishing its dominant position in practically every branch of that business. Barnes had started in 1831 with D. F. Robinson of Hartford, who moved to New York in 1835. In 1838 Barnes formed a partnership with a mathematics professor, Charles Davies, and returned to Hartford to establish his own firm. In 1844 he moved the company to New York. It was his idea to

issue national series of standard books in every department of education. His son, Alfred Cutler Barnes, joined the firm in 1858, was made
partner in 1865, and head of the business in 1888. The educational departments of the firm, together with those of a number of other big
firms, were consolidated in 1890 to become the American Book Company. The old name of the firm was continued as a publishing house
specializing in physical education and sport, directed by John Barnes
Pratt, and after his death, by his son Lowell.

Specialists in a rather particular sense were Street & Smith in New
York, founded in 1855 by Francis Scott Street and Francis Shubael
Smith. Their *New York Weekly*, advertised as "a journal of useful
knowledge, romance, historical items, amusement etc.," was one of the
first story papers published in that period. They concentrated, perhaps
more intensely and for a longer period of years than any other firm, in
the marketing of ten-cent paperbacks and various cheap "libraries" and
popular fiction serials. Frank Luther Mott has pointed out in the
Golden Multitudes that they stayed in the field long after the introduction of international copyright and the collapse of the nineteenth century piratical libraries. Their books were still on the newsstands after
World War I, almost up to the time when the Boni Books and the
Modern Age Books ushered in the new era of cheap paper books. The
firm is still active, but not in the book field.

Continuing our journey over the map in search of special publishers,
we find in Hartford, Connecticut, and in other New England cities
traditional centers of school and textbook publishing. G. & C. Merriam
Company of Springfield, Massachusetts, is of course famous as the publisher of *Webster's New International Dictionary*. In 1797 Dan Merriam and his brother had founded a newspaper in West Brookfield,
Massachusetts, and had branched out into miscellaneous publishing, including successive editions of William Perry's *Royal Standard English
Dictionary*. Upon Dan Merriam's death in 1823, his sons George and
Charles joined their uncle in the management of the business, which
they moved to Springfield in 1831, and where, the following year,
they founded G. & C. Merriam Company. Upon Noah Webster's death
in 1843 they bought from J. S. & C. Adams of Amherst the unsold copies
of his dictionary and the right to publish it in the future. That was the
foundation of their fortune. The dictionary was adopted for use in

common schools about 1850, was enlarged and freely illustrated in 1859, and given as a premium to subscribers of the *New York Tribune* early in the seventies. *Webster's International Dictionary* appeared in 1890, followed by the *New International Dictionary* in 1934. The dictionary in its many editions has remained the main enterprise of the firm to this day, but they have also in the past published Bibles, schoolbooks, law books, reference books, and other volumes of a similar nature.

In Boston, too, several important publishing houses specialized in school and textbooks. One of the most prominent firms was founded in 1867 by the brothers Edwin and Frederick Ginn, and it has remained in the front rank to this day. Edwin Ginn happened to meet a young student of the Harvard Law School, who in 1876 had graduated from Amherst. His name was George A. Plimpton. Ginn was so impressed with the young man's ability that he invited him to join the business. Young Mr. Plimpton accepted and took charge of the New York office. In a few years he was made a member of the firm and upon Ginn's death in 1914, he became head of the business, retiring in 1931, five years before his death.

In 1874 Ginn Company had accepted as partner young Daniel Collamore Heath, who later on in 1885 severed his connections with the firm and founded his own business, at the head of which he remained until his death in 1908. His main interest was in the natural sciences, in chemistry, economics and in foreign language classics.

Another leading textbook house founded in Boston is the firm of Silver, Burdett & Company, established there in 1885 by Edgar O. Silver, after a short apprenticeship with the Appletons. The firm later moved to New York City. One reason for the rapid success of this house can be seen in Mr. Silver's interest in new methods of musical instruction. In the course of time the firm developed other fields of interest, and it is today among the leading textbook houses of the country. Of similar substantial character is the house of Allyn & Bacon, located on Beacon Hill.

As we leave the publishing centers of the Eastern seaboard and turn towards the West, we find that Cincinnati, Ohio, in the days after the Civil War played a considerable part in the publishing of religious books and school and textbooks.

There was, for instance, the old Van Antwerp Bragg Company, one of the main contributaries of that all-absorbing stream, the American Book Company, which we shall discuss later on. Then there were Chase & Hall, Hitchcock & Walden and Robert Clarke & Company. This latter firm remained active until 1924, when via their successor, Stewart-Kidd Co., specializing in the field of drama and the theater, Appleton in New York bought up their rights. Robert Clarke & Company also had a well-organized retail department. The increasing specialization in the publishing activities of Uriah Pierson James has already been touched upon.

The picture of Chicago special publishing is dominated by the firm of Rand, McNally and Company. The house originated in 1864 when Andrew McNally, who was born in Ireland in 1836, joined forces with William H. Rand, a printer from the Pacific Coast. It is almost superfluous to say that their enterprise was crowned with unusual success and that they have remained to this day one of the most important American publishers of atlases and guides. Their children's book publishing program is also an active part of their business. While a natural depository point for every large educational house and the place of manufacture for enormous editions, Chicago is also the home office of such well-known textbook houses as Scott, Foresman & Co., Row, Peterson & Co., Benjamin H. Sanborn & Co. and Callaghan & Co., who, directly or indirectly, have their roots in nineteenth-century firms.

An interesting special publishing firm was started in Milwaukee a few years after the Civil War. In 1870 the Morehouse Publishing Company was founded, and in 1884 they opened a retail store there. They were among the leading religious publishers and booksellers of the country, and have continued steadily to this present day. In 1935 they opened a store in New York, and in 1938 Edwin S. Gorham, Inc. was merged with Morehouse to form the Morehouse-Gorham Company.

There is no room in this volume to do full justice to the publishing of the various kinds of theological works in America. This is regrettable, because it is a very characteristically American story. The publishing of the Bible, of prayer books and liturgical works, of theological studies and of all kinds of devotional literature occupies, of course, an important part in the publishing annals of every European country. But the singularly important role of the church in the social growth of the American nation and the tremendous number of different religious denominations in existence here have lent unique color and vigor to religious publishing and bookselling. P. Marion Simms' careful study of *The Bible in America*, an excellent, comprehensive volume, tells of the activities of the regular religious publishers as well as of the various scripture-distributing agencies, such as the American Bible Society.

One of the largest religious publishing organizations, the Methodist Book Concern, is also one of the oldest existing publishers in America. Since its foundation in 1789 it has seen a truly astonishing development. It was founded for the purposes of furthering Christian education through the distribution of moral and religious literature, and in order to take care of the publication, the manufacture and the sales of such literature.[9] The closely knitted, nation-wide organization of the Methodist Book Concern includes every type of production and distribution agency. The profits from these various activities are collected in a fund designated for the benefit of Methodist ministers, their families and survivors, and for the "traveling supernumeraries." The large Protestant churches, Methodist, Baptist and Presbyterian, divided territorially by the War between the States, built up important publishing and bookselling organizations centering in the North at Philadelphia and New York and in the South at Nashville. Other religious organizations have followed the same plan, one of the largest being the Christian Science Publishing Co. of Boston, issuing books, magazines and a daily paper.

A word should be said about the nineteenth-century music publishers, although it is easily understood that here is a field which has very little connection with general and special book publishing. There existed after the Civil War a well-diversified network of relatively small firms with their own retail outlets, many of them devoted to popular and often fairly trivial music, with centers in Boston, New York, Philadelphia, Baltimore, Cincinnati and Chicago. The seventies and eighties saw rapid and permanent absorption and amalgamation, particularly in the hands of the Oliver Ditson concern of Boston, which

[9] In 1868 John Lanahan, D.D., was elected an assistant book agent of the Methodist Book Concern. His discovery of irregularities in the purchase of raw materials, in the management of the bindery, and in several other ways, also his own trials and tribulations resulting from these discoveries, are the subject of an interesting book which he published in 1896 under the title, *The Era of Frauds in the Methodist Book Concern at New York*, at the Methodist Book Depository in Baltimore, Maryland.

soon established branches in all important centers. Among the houses which survived independently to the present day are Theodore Presser of Philadelphia, who took over the Ditson list, G. Schirmer in New York and Carl Fischer, also in New York.[10]

Sales Methods and Book Outlets

Having made ourselves acquainted with the structure of the publishing business and with some of the representative firms, we should now attempt to answer the question, how the books of these publishers reached the public. Once again a glance at European conditions is tempting, because the comparison is illuminating and instructive.

In Europe, in the second half of the nineteenth century, a large majority of all books sold to the public were sold through regular bookstores. These bookstores, as a rule, were part of a well-organized system, based on the particular traditions prevailing in each country. The most orthodox conception of what a regular bookstore should be like, existed in Germany. To become a bookseller you had to serve an apprenticeship of from two to four years, during which time you were thoroughly trained in the organization of the publishing trade, in ordering, shipping and accounting methods, in selling books to customers, and last but not least, in the appreciation of literature and in bibliographical methods. After your apprenticeship you became a junior and later a senior clerk, and if you had luck or some financial backing you became a partner or went into business on your own. If you wanted to become a publisher you would also be advised to start your career by serving a retail bookseller's apprenticeship. There were also opportunities for more formal theoretical training, such as the Leipzig School of Bookselling, which was a sort of book trade academy.

The old-time German bookseller considered himself a servant of literature, and he was proud of his training and his literary judgment. He would have felt it beneath his dignity to handle anything but books, and possibly magazines and music. Stationery in particular he felt to be outside of his realm. In England, this feeling was not as strong, although there, too, if the store did sell stationery, the tendency was to set aside a separate room for these things. It can also be said that in

[10] The most authentic source for the names and dates of the nineteenth century American music publishers is found in Dichter and Shapiro's *Early American Sheet Music*, New York, R. R. Bowker, 1941.

Europe there was, and is, very little contact between the individual publisher and the book-buying public. The publishers did not encourage direct sales to the readers of their books, but concentrated on selling to the many bookstores throughout the country.

All this was quite different in nineteenth-century America. The role of the legitimate bookstore was not as prominent as in Europe, and there were many other channels of distribution. When William H. Appleton was asked, in 1880, which was the best selling book on his list, he replied: "Webster's Speller . . . and it has the largest sale of any book in the world except the Bible. We sell a million copies a year . . . We sell them in cases of seventy-two dozen, and they are bought by all the large dry-goods houses and supply stores, and furnished by them to every crossroads store."

The question of well-trained bookstore clerks was one of the problems that worried responsible members of the book trade. That all was not well may be gathered today from the frequent discussions of training conditions in the trade journals. *Publishers' Weekly*, for instance, in its issue of October 25, 1873, published an appeal for the improvement of working conditions and a better training system, together with detailed information on the Leipzig School of Bookselling.[11]

Those who think of the sale of books in drug stores and various other non-bookish outlets as a freakish habit of the twentieth century would do well to read the title page of *Geyer's Reference Directory*, published in 1889, which has the following wording: "Geyer's Reference Directory of the Booksellers and Stationers of the United States and Canada. Including all Dealers in the Book, Stationery, Paper, Toy, Fancy Goods, Notions, Picture and Picture Frame Trades, including a complete list of Wholesale Druggists and the Purchasing Agents (Stationery) for Railroads, Also Book Publishers, Bookbinders, Lithographers, and Manufacturers of Stationers' Specialties. . . . Also Containing a List of All Paper Mills in the United States and Canada, giving Daily Capacity and Kinds of Goods Manufactured. 1889. . . . Published by M. Shirley Geyer, 63 Duane Street, New York."

This is an interesting and amusing example of the hodge-podge of trades with which the booksellers' profession was mixed up, and it gives some idea of the variety of outlets through which books in those days

---

[11] See page 375 for later developments along these lines.

reached the public. It is quite impossible to gather from the miscellaneous collection of names and firms any idea which of the listed establishments were booksellers, and where in the United States they were located. Nor have I found in any other publication a satisfactory survey of retail firms in the second half of the nineteenth century. Many bookstores were in the hands of men who were also active as wholesalers and as publishers. On the following pages are listed merely a few of the firms that were genuinely concerned with the selling of books in those days and which, in one form or another, have survived to the present time.

In the same way in which the old-time Boston publishers were more readily comparable to the literary publishers of Europe than other firms in this country, so did the booksellers of old Boston provide perhaps a closer analogy to European bookshops than the stores of other cities. We have already encountered the Old Corner Bookstore, that famous breeding place of publishing houses. When E. P. Dutton went to New York in 1869 to become a publisher, he sold the store to A. Williams & Co. In 1883 it passed into the hands of Cupples, Upham & Co., became Damrell & Upham in 1887, and in 1902 it was incorporated as The Old Corner Bookstore. Very little is really told by these dates and names. They are cold compared with the vivid recollections of the men whose memory goes back to those days. Anyone who wants to know what bookselling was like in Boston then, should not neglect to read Charles E. Goodspeed's delightful *Yankee Bookseller*. Even though it concerns itself mainly with later developments, one finds much that illuminates the old traditions. Goodspeed speaks primarily of rare book dealers, though not exclusively. He mentions, for instance, De Wolfe, Fiske & Company, then on Washington Street, now on Park Street, a store that sold new books to individuals and to libraries and acted as a wholesaler for small-town booksellers, which was a more profitable line of business then than now.

Cornhill was for years a center for New England retail bookselling, and so was nearby Washington Street, where not only the Old Corner but Little, Brown; William H. Piper, Estes & Lauriat and W. B. Clarke Co. were located.

In other cities of New England, too, we find bookstores "with a history." Israel Witkower's bookstore in Hartford, Connecticut, for instance, was founded in May, 1835. Seven times in the first century of its existence did the shop change its name and three times it was moved to a new location. Abraham Lincoln, Mark Twain, and Harriet Beecher Stowe were among the regular customers of the store. When Jenny Lind came to Hartford in 1881 to sing in a church, her manager rented the shop to sell his tickets. He sold twice as many tickets as there were seats in the church. When people realized that they had been taken in, there were broken windows and show cases.

In New York, in the days before the Civil War, the bookshop of Stanford & Swords had been famous, particularly for its religious books. Later the firms of C. S. Swords & Company and D. G. Francis developed from this store. Bartlett & Welford was a popular meeting place for collectors and literary men in the forties. In 1849 John Russell Bartlett withdrew from the firm, which continued as Scribner & Welford.

When, as the century turned, Dutton's and Putnam's had their two great bookshops on 23rd Street near Madison Square, when Scribner's was just below Madison Square on Fifth Avenue and Brentano's was just above, this section was indeed one of the retail bookselling centers of the world.

The story of Brentano's, retailers for eighty years, is an interesting record of three generations of American bookselling. The business was founded by August Brentano, a young immigrant from Austria, who in spite of the handicap of a slight physical deformity carved out a brilliant career for himself. In 1856 he was still selling newspapers on Broadway, but early in the seventies he was the owner of "Brentano's Literary Emporium." In 1873 his nephew, Arthur Brentano, then aged fifteen, joined his uncle in the business. When Arthur Brentano celebrated his eightieth birthday in the spring of 1938 he celebrated it by selling books at Brentano's bookstore, as he had done for the last sixty-five years. As assistant to his uncle, August, he had been joined early by his two brothers, August and Simon. In 1882 the younger generation took charge, with August, Jr., as president. In 1899 the bookstore was incorporated. In 1924 Brentano's moved uptown to the new retail center and undertook to extend their branch system, which had already included a large store in Washington. The depression led in 1933 to financial difficulties followed by successful reorganization.

It is of interest to note that in 1897 Brentano's opened a publishing department which was active until 1933. They were the publishers of the Merrymount Press edition of Benvenuto Cellini's autobiography and American publishers for George Bernard Shaw.

One of the mainstays of Brentano's has been the store's rich stock of books in foreign languages, imported from the various European countries. New York has always been a market for European books, and the New York book trade has always welcomed into its midst the importers of books from abroad.

An important firm in this field was the B. Westermann Company, established in 1848 by the brothers George and Bernhard Westermann, as a branch of their German publishing firm in Braunschweig. Around 1924 a consortium of twenty German publishers joined the German-American interests who wished to see the continuation of the old firm. In 1926 Ernest Eisele, who had been the manager of Brentano's foreign department since 1903, became the head of the B. Westermann Company. The firm was closed a few months after Pearl Harbor on the filing of an involuntary petition in bankruptcy. At approximately the same time a closing order was issued by the Treasurer of the United States.

Some of the men who have in later life become the heads of importing concerns which are still prospering today, received their early training at Westermann's. Ernest Steiger, for instance, the founder of the New York book importing firm of that name, entered the employ of Westermann sometime before the Civil War, and he remained with them for ten years. Another member of the staff, who subsequently established himself in a similar branch, was Gustaf E. Stechert. He founded his firm in 1872, and established purchasing offices in Leipzig, in London and in Paris. In 1889 Alfred Hafner, who had been trained in Switzerland, entered the Stechert firm. He became the manager in 1899, and later took in his two sons, Otto H. and Walter A. Hafner, as partners. The retail store of the firm is only one of the many departments of the large concern, now called Stechert-Hafner. They supply European books to a large number of universities, colleges and public libraries throughout the United States.

In an attempt to search out and mention here good booksellers in other parts of the country, one does best not to insist too much on the distinction between real booksellers and those stores which handle, along with other things, books. Reed's in New Brunswick, for instance, founded in 1848 as one of the oldest bookshops in the country and the oldest extant store in New Jersey, also carried wallpaper and window curtains, and today the books, although prominently displayed, form but one of many departments.

Apart from the old centers of culture along the Atlantic coast it is particularly in the Near West and in the Middle West that one finds, in the days after the Civil War, a good many bookstores. Missouri, Michigan, Illinois and Wisconsin seem to be pretty well provided with retail outlets, and Ohio, with Cincinnati as the center, exceptionally so. Among the bookstores of that city the James Book Store Company, already discussed for its publishing, has an interesting history. The firm goes back to the year 1831. No railroad had then crossed the Alleghenies, and, situated as it was on the banks of the heavily freighted Ohio River, Cincinnati practically dominated the Middle West. At the same time it was the gateway to the South. Uriah Pierson James and his brother Joseph commenced with a printing shop and a stereotyping establishment, and developed—like the Harpers in New York—into an important publishing house. The bookstore was opened around 1840, and is still operating.

Another Cincinnati bookstore of the old days still in operation was opened by Robert Clarke in 1863. In 1910 the firm was taken over by W. K. Stewart and John G. Kidd, and today is called John G. Kidd & Son. We have already spoken of the publishing department of the Clarke firm.

That these old firms have been able to hold their own to the present day is all the more remarkable because Cincinnati as a city lost much of its former influence and power in the further course of the nineteenth century. At the beginning of the seventies, however, this was not yet apparent. Together with New York, Philadelphia, and Boston, Cincinnati was a great center of the book trade. It was a popular convention place, where in 1873 the "Booksellers Protective Union" was founded, which soon developed into the "American Book Trade Union," and then into the "American Book Trade Association." This organization took the place of the "New York Publisher's Association," founded in 1855, which functioned under the names of "The Publishers Association" and "The Book Publishers Association" until 1861. The main task of these organizations was to clarify the conditions of the trade and the relationship between the publishers and the distributors of books. The chief problem that had to be coped with was the price cutting practiced between publishers, jobbers and retailers. Very serious efforts were made by responsible men in the trade to establish a comprehensive organization which would bring about a satisfactory solution of these difficulties. These attempts, however, brought no lasting satisfaction. We shall hear more about this presently.

Another old Ohio firm still active today should be mentioned here: The Burrows Brothers Co., Booksellers, Stationers, Engravers, of Cleveland. The store was founded there in 1873.

In Indianapolis there was the old Bowen, Merrill store which grew into the publishing firm of Bobbs-Merrill Company, but the retailing continues as the W. K. Stewart Company.

In Chicago vigorous retailing was practiced by a group of firms which also engaged in publishing and which acted as wholesalers on a very considerable scale. S. C. Griggs & Co., founded in 1848, and soon known as "The Literary Emporium of the Prairie," was considered at one time the largest book outlet in the country. A study of the record of this firm and its successors and competitors was undertaken a few years ago by Jack Cassius Morris.[12] He found that orders had been placed at Griggs for no less than 600 sets of the Waverley novels and 10,000 copies of *Enoch Arden*—indicating a sharp appetite for literary reading matter in the Middle West. In its State Street location, Griggs formed the nucleus of Chicago's famous "Booksellers Row," along with W. B. Keene, Cooke & Company and the Western News Company. Griggs himself retired from the retail end of the business after the great fire, to devote himself exclusively to publishing, and the firm was reorganized as Jansen, McClurg & Co. in a new location, which provided space for a rare book department. Here was the famous "Saints & Sinners Corner," frequented by Eugene Field and others. Jansen retired in 1886 and the firm became A. C. McClurg & Co. It was sold out in 1930, but its big wholesale house continues. The famous international bookstore of A. Kroch, although not founded until 1907, rapidly became a significant outlet through the Middle West. The Fred Harvey chain

[12] Unpublished thesis in the Library School of the University of Illinois.

now headed up in Chicago spread from Kansas City to cover the Santa Fe route.

In the Far West, too, in California and in what was then Washington Territory, there were, of course, "booksellers and stationers." Anton Roman, whose publishing activities have already been discussed, moved his bookstore from Shasta City to San Francisco in 1857, where he operated also as a large-scale importer and wholesaler, covering besides the city about a dozen interior counties. He published an extensive *Catalogue Raisonné* in 1861, which included many titles by Eastern publishers. He had his agents in New York, in Paris and London. In his lavishly equipped store in the Lick House Block, he announced, the "noble hall has its long tables covered with the choicest mental food culled from all climes and served up in the most magnificent style of binding."

In 1877 A. M. Robertson started his bookselling establishment in San Francisco. He was a staunch supporter of price maintenance on the Pacific Coast.

The largest outlet in the Pacific Northwest was started by J. K. Gill in Salem, Oregon, with stores now in Portland and Seattle. By 1885 Lowman and Hanford were established in Seattle and four years later John W. Graham in Spokane, and in 1891 Kendrick-Bellamy opened in Denver.

The southern states of the Union, and the Southwest in those years were not so well off for bookstores. By and large, these same regions have today fewer retail book outlets. There are, of course, a few notable exceptions. Hansell's opened in New Orleans in 1876, Legerton's in Charleston in 1888, Bell in Lynchburg in 1897, Mills in Nashville in 1892 and before the end of the century, 1898, the now influential chain of agencies for the Methodist Book Concern in Nashville, Dallas and Richmond started up.

We have made rather a point of showing that few booksellers showed any hesitation in adding other lines of goods to their stores. On the other hand, there were several types of shops which carried, among other things, books. There are, first, the borderline cases of the "stationers" and the "newsdealers," which carried some books in addition to their stock of paper and writing materials, newspapers and magazines, candies, cigars and cigarettes. There is also the interesting fact that already in those days the mixed warehouses or "dry goods stores" handled books. We shall see presently what a troublesome precedent was established by the inclusion of books in the stock-in-trade at these establishments.

The various retail outlets had, in the main, two sources of supply. They could buy either directly from the publisher, at a usual discount of from 40 to 46 per cent, or they could buy their books from a jobber who business it was to keep a large and representative stock from many publishers for the convenience of the retail trade. In the nineteenth century there were in existence a small number of strong and very energetic wholesalers scattered regionally about the country.

A good picture of the functions of the jobber can be gathered from an advertisement of Charles T. Dillingham, New York, in the *American Bookseller*, volume 23, 1888, which appeared five times from April to June upon the occasion of the firm's removal to larger quarters. It says there:

"We desire to call the attention of our customers and the trade generally, not only to the better warehouse room we possess for the display of the most extensive stock of books in every department of literature to be found in the country, but also to the great facilities for the prompt dispatch of all business intrusted to us, from a single 'pick-up' to that of one hundred cases, or from one volume to the thousand; offering, as we do, greater advantages to the trade as a jobber than can be found anywhere else, and always carrying a full stock in all descriptions of books. It is unnecessary to assure booksellers that we sell at the lowest prices possible; oftentimes lower than the publishers will; in fact, selling much lower than 'we like to do.'"

The activities of the jobber, like those of the bookseller were often not confined to books, nor were books necessarily their most important commodity. The American News Company, for instance, was, and still is, primarily a central source of supply for the newsdealers, but the firm also served as a wholesale house for stationers and booksellers and developed steadily a system of regional deposits of great efficiency. The firm also had its publishing department from where, since 1875, there was issued *The American Bookseller, A semimonthly Journal devoted to the interests of the Book, Stationery, News, and Music Trades*. The files of this periodical are today a very valuable source of information for the book trade conditions of those years.

The various sales methods so far discussed have in common the fact that the ultimate consumer buys his books not from the publisher directly but through various types of retail outlets. There were in addition methods by which the publishers would sell their books directly to the reader.

Foremost among these was the subscription method of bookselling, already discussed in its earlier phases. Henry Howe, the noted historian and bookman, who in the eighties called himself the "oldest publisher of subscription books in the Union," has made some interesting observations:

"This mode of circulating literature, as practiced in this country, is peculiarly an American invention. In Europe it is adapted to insure, in advance, the expense of costly works—with us, as a method—for the convenience of the purchasers—of engaging sales after a book has been issued. Our mode has grown out of the general desire at large for information, and the difficulties experienced by the mass in procuring just the kind adapted to them; for it should be remembered that the regular book merchant—the trader in ideas—is the very last man who emigrates—the very last to be established in a young community, and solely too from the absence of a demand for his services . . . millions of our people never in their lives have entered a bookstore, and millions upon millions do not annually average the possession of a single new book. . . . Ignorance everywhere rears his stupid front, and among the best weapons with which to vanquish him are books, and in the interior, with a vast number, the habit of obtaining and of using these will not be acquired unless brought to their very doors."

This statement, issued in an attempt to justify subscription bookselling, is a good explanation of its particular role in America, although it should be understood that advance subscription, too, was practiced. The absence of a well-developed, evenly distributed network of retail outlets, the same thing which in the twentieth century has aided the phenomenal growth of the book clubs, made subscription selling feasible and necessary. There seems to be some difference of opinion among expert observers on the question whether it reached its point of greatest expansion before or after the Civil War. In general, it is safe to say that the mid-century had brought an enormous increase in the number of settled communities without bookstores—towns, villages and farmsteads in which life began to offer enough leisure time for reading.

Some students of the nineteenth century have doubted that the books which subscription agents sold from door to door were really read. They have suggested that they were bought mainly for their prestige value, by quality folk and especially by those who wanted to be considered as such. In certain instances, and with some of these items, that was probably the case. It may have been true with a good many standard sets of famous authors. But there were always children around who were curious, and many of the books were planned for casual perusal, with their hundreds of illustrations and their anecdotal style of writing. So these books were read and used. Many of them were not literary in character, but practical, containing advice on letter-writing, legal transactions, medical care, housekeeping and gardening. Other groups of volumes sought to combine instruction and entertainment, usually in the form of anthologies, encyclopedias and dictionaries. Histories, general, national and regional, played a great role and so did biographies, especially the memoirs of General Grant. And then there was edification through the hundred different kinds of family Bibles and other devotional volumes.

The books were usually moderately priced, from $2.00 to $3.00. Some agents also carried cheap books, while certain sets or special editions sold for $10.00 or more. Most of the subscription books were octavos and quartos, in rather spectacular cloth bindings, heavily embossed and gilded, and with copious illustrations.

Subscription publishing was engaged in both by the regular houses, many of whom had their own departments for these activities, and by specialists in the field. Many of these specialists, Henry Howe in Cincinnati, for instance, or the American Publishing Company in Hartford, Connecticut, sold "by subscription only." One important reason for this was to defend themselves against the disadvantages of price cutting. They would obligate their agents by contract not to undersell each other, or for that matter themselves, and they could assure their customers of a steady price by not selling to bookstores.

Judging from the frequent advertisements in newspapers, through special circulars and in the backs of their books, the subscription publishers could always use new agents, to whom they offered fairly liberal terms. Controlled by regional supervisors, the agents would penetrate from their headquarters in the smaller towns into the thinly settled communities and to the isolated homesteads, providing in many hundreds and thousands of instances the only contact with reading matter. Contracts were signed on the basis of sample dummies, the required number of copies periodically supplied by the publisher on a cash basis, and delivery made on a second round of visits. It was a life similar to that of the old book pedlar, but it served to distribute a different type of reading matter on a different scheme of operation.

It was natural that subscription bookselling flourished in the Western book trade centers. Henry Howe was active from the later forties to the eighties, mostly in Cincinnati and later in Cleveland, with a branch in New Haven, Connecticut. Among the general publishers of the West, U. P. James in Cincinnati relied on itinerant agents for the distribution of many of his titles.

The most popular American author of his day, Mark Twain, was quick to recognize the special advantages of the subscription method for his own books. His connection with Elisha Bliss, Jr. of the American Publishing Company in Hartford, resulted in a vigorous and spectacularly successful sales campaign for *The Innocents Abroad*, closely co-ordinated with the lecturing schedule of the author, and later for *Roughing It* and *The Adventures of Tom Sawyer*. Mark Twain showed keen appreciation for the value of publicity and acquired a detailed knowledge of subscription selling methods. He used these, after the death of Bliss, in his own company, which succeeded in the sale of *Huckleberry Finn*, but failed later on. *Following the Equator* (1897) was the last book marketed by the American Publishing Company under a joint imprint with Doubleday, McClure. In 1895, after Harpers had begun to publish his *Joan of Arc* anonymously in their magazine, Mark Twain entered into an agreement with that firm for the publication of his books.

The San Francisco agent for the first edition of *Roughing It* had been Anton Roman, the most colorful publishing figure on the Coast. Late in his career he turned exclusively to subscription bookselling at a time, however, when various difficulties combined to decrease its popularity and the returns to be realized. "We are all familiar with the publishing 'rackets' that sprang up at that time," writes F. E. Compton in his Bowker Lecture, "high-pressure selling of cheap sets at exorbitant prices, working off antiquated works in new disguises, flooding the country with flashy books produced overnight on some spectacular event, and swindling the new-rich into buying so-called de luxe sets at ten or twenty times their real value." Nevertheless, subscription book-selling never ceased to exist. In fact, the nineties saw the beginning of a substantial subscription business of standard sets of authors which included the whole range of accepted literature. Among the firms which carried on to the end of the century and which provided valuable training for some of the later leaders in the field was the famous Boston firm of Estes & Lauriat. It was established in 1872 by Dana Estes and Charles E. Lauriat, who had both entered the Boston book trade sometime in the late fifties. They played a large role in the publishing of popular illustrated works in paper parts; Guizot's *France* and Duruy's *Rome* were phenomenally successful. They also realized that there was a market for well-edited and finely produced editions of the best English and French authors. Their set of the Waverley Novels was edited by Andrew Lang, and they published Thackeray, Carlyle, and one after another every standard author of general appeal. The partnership was dissolved in 1898. Estes carried on in the publishing end of things under the imprint of Dana Estes & Co. until his death in 1909, and in 1914 the list was bought from his sons by the then rising house of L. C. Page and Co. Mr. Page, a stepson of Dana Estes, had started publishing in 1897, having great success with such titles as *Pollyanna*, *Anne of Green Gables* and the "Little Colonel" books. He is still active as the president of his firm. When Estes and Lauriat was dissolved, the retail store became the Charles E. Lauriat Company. After the older Lauriat's death in 1920 his son took control and remained active, both as bookseller and a publisher of books on yachting and all matters of the sea, until his death in December, 1937.

A colorful person who had his start in the old firm was Walter M. Jackson, genius of subscription and mail order methods. In the nineties he branched off from the old house, sold hundreds of thousands of sets of Ridpath's *History of the World* through newspapers, joined forces with Horace Hooper, flower of Chicago's subscription and mail order enterprise, and in London bought from A. & C. Black all rights in the old *Encyclopædia Britannica*, for which they proceeded to organize an international half-price sale as a London *Times* edition. They laid the basis for a thirteenth edition of the Encyclopaedia under the sponsorship of the University of Cambridge, and the sale of this edition by direct mail campaigns was a high peak of mail order publishing. In the hands of two sons the firm is still active today, selling books by subscription throughout Latin America.

That subscription bookselling should have been watched very carefully in the other branches of the trade is not surprising. When the material offered was different from the regular products of the publishers, and as long as it was distributed in territories and by methods which did not impinge upon their own prerogatives, there was no particular reason to complain. But tension rose whenever books which the regular trade considered in their normal domain were kept away from them, or when dumping and price cutting created general confusion. There were publishers who sold indiscriminately to the wholesale and retail houses as well as to the customers directly. This seems to have been a very common practice in those days, which led to much friction and instability of trade conditions. Here, too, there were border line cases. Libraries primarily, then ministers, professors and teachers were considered as special book customers entitled to special discounts. In introducing new school or textbooks it was the practice to sell copies at a specially reduced price directly to these preferred customers for a stated period, although it was a question how long this was justified in each case.

American Book Auction Houses Since 1860

The account of colonial conditions and of the early nineteenth century includes a description of book auctions during those years. Many of the early auctions obviously served the purpose of selling newly issued works to the public and clearing the publishers' stocks of items which moved slowly. In the nineteenth century, and particularly in its second half, this function continues, but the American auctioneer assumes new importance as an agent for the American bibliophile, then entering the field as its greatest factor. The following brief summary will include the developments of the twentieth century.

In the early nineteenth century in Boston, we find Blake and Cunningham and a few others holding the field. Blake and Cunningham (later Cunningham alone) were succeeded by Howe, Leonard & Company, a firm which went through many changes until, in 1878, Joseph

Leonard retired and was followed by his assistant, Charles F. Libbie, already well known for his knowledge of books. Both he and his son, Frederick T. Libbie, who inherited the business, were genuine book-lovers and friends of the bibliographers and collectors of their day. After forty years of activity the firm of C. F. Libbie & Company withdrew from the auction business in 1920, to become dealers in rare books in Boston, where they remained active to the middle thirties. Most of the sales of important collections (Leffingwell's, Livermore's, Amor L. Hollingsworth's, etc.) of Boston and its vicinity during that period were conducted by them.

In New York the firm of McLaughlin & Blakely were advertising as early as 1823, and David Dunham and John Doyle were issuing broadside catalogs in the early nineteenth century, followed by Royal Gurley, who formed a partnership with John Pearson in 1830, later continuing alone and in partnership with H. Hill. A prominent name is that of William Gowans, better known as a bibliophile and bookseller, though he conducted a few auction sales. He began his bookselling activities by carrying books in a basket from door to door, looking for customers.

From 1860 such important sales as those of William E. Burton, George Brinley, and William Menzies were conducted by Joseph Sabin, the great bibliographer, maker of many catalogs, said to have been "killed by a dictionary" on account of his arduous labor in behalf of American bibliography. The third Brinley sale was the last at which he presided. It included the first copy of Gutenberg's 42-line Bible to be sold at auction in this country; $8,000 was paid for it. The first part of this sale also included a copy of *The Bay Psalm Book* of 1640, which then realized $1,200, and in 1947 brought $151,000.

From about 1830 James B. Cooley and Lemuel Bangs were leading figures, and in 1837 they entered into partnership, the firm of Cooley and Bangs becoming the progenitor of two houses which held the forefront of the stage in New York through the rest of the century, one of them developing, if perhaps in a roundabout fashion, into the American Art Association–Anderson Galleries of later days.

In 1838 Cooley retired from the firm of Cooley & Bangs, forming a partnership with Horatio Hill and John Keese, and later with Keese alone, the latter acting as auctioneer and attracting attention by the wit and ingenuity with which he conducted sales. Cooley & Keese sold their business to Lyman & Rawdon, later Lyman & Company, but it was afterwards reacquired by Cooley, who continued it under the name George A. Leavitt & Company. Later it became Leavitt, Strebeigh & Company, who in 1868 sold the important library of A. A. Smets of Savannah, including the autographs of the English collector, William Upcott. After other changes the firm ceased to exist in 1892.

When Cooley retired from Cooley & Bangs, Lemuel Bangs continued the firm as Bangs, Richard & Platt. It was later known as Bangs & Company, Bangs, Brother & Company, Bangs, Merwin & Company, and again as Bangs & Company, under which name it continued until purchased in 1903 by John Anderson, Jr. and reorganized as the Anderson Auction Company.

John Anderson, a commanding figure in the history of book auctions, had been in the field since 1900, winning the full confidence of collectors and dealers by his fair play, newer methods and ideals. In 1908 the business was bought by Major E. S. Turner, who had previously formed the Merwin Clayton Company. The sale of the library of Robert Hoe, in 1911-12, brought to the Anderson Auction Company the recognition of the book collecting world. In 1915 Major Turner was succeeded as its president by Mitchell Kennerley.

Meantime, in 1883, the American Art Association, headed by Thomas E. Kirby, had been organized, pre-eminently for the sale of paintings and art objects. For many years it was a great influence, not only in bringing important works of art to the United States, but in diffusing knowledge of these things throughout the country. Its first important book sale was that of Henry Ward Beecher in 1887, and thereafter it became increasingly important in the world of books.

In 1929, the American Art Association and the Anderson Galleries (then so-called) were united by Cortlandt Field Bishop, book collector. One of the most distinguished auctions of the American Art Association–Anderson Galleries was that of the magnificent library of the Marquess of Lothian, which occurred on January 27-28, 1932. In the autumn of 1937, H. H. Parke and Otto Bernet withdrew from the American Art Association–Anderson Galleries and together with Arthur Swann initiated the Parke-Bernet Galleries. In the fall of 1949 the

Parke-Bernet Galleries moved into their beautiful new building, especially designed to serve the purposes of a great modern auction house.

Old Philadelphia houses which continued under varying names into the present century were those of Thomas and Freeman, the latter being still active. In 1920 Stan V. Henkels of Philadelphia celebrated the fiftieth anniversary of his entrance into the book auction business, in which he won particular fame as an authority on autographs and a detector of forgeries. In 1876, when a boy in the employ of M. Thomas & Sons, he was entrusted with making the catalog for the sale of that portion of George Washington's library which had remained in the hands of his family, and, though Henkels' copious notes were not used, from that time he set about enhancing the interest of his auction catalogs by notes and quotations, which gave them a character new in America. Henkels set up independently under his own name in 1913, the business being carried on after his death by his son. Active Philadelphia auction houses of the present day are Samuel T. Freeman & Co., and, until 1945, William D. Morley, Inc.

Auction firms operating in the twenties and thirties included Charles F. Heartman of Metuchen, New Jersey, and later, Hattiesburg, Mississippi; The Walpole Galleries, of New York, founded by Mr. and Mrs. Edward Turnbull; J. C. Morgenthau, of New York, with which Mrs. Turnbull was associated; the Rains Galleries, of New York; and the bookselling firm of G. A. Baker & Co., Inc., of New York, which held a series of sales for seven years, commencing in 1938.

With the passing of the American Art Association–Anderson Galleries in 1939, the only major auction house left in New York was the Parke-Bernet Galleries, Inc. In 1940 the Kende Galleries was formed and since that time has held various book and autograph sales. In 1948 the firm was reorganized and its first large sale of literary properties was the dispersal of the "Paris" Library of the late Cortlandt Field Bishop. The 332 lots of this sale realized $325,900.

Two firms devoted wholly to the sale of less expensive literary properties were founded in New York in recent times. The first was The City Book Auction, started in 1938, and the second was The Swann Auction Galleries, in 1942. The City Book Auction has held close to 500 sales up to June, 1950, and The Swann Auction Galleries held its 250th sale in

January, 1950. Another "small" house in New York devoted to the sale of literary properties only is American Book Auction, founded in 1942.

Infrequent sales were held in California, mainly by San Francisco Book and Art Auctions, but on February 28, 1950, Harry A. Levinson held his first sale of literary properties in Beverly Hills. This was the beginning of a projected regular series of sales.

Trade Sales

Considering the confusing variety of means and ways of selling books in the latter part of the nineteenth century, one can understand how difficult it was going to be to bring some order into the very loose organization of the trade. There were so many opportunities for unfair competition and competitive price cutting. One particularly disrupting practice, the annual trade sales, we have not mentioned. Although in procedure this was a kind of book auction, the trade sale should not be confused with the regular practice of book auctioning as described in the previous section.

The trade sales were a clever method of the publishers to clear their stock. Once a year, usually in January, a conference of various representatives of the publishing and bookselling world was held. Upon this occasion the publishers sold their slow-moving stock at auction. Books, "sheet stock," the used plates of out-of-print books, also printing presses, type, ink, paper, binding machinery and materials—all were sent to these auctions. One could buy very cheaply there. Records show that sometimes for as little as from twelve to fifty dollars a publisher or perhaps a printer could pick up the complete printing plates of a book. Thus it was possible, by using the cheapest paper and paper covers, to sell at ridiculously low prices books which perhaps were still part of the stock of a retail book dealer. This might also be the case with the remaindered stock. The supply bought up on these occasions by jobbers and retailers, on the other hand, lasted often for months, and stood in the way of the purchase of the new books issued by the publishers. Perhaps this was the reason why publishers sometimes sold their new titles along with older stock items at the trade sales.

The trade sales originated in the first half of the nineteenth century.

They took the place of regular book fairs which Mathew Carey, inspired by the example of the Leipzig fair, had originated. He had been the secretary of the "first Literary Fair ever held in the United States" in 1802 with Hugh Gaine presiding. It had been the hope of those who had urged the fair that ways and means might be found to meet the serious competition of English books by raising the standards of book manufacture in America. Gold medals had been offered for the best specimens of printing, the best sample of homemade printing paper and ink, and for the best piece of American binding executed in American leather—all these things interesting forerunners of our current annual "Fifty Books of the Year" competitions. Charles L. Nichols in his essay on "The Literary Fair in the United States"[13] says: "The primary object of the book fair was to facilitate the exchange of books published in the different sections of this country by exhibiting them at these gatherings and taking orders for them and . . . the plan worked well for several years. Later, in spite of the precautions taken by the officers of the organization to raise the standards, the market was flooded with large editions of poorly printed books which came into competition with the finer and more costly issues of the better publishers and these, largely in the cities, withdrew from the organization."

The first trade sale, as far as we know, was held in 1824 in Philadelphia at the suggestion of Mathew Carey's son, Henry C. Carey. It had been sufficiently successful to result in the recommendation that further fairs be held semi-annually in New York in April, and in Philadelphia in October. Later, time and place of the meetings were changed, but at least until the nineties these trade sales were continued in one form or another. Cincinnati played an important role in the middle of the century, with U. P. James in a leading role. In New York, the auction houses of Bangs & Company and of George A. Leavitt & Company were particularly active in the fifties and sixties.

The Struggle against Price Cutting

The trade sales, which came to take the place of the regular, legitimate book fair, were a true expression of the evergrowing trend towards cheaper production and competitive price cutting. Along with the disruption of the price structure, they favored carelessness, haste

[13] In *Bibliographical Essays: A Tribute to Wilberforce Eames.*

and general abuse of trade relationships.[14] Conditions grew so bad after the Civil War, that early in the seventies serious attempts were made towards a reform. General A. C. McClurg, the Chicago publisher, fought valiantly against price cutting. It was he who answered Herbert Spencer in England who had launched an attack against booksellers in general, arguing that they were needless middlemen. In 1873, as a preliminary tentative step, "The Bookseller's Protective Union" was formed in Cincinnati, paving the way for the formation in February, 1874 in Cincinnati, of "The American Book Trade Association." On this occasion the following important resolution was passed: "As retailers, jobbers and publishers, we pledge ourselves to maintain and protect publishers' retail prices." At the next meeting of the Association, held in July of the same year at Put In Bay, Ohio, it was recognized that the only effective way of reform would be to kill the "trade sales" and substitute a legitimate semi-annual book fair in its place. This is the text of the resolution passed at that time: "*Whereas*, the late controversies, and distractions existing in the book trade, and the custom which has grown up on the part of the publishers and large city dealers of selling books to private consumers at very nearly the same rate at which the local bookseller can purchase them, has rendered it impossible for the local dealer to successfully invest his capital in a stock of books to meet and develop the wants of his own section; and if this evil is not checked at no distant day the whole business of selling books must fall into the hands of large city dealers or peddlers, greatly to the detriment of local communities; therefore be it . . . *Resolved*, that in view of the insufficiency of the present system of trade sales, and also of commercial travelers to meet the wants of the trade; that in lieu thereof this Convention appoint a committee with power to establish and conduct a semi-annual Book Trade Sale or Fair, at which the publishers shall offer their books during the period of the sale or fair at special terms to the trade."

So a fair was held in New York in July, 1875, a supplementary one

[14] Walter Sutton, *op. cit.*, has pointed out that one of the functions of the Cincinnati sales was to afford important Eastern houses the facilities for dumping large lots of their inactive stock. The records of U. P. James show that he complained to Eastern auction houses because the plates which he had bought from them were seriously damaged due to bad packing, some of the sets were incomplete and some, which he had already paid for, had never been shipped to him at all.

in October, 1875, and two more in 1876. But the history of Mathew Carey's fair early in the century repeated itself—it failed to become permanently established. "By the time of the third fair," writes Phyllis Bentley,[15] "the old love of the trade sale was strong in the veins of many participants; they seemed to recognize that the orderly fair was the better way, but to miss the auction that gave zest; and so, for this third fair, they reverted to just a hint of the trade sale,—a kind of post-fair auction, limited to titles not listed in the catalogs of the fairs. However, this was the re-introduction of the trade sale element." At least for thirteen years, until April, 1890, publishers continued to sell their remainders twice a year at auctions.

The failure to establish an all-embracing organization of the book trade and a fixed price level resulted in constant complaints of one group against another. The retail booksellers were annoyed because the publishers sold directly to the public at a considerable discount; particularly the bookstores in college towns felt the competition of the sale to students directly from the publisher or through special agents. Also there was the direct sale to Sunday Schools, to ministers, teachers, and even high school students, all of them enjoying special discounts.

There was besides this the competition of one kind of retail store against another, aggravated by the existence of fly-by-night cut-rate bookstores. Nor was the holiday sale of "gift books," especially at Christmas time, and to a lesser degree at Easter time, really a healthy thing for the trade as a whole. These plush-covered family Bibles and illustrated folios and volumes of picturesque views were published as nothing but gift books; they appeared spasmodically to occupy important shelf space which might have been used to better advantage for books of more permanent value at times when many people came into the stores, and they disappeared immediately after the holiday. Moreover, there was an annual cropping up of holiday bookstores, established solely to cash in on the Christmas trade and to draw customers away from the regular bookshops.

Of particular interest is the fact that even in those early days the dry goods stores—ancestors of the modern department stores—had hit upon the idea of using books as loss leaders to attract people to their store. They did not mind it if publishers, in order to protect the legitimate

[15] In an unpublished report on "The Book Fair in the United States."

book trade, threatened to cut their discounts. Their profits did not come from selling books anyway.

To boycott such members of the trade who sold to or bought from firms who did not play fair is a recognized universal remedy under such circumstances, and we know that it was continuously under consideration. "The practical cure of the evil is today in the hands of a half dozen publishers and one jobbing house, and so soon as they give up throwing the responsibility each upon the other, the evil will be cured, not before," wrote someone at the time. But then again, as the *American Bookseller* pointed out, was it fair to boycott a leading New York jobber because he had sold books to a dry goods store in Boston, when on the other hand a leading publisher, also in New York, sold directly to a Boston dry goods store?

The greatest single problem which presented itself to the trade as a whole, and which affected every branch, was of course the piratical ten and twenty-five cent paperback. We have seen that some of the well-established publishing firms met the competition by issuing their own cheap "libraries." How the average near-bookseller felt about the situation, and how a responsible trade paper reacted to his attitude, can be gathered from an article which appeared in the *American Bookseller* in 1888,[16] and reads: " 'A Retail Bookseller' writes to us of International copyright as seen from the retailer's point of view. He regards anything that will do away with 'cheap books' as detrimental to the retailer's interest, 'for,' he says, 'I can more easily sell three hundred twenty-five cent novels than twenty-five copies at $1.50 of the best authors.' He finds that many buy of him one novel a week at the low prices who would never buy at all at former prices. He thinks that the American author who complains that he can get a hearing only in the magazines ought to be satisfied with the extended audience so obtainable. Perhaps the American author would agree with him if *to be read* was the single purpose of a literary career.

"It is probable that the interests of the retailers," the article goes on, "like those of authors and publishers, would be greatly helped by the tremendous stimulus to literary production in this country that would follow the enaction of an International copyright law. The American author is bursting with good, saleable material, but there is a dead

[16] "Retailers and Copyright" in Vol. XXIII, No. 4, of the *American Bookseller*.

weight on his head and hundreds of stolen foreign books are annually dumped to make it heavier. When the law enables him to go to an American publisher and have his work considered on its merits in fair competition with foreign books, American literature will take a fresh start, and American retail booksellers will handle books far better adapted to the tastes of their customers than the trash turned out, in default of anything better, even by respectable publishers. 'Intense Americans' hold up their hands in horror at the 'Anglomaniac'; yet, when the American reader is fed with books that give him only English models, English notions, and English expressions, the wonder is that he retains anything at all that is distinctly American. A well-known English writer has said that the world never saw such an example of voluntary bondage to foreign thought as the Americans subject themselves to by their folly in respect to copyright.

"As to the price of books in the future, whatever the law, retail booksellers may trust to that to regulate itself. If 'cheap books' have come to stay, as they very likely have, books will continue to be cheap. No publisher or author will care to see his books remain on his shelves, for lack of meeting the ideas of the reading public as to what the price should be. There will be more books written, books better worth reading, and more books bought and sold than ever before; and the retailer, the publisher, the author, and the reader, will each share in the benefit. It is for all concerned a clear case of 'Honesty is the best Policy.'"

The Artistic Revival of the Nineties

THAT POWERFUL MOVEMENT of protest against industrialism and mechanization which in England found its most forceful expression in the personality of William Morris, was felt in America with hardly less vigor by all those who were at all susceptible to that kind of argument. Among those in America who followed Ruskin and the pre-Raphaelite brotherhood in both their literary and artistic endeavor, the ideas of William Morris spread like wildfire. How their enthusiasm for personal, individual assertion in literature and art tempted a group of young people into publishing, when the settlement of the copyright question in 1891 had cleared the atmosphere, will be told later on. It was in the design of the books of such publishers as Stone & Kimball and Copeland & Day that these new tendencies found a natural first field of application. There was one artist in particular to whom the new trend brought the chance to exercise his talents and energies—Will Bradley. In 1895 he founded the Wayside Press in Springfield, Massachusetts, which, three years later, was moved to Cambridge and made part of the University Press, John Wilson & Sons. Bradley was active also as art director of the *Century Magazine,* and as editor of *The American Chapbook*[1] issued by the American Type Founders Company, of personal little series like *Bradley, His Book* and of other casual publications. William Morris undoubtedly furnished the initial impulse, but it is plausible that directly or indirectly, Joseph Crawhall's forceful *Chap-book Chaplets,* published in London in 1883, was an important influence.[2] Bradley loved color and rich, ample ornament. He reveled in the succulent borders, the quaintly shaped initial letters surrounded by decorative encasements, which the fashion now allowed and demanded

[1] This *American Chapbook* is not to be confused with Stone & Kimball's *Chap Book* mentioned on page 323.
[2] See the late Paul McPharlin's "Crawhall's Chap-book Chaplets, 1883" in *Publishers' Weekly,* Nov. 7, 1942.

of him. In his staunch support of Caslon type he showed a more sober side. All his work carries the stamp of a free and forceful personality. He did not confine himself to book decorating and the design and production of periodicals. The type specimen books of the American Type Founders Company for many years showed the mark of his personal taste, and his posters and other commercial art work are eagerly sought by collectors of fine printing today.

The American Type Founders Company had been quick to sense the new trend, and they brought out types and ornaments closely based on the material designed for the Kelmscott Press. Rapidly the gospel spread throughout the country, much of it, though, in somewhat thoughtless imitation.

One printer who closely followed the example of William Morris was Elbert Hubbard with his Roycroft Shop in East Aurora, New York. His products were marketed through the far-reaching channels of a well-organized mail-order business and they enjoyed a tremendous popularity in this country. Elbert Hubbard deserves credit for showing to many people the elementary fact that the printed page could be the object of artistic endeavor, even if his own work was neither original nor really in very good taste.

There were several other smaller presses which followed along early in the century, among them the Cranbrook Press in Detroit, managed by George D. Booth. The tragic career of Frederick Conrad Bursch, who conducted the Literary Collector Press from 1903 to 1906, and the Killacre Bookhouse from 1909 to 1919, both in Greenwich, Connecticut, has recently been brought to light by Thomas A. Larremore.

Will Bradley's adaptation of the new style to the purposes of commercial printing was not the only instance of its kind. Those who are interested to see how the William Morris formulas were aptly utilized for advertising purposes, should look at the attractive examples in a little publication of Ingalls Kimball's Cheltenham Press, *The first ten years of the Cheltenham Press: 1897-1908. Being an Account of various problems in Printing and in Advertising and of their solution.* One sees there very clearly of what fundamental importance the new creed in decorative book typography has been for commercial printing. Today, the situation is completely reversed. Modern printing for commerce not only has caught up with book printing, but it is often much freer and more progressive.

Modern Fine Printing in America

It is generally recognized today that the most lasting contribution of William Morris was perhaps not so much the particular volumes which he produced and the way in which he printed them, but the example and stimulus which he gave to printers in the various European countries and in America. It is certainly true that the impression which he made upon three young Americans who were then contemplating a career in the graphic arts was of the greatest importance to them. If nothing else, Daniel Berkeley Updike, Bruce Rogers and Frederic W. Goudy have this in common, that their first steps were taken under the strong influence of William Morris and the Kelmscott Press. He had the power to attract and fire the imagination of the young. I once heard the late Rudolf Koch, in a lecture at Frankfurt, give a vivid recollection of the Morris influence and that of other English private presses upon the young typographic artists of Europe in the early years of this century. He went on to describe how these men, trained in the new schools of the arts and crafts movement and filled with the ideals and ideas of the creed, went out into the world to take their share in the day's work. They met the old-time craftsmen in the printing-houses like strangers, talking a different language; but gradually they got to know and to understand each other. Out of private press ideals and art school education on the one side, and the traditions of faithful craftsmanship in the great printing-houses on the other, there grew a broad and powerful movement which rejuvenated the entire printing world in Germany and was embraced by all the important book publishers.

In America the initial stimulus was exactly the same, and the hopes and efforts of the younger generation were directed towards very similar achievements. We shall hear of the initial frustration of these trends in the field of publishing. Whatever may have been the reasons, the early failure of the literary publishers of the nineties had, I am convinced, far-reaching consequences in bookmaking. It delayed the improvement of trade books, a matter of vital importance, for at least twenty years. As it happened, the normal publisher's product remained untouched by the new ideals in the graphic arts, and it continued, almost without exception, as a purely industrialized product of large concerns, conceived in terms of the publishers' commercial requirements. Not until after the first World War did the idea of a well-made book occur to the trade publishers.

During the nineties it was only natural, then, that the energies of the young men interested in printing as an art sought other means of expression and other channels than the trade book. So it came about that America in the new century saw a strong private press and limited editions movement. The program of these presses to some extent reflects the general literary trend of the day, with a special emphasis, of course, on the choice and the select. But there is also another influence noticeable, namely, the personal taste and the ambition of the patron of private presses. Much autobiographical material, memoirs and family histories, genealogy and the like was put into the hands of the printer for private production and distribution. Along with individual customers the presses enjoyed the patronage of universities and libraries, of the various churches, and of business and industry.

The term "private press" and "fine printing" in this connection, should not be interpreted too narrowly. It is not only a question of books set by hand, and printed upon handmade paper on the hand press; rather it is the entire realm of printing in a spirit of devoted craftsmanship, the production of small or relatively small editions of a book for other than ordinary trade distribution.

Of the three outstanding young men who were attracted to printing in the nineties, it can be said that D. B. Updike developed primarily as a printer, Bruce Rogers as typographer and type designer, and Frederic W. Goudy chiefly as type designer.

Daniel Berkeley Updike represents the happy example of a printer who became completely identified, by inclination as well as by reputation, with his press. In years of closest association with a small group of collaborators, foremost among them his partner John Bianchi; in the careful selection of types and decorative material of pleasing design and quality; and in the wise limitation of his press to proportions conveniently managed, Mr. Updike forged himself a tool that he could use with remarkable effectiveness. There is a certain something present on each page and each broadside printed at the Merrymount Press that escapes definition, a certain quality of readability and typographic grace that is unobtrusive but quite unmistakable. Nevertheless, tasteful composition and good presswork were to Mr. Updike never an aim in themselves, but always a means towards an end.

In the spring of 1880 Mr. Updike had found a position with Houghton, Mifflin & Co., where he was soon given a hand in the layout of advertisements and prospectuses which attracted attention to his particular abilities and eventually led to his working at the Riverside Press in Cambridge, under the direction of Mr. Mifflin. During his twelve years with the fine old firm he collected knowledge, experience and self-confidence. When there was the immediate prospect of an important printing commission he decided, in 1893, to start his own printing press. From the very beginning he was successful.

It is quite impossible to attempt on these pages a review of even the most outstanding books that have come from the Merrymount Press in the nearly fifty years of its existence; but a few words on the main trend displayed in them will be in order, not only because they may help to illuminate Mr. Updike's achievement as a book designer, but also because of the general significance of these typographic moods in American fine printing.

While still connected with the Riverside Press, Mr. Updike was asked to prepare a special decorated edition of the *Book of Common Prayer*, which had been printed by Mr. De Vinne in a workmanlike, but somewhat uninspired, manner. Mr. Updike had to invent a scheme of decoration that would be graceful and yet fit in with the book as a whole. He asked Bertram Grosvenor Goodhue, the gifted young architect and designer, to help him. Later Goodhue did more designing for the Merrymount Press. There was particularly the "Merrymount" type face which Goodhue designed for another important piece of ecclesiastical printing, the *Altar Book* of 1896. This time, border decorations, initials and the body type were the work of the same artist, and Anning Bell's illustrations fitted in well, and that unity on a monumental scale, which circumstances had denied Mr. Updike in the *Book of Common Prayer*, was now achieved by him.

The more immediate influence of William Morris, who in his turn had drawn on the inspiration of fifteenth century manuscripts and early printed books, soon gave way, in Mr. Updike's work, to the influence of other historical styles of printing and decoration, which he studied very carefully. One can actually speak of a sort of American revival of the renaissance in the early days of this century, not only as a typographic fashion, but as a matter of scholarly and literary interest. Updike had occasion to print a translation of Condivi's biography of Michelangelo, of Benvenuto Cellini's autobiography (for Brentano in New York) and the famous "Humanist Library" with books by Leonardo, Petrarch and Erasmus. Here was a genuine opportunity for some fine period typography, and T. M. Cleland and W. A. Dwiggins contributed some of their earliest work for this series. Some of Mr. Updike's most interesting period work was done in the colonial manner, with its careless looking (but artfully planned) title pages in a naively crowded mixture of type faces and sizes, its elaborate chapter headings and tail pieces, its introductory matter in old-fashioned italic, the text in readable Caslon. But a good deal of the work at the Merrymount Press was done in no consciously planned style at all, but in simple and natural continuation of that fine tradition which had started at the Chiswick Press, was brought to this country by John Wilson, was handed on to De Vinne and then to Updike. In yet another regard one can look upon Mr. Updike as the successor of De Vinne, namely in his capacity as a distinguished scholar and author of the history of his own craft. His *Printing Types* is an exhaustive study of the most important of the printer's working material, but it is at the same time an excellent account of the development of book designing.

One of the most important commissions of the press was a new edition of the revised *Book of Common Prayer* of 1928, an outstanding achievement in the field of liturgical printing, which was completed in 1930. Details about the many interesting problems encountered and, needless to say, solved, in the printing of this and of many other books, are told by Mr. Updike in his *Notes on the Merrymount Press & Its Work* which he wrote as an introduction to a complete bibliographical list of the books printed up to 1933.

He died on December 29, 1941. The books which he printed are his most eloquent monument. The books which he owned, which he had used, studied and loved, also remain as a permanent memorial. An important group of them form the nucleus of The Updike Collection, established in 1937 at the Public Library of Providence, Rhode Island, the town of his birth. The books which remained at the Merrymount

Press until its final dissolution late in 1948 were acquired by the Huntington Library.

The year 1947 saw the publication of two important books about Daniel Berkeley Updike, each the first in a new series of graphic arts publications. The last of his own contributions to the literature of printing was a collection of essays entitled *Some Aspects of Printing Old and New,* published the year of his death by William Edwin Rudge in New Haven. It contained a final chapter which he had called "A Last Word," the last paragraph of which ended thus: "There are those who feel that everything of value in the world is cracking about our heads. I do not believe that. *Our* world may crack but not *the* world. 'New ideas in their violence,' says the philosopher, 'and new needs in their urgency pass like a storm; and then the old earth, scarred and enriched by those trials, finds itself still under the same sky, unscarred and pure as before.' For life, in nature and in human nature, after each cosmic disaster or phase of man's folly, is renewed again and again."

Quite in contrast to Updike's steady work at the head of the Merrymount Press, Bruce Rogers has never tied himself down too firmly. Born in 1870 in Linwood, Indiana, he first became interested in the graphic arts during his student years at Purdue University. Quite early he had acquired a remarkable store of experience in handling typographic jobs both in book and in commercial printing. The year 1894 was decisive for his career: he met Joseph M. Bowles, the editor of a magazine called *Modern Art,* who introduced him to the work of William Morris. When the magazine moved to Boston, Bruce Rogers went along. There George H. Mifflin offered him a position at the Riverside Press which he accepted. In 1899 the "Riverside Press Editions" were started, a plan which was to give the brilliant young typographer a chance to show what he could do on an important scale. Later came traveling in Europe, and a year in New York City, fruitful particularly in collaboration with Henry W. Kent of the Metropolitan Museum of Art, who during his long years as its secretary made a great contribution in raising the standards of institutional printing in America. Then there came a year spent in Montague, Massachusetts, with Carl Purington Rollins, crowned by the appearance of Ives's translation of Guerin's *The Centaur,* set in Bruce Rogers's new Centaur type. In 1916 he took another trip to England, and a short period of collaboration with Emery Walker in London was followed by an invitation to advise the Cambridge University Press in typographic matters. Then there followed productive American years, which brought collaboration with the Harvard University Press, and his relations as typographic adviser to William Edwin Rudge in Mount Vernon, near New York. Again, important achievements along the years were the result of his collaboration with the Oxford University Press, both in Oxford and New York.

Though his work is best known among bibliophiles and students of fine printing, his reputation has grown far beyond these intimate circles. The public knows of Bruce Rogers as a great American book designer in the grand decorative manner. But he has done many other things besides. There are, for instance, his little water colors, which he has made from time to time during the last fifty years. Almost without exception they are landscapes, quietly seen at a fair distance, delicately balanced in composition and detail, and animated by a gentle glow. There is no visible change here in "style" throughout the years, just a quiet, private competence which remains true to itself all the time.

The same thing is true of Bruce Rogers' work as a type designer. Modestly he will not admit that he has done anything more than take a fine old Venetian roman, that of Nicolas Jenson, and adapt it to modern usage. This was many years ago, and he has gone quietly over his type again and again, gently eliminating certain beginner's mistakes, balancing weight and color, adding new sizes, fitting it to the composing machine—until this once historical Centaur type has become a really contemporary type face, because it has come to say so closely and so nobly what its living maker wanted it to say.

In great and obvious contrast to this mastership within self-imposed limitations, his work as a book designer and decorator shows the greatest possible range. Bruce Rogers' very first attempts, art work for his Indiana alma mater, betray the influence of the eighties. Then, clearly set off against them, there is the influence of William Morris, quickly tried and quickly forsaken. Thereafter, he gets rapidly into his stride, and within a very few years we see him work out his own personal solutions; the true Bruce Rogers emerges.

In Europe, early in this century, the British and the Continental book artists, who were saturated with medieval and renaissance traditions, felt that they must forge ahead and struggle for an independent modern style. In America the newly gained mastery of great historical styles in printing seemed too good a thing to throw away so readily. Bruce Rogers becomes the recognized master of "period typography." But he never just imitates the master printers of the past, he always gives something of his very own. Basking in the sunlight of the New England renaissance, his work at the Riverside Press has the warmth of complete harmony between text and format. Petrarch, Ronsard, Sir Philip Sidney, John Donne! Their words become actors on a stage which he has prepared with wise and loving hands.

Bruce Rogers has never owned a printing press, private or otherwise, and though he has worked with many institutions, he has always been free, it seems, to do the things that he likes best—live in the country and, better yet, be out in a sailboat. So whenever his work called for an expression of rural felicity, or when a book was to be made about ships and the sea—the log of an old sailing vessel in colonial days, or a novel by Joseph Conrad or Melville—he gave of his very best.

His work has a decidedly infectious quality. His period typography has frequently been imitated by the younger and sometimes the lesser person, yet it has never lost its freshness. This is so not only because of the natural superiority of his work over that of most of his followers, but also because he has steadily gone on to new fields of endeavor and to tasks of increasing importance. What could be said of American fine printing early in the century—that it preferred not to swim against the stream of the great typographic traditions and to venture into the field of modern experimentation—cannot be said of the last twenty years. Bruce Rogers would be most unwilling, of course, to accept a nomination as an outstanding modernist in typography, and not many people would suggest this. Yet I think that his example has done more than most people realize to close the chapter of period typography, when its possibilities had been fully exploited and its limitations recognized. One need only think of two of his most important books, the Homer and the Oxford Bible. The Homer breathes, of course, a very authentic classical spirit; but it has nothing to do with the way books were made and with what they looked like in ancient Greece. And the Oxford Lectern Bible in its monumental format may perhaps recall early printing days. Yet, in the beautiful clarity and simplicity of the text pages, in the total absence of typographic ornament, and in the general aesthetic economy of means, his Bible, as his *Odyssey*, is certainly "functional," if by that is meant the complete co-ordination of printing to the intentions of the text. In that sense his Oxford Lectern Bible and his *Odyssey* are as modern as the Bible and the *Odyssey* themselves are modern.

At the end of World War II, B. D. Zevin of the World Publishing Company in Cleveland, Ohio, asked Bruce Rogers to produce a Bible which would fill "the lack of a contemporary American Bible in the great tradition." He accepted and chose for this task a version of Frederic Goudy's Newstyle type, modified slightly for Monotype composition. Stimulated by the lavishly decorated first edition of the King James Bible, he chose once again the allusive style and the ornamental approach, using type ornaments and flowers "intended," as he has explained, "to give a slightly oriental flavor to the volume, indicative of the Syriac and Hebrew sources of the text."

Throughout the years Bruce Rogers has written and said very little about printing. He did permit a series of seemingly casual remarks to be elicited from him by James Hendrickson, which were published as *Paragraphs on Printing* by William Edwin Rudge in 1943. The reader will find here a most refreshing absence of the high-flung gesture and the noble generalization, but a great deal of sound, practical advice on how to get beyond the purely practical performance.

Many articles and books have been written about Bruce Rogers. The most complete record published to date is the catalog of an exhibition of his work which was shown at the Grolier Club in the winter of 1938-39, and which is listed, with some other references, in the bibliography. A notable collection of his work is being formed at his alma mater, in the library of Purdue University at Lafayette, Indiana. It is known as the Anna Embree Baker Collection, in memory of the late Mrs. Rogers, who made the original bequest in 1932, to which Bruce Rogers has since made regular additions.

Very early in his career Frederic W. Goudy recognized the inferiority of the printing types in general use in the 1900's, and with the patience and energy which stayed with him through the years, he set about, almost single-handed, to correct the situation. With so many excellent type faces available today, it is hard to realize what this meant at the time when he started. And it is easy to forget how many people in America owe him thanks for having first opened their eyes to the possibilities of type design and fine printing.

He was born at Bloomington, Illinois, in 1865 and spent student and apprentice years in Chicago. Like some of the other typographic artists who have done much for book printing, he started his career as a commercial artist. When he could not find the letters he wanted in the printer's case, he drew them. Gradually he became more and more interested in type. But he first engaged in private printing. Very much under the influence of William Morris, he started in 1903 his Village Press in Park Ridge, Illinois, which he took east into Massachusetts the following year and to New York in 1908. There a fire destroyed all his property and equipment and he had to start all over again. It was around this time that the designing and the actual production of type began to take more and more time from his other interests. The devoted support and collaboration of his wife, Bertha, were to a large extent the reason that he was able to continue to be a printer and to re-establish the Village Press at Marlborough-on-Hudson in an old mill—only again to be burnt out in 1939. He took this second disaster with extraordinary composure; once again he rebuilt his resources and continued his work as creative type designer, author on printing, and consultant to the Lanston Monotype Company. His death on May 11, 1947 ended a life that was wholly devoted to the cause of inspired craftsmanship and to the conquest of difficulties and obstacles through patience and fortitude of heart.

The year following his death, Deepdene, the Marlborough property, was bought at auction by the late Ralph C. Coxhead of the Vari-Typer Company, who has announced his intention to preserve the house as a printers' shrine.

The total number of the types designed and cut and cast by Frederic Goudy is well over a hundred—a most interesting contrast to Bruce Rogers' concentration upon one type design. Mr. Goudy early in his career decided not to count too much on the co-operation of commercial type foundries, and he worked out his own method of production, which combines some of the elements of traditional type founding with much that was developed more recently—such as the use of the pantograph. The best source of information on his types is his own *A Half-*

Century of Type Design and Typography 1895-1945, published by the Typophiles in two volumes in 1947. This work might appropriately be called an autobiographical type specimen book. It is the definitive record of the life's work of America's most beloved and most honored creator of printing type.

Unlike the type faces of many practicing designers today, Mr. Goudy's types do not originate from the realm of calligraphic experience, but are drawn in outline. He has explained[3] how the beauty of an old manuscript is often the stimulus for a new design. The world of the Gothic and the Renaissance have influenced him, as has the art of ancient Rome, particularly in its inscriptions. The names of some of his type faces—Forum, Trajan, Hadrian—testify to his almost naive admiration for the glory that was Rome. There is a rich variety in his type faces, which range all the way from inscriptional stateliness to friendly and homelike italic, from the even gray of a carefully balanced Roman to the crisp light and heavy of liturgical Gothic. He has done some very fine Gothic type. His *The Alphabet, Fifteen interpretative designs drawn and arranged with explanatory text and illustrations,* first published by Mitchell Kennerley in 1922, is on the shelves of many students of lettering and printing. In the flood of books, pamphlets and articles that have been written about Fred Goudy, a little volume by Vrest Orton, entitled *Goudy, Maker of Letters,* stands out. It avoids the kind of blind devotion which pervades too many of these writings, and it portrays with striking likeness Goudy's idealism, his refusal to accept things as he found them, his restless, ingenious struggle to beat the machine age with its own weapons.

Fine book printing, to be sure, depends on the intelligent forming of a plan, on tasteful selection of materials, and on skillful and conscientious execution. However, there is no single material so important for the eventual success of a book as the type face chosen for the job. It is unfortunately impossible to include in the present account the work of those firms and individuals who have contributed type faces of lasting importance, or to review the rapidly changing fashions in twentieth century typographic style. Such an account should consider the Cheltenham and the Cloister types; the revivals of the great historic type faces by the American Type Founders Company, by Linotype, Inter-

[3] In an article in *The Dolphin,* Vol. I, entitled "On Designing A Typeface."

type, Monotype and Ludlow; the contributions of these companies to typographic refinement; the work of such men as Benton, Orcutt, Cooper and Cleland; the importation of many excellent type faces from abroad by the Bauer Type Foundry and the Continental Typefounders Association, both active in the period between the two world wars. There will be an opportunity, however, to speak of recent trends in creative type design in the next section.

Before reviewing those presses which within the last forty years have made unusual efforts to produce books of lasting typographical distinction, we should speak of a man who over a long period of years has moved into a position of ever increasing intellectual leadership in American printing and bookmaking, Carl Purington Rollins. Like other distinguished men in his field, he was a disciple of William Morris, particularly impressed with Morris' emphasis on the social importance of the modern printer as a craftsman. After apprenticeship years at the Heintzemann Press in Boston, Rollins early in this century organized the Montague Press, in Montague, Massachusetts, which became the organ of the small town's community life. It was during that phase that he enjoyed the companionship and collaboration of Bruce Rogers, who has recently said of his work that in it "the decorative features, the touches of phantasy, the ingenious arrangement of details, the bits of typographic humor, are all subservient to the main purpose and add immeasurably to that purpose—to be read . . . Like Emery Walker and T. E. Lawrence, Carl has always had a predilection for Caslon's types . . . Carl used it with even more variety than did the eighteenth-century printers, or than Pickering and Whittingham in their revival of it, and always with more vigor and freshness. Even Updike did not explore its possibilities so thoroughly." In 1918 Rollins went to the Yale University Press. He has made his mark there not only in the steady maintenance of typographical standards, but also in difficult and complicated tasks, such as bibliographies and other special projects. Scholarly works with a complex body of documentary material, such as plans, maps, tables, photographs, he handled in a manner both technically sound and aesthetically pleasing. Carl Rollins is keenly interested in the complete picture of the graphic arts in America today, and particularly in the relationship of craftsmanship and machine. He has frequently collaborated with the American Institute of Graphic Arts in the annual selection of the "Fifty Books of the Year," has conducted a typographic column in the *Saturday Review of Literature* and has repeatedly contributed appraisals of contemporary American book production to various typographic yearbooks. A collection of his addresses, reviews and verses was published under the mysterious title *Off the Dead Bank* by the Typophiles in 1949. He retired from active duty in the summer of 1948.

It is only natural that in New England one should encounter the strongest traditional influences, the closest ties with the past. Immediately upon entering the New York area, the picture changes. Here, in the metropolis, one finds reflections of probably every single tendency in the contemporary typography of America as well as of the various European countries. These trends often exist alongside of each other without visible conflict and they are cultivated by quite different groups. There is continued readiness for the new and combined willingness to experiment. The West, by and large, cannot as yet be said to have developed decisive regional characteristics. Both the New England love of tradition and New York's cosmopolitan attitude can be seen reflected there. There are indications that the Middle West with Chicago as a natural center is becoming the focusing point of a strong native American school of taste, in the realm of the graphic arts as in other fields. On the Pacific Coast, in California, there are recognizable signs of a regional school of fine printing. There is a succession of enterprises there that have depended upon each other for inspiration and guidance. It may be that the colorful and generous quality of the best of Californian printing is somewhat indebted to the climate. But at least of equal importance, I should think, is the existence there of an old, settled cultural foundation, nourishment to be derived from the formative power of the Latin race. If this is true, one should look for similar developments in the Southwest, where Indian, Spanish and Anglo-Saxon traditions seem to live on in a unique condition of mutual tolerance and fructification. The last decade has not, however, brought many new signs of such a development.

A brief survey of individual printers and presses of distinction active in the thirties and continuing in part to the present time, takes us first to the Northeast of the union. In Portland, Maine, we find the successful continuation of local traditions. Thomas B. Mosher had shown a very unusual flair for delicate and appetizing bookmaking. Today, the Anthoensen Press cultivates the solid New England traditions in printing. The press is headed by Fred Anthoensen and is the successor, since 1947, to the Southworth-Anthoensen Press, which in its turn had grown out of a printing firm which Constant Southworth had inherited from his father. That their taste should have been influenced by the Merrymount Press, the strongest typographic power in the New England region, is perhaps only natural. They have developed bibliographical work as one of the specialties of the firm. *Types and Bookmaking* is the title of a volume which describes the work of the press and lists the books printed there.

There is no need to stress again the contributions of D. B. Updike and Bruce Rogers in the typographic achievements of Boston and Cambridge. Both men had successively been connected with The Riverside Press, which continues to be the manufacturing division of the Houghton Mifflin Company. The Riverside Press has described its history in *The Annual of Bookmaking 1927-1937*, published by *The Colophon* office. This volume, although not exactly a complete and co-ordinated account of that decade, presents information about some of the well-known presses, and, perhaps most valuable, accounts of several enterprises which started during those years. A genuine Massachusetts private press of small dimensions but high ideals is the Cummington Press, affiliated with the Cummington School of the Arts. Active for a number of years now, the press, under the direction of Harry Duncan and Wightman Williams, is engaged in issuing books of new literature printed by hand.

Not so very far from New Haven, in the countryside back of Stamford, is the Overbrook Press, which comes as close to being a private press in the real sense of that word as any similar establishment in this country. Frank Altschul, the proprietor who prefers to remain in the background, has a clear conception of what a private press could and should be today. The Overbrook Press both prints and publishes its selections, alternating from illustrated editions such as *One More Spring* and *The Happy Prince and Other Tales* or Stevenson's *Inland Voyage*, to brief texts of political or economic significance, such as the text of addresses by Wendell L. Willkie and General Eisenhower or *An Exchange of Letters* by Thomas Mann.

Another personal press in Connecticut was Hawthorn House in Windham, which was established in 1932 by Edmund B. Thompson, a former Rudge disciple, and once associated with Peter Beilenson. The press has become known for the delicate beauty of its small-sized volumes, many of them treating with matters of local tradition. Here is a genuine "regional press."

In the New York area the variety of printers and presses committed to fine book printing has always been considerable, including the free-lance typographic artist, the small individual press, and the large industrial printing concern with an interest in the limited editions field. However, it is impossible to overlook the fact that few of the presses active between the wars have survived to the present time. Their place has not been taken by newcomers to the field of fine printing. There is no question, the emphasis is changing.

One of the first free-lance artists who since the turn of the century has done excellent work for various printers and publishers is Thomas Maitland Cleland. Born in Brooklyn in 1880, he did not take his formal schooling and art education very seriously, but preferred to find his own way. He did some of his early work, before the first World War, for the Merrymount Press; for instance, title page decorations for the "Humanist Library." Like Updike and Bruce Rogers he drew inspiration and nourishment from the great decorative traditions of the sixteenth, seventeenth and eighteenth centuries. His mastery of historical ornament lends a stately yet personal charm to his title pages and border decorations, to his period illustrations, his bookplates and publishers' marks. Even his commercial work, such as railroad and automobile advertisements, he has endowed with the cavalier grace of the eighteenth century, in a supreme indifference to anachronisms.

A discussion of New York owners of presses must begin with two men, each of whom in his own way did much valuable work—Hal Marchbanks and William Edwin Rudge. Hal Marchbanks came as a young man to New York from Texas. He was active in the printing department of the Hill Publishing Company, which later on he bought, when John A. Hill joined forces with James McGraw in forming the McGraw-Hill publishing house. This was the origin of the Marchbanks Press. Some of the most colorful and lively work of the press was done in collaboration with talented artists such as Fred G. Cooper, A. Allen

Lewis and many more. Marchbanks was a master of letterpress printing in color; his posters and charming monthly calendars are the pride of those who own them. Marchbanks believed in high prices, but was most liberal personally. Many a printer who is on his own today owes to him his first opportunity to play with type and to pull a proof. Since his death in 1934, Emily E. Connor has carried on at the Marchbanks Press with courage and vigor. She is one of the country's outstanding woman printers.

Under the direction of Roland Wood, and with John Fass as the responsible typographic designer, the Harbor Press in New York became well known for the quality and taste of its printing, which has included some charming little volumes of local New York interest, published under their own imprint until World War II. There is a flavor of good breeding and tradition in the books of this press which is pleasantly mixed with a sense of humor and intimacy.

William Edwin Rudge deserves particular recognition in these pages because in the course of many successful years at the head of a large industrial plant he made a point of cultivating fine book printing. He had a keen interest in new technical developments, particularly in the field of pictorial reproduction, and he gathered around him a staff of unusually able and promising people. A visit to the Rudge plant in Mount Vernon was a real experience, with its low buildings, which looked more like a country estate than a printing plant, in pleasant suburban surroundings, with a group of small dwelling houses for the older members of the staff, and a private railroad track leading to the loading ramp where an old iron hand press braved the elements in rain and shine. Inside, there was the large, well-stocked composing room, there were Linotype and Monotype, a complete equipment for the "Aquatone" variety of offset printing, a row of small job presses for rapid four-color relief printing, a variety of middle and large size cylinder presses, an excellent hand bindery, a rich typographic library, and a cafeteria restaurant. Among the many important commissions carried out there in the course of the years, two large undertakings are of particular literary interest. When some years ago important and completely unknown manuscripts of Boswell, Doctor Johnson's famous biographer, came to light at Malahide Castle in Ireland, William Edwin Rudge was commissioned by Ralph H. Isham, the owner of these precious papers, to bring out the complete text, illustrated with many fac-simile reproductions from the papers. Another major commission was the printing of a complete edition of Milton's works for the Columbia University Press.

Rudge had been both wise and fortunate in his collaborators. He very clearly saw the importance of the designer within the framework of the large industrialized plant. Of the collaboration of Bruce Rogers we have already spoken. A similar position was held there for some time by Frederic Warde, whom one may consider Rogers' outstanding disciple. He compiled a fine bibliography of books printed by Bruce Rogers. Warde's "Arrighi" type face, the successful revival of a fine calligraphic italic type of the renaissance, is used as a companion italic with Bruce Rogers' "Centaur." Frederic Warde combined artistic interest and ability with an unusual scientific curiosity about printing. His knowledge of paper, ink and presswork together with his typographic taste lend a particular distinction to his work. Later in his life, he was associated with an old-time firm of upstate New York printers, under the imprint of McFarlane, Warde & McFarlane. He was also typographic adviser to the Oxford University Press in New York.

A successful Rudge disciple is Peter Beilenson of the Walpole Printing Office in New Rochelle. Beilenson first printed for himself in 1928, using the imprint Peter Pauper Press, a year before the depression. In the fall of 1929 he and Edmund B. Thompson, also formerly of the Rudge staff, established the Walpole Printing Office. Thompson left in 1932 to start his own Hawthorn House in Windham, Connecticut. The Walpole Printing Office, where a steadily increasing number of volumes have been printed each year, works for its own imprint, for private customers and for publishers and rare book dealers. Peter Beilenson, actively assisted by his wife Edna, has pursued a policy of keeping his rather long list of titles constantly in print at low prices, and of distributing them through regular trade channels, with his own sales force on the road. As a result his books, found in nearly every good bookshop in the country, and especially in the college stores, have had an enormous influence in shaping people's taste.

Samuel A. Jacobs' Golden Eagle Press, also in Mount Vernon, has gained a reputation for the originality of its progressive, experimental typography.

Another Rudge alumnus of considerable typographic ability, who held a responsible position in the large organization, is Melvin Loos. He came to the Columbia University Press after the death of William Edwin Rudge in 1931. The Rudge plant was liquidated in 1936, when the two sons, who had previously started out for themselves, took over the name and trade-mark of their father's organization. Later on, the brothers separated, Frederic G. Rudge to stay in New York in the commercial printing field, William E. Rudge, Jr. to become the printer and publisher of *Print Magazine,* first near New Haven, Connecticut, then in Woodstock, Vermont.

For many years, Elmer Adler's Pynson Printers enjoyed the distinction of being the most substantial and progressive of the New York printing presses exclusively devoted to fine book work. Relatively late in his career Mr. Adler took up printing, and from the start he devoted his energies to the artistic and creative aspects of book production. Liberal in mind and international in taste, he has collaborated with Rockwell Kent and other American artists, and with such men as Lucian Bernhard, Richard Floethe and Hans Alexander Mueller from Germany. In his selection of type faces he has shown a similar cosmopolitan taste. He made particular efforts in the production of limited illustrated editions of great works of world literature, adding, however, occasional smaller volumes at moderate prices. He has printed both for publishers and for his own Pynson Printers imprint. The most notable of his publishing ventures is *The Colophon,* a bibliophile quarterly which first appeared in 1930 and was resurrected after a wartime lapse as *The New Colophon* in 1948. For many of its issues Elmer Adler devised the interesting scheme of inviting different designers and presses to plan and produce the articles, reserving a share in each issue for his own press. The Pynson Printers ceased operation when Elmer Adler moved to Princeton University, where he was appointed an associate-in-residence attached to the staffs of the university's library. His beautiful and famous library of printing history and great examples of printing was presented by him to Princeton, and is separately housed.

The Pynson Printers also printed and published some of Dard Hunter's volumes on the art of papermaking by hand. Dard Hunter has traveled far and wide to record the existence of old-time paper craftsmen in the modern world, to collect specimens and to illustrate their various methods. The establishment of his Paper Museum at the Massachusetts Institute of Technology in Cambridge took place in 1939.

In several regards the existence of the Spiral Press in New York is encouraging to those who look for sincerity and originality in typography. Too often, one finds either a somewhat strained effort to be different and "modern" at the expense of sound execution, or one finds meticulous craftsmanship that is uninspired and over-traditional. Joseph Blumenthal, of the Spiral Press, submitted himself to a rigidly disciplined personal training. He designed his own type face, which was cut for him at the Bauer Type Foundry and, incidentally, has been taken over by the Monotype Corporation; he learned the operation of a hand press with Dr. Wiegand of the famous Bremer Presse in Munich; on his own hand press in the country, he printed books, on moistened sheets of handmade paper, that are a sheer delight to the eye and the hand. But he also went on to apply his experience to the successful production of books for publishers in his small but well-equipped modern plant in the big city. He has also made a specialty of printing exhibition catalogs for museums and art dealers.

The late Melbert B. Cary, Jr.'s private printing press went by the name of the Woolly Whale. It was founded in 1928 "merely as a means of experimenting with type and paper and as a pleasant method of turning the annual problem of providing Christmas gifts for one's friends into the highly delightful experience of choosing, designing and preparing Christmas books for them." The press on several occasions enjoyed the collaboration of Frederic Goudy.

There is one excellent press of rather modest dimensions in New York which until recently was not well known outside a small circle of experts, the Press of A. Colish. Abraham Colish came to New York early in the century and set up in business for himself in 1907. The special equipment and the interests of its owner made the press ideally suited for limited editions work, a field in which A. Colish has been active since the twenties. In announcing his new Lectern Bible for the World Publishing Company, Bruce Rogers, who has worked with Colish for many years, wrote about him: "Mr. Colish is a remarkable man, and his printing has not gone without remark. He is a combination of the keen practical commercial typographer and the artist-printer. To meet him at a business conference round a luncheon table at one of the New York clubs you would hardly suspect that half an hour earlier, clad in an old blue smock-frock, he had been setting type at the case or making up pages in his own composing room. His establishment is small, so that he supervises every detail of the work; yet from it for many years have issued splendid volumes for private clients, Yale and Texas Universities, the New York Public Library, and the Limited Editions Club, including the 39-volume Shakespeare in small folio. He is the favorite printer of T. M. Cleland, Rockwell Kent, and many other artists."

In turning from New York to other places where books have been and are being printed with exceptional care and success one realizes that it is more often a matter of an individual printer or firm than a local tradition. Those who know the twentieth century development of the graphic arts in America think, for instance, of the city of Baltimore in connection with Norman T. A. Munder, who has made some remarkable efforts there in the field of fine halftone printing, and, for a brief period in the thirties, acted as consultant of the Enoch Pratt Free Library. They think of Pittsburgh because of the existence there years ago of the late Porter Garnett's Laboratory Press, an experiment conducted in connection with the Carnegie Institute of Technology and its important department of printing. In Rochester, New York, Horace Hart, inspired as a Harvard student by George Parker Winship, is making a contribution both to fine bookmaking and the literature of the craft with his "Printer's Valhalla Series."

The progressive and independent character of some of the good printing done at Chicago today testifies to the existence there of a group of enterprising and forward-looking typographers. However, their effect is seen more clearly in commercial printing than in either limited editions or trade books. For many years the best work in the field of fine printing has come from R. R. Donnelley's Lakeside Press, that great old establishment which has existed now for about three-quarters of a century. The remarkable thing about this giant organization, where the New York City Telephone books are forever revised and reprinted, and where the fourteenth edition of the *Encyclopædia Britannica* saw the light of day in 1929, is that it has maintained throughout the years a high standard of taste and competence in fine book work. In 1903 there appeared the first volume of "The Lakeside

Classics," a series of Christmas volumes inaugurated "to present to the friends and patrons of an old-established press an occasional book of the best English prose, representing in its mechanical details the ideals of that press in workaday bookmaking." Since then, the Lakeside Classics have appeared annually, "—a pleasant habit on the part of the publishers and a sort of vested expectancy on the part of the friends and patrons." The influence of William A. Kittredge, who came West from New England to take charge of the Lakeside Press typography in 1922, was responsible for the progressive character of many Lakeside books, and in particular for a series of distinguished volumes, for which W. A. Dwiggins, Rockwell Kent and others made the illustrations. "His mind had a freshness, an originality, an unexpectedness that made his conversation both difficult and delightful," said Pierce Butler of Kittredge in a memorial address delivered on July 28, 1945. Also in Chicago was the Black Cat Press, directed by Norman W. Forgue, which until World War II printed and published books on bibliographical and typographical subjects, with a particular interest in the local Chicago traditions. Herrin, Illinois, has become known to lovers of amateur printing as the seat of the oldest existing private press in the country, the Trovillion Private Press, conducted continuously for over forty years by Hal and Violet Trovillion "at the Sign of the Silver Horse." Thomas Bird Mosher's style is still their chief typographic model.

Turning now to California one is struck with the satisfactory and promising existence there of something like a real school of fine bookmaking. It is not merely a question of one or two individuals who like to play with type and presses, but the gradual unfolding and branching out of enterprises which seem to thrive on the same soil and on similar nourishment, though they differ otherwise. There seems to be a "genius loci" which even in the nineteenth century had tempted some of the restless pioneer printers to turn from their newspaper printing to bookmaking.

The pioneer and dean of modern fine printing in California was John Henry Nash. Years ago, he must have felt the influence of the Kelmscott Press and, back of it, of Ratdolt and other fifteenth century printers, keenly and spontaneously. He set out to print in the grand medieval manner, as have many other private press printers, but he never freed himself from what in his case became a rigid and, eventually, a frigid pattern. Nash never learned to unbend and to admit some warmth and humor or intimacy onto the pages of his books. But he evidently gave his patrons what they wanted, for he was enormously successful. It would be ungracious to deny that John Henry Nash has had a decided influence, and that in his manner he has done much to prepare the way for the younger generation,—demonstrating the possibilities of private press printing and publishing for individual patrons.

The brothers Edwin and Robert Grabhorn in San Francisco, the leading figures of the California group, are among the most capable book printers in America. Like so many others they, too, emerged from the realms of eclecticism, from the initial stimulus of William Morris and the cult of Colonial typography. They have steadily developed and progressed upon the path of natural and contemporary articulation. If they occasionally strike a note of gentle historical allusion, they do it with such grace and independence that it turns out, in the end, to be more a piece of Grabhorn printing than anything else. In their literary program, too, they have gone their own way. Their particular field is the adventurous, colorful and ever changing panorama of the life and history of the West and the Far West. Their series, "Rara Americana," attractive alike in contents and in format, contains a number of volumes of lasting value.

The Grabhorns, in turn, have influenced a further group of typographers and printers. I am thinking particularly of Helen Gentry, who left California and came East to New York in the thirties, to become a co-founder and the designer of Holiday House in 1935. She has demonstrated a very particular knack with what we might call the modern chapbook, diminutive formats, clear, well-defined colors in connection with sound and strong little woodcuts, bold type with plenty of air to breathe. In association with the Holiday House imprint she brought into the nursery tiny books, which the children loved and which at the same time were acceptable to even the hard-boiled aesthete. Helen Gentry has also been recognized as a capable general book designer. She has done fine work for the University of New Mexico Press.

Ward Ritchie, who graduated from Occidental College, Los Angeles, in 1928 and studied books and printing both at home and abroad, started a private press early in the thirties. He has steadily grown in competence and skill, both typographically and editorially. The books which are offered under the imprint of Anderson and Ritchie in Los Angeles are fine examples of discriminating taste in regional publishing on an intimate scale. In Oakland at Mills College the Eucalyptus Press has done highly creditable work.

In the Southwest there was the Rydal Press in Santa Fe, directed until 1942 by Walter Goodwin. The press was established in 1933 in response to the enthusiasm of a group of resident authors who felt the need for a local press that would make them less dependent on far away centers of printing and publishing. The press is no longer active in the fine book field. In its informal, slightly erratic way the Peripatetic Press has made lively and handsome contributions to Southwestern printing. E. De Golyer and Elizabeth Ann McMurray are its founders and owners; Carl Hertzog, the printer.

It would be possible to go on and mention by name some of the private presses and smaller printing firms throughout the country which in one way or another have been striving for improvement. Unfortunately, considerations of space make this impossible. Detailed information about these developments is found in the publications of Will Ransom and Irvin Haas.

There is one other group of organizations which is making an increasingly significant contribution to fine bookmaking throughout the country, the University Presses. Such presses as the Harvard University Press, and somewhat later, the Yale University Press, have emphasized sound craftsmanship and intelligent planning for years. But more recently, the work of many of the university presses throughout the country has assumed significance as the most consistent, regionally diversified effort towards lasting typographic and manufacturing achievements. Such men as P. J. Conkwright at Princeton, the late Samuel T. Farquhar and A. R. Tommasini at California, Earl Schenck Miers when at Rutgers, and Will Ransom at Oklahoma have made and are making an important contribution even if they are not engaged in "fine" printing, and although their function is more closely related to that of the trade and textbook designer.

The picture of fine bookmaking would also be incomplete without at least the mention of publishing organizations which have made a particular point of encouraging the quality group of printers. Toward the beginning of its career, Random House was the American representative of the Nonesuch Press and issued a number of finely printed limited editions. In recent years they have been noted for attractive trade book production.

The Limited Editions Club, a bibliophile publishing house organized on a yearly subscription basis in 1929, sends to its members each month a volume designed to represent a valuable work of literature artistically printed, illustrated and bound. Membership in the club has been limited to 1500, plausibly enough explained by the policy of the club to issue only books printed from type and from the original illustration plates. The club has gone out of its way to engage the best designers and printers not only of this country but from all places where worthwhile work could be expected to result from a commission. The series thus presents an interesting cross section of contemporary methods and styles and certain of the volumes are real monuments of the arts of the book in the twentieth century. The Limited Editions Club has among its members many persons who have not previously concerned themselves much with book collecting and the appreciation of fine printing, and there can be no doubt that in this regard the club has done some real pioneering. On the other hand, the point of view of impressing one's friends, less fortunate because they do not happen to be subscribers, and the lure of "worthwhile investment" is one of the talking points in the club's promotion campaigns. From here stems an element that is not always agreeable in the format of the books: the visible desire to look worth the subscribers' money, or more.

From time to time the club has held a competition in book illustration or in essay writing on the subject of fine printing. For a number of years the director of the club, George Macy, undertook the task of publishing a typographic yearbook, *The Dolphin, a Journal on the Making of Books*, of which three yearly volumes and some smaller issues appeared. In some regards the *Dolphin* took the place of Stanley Morison's famous *Fleuron*. However, it was not directed to printers and typographers primarily, but to the book collecting public in general, and the members of the Limited Editions Club in particular. The *Dolphin* was read by printers and typographers as well, and it offered a much needed platform for the discussion of technical, artistic and historical questions.

The Heritage Press, another division of George Macy's publishing organization, has pursued a policy that is very similar to the Limited Editions Club in its literary and typographic aspects, except that the editions are not limited and the prices more moderate. There are some very interesting books in this series. The famous English Nonesuch Press has been added to this group of bibliophile publishing activities through the acquisition in 1936 of a controlling interest by the Limited Editions Club.

It is possible today to trace the full course of the forces originally set in motion by William Morris in the 1890's. The energies generated by him were caught up in the private press movement, which carried the main responsibility for fine printing in the first quarter of this century. In the period between the wars this responsibility was handed over, to a considerable extent, to the small or medium large printing plant organized for quality production. This happened in England, on the European continent and in the United States. From there the reform spread to the trade book, first in Europe, later in America, where the last fifteen to twenty years have seen a powerful revitalization of the day-by-day products of many commercial publishing houses, university presses and also of certain textbook houses.

It might very well be asked what, if any, is the remaining legitimate function of the amateur effort today. The private press as a hobby, as the personal gratification of a creative urge, needs of course no justification. Yet, if the owner of a private press today is forever content to emulate an example first set over half a century ago, in attitude and style of work, his product will fall short of a desirable and an obtainable goal. Peter Beilenson, in the Harvard University Press symposium, *Graphic Forms*, published in 1949, has dealt with this question with great clarity:

"Now that mechanization is becoming more and more complete in more and more places," he argues, "we can begin to see clearly the greatest disadvantage of all: under such mechanization individual workers have lost pride and satisfaction in their work, because they have become mere replaceable units of less and less importance; whereas the machines they operate are more and more important, and have become the essential units. . . . The amateur printer has a duty which, if he will accept it, will in the long run return to him the greatest satisfaction." But there are some pitfalls: "They are romantics, romantics who turn away from the impersonal machine world of the present. . . . The trouble is, such amateurs think that because printing in the past was done by hand, and because there is something more satisfying and human about printing by hand, they must therefore work in an antique printing style. . . ." Instead, they should be pioneers in modern design, in the forefront of experimentation: "The time is ripe for amateur book-experimentalists to prod and teach. . . . The amateur can do it."

A case could also be made for the private press on editorial grounds. The current publishing scene is not favorable for literary experimentation, for the poet and the avant-gardist. I know of at least one such group which demands a certain quota of typesetting by hand from each member as a condition of publication. Obviously, the members of this group do not feel that the mimeographing machine is an adequate substitute for the printing press.

Creative Craftsmanship, Education, Organizations

The direct effect on the printer and his press were not the only important results of the reform of William Morris. His reviving and generally stimulating influence on the personal, creative forces in the graphic arts was at least of equal significance.

Nowhere can this be seen more clearly than in the twentieth century renaissance of calligraphy and hand lettering, which by now has reached considerable proportions in the United States. William Morris himself, it will be remembered, was interested in hand lettering, in his Victorian, somewhat amateurish way. His younger contemporary, Edward Johnston, created professional foundations which lie at the back of the work of such skilled masters of the craft as Eric Gill in England, Anna Simons and Rudolf Koch in Germany, Jan van Krimpen in Holland. In America, the legendary Hermann Püterschein, alias of William Addison Dwiggins, and his near-mythological Society of Calligraphers have done wonders. Dwiggins in his early beginnings owed much to that distinguished artist and craftsman, Rudolph Ruzicka. Frederic Warde was an early addict of the calligraphic pen. More recent English influences, stimulated by Stanley Morison's interest in the Italian renaissance "cancelleresca" and propagated there by Alfred Fairbank, were felt here by such men as Paul Standard and

George Salter. A direct influence from the Offenbach workshops of the great Rudolf Koch was brought to America by Warren Chappell, who together with young Dard Hunter and Victor Hammer, knows how to cut a punch by hand. J. H. Benson and A. G. Carey in Newport, Rhode Island, have brought psychological and philosophical depth to the practice of hand lettering and, incidentally, the cutting of letters in stone. Oscar Ogg is one of the most able and versatile masters and teachers of calligraphy today. Arnold Bank, and a large group of promising young people, are active in the field.

What do we owe to this movement and to these men? Perhaps the broadest importance of these efforts can be seen in its effect on everyday handwriting and, more particularly, on the way it is and will be taught in our schools. That is a matter which reaches far beyond the scope of the present volume, unless one believes, as this author does, that the general acceptance of such a reform can have decisive consequences on the future creative growth of the graphic arts in general. More immediate effects of the movement have been an increased skill and freedom in preparatory typographic layout; the more general, intelligent use of hand lettering on book jackets, title pages, initials and various other display features in current books; also some very charming experiments with handwritten pages reproduced by offset lithography. Dwiggins' *Marionette in Motion* is a modest demonstration of a procedure which could become a valuable technique in the coming age of book production by offset. It would be especially suitable in the inexpensive publication of poetry.

The seeming paradox that increased mechanization and industrialization only emphasize and enhance the importance of creative, personal design is worth remembering. The most important demonstration of this situation lies in the field of contemporary American type design. In the advance from the everlasting revival of the great type faces of the past and from a general academic design approach toward genuine contemporary articulation, calligraphy proved a wonderful training ground. Behind the work of such valuable type designers as Dwiggins and Ruzicka, Joseph Blumenthal, Lucian Bernhard, Warren Chappell, Victor Hammer and Howard Trafton lies the calligraphic experience. Nor should it be overlooked that these men have not only produced foundry type for hand composition, but they have designed fonts which are available on various composing machines for trade book production. Dwiggins' Electra and Ruzicka's Fairfield, produced by the Mergenthaler Linotype Company, are important milestones on this road.

Perhaps some readers will feel that all this is a rather subjective and, perhaps, slightly exaggerated view of the situation. An examination of the type faces employed in the "Fifty Books of the Year," selected annually by the American Institute of Graphic Arts, furnishes some hard facts which are decidedly illuminating. In the 1939 catalog we find that in forty-two out of the total of fifty books, such historical type faces as Garamond, Estienne, Granjon, Janson, Caslon, Baskerville, Bodoni and Scotch Roman were used. Only two books were set in a type face designed by a contemporary American artist with a strong calligraphic background. In the 1946 catalog, this latter group is represented in no less than eighteen books.

It is of course true that in the field of calligraphy and type design the situation is particularly favorable for a close application of personal skill to mechanical production. In the field of hand binding, for instance, it is not nearly as favorable. Experts in the field have recognized that an apprenticeship in hand binding can be immensely valuable to the designer as well as the producer of machine binding. Hand binding also has a vital and not sufficiently recognized function in the preservation of materials worth keeping. But above all, it is a field of craftsmanship that offers peculiar challenges and special rewards to its devotees. Against many skeptics the art of hand binding has survived the first impact of industrialization. When we organized an international exhibition at Columbia University in 1935, more than half a dozen countries sent collections of books which were bound with immaculate technical perfection and at the same time showed genuine originality of design. Nor has World War II eradicated this art from the surface of the globe.

In America at the present time, the number of professional hand binders whose work shows both originality of design and technical excellence is small. The nineteenth century tradition of luxurious, often over-elaborate design, imitating the great historical styles in bookbinding, still lingers on. This precious eclecticism still seems to dominate the taste of wealthy patrons and amateurs, including a good many lady binders. Certain commercial binding firms also cater to this group. It will be interesting to see if the efforts of a few forward-looking men and women eventually will bring about a more general reform and acceptance of the contemporary idiom, or if they will remain isolated experiments. There are a few hopeful signs. The Guild of Book Workers, since 1948 an affiliate of the American Institute of Graphic Arts, is undergoing a reorganization which it expects will have beneficial results. The classes in hand binding conducted since the early thirties at Columbia University by Gerhard and Kathryn Gerlach, have opened up new vistas to a considerable number of individuals, some of whom are working seriously in the field.

Laboratory courses in the graphic arts have greatly increased in number and variety of offerings throughout the last decades. A young man or woman coming to New York in the fall of the year can select all the various workshop courses necessary in building the foundations of a genuine creative career. This type of instruction is now being offered by several of the universities and colleges and by various other educational organizations and institutions. Some such opportunities exist also elsewhere in the country. Undergraduate colleges have increasingly adopted the graphic arts into their curriculum, or have arranged for informal, intimate contact with the world of printing and bookmaking. The work of Ray Nash at Dartmouth, of Elmer Adler at Princeton, of Philip Hofer at Harvard, may be cited as examples of such developments in the East; they too have their counterpart here and there throughout the country. Book arts courses in library schools in many states are steadily increasing the appreciation of the art of printing and of its vital function in our society and our culture.

The printing industry at large has been slow to recognize the value of such developments. Its approach to education has been far too much of a purely technical nature, emphasizing mechanical proficiency, management and salesmanship. There is a very real need for much closer co-operation and co-ordination of the educational efforts of the industry with those of the cultural institutions. Here is the only practical way of mastering the threat of the machine age and of safeguarding human dignity and freedom in this important field of endeavor.

Certain groups and organizations have rendered valuable services in

these directions. With robust sincerity, Paul A. Bennett of the Mergenthaler Linotype Company has held together a Wednesday luncheon
group in mid-Manhattan, known as The Typophiles, and in existence
since the early thirties. Through a remarkable series of chapbooks, informal in approach, small in format, and big in substance, this group
has exerted a considerable influence.

In Chicago, there is the Society of Typographic Arts, organized in
1927. Its stated objectives are: "To promote high standards in the
typographic arts by all possible means; to foster and encourage education in these arts; to elevate public taste in matters typographic; and
to co-operate with all other organizations and institutions having
similar aims." The Bookbuilders of Boston have also been a lively and
active group, with a well-integrated program and visiting lecturers of
national renown. The Philadelphia Book Clinic has been the meeting
ground for all those interested in the graphic arts in that region.

An organization whose steady influence from year to year has been
a factor of great significance in book production is the American Institute of Graphic Arts. The Institute was organized in February, 1914,
when the United States was invited to participate in the famous international "Bugra" exhibition of graphic arts in Leipzig. Although it was
too late then to arrange for a representative American participation,
the Institute became a permanent organization "to stimulate and encourage those engaged in the graphic arts; to form a center for intercourse and for exchange of views of all interested in these arts . . . and
generally to do all things which will raise the standard and aid the extension and development toward perfection of the graphic arts in the
United States."

The functions of the Institute include the organization of exhibitions,
both national and international in scope; the circulation of many of
these throughout the country, and some of them in foreign countries;
the issuing of various publications and newsletters; the distribution of
awards; and, more recently, the organization of workshops in the
graphic arts.

Of the many stimulating activities the annual selection of the "Fifty
Books of the Year" has probably been of greatest influence in book
production. The first selection was made in 1923, and was so successful
that the idea since then has been taken up in many European countries.

One of the important lessons taught by this annual event, through the opportunity to compare "limited editions" and "trade books," was the demonstration that trade books and also textbooks in their own way can be made as attractive as many of the books produced under special circumstances, and that books are not attractive simply because they have been done expensively. The "Fifty Book" exhibitions which are reviewed, discussed and criticized each year, have done much to break up antiquated traditions which stood in the way of a normal and natural development toward contemporary expression; they have also helped to curb too violent activities along the lines of experimentation.

In order to provide a platform for detailed discussions of the problems of trade book design, a Book Building Clinic was organized by the Institute in 1931 under the original chairmanship of Harry L. Gage. The idea of these "Book Clinics," as they soon came to be called, was taken up in several cities. Later on, there was a division of functions, resulting in the separate establishment of a Trade Book Clinic and a Textbook Clinic, which assumed the very worth-while task of removing the seemingly unsurmountable barriers which had prevented textbooks from sharing in the general revival of book design. Both groups have held and are still holding periodic exhibitions and they have published catalogs which are eloquent documents of progress.

For a considerable number of years progressive typographic design has been encouraged by Dr. Robert Leslie of the Composing Room in New York, through exhibitions at his A-D Gallery and various graphic arts publications.

The Trade Book

A description of the design and production of contemporary trade books is difficult because the picture is both uneven and changing. Within the last twenty years there has been a noticeable improvement of standards, but even today there are publishing firms which have remained indifferent towards the attractive and intelligent designing of their product. The difficulties which stand in the way of more rapid and general improvement frequently arise from the organization of production. The physical preparation of the average trade book is the job of the publisher's manufacturing department which, however, does not necessarily have final authority in deciding the details of production. The word of the sales department, often in the person of an influential traveling representative, carries a great deal of weight. In some instances this can be a rather disturbing factor, particularly when the staff of the publisher's production department, as is sometimes the case, consists of people without any particular typographic training and taste, and where the emphasis lies too heavily on meeting production schedules and in saving as much money as possible. In such cases much of the responsibility for design and execution falls, of course, to the printer. It is not infrequently a matter of chance whether anyone, in the course of the production of a given book, has had the opportunity to visualize ahead of time the final, combined outcome of the various manufacturing stages. Quite often a book is pushed through without a plan, and it is easy to imagine the result in cases where printing, binding and the jacket are in the hands of separate firms who know nothing of the other features of the book. All that matters, under such circumstances, is low production price, speed, and an effect which will help to sell the book. Good taste is only one of a number of devices which the publisher who is essentially indifferent in these matters may employ as a means to interest the public in a book. In many cases the most important thing still is that the book must look its price, and possibly a little more than that, so that the customer feels that he is getting more than his money's worth. Binding and jacket are designed not to give permanent satisfaction to the reader, but merely to attract attention in the window and on the counter. Even with publishers who in other regards have fallen in with the trend towards better made trade books, the binding has remained a rather drab affair until quite recently. The last years, though, have seen some very real improvements in book jackets and binding.

In the jacket field, no one person has done more, by example, as a patient teacher, both of his students and of his printers, and by stubborn refusal to cut corners, than George Salter. He was instrumental in the establishment of the Book Jacket Designers Guild in 1947, which the following year held its first annual exhibition, including the work of some seventy artists. The guild believes in the combination of high artistic level and mechanical perfection, but allows that the forcefulness of an idea can compensate for lesser skill. Convincing portrayal of the book is given heavy credit, an emphasis which will be welcomed by all the users of books, including many public librarians, who have been misled by the frequent misrepresentations of a book's content through its jacket. The guild also disclaims all connection with "top-heavy ladies draped in undress," no doubt a wise decision.

One bad habit, the bulking of paper to add artificially to the weight and thickness of the volume, disappeared during the war, but is unfortunately coming back as a sales prop. The deliberate roughing of the edges of the pages, simulating the deckle edge of handmade paper, is one of the gentle deceptions still practiced here and there. One should further consider that all trade books are printed rapidly from plates, and that in the case of a best seller, speed of production becomes the paramount factor in determining the kind of presswork to be employed.

The question may arise in the mind of the reader why the less happy aspects of contemporary trade book design should be dwelled upon. For one thing, it is difficult to write of current conditions with the same detachment with which one describes past developments. Also, such detachment is undesirable when one believes that to give information about unsatisfactory conditions is one way of inducing a change to the good. Furthermore, these difficulties are typical not of the entire realm of trade book production today, but of those circles that have remained indifferent to the reform movement of recent years.

It is not easy to understand why this reform should have set in so late in the twentieth century. Once more one cannot help but regret that the improvements in trade book design which the literary publisher of the nineties had brought about failed to make a lasting impression. The fact remains, whatever may have been the reason, that when these personal publishing ventures came to an end around the turn of the century, the interest in trade book design died down completely. Neither the older nineteenth century publishing houses which were now reorganized and in new hands, nor the newly established firms, such as Doubleday, Page and others, felt any appreciable interest in raising the physical quality of their trade books.

So everything had to be done from the start when people began to realize what had been overlooked. The real pioneer of the modern trade book reform is William Addison Dwiggins. In 1915 he brought out, together with his cousin Laurence B. Siegfried, a pamphlet entitled *Extracts From An Investigation Into the Physical Properties of Books*

As They Are Now Published, a flaming protest against the current indifference and neglect.

Dwiggins, who was born in Martinsville, Ohio, in 1880, had studied in Chicago and came east to Boston in 1904, where from 1917-18 he was an acting director of the Harvard University Press. He also worked for the Yale University Press, designing jackets, end papers, bindings and posters. Then his influence began to be felt among the New York publishers, and Alfred A. Knopf in particular recognized his power and his skill. Dwiggins also worked in the limited editions field, where his brilliant designing and illustrating attracted a great deal of attention. He has also written humorously and imaginatively about printing. *Mss by WAD* is the title of a Typophile Chapbook (No. XVII) in which some of his most interesting writings have been collected.

He gives perhaps of his very best as a calligrapher. His hand-lettered title pages, running heads, picture captions and book backs, in slanting delicacy, have an individual touch. He is also very much interested in ornament, where he has been daringly independent. His bindings have paper covers in warm, soft shades and strong black calico backs with delicate gold lettering and very rich decoration. Most of his designs, by the way, are really much too original and too personal to be ideal solutions of the book designing problem; but they have a power of their own which is always refreshing and wears well. Dwiggins is undoubtedly the most talented book artist of the middle generation in America. He has had the satisfaction of seeing the effects of his efforts on the younger book designers as well as on publishers. Not that he has actually been imitated very much, in the way in which Updike or Rogers have been imitated—but his wonderful way of working with plenty of white space, his attainment of strong effects with often the most sparing means, all this has been a most salutary and inspiring influence.

Most of the typographers and designers who are responsible for trade book design today are, like the publishers, located in New York. Their functions and activities differ in accordance with their positions. They are either publishers' manufacturing men, or associated in various ways with printing and binding firms. There is also a chance for the free lance in the field, and specialization upon certain fields is not infrequent.

A list of the men and women who have been prominently associated with good book design since the thirties would include such publishers' manufacturing men as John Benbow, Arthur Rushmore, Milton Glick, Evelyn Harter, Sidney R. Jacobs, Philip Van Doren Stern, Anthony P. Tedesco, Arthur Williams, Daniel F. Bradley and John Begg, who established his reputation as a textbook specialist; and among the people who have either worked with manufacturing plants or as free lance designers, Richard Ellis, formerly in the limited editions field. Ernst Reichl, Andor Braun, Paul Johnston, also known as author and publisher in the typographic field, and Robert Josephy, who has made an outstanding success as a free lance in addition to his cultivation of a Connecticut apple and peach orchard and of the Book and Magazine Guild, a white-collar union for people in the book trade. Of these, John Benbow is no longer with us, some have since taken on added editorial responsibilities or have moved to other fields or have retired; but several of these people are very much in the picture today. New talent has of course found its way into positions which are offering opportunities for worth-while book designing, including such names as Stefan Salter, Morris Colman, Maurice S. Kaplan, James Hendrickson, Abe Lerner, Peter Oldenburg and Alma Cardi. Alvin Eisenman, one of a small group of designers specially interested in textbook production, has now moved on to the Yale University Press.

Paul McPharlin's highly promising appearance on the typographic stage—only one of the innumerable fields of creative design that held his attention—was unfortunately much too brief. One of the world's greatest authorities on puppets, the moving spirit of a "Fine Book Circle," keenly interested in the history of printing, wielding a facile pen, he died in 1948, much too early.

The designer employed by a publisher has the welcome opportunity to follow up his designs through various stages of production and to preserve, in case of corrections or change of plans, the harmonious entity of the work, although this does not mean that he is always the final authority in matters of production. Also he is often burdened down with such an overwhelming mass of routine and detail work that he sometimes has no time, at least during office hours, really to develop a plan for a given volume. Much depends in such cases upon a quick eye, a rapid sketching hand, luck and the chance to make corrections at various stages of the manufacturing process. Particular conditions prevail, of course, when the publisher has his own manufacturing plant.

The free lance typographer has the possibility to concentrate upon worth-while projects and to select the jobs which will give him an opportunity to solve an interesting problem in an interesting way. But of course he, too, has to make a living. One disturbing element, once he is at work, is the lack of opportunity to see his plans carried consistently through the various manufacturing stages. Not all designers are as skillful as they might be in anticipating production difficulties. Not infrequently the services of the free lance end upon his delivering the layout, and he may not see his work again until it appears, often with arbitrary changes, in the final product. Since he is judged by his products this can be quite a hardship. At the basis of this practice is an older notion, fortunately on the wane, that design is an element which can be deliberately attached, in the form of a fancy title page and a little ornamentation here and there, to an otherwise routine production. There are, even today, a number of publishers who are satisfied with this procedure. However, such publishers as Alfred Knopf and the Viking Press have long ago recognized the value of careful and attractive book design, not only of individual volumes, but of their entire list. There is no doubt that there is an increasing number of publishers who realize that a certain consistency of style and quality does much to identify the individual volumes in a desirable way with the general policies of their firms.

A large portion of the country's trade book production lies in the hands of a comparatively small number of book manufacturing concerns which are definitely organized for this work. These firms include, in or near the New York City area, the H. Wolff Book Manufacturing Company; J. J. Little & Ives Company; the Van Rees Press; the American Book-Stratford Press, with which the Knickerbocker Printing Corporation was merged in 1950 to form the American Book–Knickerbocker Press; George McKibbin & Son; in New Jersey, Quinn & Boden; the Haddon Craftsmen, formerly in Camden, New Jersey, now in Scranton, Pennsylvania. The George Grady Press in New York City works primarily for institutions of higher education and the government. Then there is a considerable number of small town printing firms which work or have worked for the New York publishers, such as, to name only a few, E. L. Hildreth & Co. formerly of Brattleboro, Vermont, now in Bristol, Connecticut, as the Hildreth Press; the Plimpton Press and the Norwood Press in Norwood, Massachusetts; the Colonial Press in Clinton, Massachusetts; Braunworth & Company in Bridgeport, Connecticut, active until 1941; Vail-Ballou in Binghamton, New York; and the Kingsport Press, Inc., in Kingsport, Tennessee. The Athenaeum Press in Boston occupies an important position in textbook production; Taylor & Taylor in San Francisco, established in 1896 by Edward DeWitt Taylor, is another example of a book printing firm in a large city other than New York.

The interests of the book printing industry with its various collateral branches are represented by the Book Manufacturers' Institute, first organized in 1932. The Institute has been active in the public relations field, in conducting co-operative research into reading and book buying habits, in stimulating book promotion schemes, and in watching over the relationship of its members with the publishing industry.

Recent Trends and Developments

What effect did World War II have on American book design and production? That is a very interesting question. It can be said that by 1939 matters had reached a high point of dynamic forcefulness. The stiffly conventional colonial pattern had largely given way to a freer and more natural expression and there was great willingness to experiment, to branch out, to include new groups of books, new tasks into the area of experimentation. Pictorial material was handled with unorthodox ingenuity. The war stopped all this. An era of severe austerity cast its shadow on bookmaking. Painful production bottlenecks, material shortages, lack of skilled labor, concentration of publishing on a small group of war-vital titles in exceedingly large editions, all this presented an unprecedented challenge. It acted like a chemical solvent. With an almost audible sigh of relief the half-hearted and the unconvinced dropped what had plainly been an awkward responsibility. Under these wartime restrictions and the legal limitations imposed by an anxious government, the element of design simply disappeared in many instances. But the genuine designers, the really sincere and capable people rose to new heights. They produced masterpieces of economical, stringently forceful bookmaking, as effective, and often more so, than what they had produced under easier circumstances.

Rather slowly, the losses sustained during the war have been repaired. It is a somewhat melancholy, but nevertheless accurate fact that good bookmaking suffered more severely in the United States than in many European countries which were hit more directly. There are probably two main reasons for this, both of them rather simple ones. Everyone knows that the high level of modern bookmaking in the European countries rests on a long continuity of experience and a carefully co-ordinated education and training program, in other words on very firm foundations. In America, these very foundations are still being laid, simultaneously with, and largely in terms of, current problems—altogether a much more vulnerable situation. Secondly, the first stage of a new mass production era in bookmaking coincided with the war, was in fact precipitated by the war.

The urgent need for a vigorous, fresh attack on aesthetic indifference, on convenient laissez-faire, on stupid conventions is being felt not only by the professional book designers who work from within, but also by the designers at large. Because of the breadth of his vision, the strength of his convictions and the energies which he is able to set in motion, the general and industrial designer has an extremely valuable contribution to make. Merle Armitage is recognized as one of the leaders of this movement, which is supported by such artists as Paul Rand and Alvin Lustig.

The potential contribution that can result from this approach is an exceedingly important one, but there are certain distinct dangers here. There is a temptation to disregard technical limitations, the economic element, and the special problems of bookmaking and, above all, the habits of book readers.

If the contribution of the general designer to the field of bookmaking is to be truly effective, it must not attempt simply to jump ahead, to bypass all the fundamental basic training which the study of traditions provides. To reconcile him to these special conditions, to utilize and properly to channel his energies is one of the most important tasks of the future.

The particular urgency of these matters is rooted in the spectacular increase of mass production since the end of the thirties. The large printing of certain individual titles badly needed in the war effort was only one of the factors. The Pocket Book venture, it will be remembered, started in 1939, and other twenty-five cent editions followed promptly. In the paper-covered Armed Services Editions, these first experiences were utilized and adapted to a program of incalculable influence. A format was decided upon which made possible the rapid, inexpensive and uniform production of a great variety of titles on rotary magazine presses. It also presented these books in a deceptively non-bookish garb, shrewdly designed to overcome resistance of large groups of youthful readers brought up on a diet of magazines and comic books.

The new, inexpensive mass production projects have alternatingly depended upon and have stimulated new technological developments in the printing industry. For instance, Pocket Books had to take a chance on their early runs and produce their books at a higher cost than they could be sold for, in order to demonstrate the new markets. When they succeeded, they were able to order their own printing presses, built to satisfy their particular requirements. Other printers installed similar presses in order to be able to serve other publishers of paper-covered reprints. The comic books, first produced on existing newspaper presses, and *Readers' Digest*, first limited to available equipment, were likewise able to stimulate construction of new presses which were then used by other concerns with similar publishing programs.

"Perfect" binding, which eliminated sewing needle and thread and depends upon adhesives only, is a basic process in the production of paper-covered reprints. Metal plates have been supplanted successfully and on a broad scale by rubber and plastic plates at substantial savings. In photoengraving, the Fairchild Engraver, which produces plates by a radically new method, is finding increasing use.

One of the most conspicuous developments is the printing of entire books by offset. This procedure has long been used as an inexpensive means of reprinting out-of-print editions which required little or no resetting of the original text, and, of course, in the printing of children's picture books. In textbooks which called for the reproduction of a variety of documentary material, such as graphs and charts, drawings and photographs in various combinations, the offset process was soon recognized as a practical solution. From occasional, special use it was a relatively simple step to a broader, more general employment of the offset process in book production. The general significance of these developments was recognized by the American Institute of Graphic Arts in 1942, when a selection of ninety outstanding offset-printed books was shown in its "Books by Offset" exhibition. In 1946, "Books by Offset Lithography, Inc." was set up by the lithographic industry as an educational, non-profit organization which held a number of annual exhibitions.

The use of the offset process as a practical alternative to relief printing in the production of trade and textbooks is a characteristic American development. On the other hand it must be said that American publishers have been less inclined to rely on offset for high quality color reproduction work than have their European colleagues.

Another interesting development has come along with the use of offset in trade books—the elimination of conventional typesetting through the use of special typewriters with which to prepare copy. The IBM typewriter, the Varityper and now the Justowriter are being used in this connection. With the Justowriter, typewritten copy with an even right margin is now possible without the necessity for double-keyboarding. The production of better type designs for these machines is also under way. The Intertype Fotosetter, and the American Type Founders Company's Hadego, are the first successful steps towards photographic typesetting, revolutionary new means of producing text matter without the use of metal types for direct photomechanical plate production. Although at present offset is the favored method of reproducing typed or fotoset texts, the introduction of the low-cost etched magnesium plate offers the possibility that the letterpress process will also be able to compete.

At long last paper is finding increased use on the covers of trade books, often in combination with cloth spines, and the use of one kind of cloth for spine and hinges and another for the rest of the case is no longer a luxury. Alert designers are taking advantage of these new opportunities which are in part due to a new case-making machine into which cloth is fed with the spine instead of across it.

These are only some of the more advanced innovations from among a vast variety of new experiments and approaches. These developments are being watched with keen interest and anticipation by the publishing industry, as a possible help in the seemingly insoluble problem of excessive production costs. Some of the prognostications have been over-optimistic and obviously the result of wishful thinking. Some of the most tangible economies in regular trade book production to date have been effected by larger runs and by voluntary standardization of book formats (regular trade as well as book club editions and reprint series) in combination with the placing of printing orders for entire groups of titles with the same manufacturing concern. The use of plastic plates, too, has helped to cut costs.

To what extent not only the mass media, such as magazines and the twenty-five cent books, but also regular trade and textbooks and university press books will be caught up and benefited by the revolution of the graphic arts, remains to be seen. There are some definite indications that these groups of books, too, will be affected. One thing is certain—the more successful this technological revolution turns out to be, the greater will be the need for the guiding hand of the creative designer.

A Note on American Book Illustration Since 1860

Book illustration does not play a very important part in the development of the book in America. It does not influence the course of events in the sense in which the woodcut, for instance, has influenced the books printed in the fifteenth century, or in which the copper engraving became part of the essential structure of the book in the later renaissance.

That the work of early American engravers on copper and wood, the rise of steel engraving and lithography after 1800, and nineteenth century pre-photographic illustration are nevertheless worthy of the attention of students and collectors, has been made clear in the earlier sections of this volume.

There has already been mentioned Felix Octavius Carr Darley, the outstanding American illustrator of the mid-nineteenth century. His illustrations for Washington Irving (1848 and 1850) and for Hawthorne (1879) are outline drawings in the general classical manner, but with a good deal of attention to local detail; they appeared as lithographs. For his famous Cooper illustrations (1859–61) the best bank note engravers of the day were employed. As the publishers explained, this was the first attempt to introduce into book illustration the deep cutting and the clear, detailed line-work that was customary in bank note engraving and which was obtained at about double the price paid for ordinary steel engraving.

Bank note engraving was a distinct American specialty, drawing into its realm some of the best talents. The portraits and the ornaments on the paper money and securities of the nineteenth century were done with extreme skill and a great deal of love. Every stamp collector knows the series of portraits of the American presidents. Even today, as a glance at our paper currency will reveal, steel engraving carries with it the ornamental traditions of the romantic period, an interesting example of an apparently inseparable liaison between a technique and the artistic fashion dominant at the time of its first flourishing.

Within the realm of the wood engraving the development led to a rapid technical refinement, simultaneous with the loss of much of the genuine character of that process. Soon after the middle of the century, wood engraving became purely a method of reproduction with little artistic character of its own. At the same time the artists who drew the pictures emancipated themselves from the engravers, who became more and more technicians only.

Illustration was decidedly a popular art in those days. It was an indispensable element of the lavish gift book which lay on every parlor table. It greatly helped the subscription agents traveling through the rural districts to convince the housewife that his volumes would appeal to everyone in the family. Wood engraving was the broad medium through which many generations of young Americans first visualized the things that had come to pass in this world before they were born and which brought them the first images of the realms that lay beyond their own horizon.

The American nineteenth century comic book has a history of its own which has yet to be written. One of the best known examples is the *Journey to the Gold Diggins* by one Jeremiah Saddlebags, reported in comic pictures by the brothers James A. and Donald F. Read, New York and Cincinnati, 1849. Illustration also played a considerable part in the first publication of many works which we now consider of literary significance. Bret Harte's *The Heathen Chinee*, to mention only one example, came out first as a series of nine lithographed cards in an envelope, drawn by Joseph Hull, and published in Chicago in 1870.

An entire group of artists and engravers collected around the Harper publishing firm to such an extent that one can almost speak of a Harper school of wood engraving. These artists and engravers worked mainly for the many magazines of the firm. Much of their work, in these days before the printing of photographs had become a practical reality, was documentary in nature. Winslow Homer, for instance, covered the Civil War from the home office, while other artists worked in the field. One of the greatest talents working for Harper's and also for Scribner's was Thomas Nast, characterized by John A. Kouwenhoven as that "earnest little German-American" who created "such symbols as the Tammany tiger, the Republican elephant, and the Democratic donkey." This man was, however, not a book illustrator at all. We will find again and again that some of the best graphic talent in America works chiefly for the newspapers and the magazines, and only incidentally for books. It is often impossible, among the artists and engravers of those days, to distinguish book illustrators from magazine illustrators and newspaper cartoonists. Among the most capable engravers of the latter nineteenth century we find William James Linton, A. V. S. Anthony, John P. Davis, Frederick Juengling, Richard A. Mueller, John Tinkey, Henry Wolf and Timothy Cole, who died only in 1931.

An important book publication of Harper's to which many artists and engravers contributed was the Bible of 1843, illustrated with no less than 1400 wood engravings. Similar voluminous works appeared later, such as Appleton's *Picturesque America*, published 1872-1874, which still contained a number of steel plates along with the much more successful wood engravings. Among the many artists of this group, Benson J. Lossing, with his *Pictorial Field-Book of the Revolution* has already been mentioned by Mr. Wroth. His book of travels and of views, *The Hudson from the Wilderness to the Sea* (1866), combines graphic charm with the interest of the subject matter. Lively and natural illustrations, somewhat uneven in artistic quality, are found in David Hunter Strother's *Virginia Illustrated*, which Harper published in 1871 under Strother's favorite pseudonym, "Porte Crayon."

The books with wood engravings of this period show the same organic fitting together of picture and text which the collectors enjoy in the European books of this period. In the course of the seventies and eighties a new style of book illustration came about. There appeared an increasingly free and sweeping pen and ink manner, which coincided with the change from wood engraving to photomechanical line engraving. The surviving wood engraving soon began to reflect the tonal gradations of photography and of photographic halftone engraving. There are late wood engravings by Timothy Cole which one may almost look upon as manual reproductions in wood of halftone engravings.

The illustrative work of Winslow Homer stands midway between the older and the newer school. There is increasing freedom in his art, the gradual displacement of the episode and the anecdote by powerful dramatic concentration. But although his talent leads him away from applied illustration to free painting, even his most mature oils and watercolors betray a strong illustrative instinct. The change from the old school of careful, detailed line work, that was intended to be cut in wood, to the new freedom of pen and ink illustrations, which were easily reproduced photomechanically, characterized the work of Edwin A. Abbey, the illustrator of Robert Herrick's poems (1882) and of *Old Songs* (1889).

The best representatives of the pen and ink school in this country are at the same time specialists of the American scene. One feels in their work the love and warmth of personal observation, and a knowledge of detail, which compensates for an occasional lack of originality and artistic consistency.

Genuine illustrations, in the best sense of the word, are E. W. Kemble's pictures for Mark Twain's *Huckleberry Finn*. Once you have read an edition with his illustrations, you will continue to see the people and the scenes of this book as Kemble saw them. Kemble reveals himself as an observing expert of the life of colored folk in the South in his illustrations for Joel Chandler Harris' *On the Plantation, A Story of a Georgia Boy's Adventure During the War*. Harris' famous Uncle Remus stories were illustrated by another member of "the free pen and ink school," A. B. Frost, whose humorous pictures for that book have not been forgotten. His illustrations for H. C. Bunner's *The*

Story of a New York House are a little more reserved. Into this group belongs also C. S. Reinhart, who made, for instance, amusing and freshly drawn sketches of travel and summer resort life for Charles Dudley Warner's *Their Pilgrimage* (1893).

A distinguished connoisseur of Indian and Western life is Frederic Remington. For Longfellow's *Hiawatha*, for instance, he designed innumerable marginal drawings, which show details of Indian life with such exactness and expert knowledge that they may well be considered as reliable ethnological source material. The very extensive body of his work, the books which he has written and illustrated and his individual contributions to books and magazines, have been carefully collected and listed in Harold McCracken's biography, which appeared in 1947.

In the eighties we encounter the first monumental illustrations reproduced by the aid of photography, in a somewhat weighty symbolic and classical style, such as Will H. Low's Keats illustrations of 1885 and 1886 and the rather awkward illustrations for Rossetti's *Blessed Damozel* by Kenyon Cox, which appeared in 1886. In this group belongs also the Rubáiyát edition of 1884, handwritten and decorated by Elihu Vedder in a manner somewhat reminiscent of Blake, but so full of ornamental allusions and hidden symbols that the decorations have to be explained in detail at the end of the volume. A comparison of these illustrations with the ones which he and John LaFarge had made for an 1865 edition of *Enoch Arden* shows a long road traveled since then.

If one is looking for a good example of illustration by the halftone relief process so popular at the turn of the century, Sarah Orne Jewett's *Deephaven* will answer the purpose nicely. There appeared in 1894 an illustrated gift edition of this nostalgic story of a New England fishing village. Friends of the authoress, the Woodburys—Charles Herbert, the marine painter, and his wife Marcia Oakes, specializing in "Dutch genre"—made the illustrations. They drew gently realistic sketches with the brush, which were reproduced rather timidly and with excessive reduction.

Howard Pyle is the most representative American illustrator of the late nineteenth and the early twentieth centuries. His first work appeared in *Scribners' Monthly* in 1876 and for many years his illustrations were a leading feature of *Harper's*. Upon his death in 1911 he left behind him a very many-sided and voluminous body of work. His early academic training brought him under the influence of the Pre-Raphaelite school of black and white drawing; then, for a while, he practiced the realistic and free pen and ink manner; but he soon returned to medieval allusion and to symbolic representation. The development of four-color halftone printing stimulated his painting interests, and for a while he fell in with the artists who, like Rackham and Dulac, explored the possibilities of photomechanical color printing. The flexibility of his style is equalled in the variety of his subjects; he has revived in his pictures the colonial period, the Revolutionary Wars, the Middle Ages, pirate life, Indian warfare, fables, fairy tales, and allegory. Howard Pyle is still one of the best known of all American illustrators. In his Wilmington, Delaware, studio he had a great influence also as a teacher of such well-known artists as Maxfield Parrish, Jessie Wilcox Smith and N. C. Wyeth. These were in the early group to explore the new possibilities of four-color halftone printing. Not all of their work would pass current standards, technically and aesthetically, but they had a considerable effect in their day, especially on illustration for children.

The amazing Joseph Pennell (1860-1926), prominent etcher and painter of the impressionistic era, achieved remarkable success in illustration. He left behind a substantial body of work to testify to his brilliant, nervous talent.

Charles Dana Gibson, who illustrated both magazines and books, made pen and ink drawings which will always be remembered as witty and spontaneous documents of a definite era of American life.

Illustration early in this century seems to lack direction and distinction. It appears that comparatively little work done during those years is likely to survive. The contemporary school of book illustration, too, does not present itself as clearly outlined as that of the nineteenth century, but this may be due in part to the lack of perspective. In the general publishing picture illustration has not fared badly in the last two decades. The role of the illustrator in developing the program of both the Limited Editions and the Heritage Club has been an essential one. The Book-of-the-Month Club has drawn heavily on the appeal of the printed picture in various dividends and premiums. The Illustrated Modern Library was launched as a special medium for the pictorial enhancement of literature. Mass production of illustrated children's books can now be seen as one of the major developments of the forties. This does not, of course, take into account the comic books —an altogether different story.

The question whether a definite American style in book illustration can be said to have evolved, is not easily answered. "It is doubtful," wrote Carl Zigrosser in the catalog, *International Book Illustration 1935-1945*, published by the American Institute of Graphic Arts in 1946, "whether this can be affirmed without qualifications. The United States by its very nature is a melting pot, a conglomeration of heterogeneous and as yet unfused elements in a vast and varied country. As a freedom-loving democracy we have always welcomed visitors and colonizers from older countries. We are receptive to the cultures these people brought with them; we are curious to read the classics produced by other cultures; we contrive to print these classics with illustrations not only by our native artists but also by those from afar who have found refuge in our land. These varied cultural strains are a fructifying impulse, and add greatly to the richness and diversity of our panorama. Therefore, although we may not boast of an American style or language, we are justified, I believe, in speaking of an American accent. We can discover subtle traces of a new approach and a distinctive way of doing things. . . . Our tradition is not behind us: it is still in the making."

One aspect of modern American book illustration that can be seen as a characteristic achievement is the success in the fields of travel and adventure. In books of discoveries, in tales of the sea for young people and for older ones, the American illustrator is greatly at his ease. Edward A. Wilson has been particularly happy in this field. He has become closely identified with contemporary American book illustration, and the fact that he was born in Glasgow and came to this country in 1893 is not known to many of his admirers. He spent two years with Howard Pyle in Wilmington. His illustrations for *Two Years before the Mast* for the Lakeside Press and for the Limited Editions Club's *Treasure Island* and *The Tempest* are among his best. Rockwell Kent, himself an ardent sailor and explorer, is a purist, who believes in the clear discipline of black and white drawing, carefully placed into the text. His sophisticated and witty drawings for *Candide* belong among the best American illustrations of this century.

Valenti Angelo, too, is much concerned with the aesthetic unity of text and picture, and there lives in his work a feeling for symmetry and harmony that seems a part of the Latin heritage. William A. Dwiggins has done excellent things in the field of book illustration. His drawings for Poe's *Tales* and for Stevenson's *Dr. Jekyll and Mr. Hyde* are masterpieces of intelligent and discreet interpretations. Anyone interested in the eternal question of what illustration should, and what it should not be, ought to read his *Form Letters: Illustrator to Author*. Dwiggins has always understood very nicely the sparing use of a little color along with black and white illustrations. In line with the printers' increasing skill in handling color in the press, his color work has gained in strength and breadth, and his Rabelais illustrations and the pictures for Robert Nathan's *One More Spring* are masterpieces of modern color printing.

Particularly interested in the woodcut, black and white and in color, are A. Allen Lewis, J. J. Lankes, Charles W. Smith, Norman Kent, Ernest and Eva Watson, Paul Landacre, Thomas W. Nason, and several others. Lynd Ward has made many contributions to book illustration. He was the first to develop in America the idea of the picture novel, which originated with the Flemish artist, Frans Masereel. He later added to the strict discipline of wood engraving a freer expression in color lithography, where he soon developed his own style. He has been very active in the juvenile field.

European artists have forever been well received and quickly made to feel at home in America. They usually bring along a developed sense of style, competent craftsmanship and definite knowledge of the possibilities and limitations of book illustration. America has offered them not only the chance to show what they can do, and an opportunity to make a living, but has often inspired them with new ideas and fresh powers of perception and of expression. It is so long ago since Rudolph Ruzicka came as a boy of eleven to America from Czechoslovakia, where he was born in 1883, that nobody thinks of him as anything but the recognized American master of polychrome wood engraving. His inborn sense of color and line, his solid and intelligent workmanship, his integrity and modesty have won him universal respect and admiration. The wood engravings in his *New York*, his *Fountains of Papal Rome*, both issued in 1915, the *Newark* volume issued in 1917, illustrations for Washington Irving, 1921, La Fontaine, 1930, Thoreau, also 1930, and for Oscar Wilde, 1936, his contribution to *Three Monographs on Color*, 1935, are his most important works to date. In 1948 the Grolier Club held an extensive exhibition of his engravings and typographic contributions, the catalog of which contains a useful check list.

At various times since the early thirties successful German graphic artists have come to make their home here. Richard Floethe, George Salter, the painter George Grosz, and such mature masters of the woodcut as Fritz Kredel, Hans Alexander Mueller, Fritz Eichenberg and Louis Hechenbleichner have made a substantial contribution to book illustration in America.

Fritz Eichenberg has gained a special reputation for his illustrations of the great nineteenth century Russian novelists and of the Brontës, into which he has poured immense energies of psychological penetration and of factual study. He has been active as a teacher, in creating artists' organizations, and he has taken a militant stand against the threatening standardization and mechanization of book illustration through mass production and mass distribution. The many children's books which he has illustrated have added to his reputation.

Boris Artzybasheff came here from Russia, and his decorative eccentricities have pleased collectors of book illustration as well as the children, for whom he has made some very successful picture books. Feodor Rojankovsky has also been especially welcomed in the juvenile field, where his vivid sense of color and his instinctive understanding of current production methods have quickly carried him into the first rank since he arrived here in 1941.

Roger Duvoisin, the son of a Geneva architect and trained as a textile designer, came to New York early in the thirties. He is perhaps the best representative of the French temperament in book illustration. Thoroughly spontaneous, with an innate sense of form and color, a lively imagination which expresses itself easily and naturally in the graphic medium, he has illustrated *Robinson Crusoe*, stories about Java, Bali and India, the homely maple leaf and the winter's snow in the American countryside.

The thing that surprises one again and again is the number of artists and designers who, without cultivating this field particularly, have occasionally turned to illustration and been remarkably fortunate there. For instance, the painters Grant Wood, Thomas Hart Benton, and Charles Demuth have illustrated books, and the architect Percival Goodman's drawings for *The Golden Ass* (Limited Editions Club, 1932) are interesting and delightful.

The revival of aboriginal American art in the hands of the Mexicans has added a striking note to contemporary book illustration. Covarrubias and Orozco have led the way with some interesting experiments in color. Also, book illustrations by artists of American Indian descent are not as rare today as they were one or two decades ago. Some of this work is of high integrity and forcefulness, in contrast with many illustrations which deal sentimentally or patronizingly with Indian life.

Pure photography, too, has found its place in American book illustration. Books have, of course, been illustrated with photographs for many years now. It is the natural medium for pictorial documentation. But the use of photographs to illustrate and interpret literature is a more recent development. Edward Steichen, for instance, has been successful with his photographic illustrations for *Walden*.

In children's illustration all the tendencies outlined above are reflected. Many of today's illustrators work in both the adult and the juvenile field. There is also a large group of men and women who devote their time and energy exclusively to children's illustration, which is a very active field indeed. There is not room in this brief note to go into details. The best source for information about the artists and the books which deserve to be known and remembered is the Hornbook's *Illustrators of Children's Books*, published in 1947. The Caldecott Medal, donated by Frederic Melcher and awarded by the Children's Library Association of the American Library Association to the artist who has illustrated the most distinguished picture book of the year, brings the opportunity for an annual review and evaluation.

In book illustration, too, the privileged position of the newspaper and the magazine in American life has been a very important factor.

The illustrator finds far better financial returns for his work in the magazine field, where his drawings are reproduced in editions far outnumbering any figures that he might hope for in the book world. It is no wonder, therefore, that many illustrators accept the standardizing and often commercializing influence of work for the magazines and, of course, for the advertising world. It can probably be said that the best graphic talents, the people who can, or could, do some of the most interesting work, do not always find their way to book illustration.

In his book on American illustration Henry C. Pitz speaks of these trends: "America," he says, "is a land of prodigious appetites. It is young enough to want to taste everything and young enough to draw strength from even an injudicious diet. Its strong gastric juices triumph over the strangest brews and the most cloying mixtures . . . Insistent demand for a never ending stream of easily read pictures has brought into being a giant mechanism for their production and distribution . . . The emphasis, however, is upon speed and size, not quality . . . The unique products of these presses are the large magazines—the great weeklies and monthlies of national circulation. They are without counterpart in the world of today. They are characteristically American . . . Although the separate categories of book, magazine, advertising and newspaper illustration exist, no one of them can be reviewed in complete isolation from the others, for the same types of pictures are found throughout. In fact, many illustrators work in two or three of these fields, sometimes in all of them. The categories interlock and together form a great popular art . . ."

How much talent is hidden, successfully, I admit, but nevertheless noticeable, in the comic strip! And one must not forget that amazing wonder child of the comic strip, the singing, dancing, colored motion picture cartoon. In the hands of Walt Disney and his faithful collaborators, the technicolor film has quite often become a happy and spontaneous field for the graphic phantasy and imagination of the American illustrator today. It is true that the recent mass production and mass distribution of inexpensive picture books has drawn to a considerable extent on the Disney studios and on similar sources. Elementary textbooks too have become a vehicle for this type of simplified graphic expression. How healthy these developments will prove to be in their ultimate effect on the visual habits and the emotional growth of children remains to be seen.

Simon and Schuster's "Little Golden Books," for instance, have been generally accepted by harassed parents and by visiting uncles and aunts as a marvellous solution of the gift problem. The individual volumes are usually well designed, with art work of acceptable quality, and fairly well reproduced. Nevertheless, some close observers view the scene with a certain degree of apprehension. When a discriminating saleswoman in a children's book department declares her boredom over the tedious monotony of such volumes as she handles them in quantities, when a publisher fears the decline of the publishing of individual juveniles by trade publishers because of mass production competition, when a book illustrator complains that he can no longer work on new problems and develop his style as he would like to, each of them is afraid of the same thing: of the possibility of a serious loss of cultural freedom.

PUBLISHING AND BOOKSELLING SINCE 1890

General Publishing Trends in the New Century

IN THE ORIGINAL EDITION of this book I attempted, at this point, to describe somewhat the mood of optimism which prevailed in America at the end of the last century—to explain, in other words, why the nineties were gay. I have spoken there of the progress in foreign policy, of the acquisition of new territories, of the magnificent achievements in industry and business and of the enjoyment of the large fortunes which had been made. All this is too well known to need rehearsing again before an American audience. Well known, too, is the fact that the very decade which is popularly remembered as the gay one, saw, from 1892-1898, one of the country's worst business depressions. The first symptoms of a critical attitude towards the age of materialism have been carefully observed by various students of American intellectual history. Anti-trust laws, election reforms, fight against corruption, rising taxation of the great fortunes, increasing organization of labor, minimum wage laws, use of government funds for public purposes—these are the first steps in the new orientation of the country early in the twentieth century. These steps had been preceded in the nineteenth century by discussions which were carried on particularly in the theological field. The emancipation of science and philosophy from the previous narrow dictatorship of the church was of great consequence. But also among the theologians themselves interest in social problems began to be felt. The universities, on the contrary, defended in closed formation the conservative point of view. But gradually in academic circles, too, a more critical attitude arose. Important authors devoted themselves to the study of the social theme, from a philosophical and theoretical point of view. Literature itself began to take up the subject. Particularly in the new novel and in the short story, fresh powers of thought and of expression broke forth.

An entirely new generation came to the fore. Henry James and William Dean Howells can perhaps be called the most prominent pioneers of the movement. They were joined by such popular authors as Hamlin Garland, O. Henry, Stephen Crane, and Jack London, who had risen successfully above the level of the "local color" tradition, and had made themselves heard in England and on the European continent as well as at home. They were the pacemakers of entire new schools of writers, of whom such men as Dreiser, Hergesheimer, Sinclair Lewis, Upton Sinclair, and Sherwood Anderson, were well known abroad. Others were better known at home, such authors as Edith Wharton, Willa Cather, Robert Herrick, James Branch Cabell, Edgar Lee Masters, and E. W. Howe. But whether nationally or internationally recognized, the main thing about the new generation of authors was that it existed. There can be no doubt that the passing of the copyright law of 1891 had done much to release these forces. It had freed the American author from the humiliating necessity to compete constantly against English authors under the most unfavorable circumstances, and to see their writings used as stop-gaps in magazines that were often patronizing rather than encouraging in their attitude.

The rise of the novel and the short story after the passing of the copyright act is most interestingly reflected in the publication statistics. In the decade 1890-1900 the number of new fiction titles published each year shows a slow but steady increase. In 1894 the figure is 729, in 1900 already 1278. The next year, in 1901, the figure is almost doubled, to 2234. In this record year the total amount of fiction published makes up as much as 27.4 per cent of the entire book production of the country. During all of the decade 1900-1910 the figure remains at a steady high figure. However, from 1911-1916 the annual output sinks again to about 1000 editions, approximately the level of the nineties. In 1914 fiction makes up only 8.77 per cent of the total output.

These figures seem to indicate that the new opportunities for authorship began to attract new talents and, in a general way, to stimulate the reading of fiction, until in 1901 this movement reaches a culmination point. Then saturation seems to occur, followed by a decade of stability, and then a slight reaction.

Fiction was of course only one part of the total book reading of the nation. One way of gaining an impression of the fluctuating tastes and preferences of readers is the study of best sellers. In 1895 Harry Thurston Peck, the editor of *The Bookman*, first conceived the idea of formulating systematic best seller lists in America, and he issued periodic summaries based on reports received from representative bookstores throughout the country. The idea was later taken up and developed through such media as *Publishers' Weekly*, the *Times Book Review*, the *Herald Tribune Weekly Book Review* and other book reviewing media. Alice Payne Hackett's *Fifty Years of Best Sellers 1895-1945* contains an illuminating year-by-year listing of best-selling fiction and of the war books published during World War I. The later chapters in Frank Luther Mott's *Golden Multitudes* trace the various reading trends which produce a best seller, and they interpret their meaning in the general life of the nation.

The study of reading habits by now has become almost an exact science. It would serve no useful purpose to duplicate in this volume the work that has been done by the many experts in this new field of social studies. The various volumes of the Public Library Inquiry, edited by Robert D. Leigh and a committee of highly qualified collaborators, contain valuable and up-to-date observations. Bernard Berelson's *The Library's Public*, in particular, conveys much information relevant to the total picture of reading in the United States, both in historical perspective and in its current aspects. Important statistical breakdowns, as well as other essential information, is also found in Cheney's *Economic Survey of the Book Industry 1930-31*, reissued in 1949 with a supplement.

The total number of new titles and new editions published annually in each field is also a valuable key to an understanding of the broad trends in publishing and reading. For this reason the figures for characteristic years since 1869 are shown on the table on page 321.

Interesting is the fact that while 1901 was a record year for fiction, a high all-around figure was reached in 1910. One notices on the chart that particularly the group "General Literature, Essays," shows an enormous increase. Fred E. Woodward[1] has pointed out that in 1909 an unusual number of anniversaries were celebrated and that this has influenced the production figure of the following year. The year 1909 saw anniversary celebrations of Calvin, Samuel Johnson, Haydn, Mendelssohn, Gogol, Tennyson, Mrs. Browning, Fitzgerald, Darwin, Gladstone, Lincoln, Poe, and Oliver Wendell Holmes!

[1] In his *A Graphic Survey of Book Publication*, 1890-1916, Washington, 1917.

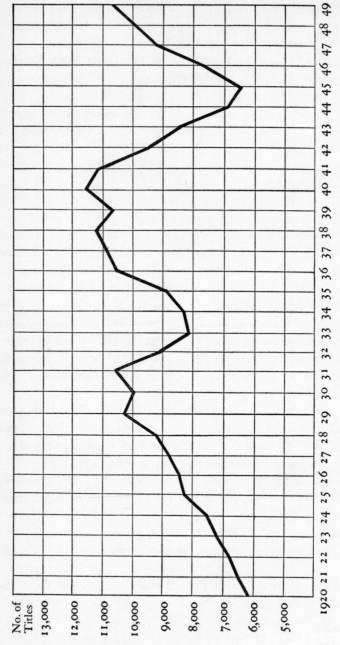

TOTAL NUMBER OF NEW TITLES AND NEW EDITIONS ISSUED ANNUALLY FROM 1920-1949.

Diagram prepared by W. S. Budington, Librarian of Engineering and Physical Sciences at Columbia University, as part of an unpublished study, *A Graphic and Statistical Picture of U. S. Book Publication, 1920-1948.*

International Classification	1869	1880	1900	1901	1909	1910	1914	1916	1919	1922	1929	1931	1933	1936	1937	1938	1939	1940	1942	1945	1946	1947	1948	1949
Philosophy	31	22	11	101	114	197	265	110	322	266	269	306	296	219	219	120	152	104	102	84	207	290	308	325
Religion	334	239	467	448	533	903	943	843	755	695	593	806	786	632	632	710	811	821	697	843	656	438	677	720
Sociology, Economics	30	99	183	269	628	784	1038	767	846	436	484	632	621	535	753	838	854	876	620	301	311	387	461	548
Law	140	62	458	543	591	678	507	274	204	163	116	126	91	149	149	148	163	202	112	117	124	214	231	267
Education	128	131	399	641	560	{423	268	324	244	211	125	255	165	332	334	313	315	349	217	124	147	156	199	254
Philology }						{200	711	330	259	250	211	264	264	211	222	295	319	280	151	108	156	149	199	166
Science	69	56	93	184	292	620	711	677	639	586	315	424	452	357	481	473	525	523	493	397	341	350	442	592	676
Techn. Books (Useful Arts)	70	63	133	153	197	775	707	595	587	401	410	359	354	419	360	390	406	485	452	454	472	611	393	466	455
Medicine, Hygiene	102	114	117	218	292	756	544	516	401	258	402	419	360	406	390	431	452	472	443	302	300	322	433	450
Agriculture, Gardening }	33	43	29	76	65	204 {	{200	371	383	407	57	82	93	60	140	130	136	129	100	100	139	50	55	97	162	191
Domestic Economy							132	135	157	98	49	53	81	71	71	110	93	89	100	94	112	116	144	201	183	263
Business	8	··	··	··	150	229	272	337	231	213	199	139	234	318	359	357	402	261	152	216	228	223	306
Fine Arts	25	44	135	167	216	245	310	238	586	103	205	221	196	230	302	287	288	222	187	178	267	249	336	347
Music	26	24	··	··	··	100	112	113	63	44	71	80	72	127	92	124	124	67	55	71	94	104	95
Games, Sport	26	32	82	51	70	109	145	194	127	64	80	130	170	154	243	230	219	182	149	68	134	168	199	235
General Literature, Essays	70	106	183	543	720	2042	732	461	339	337	572	494	295	560	337	562	584	536	400	265	377	400	473	535
Poetry, Drama	119	111	168	400	448	671	752	902	860	500	494	727	711	501	808	754	744	653	738	594	380	441	511	563	574
Fiction	420	292	1118	1278	2234	1539	1053	932	904	1089	2142	1042	1806	1899	1896	1663	1547	1736	1663	1293	1722	1066	1643	1644
Juvenile	369	270	408	527	595	1010	633	670	433	514	931	1018	626	843	967	1041	949	984	864	691	877	933	929	979
History	114	72	153	257	283	565	581	754	812	428	417	487	464	753	934	857	804	853	646	343	359	413	503	527
Geography, Travel	108	115	162	192	220	474	599	542	354	373	387	243	345	327	366	357	308	259	98	133	196	214	248
Biography	68	151	218	274	428	563	644	604	469	367	738	775	545	699	660	662	628	647	542	392	456	518	513	595
Humor and Satire	26	30	42	34	46	73	141	110	49	36	55	65	46	100	76	76	78	88	81	110	124	180	336	··
Miscellaneous	286	··	··	31	113	42	··	··	··	··	··	··	··	··	··	··	··	··	··	··	··	··	··	492
TOTAL	2602	2076	4559	6356	8141	12010	12010	13470	8594	6863	10187	10307	8092	10436	11912	11667	10640	11328	9525	6548	7735	9782	9897	10892

This table is based upon compilations published annually in the *Publishers' Weekly*. The total for the year 1916 and for a number of preceding years includes pamphlet material; for 1914, for instance, 1,662 pamphlets, and 1,041 for 1916; after that date pamphlets are no longer included. The adoption of the Brussels Classification in 1910 accounts for certain changes in subject groups; for instance, for the separate listing, from that year on, of Education and Philology, and of Domestic Economy and Agriculture, previously listed together as Domestic and Rural Economy. On the other hand, groups sometimes listed separately, such as Reference in 1901, and Military and Naval Science in 1916, are here included in more general groups.

The figures for 1869 were estimated by James A. Hulbert, Librarian, Virginia State College, Petersburg, Virginia, on the basis of data in *The American Catalogue of Books* for 1869, New York, Leypoldt & Holt, 1870. This appears to be the earliest tentatively classified list of titles to appear in print after the Civil War.

The diagram on page 320 will help the reader to visualize the year-by-year trend of the total output of new titles and editions from 1920 to 1949. It should of course be understood that neither the table nor the diagram give an indication of total sales. During World War II, it is well known, fewer titles were published, but the number of copies sold of each new volume showed a marked increase.

The diagram demonstrates very clearly the effect of world history and of its economic consequences in the United States. We see the steady rise of publishing figures during the boom of the twenties; the delayed effect of the crash of 1929 between 1931 and 1933; the recovery and new prosperity of the thirties; the effect of the outbreak of World War II in Europe; the steady decline in the number of new titles issued during the war; and the new postwar prosperity of the late forties.

A comparison of these over-all statistics with the individual trends in the various subject divisions shows one thing with impressive clarity: The majority of all subjects follows the over-all trend very closely. The decision on what to publish each year, in other words, is primarily governed by the general conditions prevailing in the trade.

There are, of course, some significant exceptions. Fiction, for instance, does not share in the prosperity wave of the late thirties, but declines fairly steadily from 1935 to 1945. Technology and military science do not participate in the boom of the twenties, but they make up amply for lost ground between 1934 and 1942. Domestic economy shows a steadily increasing tendency since 1920. History remains on an even level or declines slightly during all of the twenties and the early thirties, when most other subjects are booming. Also, the recovery boom of the late thirties does not affect philosophy and ethics, agriculture and gardening, and business. Law shows a completely different, seemingly erratic pattern.

Some of these exceptions from the general trend are easily explained. Others offer a challenge to the analytical skill of the observer.

The Literary Publishers of the Nineties

The international copyright regulation of 1891 had a beneficial influence not only upon the new generation of American authors, but it also clarified and furthered the relationships towards the English literary circles. The American publisher of an English book was no longer dependent upon the good will of his colleagues; he could rely upon the government's legal protection. This clarification of conditions must have been one of the reasons why a number of enterprising young literary men in Boston, Chicago and New York decided to become publishers. There arose in the nineties a number of small publishing houses, which had in common their determination to publish only works of literary quality and to bring out their selections in an attractive and distinctive format. They were somewhat influenced in their ideas as well as in their methods by such London publishers as Elkin Mathews and John Lane. The program of two outstanding young American publishing firms of this group, namely, Stone & Kimball in Chicago and Copeland & Day in Boston, shows quite clearly what they were after.

Herbert Stuart Stone, born in 1871, the son of a distinguished journalist, met his future publishing partner [Hannibal] Ingalls Kimball (1874-1933) in Harvard College. They helped to get out a student paper, both in characteristic roles, Stone as an editor, and Kimball as business manager. In 1893, while still in college, they made their publishing plans public. The first book issued jointly with the imprint Stone & Kimball was a bibliography of American first editions, compiled by Herbert Stone. From the start they emphasized their policy of accepting only manuscripts of literary merit, which were to be brought out in careful and artistic form. In August, 1894, the firm moved to Chicago. They took with them their literary-artistic magazine, *The Chap-Book*, begun in May of that year in Cambridge. They received contributions from, among others, Aubrey Beardsley, Max Beerbohm, and Georges Pissaro. No less an artist than Toulouse-Lautrec was among those who designed posters for their publications; Will Bradley and Bertram Goodhue were distinguished among their American artistic collaborators. Among the authors on Stone & Kimball's list were Hamlin Garland, whose *Main Travelled Roads* appeared with a foreword by William Dean Howells, George Santayana, with an early volume of *Sonnets*, Gilbert Parker and Robert Louis Stevenson.

Even to the present-day beholder, the books of this publishing house have the fresh charm of the personal and the individual, and seen against their nineteenth century background, they do represent something new and striking. Their typography is unpretentious yet attractive, with the brightly colored end papers and amusing bindings in rich ornamental and floral patterns of the period. Most of the books were printed by John Wilson in Cambridge and at the Lakeside Press in Chicago.

In 1896 Kimball purchased the entire business and removed it to New York, but in 1897 the promising enterprise came to a premature end. Ingalls Kimball then founded, in New York, the Cheltenham Press, where he succeeded in applying the new typographic ideas and inspirations of the period to commercial and advertising purposes.

Stone immediately entered publishing again in Chicago as Herbert S. Stone & Co., with the assistance of his younger brother, Melville E. Stone, Jr. He won George Bernard Shaw for this venture, and so it came that Shaw's authorized American editions appeared from Chicago. The firm, which also published the magazine *House Beautiful*, continued until 1905.

A very similar experience was that of Copeland & Day on Cornhill in Boston, conducted by Frederick Holland Day and Herbert Copeland. The eccentric and picturesque Day came from a wealthy family and had the means to pursue his many artistic and literary interests. A successful photographer and collector of Keats, he had served as secretary to the Boston branch of the A. S. Barnes publishing firm from 1884 to 1889. Copeland had been in Harvard during the time when Herbert Stone, Ingalls Kimball and W. B. Wolffe were there, all of them vitally interested in creative publishing. Their office opened in August, 1893, but the enterprise did not outlast the turn of the century.

In their literary offerings they were at first quite dependent upon Mathews and Lane and the famous *Yellow Book* magazine, but they soon built up an impressive list of American authors, deliberately encouraging the young writer with a first book to publish. Their total output of ninety-six volumes included no less than fifty-four books of verse, and translations of interesting foreign works played a considerable part in their program.

Their volumes, too, were largely done by the University Press in Cambridge, under the direction of the younger John Wilson and William Dana Orcutt. Other Boston printers, such as Rockwell & Churchill and the Everett Press also worked for them. Mr. Updike has said of these books that they belong among the best printed volumes of their day. Small and light, they are real reading volumes, favorably distinguished in their charming bindings from the drab mechanical carelessness of the ordinary editions of those years. Here, too, one finds the use of color and ornament, gold or silver stamped upon simple cloth covers, or boards completely covered with paper, gray or in colorful ornamental patterns.

There were other publishing houses who fell in with these tendencies, either in literary program or in the colorful decoration; for instance, in Boston, the new firm of Lamson, Wolffe & Co., which published some seventy titles or more between 1895 and 1899. The partnership was temporarily dissolved in 1895, because young W. B. Wolffe was presented by the Harvard authorities with the not unreasonable request that he withdraw either from the firm or the college. Another enterprise with the same ambitions, the house of Small, Maynard & Company, survived well beyond the turn of the century.

In Chicago, alongside of Stone & Kimball, Way & Williams followed suit. W. Irving Way was a well-known bibliophile, friendly with English collectors, and himself a writer on printing and binding. Chauncey Williams, graduating from the University of Wisconsin, put a considerable sum of money into this publishing firm. Between 1895 and 1898 they issued well over fifty handsome volumes, designed by some of the best men of the private press movement. They shared the fate of the other young publishers of the decade, and had to cease operation after an all-too-brief period of experimentation.

A brilliant decade of publishing was begun in New York in 1893 when Robert Howard Russell, of the De Witt Publishing House, launched into trade publishing as R. H. Russell & Son (later R. H. Russell), building with imagination and success a yearly list of books which included the immensely popular books of Charles Dana Gibson, followed by similar volumes of Remington and Penfield, the plays of Rostand, Pinero and others and volumes by Richard Harding Davis. The younger Russell, the son, was a man of artistic training and cultivated taste with high ideals for his list. In 1903 he turned his selling over to Harper & Brothers.

It is a somewhat melancholy fact that these enterprising individualists could not make a permanent impression. From the standpoint of physical excellence alone, their volumes might have become the turning point towards better trade book design. From the literary point of view, too, the continuance of a group of individualists in publishing would have been distinctly desirable. However, economic conditions both within the realm of the publishing and printing industry and, in a wider sense, the general trend of business favored not the small, personal enterprise, but big, expanding business organizations. Sidney Kramer, who has made a special study of the publishers of the nineties, feels that it was in the main a certain lack of commercial enterprise in each case, which ended these ventures.

Not lacking in commercial enterprise and fully as individual and discriminating as the young men just discussed was Thomas Bird Mosher, the much discussed sea captain and literary pirate in Portland, Maine. Nonchalantly he disregarded the rights of British authors and proceeded with the good old custom of printing anything that pleased him without asking for permission and without paying a cent of royalty. Said Richard Le Gallienne: "He waylays the unprotected copyright with such grace that it hardly seems like piracy at all. In fact I suppose, technically speaking, it is not. Else Mr. Mosher would not be permitted to delight us with perhaps the daintiest editions at present being published by any publisher." The praise is hardly exaggerated. Mosher was a fanatic believer in the value of cultivated and individually thought-out book designing. His diminutive volumes are most inviting, agreeable to hold and to read. Almost all of them are set in Caslon type, a little red or green on the title page and a delicate decorative head piece on the opening page. They are mostly bound in white vellum paper or in gray paper over thin boards with a little printed label for the title on the back. Mosher's printing was done by Smith & Sale or by George D. Loring, both in Portland.

His first book, an edition of George Meredith's *Modern Love,* appeared in 1891, when, after restless seafaring years, Mosher was nearly forty years of age. Without asking too much what the public liked, he indulged in the luxury of following his own taste, and he was successful —obviously so because his taste was good. He started a selection of contemporary English poetry, politely called *English Reprint Series,* including, among others, poems of Rossetti, Swinburne and Morris. His famous *Bibelot Series* appeared 1893-1897, and from 1897 to 1902 he brought out *Reprints from the Bibelot,* with a special emphasis on the writings of William Morris. From 1895 on to his end, there appeared a further colorful string of lovely little books. He died in 1923, "the potential author of one of the most fascinating autobiographies that was never written." (Christopher Morley.)

American Branches of English Publishers

More durable than the publishing experiments of literary young men in the nineties were the branches of English publishers established in America. The idea suggests itself that these enterprises, two of which were started in 1896, were encouraged by the copyright legislation of 1891. Obviously, the sale of English books in America assumed at once a more promising and secure aspect, now that piracy was a thing of the past. As a matter of fact, there are evidences that a certain fear of the competition of British publishers had previously played a part in delaying copyright legislation for such a long time. Only a few years before the bill was passed there appeared in the *American Bookseller* an article which actually warned against the threatened "invasion" of the London publishers.

If we look closely, however, we see that the establishment of these branches was really just another logical step in a development which had older roots. These branches were devoted not so much to the propagation of novels and books of a general nature, as to the promotion of scholarly works, school and textbooks, and the special fields of theology and medicine. In these fields even in the days before the Civil War there had been a steady influx of the books of certain English houses, and in the second half of the nineteenth century Cassell & Co., George Routledge & Sons, Frederick Warne & Co. and Thomas Nelson & Son had maintained flourishing New York branches. Nelson played a special part as publisher of American Standard Bibles and in the first adaptation of the loose leaf process to reference books. The American market was so important then, that it had a very decided influence upon the publishing program of these firms even in England; it also led to frequent invitations to American scholars and educators to write a book for them to publish. In line with this policy the establishment of a New York branch was a logical step towards the reinforcement and further development of these connections. It made it possible to add to the books imported from abroad special editions for the American market, actually produced in this country, and even to publish, with a measure of independence, books by American authors calculated primarily for the sale in America.

We have already mentioned that as early as 1869 George Edward Brett had founded the New York branch of the London publisher, Macmillan & Co. In 1890 his son, George Platt Brett, became American partner of the firm, which in 1896 was incorporated as a separate American house under the name of The Macmillan Company with Brett as president, and under his guidance it became for many years the largest publishing house in the country. In 1931, five years before his death, he was succeeded by his son, George P. Brett, Jr., while the second son, Richard, became treasurer, a position which he held, together with other responsibilities, until his entry into the Air Force in 1942. Richard Brett is now business manager of the New York Public Library. T. C. Morehouse, one of the vice-presidents, served the company for half a century until his retirement in 1949. Harold S. Latham has held for many years a leading position as a vice-president and editor of the trade department. J. Randall Williams, with the firm since 1939, combines the responsibilities of a general manager and treasurer.

The most important early publishing success of the new American firm was Winston Churchill's *Richard Carvel*, which appeared in 1899. Owen Wister's *The Virginian*, published in 1902, and Jack London's *Call of the Wild* were other significant early milestones. To name even in the briefest form the distinguished list of authors and the many series of books published by Macmillan would be impracticable in this volume. An exception must of course be made for Margaret Mitchell's *Gone with the Wind*, one of the most profitable books published by the younger generation. The Macmillan Company owns its large building on lower Fifth Avenue, and has established branches in several American cities and in Toronto.

Macmillan has played a significant part among contemporary American publishing firms as one of the most important scholarly publishers. The firm has always belonged definitely in the "quality group," meaning that they maintain a definite standard of merit in all their general works. They have been the publishers of several leading contemporary poets. Various special departments enjoy the advice of experienced authorities. A strong trade department, covering a broad variety of subjects, includes divisions devoted to religious books and general outdoor books. There are also special departments for educational, college, medical and public health books. They were the first house to organize a juvenile department with a woman, Louise Seaman, as head.

For years Macmillan has represented here various other English firms in addition to their own mother house, notably the Cambridge University Press. This arrangement was initiated in 1921. Ten years later Ronald Mansbridge became the head of this department. In the spring of 1949 the Cambridge University Press established its own branch here, with Ronald Mansbridge in charge.

Longmans, Green & Co. founded their New York branch in 1887. The English house goes back into the early eighteenth century: young Thomas Longman, in 1724, bought the publishing business of the late William Taylor, who had published among other books the original edition of Daniel Defoe's *Robinson Crusoe* in 1719. Through six generations down to our own times the house has remained in the hands of the Longman family. Under their imprint had appeared books by Coleridge and Wordsworth, Scott, John Stuart Mill, Macaulay, Disraeli, the *Edinburgh Review* and *Longman's Magazine*. As early as the Colonial days the American connections of the Longman firm were lively and lucrative, and later on *Longman's Magazine* enjoyed the collaboration of such distinguished Americans as William Dean Howells, Henry James, Bret Harte and Brander Matthews. In the hands of Charles J. Mills and then of his son Edward S. Mills (with the third generation Edward Mills also in the business), the New York house acted as agent for the English mother firm, but from the start it sought and found the collaboration of American authors of rank. William James, the philosopher, wrote for Longmans, and for years Brander Matthews was active as literary adviser and friend of Mills. Theodore Roosevelt and Woodrow Wilson each wrote a volume for their series "Historic Towns." Other successful series were the "Epochs of American History," the "American Teachers Series," and the "American Citizen Series," to which A. Lawrence Lowell, president of Harvard College, and E. R. A. Seligman, the famous economist, contributed. Along with these series of a more general cultural and scholarly level the firm maintains a broadly organized textbook department.

In the famous incendiary raid on the City district of London on December 29, 1940, the English mother house of Longmans, Green suffered severely. The firm, which on December 28th had between 5,000 and 6,000 different titles to offer, had but 12 left on December 30th. Reprinting orders were issued immediately, and the rebuilding of the list was begun promptly. The desirability of giving the fullest support to the heavy postwar program of the London house has had decided effects upon the management of the American branch. One among several changes of policy announced by the firm in the spring of 1950 was the decision to curtail the future publishing of Catholic manuscripts.

The transatlantic trade of the famous Oxford University Press reached very considerable proportions years before the establishment of an American branch. Their business here had been in the hands of Macmillan in New York. But when, in 1896, that branch became incorporated as a separate American firm, John Armstrong (d. 1915) took charge of the business. An important part of the income of the firm has come from selling the Oxford Bibles, imported from England or manufactured here, which required extensive stock and experienced traveling representatives throughout the country. There is also the important responsibility of marketing the general Oxford list and standard series and the task of preparing the great Oxford standard works for the American market. This entails a revision of the dictionaries, and of most of the textbooks. In the course of years the independent publishing activities of the New York branch have reached large proportions, starting in earnest in the early 1930's and gaining momentum toward the close of the decade. Between 1937 and 1945, 661 publications originated in the New York office. Highlights of this program include S. E. Morison and H. S. Commager's *The Growth of the American Republic*, important studies in American literary history and criticism, and distinguished contributions to art and archaeology by such authorities as Erwin Panofsky, Talbot Hamlin, the Richters. The American promotion of Arnold J. Toynbee's *A Study of History*, an abridgement of the first six volumes of his monumental project, resulted in wide distribution of this work.

The present "Publisher to the University of Oxford," Geoffrey F. J. Cumberlege, was manager of the New York branch from 1927 to 1934. He was succeeded by Paul Willert (1934-1939) and since 1939 by

personalities in American book publishing, and among the authors whose books he published were many who owed him their first start to fame. At about the same time he established, as a retail outlet for his own publications, The Little Book-Shop Around the Corner, where he brought Laurence T. Gomme into partnership. Bookstores in connection with publishing houses were then the common practice, and Dutton, Putnam, Dodd, Mead, and Scribner's had them. In a short time Mr. Gomme gave the store an atmosphere of bookselling competence and literary taste which attracted many of the most interesting literary figures, both American and English, to the shop. Around 1908 Kennerley bought *The Forum,* and the publishing firm grew so rapidly that he sold the bookshop to Gomme and Donald Vaughan, who carried on there until 1917. An important friend of Mr. Kennerley's was Frederic W. Goudy, who named one of his best-known types "Kennerley." Among his early authors were Edna St. Vincent Millay, D. H. Lawrence, Joseph Hergesheimer and Walter Lippman with his *Preface to Politics.* He published Frank Harris' *The Man Shakespeare,* books by Van Wyck Brooks, and such poets as Bliss Carman, Richard Le Gallienne, Witter Bynner, and Vachel Lindsay. In 1915 Mr. Kennerley became the director of the Anderson Auction Company, which in 1929 was merged with the American Art Association. He continued his publishing firm for some years, but gradually disposed of his list. The highwater mark of his career was perhaps the fabulous Kern Sale, with its all-time high of $1,729,462.50. His connection with the great book auction firm ended soon after Constant Field Bishop, owner of the American Art Association, bought out the Anderson Galleries. Life gave him a great deal and took away a great deal. When he ended his life early in 1950, his estate was valued at $50.

At the turn of the century the first large new foundation to accomplish permanence, the firm from which eventually the house of Doubleday & Co. emerged, stands in its program about midway between the older and the newer school.

The large organization of Doubleday & Co. in its early roots goes back, on one side, to the ability, the energy and the literary flair of an Irishman, Samuel Sidney McClure. Born in the old country in 1857, he spent his youth in Indiana, and in 1882 he edited *The Wheelman,* the house organ of a Boston bicycle factory. In the winter 1883-84, Mc-

Clure for a time was working with Mr. De Vinne, and in the fall of 1884 he founded, in his name, the first American newspaper syndicate. In 1893 there followed *McClure's Magazine*, a pioneer in the ten and fifteen cent magazine field. Here he began really to explore his literary leanings. He took a special interest in O. Henry and in a number of English authors of distinction—Kipling and Stevenson, for instance.

In 1897 he joined forces with Frank Nelson Doubleday, to found the firm of Doubleday & McClure Company. The collaboration, however, did not last very long; in 1899 McClure withdrew and combined with John S. Phillips. McClure, Phillips & Co., though it developed a fine list, did not last more than about five years, when they were absorbed again by the Doubleday enterprise.

Frank Nelson Doubleday was born in Brooklyn in 1862. A powerful and creative personality, he had enjoyed an early start in the world of books and printing, since it was in his parents' home that he successfully conducted a little job printing establishment. He entered into the Scribner firm as an apprentice, and in the course of time became business manager of the resurrected *Scribner's Magazine*. He remained with this house for twenty years, until the founding of his publishing house with McClure in 1897. This connection brought into the new firm a number of very valuable authors. Kipling in particular was the first great success, and he has been called the cornerstone of the firm. O. Henry's short stories, as they appeared in the magazines and newspapers, had already made his name famous. Collections of these stories were published by Doubleday. The contribution of Mrs. Doubleday should not be forgotten, for under the pseudonym of Neltje Blanchan she supplied the house with *Bird Neighbors*, sold in enormous editions, and *Nature's Garden*. The firm also developed the American sale of Joseph Conrad. Selma Lagerlöf was another of the successful European authors who shared honors on the Doubleday list with the native Booth Tarkington, Steward Edward White, Upton Sinclair, Sinclair Lewis, Gene Stratton Porter, Edna Ferber and Christopher Morley. After the separation from McClure in 1899, Doubleday entered into partnership with Walter Hines Page, who later was ambassador to Great Britain, and from 1900 on the firm was called Doubleday, Page & Co. Page had been occupied with the editorship of the *Atlantic Monthly* and now edited *World's Work* for the new house while *Country Life* was another important enterprise. We owe to Page in his book, *A Publisher's Confession*, a lively picture of bookselling and publishing during those years. In 1924 his *Life and Letters*, edited by Burton J. Hendrick, made a profound impression in both America and England. He has a characteristic way about him, of seeing people and things which lends a hard reality to his account. He writes consistently from the business point of view.

Success was with the Doubleday colors from the very start, and the house grew rapidly in size and importance. The publishers had their offices in New York, and their manufacturing kept a number of concerns busy. As time went on, the need and the desire for their own plant made itself felt with increasing acuteness. The year 1910 brought the decisive step: transfer of the organization to Garden City, Long Island (except a small Madison Avenue office), and the establishment there of a complete manufacturing plant. This was an unusual step, but success justified the courageous move. The grounds were purchased in March, 1910, and by September the rumble of the presses could be heard in the well-planned wings, which were surrounded by beautiful gardens. In 1938, executive offices of the publishing firm returned to New York. The manufacturing department then became incorporated as a completely separate organization under the name of the Country Life Press Corporation. It did not take many years for the realization that Doubleday still needed their own manufacturing facilities, and in the summer of 1948 a model plant at Hanover, Pennsylvania, geared to the economical production of large editions, was added to the Garden City establishment.

When in 1920 Doubleday, Page & Co. had taken over a large part of the shares of the big London publishing house of William Heinemann, they had brought about there, too, the removal of the plant to a suburb. The control of the Heinemann firm was returned to English hands in 1933.

Always experimenting, the firm began the policy of publishing reprint series of older works, such as the Star Dollar Books, the Sundial series and the De Luxe Series. They also put many new books into series such as the Crime Club and the Dollar Mystery Club. A subsidiary, the Garden City Publishing Company, was organized in 1920 to devote itself exclusively to the low-price book field. In 1920 also, a finely conceived juvenile department came into existence. The year 1927 once more brought a new partner to the firm, resulting in changes of organization and of the firm's name to the form of Doubleday, Doran & Co. Arthur Page, the son of the late Walter Hines Page, withdrew from the organization.

The new partner, George H. Doran, had grown up in the American book trade, and at the time of the merger with Doubleday he could look back upon many successful years in the publishing business. He brought out a volume of memoirs in 1935. *Chronicles of Barabbas* has the quotation from Byron on the title page: "Now Barabbas was a publisher." The satanical streak which, fortunately, is not confined to the title page secures to these memoirs an almost unique position. They are refreshingly free from the sentimental garrulity which seems to befall worthy and shrewd businessmen when they come to contemplate their own achievements. Publishers' memoirs, although the work of men who have spent their lives with books and authors, usually provide no exception to this rule; George H. Doran's book does. It is full of intimate observation and personal touches.

After an apprenticeship in the theological book field in Chicago, Doran started out in business for himself in Toronto, soon adding a branch in New York. In 1908 he settled altogether in New York and headed the George H. Doran Company, the strength of his first list being based on the close connections with Hodder and Stoughton of London, with their important religious list. The early years were successful and prosperous. An important early success was Arnold Bennett's *The Old Wives' Tale*, issued in 1909, which secured a respected place for the young house among the older publishers. The first years of the World War brought new enterprise and new plans, with war books as a specialty of the firm. Towards the end of the war Mr. Doran felt the need for younger collaborators who would be ready to take some of the responsibilities. His son-in-law, Stanley M. Rinehart, Jr., son of Mary Roberts Rinehart, became a member of the firm and so did John Farrar, the young but experienced editor of *The Bookman,* with his enthusiasm and literary common sense. The epoch of postwar prosperity which started around 1924 found the Doran firm well prepared.

Looking back to the time when the merger was effected, John Farrar described the two principal characters: "The all-embracing imaginative drive of F. N. Doubleday was always back of the scenes, even when he was an invalid . . . He could invest the stark mathematics of percentages with an almost spiritual glow . . . George H. Doran was dramatic in both mind and figure. His intuition, charm and force had produced a great list of books. He had a way with people, and it was his greatest talent, for he had swift intuitions about them and because they fascinated him, he took enormous pains to fascinate them."

The merger in 1927 included a plan for placing the actual management of affairs into the hands of the younger generation—Doubleday's son, Nelson, and his collaborators on the one side, and Farrar and Rinehart, with his younger brother, Frederick, on the other. F. N. Doubleday and George H. Doran were to advise and generally supervise rather than take active part in the management. In spite of the firm's generous proportions the collaboration of so many outspoken personalities proved impractical. In 1929, unconscious of the impending depression, the young men of the Doran group left the firm and founded their own publishing house in New York City.

The inventory, contracts and entire business of the Blue Ribbon Books, Inc., a co-operative reprint house, were bought by Doubleday, Doran & Co. in 1939, the same year which saw the publication of Daphne du Maurier's best seller, *Rebecca*, which was followed by a steady succession of best sellers, including the works of Kenneth Roberts, Somerset Maugham, and others. In the midst of the war pressures, The Blakiston Company, the old Philadelphia medical house, was purchased, shortly after that firm's celebration of its one hundredth anniversary. Blakiston were publishers of the *Red Cross First Aid Manual*, selling over a million copies in 1942. The acquisition of this firm brought Doubleday a huge additional paper quota. In 1946 the name of the firm was simplified to Doubleday & Company. Nelson Doubleday was succeeded as president by Douglas M. Black, but continued as board chairman until his death in 1949. New book clubs were continuously being developed, until in 1950 there were ten book clubs, including the two divisions of the Junior Literary Guild.

Farrar & Rinehart made a go of their new firm almost overnight. The overwhelming success of Hervey Allen's *Anthony Adverse* brought financial security and helped greatly to carry the new firm into the more prosperous era of the late thirties. The second world war took John Farrar from his publishing activities, or so it seemed, when the Office of War Information sent him overseas to the Mediterranean Theater on a psychological warfare mission. He was soon back, however, in the United States, where he rendered valuable professional services as editor of OWI's *U.S.A.* magazine and of the *Amerikanische Rundschau*, officially published by the government as a step in German postwar reorientation. On his return from overseas John Farrar had separated from his old partners, who continued as Rinehart & Company, Inc. Soon after the war, in January, 1946, Farrar, Straus & Co. came into being as a new general trade house, with John Farrar as chairman of a strong board of directors and Roger W. Straus, Jr., recently returned from the Navy, as president. In December, 1950, the firm became Farrar, Straus & Young, Inc. One of the steps taken to insure greater stability of income against the very high risks of postwar trade publishing was the absorption of Hendricks House, a college textbook firm. Like other publishers they have developed close and profitable contacts with the motion picture industry. John Farrar's long-standing interests in the fate of writing and in the development of a professional book trade in this country brought him an active share in Columbia University's training program in the field of bookselling and publishing.

One of the most talented and enterprising of America's twentieth century publishers also started years ago from the fold of Doubleday, Page & Co.: Alfred A. Knopf, who had entered there in 1912 after completing his studies at Columbia University. In 1914 for a short time he joined Mitchell Kennerley, and in 1915 he went into business for himself. In an amusing *New Yorker* profile, which ran through three issues, he has been aptly described as bold and piratical in appearance, wearing clothes of startling originality, and with an expression both challenging and reproachful. His wife, Blanche, is an important influence in the firm, as director, vice-president and part-owner, acting as a talent scout who brings into the firm many new authors. Their son is now also active in the business.

The program of Mr. Knopf showed from the start a distinct leaning towards European, and especially Russian literature. Tolstoi, Gogol, Dostoievsky and Gorki appeared on the list, together with Spaniards, Frenchmen and Scandinavians; Knut Hamsun and Sigrid Undset leading the latter group. He has published Nietzsche and Thomas Mann. Since the great German author's immigration to the United States, Mann's writings have taken an important place on the Knopf list. Of English authors, Beerbohm and Bridges should be mentioned, and Cather, Hergesheimer, Mencken, and Robert as well as George Jean Nathan from among the many distinguished American authors. When André Gide was awarded the Nobel Prize in literature in 1947, he was the ninth author on the Knopf list to be so honored. With this splendid program Knopf may perhaps be called the most outstanding representative in America of the literary publisher. "He is a professional phenomenon among publishers," wrote the *New Yorker*, "because his list is more a projection of his own personality than the list of any other publisher of comparable scope."

He shares with his European colleagues, who have influenced his policy to some extent, the interest not only in his authors, but also in the design of his volumes and the desire to give each of them a distinct, attractive garment which will make them readily recognizable as members of his book family. "The Borzoi" has come to mean something in this regard. In retaining W. A. Dwiggins as a consulting designer he had set a pace, within the realm of the "trade book," for that type of collaboration between the free lance artist and the publisher's production department. Sidney R. Jacobs for many years has been in charge of production at Knopf's.

Chronologically the next foundation, the firm of Boni & Liveright, established in 1917 by Albert Boni and Horace Liveright, appears on the scene with a similar, exclusively literary and progressive program. Albert Boni had begun his business career with his brother Charles in a Washington Square bookshop. Together they had founded the "Little Leather Library," a set of thirty tiny volumes of classics and abridgements planned to be sold by mail at $2.98, which Harry Scherman and Robert Haas later took over. The chief concern of the new firm of Boni and Liveright at the start was the "Modern Library," a generously conceived reprint series of masterpieces of contemporary world literature, including, however, certain older works which the publishers considered of vital importance to the present generation. The volumes, selling originally for sixty cents, were uniformly printed in a pocket-size format with attractive end papers and flexible covers.

In 1918 Boni & Liveright were joined by Thomas Seltzer, who had recently come from Russia and had made a name for himself as translator of Gerhard Hauptmann and of Russian and Polish literature. He separated from them in 1920 and established himself as Thomas Seltzer, Inc., with a brilliant list of authors, including Ford Madox Ford, D. H. Lawrence, Waldemar Bonsels, Arthur Schnitzler, for whose *Casanova's Homecoming* he fought a valiant censorship battle, and Evelyn Scott's *Escapade*. It is a very interesting thing about his publishing career that he achieved financial success with books of literary merit, but when he tried the popular fiction field, he failed. His firm was taken over in 1926 by the Boni's, until in 1935 he once more ventured forth for himself. He died in September of 1943.

In 1918 Boni and Liveright had separated, the firm, however, retaining its original name until 1928, when it was changed to Horace Liveright, and again Liveright, Inc., and Liveright Publishing Corporation. Liveright's reputation for brilliance and daring attracted able collaborators, Julian Messner, T. R. Smith, Isador Schneider, Bennett Cerf, and Richard Simon. Among their authors one finds Theodore Dreiser, Eugene O'Neill, Edgar Lee Masters and Rose Macaulay. He retired from publishing in 1930, and until his death three years later his interests centered mainly on the theater.

Boni in the meantime took to traveling in Germany and Russia, where he engaged in journalism and literary agent work. Back in New York he purchased in 1923, together with his brother, Charles, the New York firm of Lieber & Lewis, and called the new firm Albert and Charles Boni. The house brought out both American and European authors, among them Upton Sinclair, Thornton Wilder, Will Rogers, Carl Van Doren, from at home, and D. H. Lawrence, Proust, Unamuno, George Brandes, Paul Wiegler, from abroad. In 1929 they started a new venture, not tried before in that manner—the publishing, in cheap fifty-cent editions, of good books in paper covers, attractively designed by Rockwell Kent, which went out into the world under the name of the "Boni Paper Books." This plan can be considered a predecessor of the later twenty-five cent books. However, they were not given quantity production nor marketed for the newsstand and drug store trade, which later absorbed such large printings, and the project had to be abandoned. By 1932 Albert Boni was the president and chief editor of the firm, while Charles Boni was inactive vice-president. In 1939 Albert experimented with his "Readex Library," a plan for the publishing of microprint books to be read with a projector.

Charles Boni returned to publishing in 1946 in a new association with Joseph Gaer, in the firm of Boni & Gaer. They started out at a time when the wartime boom in the book trade was decidedly slowing up, but felt certain that there was a public sufficiently large and interested to support a program of books dealing fearlessly with the most controversial issues of the day. Gaer, himself a recognized author, had taught at the University of California, had been busy for several years on the Federal Writers Project in Washington, and was in charge of a pamphlet publishing department at Reynal & Hitchcock during 1945. They did not meet the anticipated support, in spite of some initial success. Charles Boni withdrew in 1948, early in 1949 the firm was changed to Gaer Associates, and later that year Gaer himself resigned.

The Modern Library, to resume its story, until 1925 remained in the hands of Boni & Liveright, and then was bought by Bennett Cerf on the day of his departure for a European trip. Before the boat sailed, he had gotten Donald Klopfer to come in on a fifty-fifty basis. They incorporated a separate firm to carry on and extend the sale of the Library. The original plan for the series was not altered but amplified. By 1950, 270 titles have appeared in the Modern Library, 74 in the series of Modern Library Giants and 9 titles in the Illustrated Modern Library. In 1927 Cerf and Klopfer expanded by starting Random House, with Robert Haas joining the firm in 1936, as a result of a merger with Smith & Haas which in turn was the successor of the firm of Jonathan Cape & Harrison Smith, founded in 1929. Although over the years it has become something quite different, Random House was originally conceived as a sort of American parallel of the English Nonesuch Press, for which they indeed were agents here for a time, as they were for Golden Cockerel Press and the Bremer Presse of Munich. Their very first book under this new imprint, Voltaire's *Candide*, with brilliant illustrations by Rockwell Kent and printed by Elmer Adler at the Pynson Printers, made a lasting place for itself as one of the outstanding illustrated books of the decade. An edition of the *Leaves of Grass* for $100 a copy was another predepression item on the list. Random House took the panic of 1929 in their stride, and quickly changed into a regular trade house of high standing. They have retained their interest in good-looking and well-made volumes. Among their authors are Eugene O'Neill, Sinclair Lewis, Vincent Sheean, William Faulkner, Havelock Ellis, W. H. Auden, Robinson Jeffers, Louis MacNeice, and Stephen Spender. In 1947 they published the *American College Dictionary*, which has had wide acceptance.

Bennett Cerf, "the buzz bomb of publishers' row," is a native New Yorker, a graduate of Columbia, where he was a classmate of Richard Simon; for two years he was with Horace Liveright. "That reddish glow you may notice in the atmosphere is caused by all those irons Bennett Cerf has in the fire. He is, at the moment, publisher, editor, columnist, book reviewer, and radio commentator." This is the description of him on the jacket of his best-selling super-joke book, *Try and Stop Me*. He runs the "Trade Winds" column in the *Saturday Review of Literature*, has edited *The Pocket Book of Cartoons* and *The Pocket Book of War Humor*. He is also a popular lecturer in the Colston Leigh stable.

We are apt to forget, with the passage of time, what golden opportunities the years preceding the fatal 1929 had offered. The years 1924 to 1928 constituted a real boom period in American publishing, as in many other fields of enterprise. But before telling of the firms established during those years, one house which started in 1919 deserves attention. Harcourt, Brace & Co. (for the first year Harcourt, Brace & Howe; then Will D. Howe transferred to Scribner's until his retirement and death) was organized by Alfred Harcourt and Donald Brace, who had previously been connected with the old firm of Henry Holt & Co. At this time Holt excelled in scholarly works and in textbooks, with a general program of a rather conservative nature. During his connection with Holt, Harcourt attempted to bring his somewhat more modern point of view to bear upon the firm's editorial policy, and in order to have more scope for their creative ability, he and Brace, after an unsuccessful attempt to buy the general trade department of the firm, went into business on their own. Their first striking successes were John Maynard Keynes's careful study of postwar conditions, *Economic Consequences of the Peace*, Sinclair Lewis's *Main Street*, and Lytton Strachey's *Queen Victoria*. All three works gave to the public and the trade at once a clear picture of what the firm wanted to do. To the publishers these first successes brought the means to carry on along the lines which the partners had laid out for themselves; that was, to publish a moderate number of books each year of as high quality as possible, with a confidence that careful selection and continuing effort would result in a comparatively long life and large total sales for each title. This publishing house too has enjoyed good relations with Hollywood. Alfred Harcourt has come to be considered as one of the most far-sighted and penetrating minds among this generation of American publishers. In 1942 he resigned as president, but continued as director of the corporation. He was succeeded as president by Donald Brace, who became Chairman of the Board in 1948 and retired the following year. S. Spencer Scott was elected the new president. An important merger took place the same year, 1948: Reynal & Hitchcock was absorbed, after Curtice Hitchcock's death. Eugene Reynal became vice-president and head of the trade department of Harcourt, Brace.

The procession of new personalities which entered the publishing field during the prosperous 1924-1929 period was led by a former collaborator of Boni & Liveright, Richard L. Simon, and a young journalist, M. Lincoln Schuster. They were later joined by Leon Shimkin, described once by Bennett Cerf in his "Trade Winds" column as a cross between Babbitt, Houdini and Count Metternich. Albert Rice Leventhal, sales manager since 1938, became a board member in 1950.

Nobody today needs to be told who Simon and Schuster are. If one can perhaps say that Knopf is the most typical representative among the successful young firms of the literary publishers, Simon and Schuster represents perhaps most clearly the type of the success-publisher. They have made a specialty of books dealing with scholarly, artistic and scientific subjects in a popular and easy manner. Will Durant, Thomas Craven, Hendrik van Loon were some of the early stars on their list. But other things come into the picture. One fine day in 1924, the story is, an elderly aunt called up one of the two partners to ask if her nephew could not send her some unsolved crossword puzzles to keep her busy over a boring week-end. This started an idea, and within two years the house of Simon and Schuster had sold over a million crossword puzzle books! In 1930 they followed the depression trend towards cheaper books by bringing out a series of one dollar volumes in paper covers, but like Boni, withdrew from the experiment for the time being. They were also among the first to recognize the public appetite for more pictures and fewer words. A glance at the number of the Simon and Schuster imprints among the best sellers of the last twenty-five years shows this very clearly. An important change in the financial structure of Simon and Schuster occurred in 1944, when Marshall Field acquired a substantial interest in the firm and simultaneously in Pocket Books, providing new capital for intensive postwar development.

The appearance in 1943 of Wendell Willkie's *One World* in large paper format at $1.00, as well as a cloth-bound $2.00 edition, set a pattern for the wide distribution of current informational material, such as General Marshall's wartime reports, the J. K. Lasser Income Tax books, etc. Their project of publishing inexpensive books for children, the Little Golden Books, in cooperation with the Artists and Writers Guild, a subsidiary of the Western Printing and Lithographing Co., began in 1942. These books, selling for twenty-five cents, have phenomenal success and have been followed by a more expensive series, the Giant Golden Books. In the spring of 1950 Simon and Schuster issued six of their new titles simultaneously in both cloth and paper covers in regular novel-size volumes, an experiment which the trade is watching with interest.

Two other publishing firms share 1924 as their founding date, Dial Press and Greenberg: Publisher. Dial Press' founder and president for its first ten years, was Lincoln MacVeagh, who had gained publishing experience with the firm of Henry Holt. Its distinguished list included the first books of W. R. Burnett and Glenway Wescott's second book. MacVeagh retired from active participation when he was appointed Ambassador to Greece in 1933. In 1934 Dial was sold to Max Salop. In 1938 Burton C. Hoffman bought Dial and is its president today. J. W. Greenberg is still active as head of the firm bearing his name. His list is a varied one, including books on games, the theater, how-to-do-it books, and many of the Tony Sarg items.

In 1925 two new publishing houses were founded. One of them, the John Day Company, so named after the famous early English printer-bookseller, was started as a general publishing firm by four young men, Richard Walsh, Guy Holt, Cleland Austin, Trell Yocum. Books on progressive education was one department of their business. In 1931 came the great success of Pearl Buck's *The Good Earth*. This author became active in the business as vice-president. Richard Walsh, whom she married, is the president and the only one of the original four still active in the business. In due course, the John Day list became somewhat overbalanced on the side of books about East Asia. A new imprint was created in order to set things right in their proper perspective: Asia Press, largely to be directed by Pearl S. Buck.

The other 1925 foundation was Harold Guinzburg's Viking Press. When he had decided on the new venture, he asked his friend Rockwell Kent for some sketches for a press mark. Among them was a fine Viking ship, from which the new firm got its name. Within the first year of its life it took into its fold B. W. Huebsch and the firm which he had started around 1905. Mr. Huebsch had cultivated an important circle of early modern Europeans. He had brought out in America Gerhart Hauptmann and Sudermann, Strindberg, Chekhov and Gorki. He had published James Joyce, the Irishman, and Sherwood Anderson, the American. This literary program continued to be cultivated within the framework of the new Viking Press, other authors, of course, being added to the list. Among their other series is a group of books on contemporary political and economic questions, and, since 1933, a very active juvenile department, with May Massee capably at the helm.

Harold Guinzburg was the founder of the Literary Guild. He had observed book clubs operating successfully in Germany and worked on the adaptation of this idea to American publishing around the same time that the Book-of-the-Month Club saw its inception. Viking Press sold the Literary Guild to Doubleday, Doran in 1934. In 1938 Viking took over from Covici-Friede the publishing rights to John Steinbeck's works, the most valuable literary property on its list. Pascal Covici was taken in as a member of Viking's editorial and executive staff.

During the war, in 1943, the "Viking Portable Library" was announced as a new departure. It took its start, somewhat incidentally, from Alexander Woollcott's anthology, *As You Were*, designed in a single volume as "a portable library of American prose and poetry, assembled for members of the Armed Forces and the Merchant Marine." The neat volume, compact, durable, readable, was so successful, that the idea was tried with other titles. Something like an omnibus series in miniature evolved, featuring the writings of John Steinbeck, Dorothy Parker, Ernest Hemingway, in one-volume editions, or comprehensive anthologies of writing in a special field. In its juveniles, in the "Portable Library," and very much in its regular trade editions Viking has maintained high standards of taste and manufacturing skills. Milton Glick, for many years in charge of production, deserves much credit for a long sustained performance.

A word should be said about Harold Guinzburg's distinguished wartime activities. By 1942 he was associated with Colonel William Donovan, then Coordinator of Information, and later head of the OSS. Guinzburg subsequently went with OWI, and early in 1944 became Director of the London Publications Division, where he did vital planning both in the immediate use of the printed word in the task of winning the war and in long-range information and reorientation programs directed at both our European Allies and the conquered enemy. In particular, he helped develop the Overseas Editions program, on which the Council on Books in Wartime had been working. He returned late in 1944, but continued as general publishing consultant to the OWI.

The year 1926 saw the start of William Morrow & Company, W. W. Norton & Company and the Vanguard Press. W. W. Norton came into the general publishing field from an unusual angle. He was greatly interested in adult education, was chairman of a student group at the New School for Social Research and member of the board of Cooper Union. He saw no reason why serious modern subjects should not be presented in well-written and well-designed books especially prepared for the average person who wishes to acquire exact knowledge without too many trappings of the academic. The firm started as "The People's Institute Publishing Company" and soon grew into a substantial firm noted for the quality of its list and its strong and lasting backlist. Spectacular success was achieved with such books as *An American Doctor's Odyssey, Mathematics for the Millions* and *Burma Surgeon.* Through editorial preference and accumulating experience of ranking staff members, four specialties have come to be favorably developed at Norton's: musicology, psychology, books about the sea, and college textbooks.

Norton died in November, 1945, highly respected by his fellow publishers. He had rendered conspicuous public service as chairman of the Council of Books in Wartime, where he originated the slogan, "Books are weapons in the war of ideas." He had also been chairman of the

Joint Board of Publishers and Booksellers and president of the National Association of Book Publishers. Storer Lunt, vice-president since 1938, succeeded him after his death in 1945.

Vanguard Press, too, is the outcome of special circumstances. When Charles Garland inherited a considerable fortune his acute social conscience prompted him to refuse it for his private use and, instead, he established with it the "American Fund for Public Service," which he devoted to the promotion of the labor movement in this country. Within this organization the Vanguard Press was called to life in 1926, and it gained independence with James Henle at the head when the original Garland foundation was dissolved. Socially useful books at low price was the original program which has been adhered to through the years. Vanguard had spectacular success with Kallet's book, *100,000,000 Guinea Pigs*, in collaboration with F. J. Schlink of Consumers' Research, and is the publisher of the fiction of James T. Farrell and Vardis Fisher. When *Our Fair City* appeared in 1947, it was pointed out that this was the first full-fledged study of the politics of American cities to be issued since Lincoln Steffens' *The Shame of the Cities*, published back in the muckraking days.

William Morrow, born in Dublin, had joined Stokes as an editor in 1906, after six years in the magazine field. In 1926 he established his own imprint for a successful general publishing house, which since Morrow's death in 1931 has been directed by Thayer Hobson. Women have been active in the development of this firm, with Frances Phillips, Emily Street, Eva Colby, and Elisabeth Hamilton on the board of directors. The books of Mr. Morrow's wife, Honoré Willsie Morrow, have been conspicuous on their list, and the mysteries of Erle Stanley Gardner are a year-round activity.

Also in 1925 the Macrae Smith Company was established in Philadelphia, when Durant L. Macrae and Allan M. Smith purchased the publishing business of George W. Jacobs, with which they had both been associated. The list the new firm took over included three series of classics. Mr. Jacobs, who had been in business since 1892, thereafter confined his activities to bookselling until his death in 1936.

In 1928, at the culminating point of the postwar boom, Covici-Friede began their activity as publishers of works of a bibliophilic nature, venturing into the limited editions field, and specializing on works of unusual character which would not fit readily into the normal program of a general publisher. Pascal Covici had published previously in Chicago under his own name. The new house was sufficiently successful to weather the storm of 1929. In 1938, however, this firm came to an end. As has been noted, Mr. Covici joined the Viking Press, and the list, except for the Steinbeck titles, was absorbed by the Outlet Book Company, a group of publishing interests from which Crown Publishers took its origin.

The number of important general publishing houses founded since the depression has been small. In 1933 the publishing firm of Reynal & Hitchcock was organized "to publish a small but distinguished list covering many fields," including some fiction, but with the emphasis on such subjects as political economy, social science, history and biography. Eugene Reynal had joined the Harper firm in 1926, and in 1930 he had become head of Blue Ribbon Books, a co-operative reprint house organized by Harper and a group of other publishers, of which Reynal purchased complete control in June, 1933. Curtice Hitchcock had joined the Macmillan staff in 1924 and, in 1931, the Century Company. Reynal & Hitchcock, as has been told already, were absorbed by Harcourt, Brace in 1948.

The year 1936 saw the establishment of a new publishing house which recalls the literary publishers of the 1890's both in its sole emphasis on literary and artistic quality and in the fact that it, too, was started by a Harvard undergraduate. The New Directions Press was begun in a reconverted stable in 1936, at Norfolk, Connecticut, by James Laughlin, who is the chief editor and owner. The firm is fortunate in its economic position, commanding such strong capital resources that profits from sales are not essential for its survival. As a Harvard undergraduate, Laughlin issued his first annual *New Directions Anthology*, a collection of experimental works of promising young authors and poets of the avant garde. The firm is small in size but not in ambition. By 1950 it had published approximately 200 books, with about half of these titles still in print. New Directions believes, as do many thoughtful observers of the current publishing scene, that the good books are not necessarily those which have seasonal sale only, or disappear quickly. The Press has sales and production offices in New York with a staff of a half dozen people, mostly without titles, since informality is the keynote of house and personnel. In recent years the firm has experimented with production in Europe, placing work with some of the high-quality presses of Italy, France, England, Switzerland and Germany. It has steadily promoted the work of William Carlos Williams, Henry Miller, Tennessee Williams; of Kafka and many other European writers. In 1949, in partnership with Richard T. Smyth, Laughlin established a college textbook department, active in the fields of history, the social sciences and the humanities.

It is an interesting observation, although hardly more than a coincidence, that Crown Publishers, the other new concern which came into being during the same year as the New Directions Press, is based on diametrically opposed intentions, policies and modes of operation. New Directions is the creation of one man who publishes what he believes is valuable, regardless of profit, especially concerned with writers whose literary standards place them apart from the current commercialization of publishing. Crown Publishers has reached its present stature as the result of a curious process of accretion, by wholesale acquisition of publishers, imprints and individual titles already established and published, and capable of further commercial promotion. Early in the thirties, the Greenberg publishing firm owned as one of its many assets Outlet Book Company, a group of interests mainly dedicated to the distribution of publishers' remainders. Nat Wartels was the manager in 1934. Together with a salesman in the Greenberg organization, a young man named Robert Simon, Wartels bought the stock and the name of the Outlet Book Company. Among the additions made to their fast-growing organization were most of the assets of Covici-Friede and, in the forties, the venerable old Boston firm of Lothrop, Lee & Shepard, continuing and adding to their established juvenile list. Crown Publishers is actually one of several branches of the Outlet Book Company, but it came into prominence during the war, when the rapidly dwindling remainder stocks called for initiative and the creation of original assets. Various how-to-do-it books, collections of folklore, tourists' guide books, popular volumes about music and art, various digests and anthologies and, of course, regular trade fiction are the items on which the Crown program is built.

Pocket Books started in the late spring of 1939, a few months before the outbreak of the second world war in Europe. No one needs to be told that this was not just the start of another publishing concern, but the beginning of a major revolution in American publishing. Some data will be given at this point, but we will return to this fascinating story in connection with the new developments in book distribution and reading habits. On June 19, 1939, Robert F. de Graff published the first ten titles of his new twenty-five cent series. He had been a pioneer in the development of low-priced book publishing. He knew the experiments made with the Boni paper books and the Modern Library. He was well acquainted with the continental European tradition of cheap book publishing and especially with the British Penguin Books. In the mid-twenties he had originated the Garden City Publishing Company's line of Star Dollar Reprints. He left to become president of Blue Ribbon Books, specializing in low-priced reprints. He thus enjoyed unusual opportunities for gauging the widening market with each successive lowering of the retail price. He resigned from Blue Ribbon in 1938 to make exhaustive studies of what kind of reading matter and what shape of a book people at large needed and would buy and where they would be apt to make their purchase. He sensed an enormous untapped market. To eliminate guesswork, he carefully described his plans, set up a tentative list and asked for criticism. A sample pocket book, for which Pearl Buck's *The Good Earth* was chosen, was sent out to those who seriously responded to his inquiry. That he was on the right track was immediately apparent. A first experiment in distribution was made in New York. Within one day and a half a little cigar store near the Pocket Books office sold 110 copies, Macy's 695 the first day, and Concord Books re-ordered 1,000. The same happened in other cities. Higbee's in Cleveland had an initial order for 2,000 copies. Backed by a $100 ad in the *Plain Dealer*, they had sold every book by four P.M. of the first day. By July, Pocket Books were nationally established.

Almost from the beginning, the offices of Pocket Books were located in the U.S. Rubber Building at Rockefeller Center with Simon and Schuster, who owned the minority stock of the new company. Philip Van Doren Stern was editor until called to head the manufacturing end of the Armed Services Editions. His place was taken for a time by Donald Porter Geddes, formerly of the Columbia University Press. He made publishing history with the Franklin Delano Roosevelt memorial volume, shipped out within six days after the president's death. In 1944

Marshall Field purchased a major interest in the company, as also in Simon and Schuster, under a plan which left the publishing policies of Pocket Books in the hands of Robert de Graff and the Simon and Schuster partners. In 1950 de Graff became chairman of the Board, with Leon Shimkin as president and Freeman Lewis as executive vice-president.

In the first ten years, 600 titles were issued, totaling sales of 260 million volumes—more, Pocket Books claims, than the combined total of all best sellers published since 1880, including all major book club selections and all reprints other than Pocket Books. Fifty-six titles have sold over a million copies each. Pocket Books describes its program as ranging from social, economic, religious, political, and inspirational subjects to mysteries, romances, westerns, quiz and fun, histories, poetry, dictionaries, reference books, and the classics. Mysteries account for about 20 per cent of the titles, westerns for 15 per cent. The sales proportion of these categories is of course a different story. Top individual sellers on the list so far have been *How to Win Friends and Influence People; See Here, Private Hargrove; The Pocket Cook Book; The Pocket Book of Baby and Child Care; Merriam-Webster Pocket Dictionary.*

One more publishing concern started out in the period between the depression and the winter of the "phony war" at the end of 1939, the firm of Duell, Sloan and Pearce. The differences in the policies and methods of each of the new firms of this period offers interesting opportunities for comparisons: the uncompromising idealism of the New Directions Press, Crown Publishers' keen salesmanship of pleasant and useful packages of entertainment and instruction, the Pocket Books' revolutionary attack upon the non-book-buying citizen! Duell, Sloan and Pearce are perhaps best described as the most typical general trade house in the group. They are not very different in structure and program from other houses started by groups of young men who have earned their spurs and are eager to demonstrate their own talents and courage. C. Halliwell Duell, president of the new company, had been with William Morrow. Samuel Sloan, the new vice-president and treasurer, came over from Harcourt, as did the third partner, Charles A. Pearce, secretary and editor-in-chief of the new company. Sloan died in 1945, as a result of an accident.

Their first book, Archibald MacLeish's *America was Promise,* was published December 1, 1939. Emphasis from the start has been on a balanced program which would secure a reasonably stable income from serious fiction, nonfiction, mysteries and murders, but would also allow consistent cultivation of the new writer and the unusual book.

The long procession of immigrants who sought and found refuge in America from the persecutions of National Socialism included much colorful book trade talent. Many illustrators and designers, speaking the international language of art, were quickly absorbed and found ready reception here. For those who had been publishers abroad, the transition was somewhat more difficult, but some succeeded in establishing themselves. No one adapted himself more skillfully to the American scene than Kurt Wolff, the publisher of Pantheon Books.

Kurt Wolff was one of the most successful German publishers of the Weimar republic, appealing with a distinguished international list of unusually high standards to a fairly broad and popular audience. The very significant thing about his American publishing house, established in New York in 1942, is the fact that in eight years of existence it has not issued a single trivial or merely popular title, nor a book chosen primarily because of its income-producing possibilities. Every book on the list is of unquestionable cultural value, or of decided artistic significance, or a genuine attempt to contribute to the solution of the intellectual and spiritual dilemma of these difficult years. This is an almost unique record, made possible by modest beginnings, low overhead, contentment with moderate profits, skillful promotion of those items which appealed to the larger audiences, and above all, faith and courage. Kyrill Schabert is the president and treasurer of Pantheon Books, Kurt Wolff vice-president and editor, his wife, Helen, in charge of editorial work and promotion. Jacques Schiffrin, former French publisher of the Pléiade Editions, who came here after the fall of France, is a partner.

Pantheon Books also publishes the "Bollingen Series," founded and edited by Mary Mellon within the framework of Paul Mellon's Bollingen Foundation. The series cultivates philosophy, anthropology, art, comparative religion and symbolism, for a small scholarly audience which in itself could not support such titles.

The most promising new publisher of the 1940's in the United States is the house of William Sloane Associates, which began in 1946. It started as a secession of William Sloane and his major associates from the firm of Henry Holt and Company. During his seven year association with Holt, Sloane had brought vigorous new life to the trade department of the dignified but conservative firm. Himself a promising author of plays and novels, Sloane showed imagination and common sense. It is true that at one time he turned down a 1,000,000-word manuscript by an unknown North Carolina author, which under Maxwell Perkins' skillful administration evolved as *Look Homeward, Angel*. But he did buy *See Here, Private Hargrove*, Bill Mauldin's *Up Front* and two books by Ernie Pyle, and also poetry by Mark Van Doren, for the Holt list. In 1943 he went on an important book trade mission to China, representing the Book Publishers' Bureau and the OWI.

In 1946, following the distribution of the holdings of the Bristol family, long active in Holt's, to Clinton Murchison, a Dallas oil man and financier, William Sloane quickly decided, after conferring with his close associates, Helen Taylor, Keith Jennison and Norman Hood, to start an independent new firm. Their very first book, *Thunder out of China* by Theodore H. White and Annalee Jacoby, became a Book-of-the-Month Club selection, and in 1950 their author, A. B. Guthrie, Jr., won the Pulitzer Prize with *The Way West*. From the first the list was nicely balanced between prestige and popular selections. In December, 1947, Sloane bought from Holt the "American Men of Letters Series," planned by himself and Helen Taylor while still with Holt. In 1948 a college textbook department was started. William Sloane was one of the group of American publishers sent over to Germany on a mission of exploration and information. In the fall of 1949 the team of four disagreed, and Helen Taylor and Keith Jennison left the firm and joined the Viking Press.

While regional dispersion of specialized publishing has made steady progress in the last twenty or thirty years, general publishing has remained pretty much concentrated in New York. As one of the few general publishers carrying on west of the Alleghenies, one must mention the Bobbs-Merrill Company in Indianapolis, which developed from a bookstore started in that city in 1838. This house came to book trade prominence at the turn of the century, with its successful handling of such popular titles as Charles Major's *When Knighthood*

Was in Flower. While the firm has given success to many Hoosier authors, from James Whitcomb Riley on, it has maintained a list of national scope. D. Laurance Chambers has been president since 1935.

Another mid-western imprint is the Cleveland firm, The World Publishing Company, formerly called the World Syndicate Publishing Company, founded in 1905 by Alfred Cahen as the Commercial Book Bindery. Mr. Cahen devised many improvements for high speed book production, and his company produced books by the millions for premium distribution by newspapers and mail order houses. They had a line of popular-priced dictionaries and Bibles, inexpensive juveniles and self-help books. In 1934 Benjamin D. Zevin joined the company, and five years later was made vice-president. In 1940 a new hard-bound reprint line, Tower Books, planned to retail at forty-nine cents, was introduced. The firm has since inaugurated several other reprint series, of which Rainbow Classics, and the Living Library are still active. Mr. Cahen is now chairman of the Board, his daughter, Mrs. Zevin, is active in the editorial department, and Mr. Zevin is the president. In 1949 World issued a folio size Lectern Bible, four years in the making, designed by Bruce Rogers.

The reader of these pages will understand, I hope, that this rapid chronicle of modern publishing firms is not intended to be complete either as to the number of houses listed or in the information given for each publisher. It is an attempt to illustrate the general trend of the times with some characteristic examples. But even within this limited plan we must not overlook the specialized publishing organizations of today, nor the great old publishing firms which continue to carry on.

Contemporary Special Publishers

The nineteenth century history of publishing in America seems to indicate that specialization may be read as a sign of some stability and maturity in the intellectual life of a country. This should not be understood as an endorsement of the ideal of narrowness nor as disregarding the desirability of making special information available in generally understandable terms. It does mean that there is a logical place for a book that does not deal with matters of general interest and is not necessarily intended for the general reader. The question whether specialization in modern American publishing is growing or decreasing is therefore perhaps an interesting yardstick of maturity. An extensive statistical analysis of imprint lists would require machinery and effort out of proportion to the value of the results in this present study. But certain impressions may be recorded. The current scene does seem to indicate a tendency towards greater specialization. A large number of books dealing with specific topics are being published not as isolated items on a publisher's list, but together with other related titles, either in special departments of a general house, or by publishers concentrating in a given area. Moreover, the areas of concentration seem to be increasing in number.

It would obviously be impossible to include here a complete listing of special publishers and their programs. *The Literary Market Place* does this in precise and concentrated form. A few observations, however, can be made.

One of the most striking developments has been the growth of scientific and technical book publishing since the beginning of World War II. The challenging conditions which faced the technical book publisher are recalled by the men at Van Nostrand in their 1948 anniversary volume: "The war years of 1941 to 1945 remain so vividly in memory that it is difficult as yet to assess them as history. They were years of stress and strain to all publishers, no less than to the Van Nostrand firm. The imposition of government controls and paper quotas; the incessant trips to Washington to obtain extra-quota paper for essential books, the terrific demand born of war needs for books on radio, navigation, aircraft engineering, and a hundred other subjects suddenly a part of our mobilization program; the virtual elimination of the normal college curriculum and the shift of emphasis subject-wise from the arts of peace to the arts of war; the dislocation of manufacturing schedules because of labor shortages on the one hand and increased demand on the other—all of these problems and a thousand others kept company activity at fever pitch."

A vivid picture of these conditions can also be gained from the seventh Bowker Memorial Lecture, *The Technical Book in War Times* by James S. Thompson. He points out that in 1940 only 2 per cent of all technical books published had a direct connection with the war; in 1941 the rate had risen to 14 per cent; but within a year of

Pearl Harbor it jumped to 50 per cent for 1942. Aeronautics and air-craft manufacture, automotive construction and maintenance, radio, television, navigation, radar, frequency modulation and meteorology, those were the favored topics. We can now add to these the vast new field of nuclear fission as a continuing strong need in the technical publishing field. The fact that it was possible for the government to cause publication of new titles by suggestion rather than by actual commissioning is one of the many wartime achievements that one wishes could be carried over into the peace effort.

James Thompson wrote from his first-hand experience as president of the largest special publishing house in the country, the McGraw-Hill Book Company in New York. This firm originated in 1909 through the merger of the book department of the McGraw Publishing Company and the Hill Publishing Company, Martin M. Foss becoming director of the book business. Foss was active from 1927 to 1944, and was succeeded by James S. Thompson, president until 1946. The systematic attention of the editors was directed at the start towards engineering and industrial management. For the decade 1910-1920 this was a fortunate choice, corresponding to an ever-increasing demand. Within twenty-five years the McGraw-Hill Book Company had published over 2,000 titles. The firm developed its special policy of retaining academic instructors and other experts in the various fields as special advisers, and of training its staff by courses designed to familiarize them with the many special fields cultivated by the firm. In their various book departments and in their extensive maga-zine family McGraw-Hill covers today approximately the following subjects: mathematics, physics, chemistry, astronomy, nuclear energy, botany, zoology, pharmacy, agriculture and forestry, metallurgy and mining, general engineering, chemical and electrical engineering, radio, transportation and aviation, the textile world, economics, business management, salesmanship, public health, dentistry.

In 1930, McGraw-Hill entered the general publishing field by establishing its Whittlesey House, with Guy Holt, who had been partner in the John Day Company, as director. He has been succeeded by George Stewart, then Hugh Kelly, and again William E. Larned. In 1950 the firm announced that the imprint Whittlesey House would be retained only for juveniles and certain types of specialized books, and that its trade book activities would be carried on under the McGraw-Hill imprint. In 1931 the McGraw-Hill building was completed, one of the most beautiful and original of the New York skyscrapers, with Raymond Hood as architect. Top executives of the McGraw-Hill Book Company today are Curtis W. McGraw, chairman of the board, and Curtis G. Benjamin, president. An indication of the size of the firm is seen in the fact that it published some thirty technical and business periodicals, distributed to a total of over two million readers. Yearly, 250 to 300 new books are published by the firm, which employs a staff of over 2,500 people. McGraw-Hill is not only the largest special publisher in America, but also the third largest publishing house in the country, with a volume of business that is exceeded only by Doubleday and by Macmillan.

Somewhat comparable in scope, though not in size, is the old Baltimore house of Williams & Wilkins. They entered the field of scientific and medical book and periodical publishing in 1909, the same year that McGraw-Hill started. Edward B. Passano, who had joined the firm in 1897, was the president. In 1925 he incorporated the Waverly Press as the firm's printing department, allowing for the carrying on there of a considerable volume of printing for important institutions and foundations. In 1932 William Wood & Co., the oldest of New York medical houses, was taken over. In 1933 Passano helped to organize the publishing firm of Reynal and Hitchcock of New York as a member of their board of directors.

Such vigorous old-established firms as D. Van Nostrand, Saunders, and John Wiley, whose history has been told in an earlier chapter, took their natural share and made their contribution in the expanding technical book field. Wiley is now in the hands of W. O. Wiley as chairman and Edward P. Hamilton as president, and a member of the fifth generation, Bradford Wiley, is active in the business.

Along with the noticeable expansion in the technical book field, certain new areas of specialization are developing. The urgent quest for greater knowledge of the human personality, clearer insight into the structure of his character, his inner motives and conflicts, is finding expression in the many publications in the fields of mental hygiene, psychology, psychiatry and psychoanalysis. An extensive publishing program is developing, ranging all the way from the strictly scientific to broadly popular treatment. During the thirties no one firm concentrated in the area, but houses like Harcourt, Greenberg, and especially Norton were active and are still active. Knopf has demonstrated his interest with a group of a dozen or so titles, with intellectual appeal to the well-informed lay audience. One small firm, International Universities Press, has some 70 titles in print, of which 32 are psychoanalytical books, an example of clearly defined specialization.

One important field of American publishing which has had a notable recent growth is that of art books. Art publishing had seen a boom at the time of the Centennial Exhibition of 1876, but this field never became large or significant. More art books were imported than initiated locally, and today, in the present expansion, the market takes advantage of the output of many countries. The new techniques of photography and processes of color reproduction have enriched the lists.

The Weyhe Galleries in New York, active in art publishing since 1919, have done pioneer work in broadening the interest, and younger houses, Wittenborn & Schultz, H. Bittner, Curt Valentin at the Buchholz Gallery, Harry N. Abrams, Watson Guptill and others have followed the line. The entrance of The Museum of Modern Art into book publishing has been a tremendous stimulus, and general publishers have had increasing success with important and beautiful art books. This success where earlier attempts failed is due to the great upsurge of the interest in art in every aspect of American cultural life. The establishment of three art book clubs is equally symptomatic. The mass market has also shown receptivity to art books with several titles available in twenty-five cent and thirty-five cent lines.

Appealing to much the same market is the list of Hastings House, a firm which pioneered in the photographic picture book field. The house was founded in 1936 by Walter Frese, who at that time was vice-president of the Architectural Book Publishing Company, founded by his grandfather. Hastings House's first success was Samuel Chamberlain's collection of camera impressions, "A Small House in the Sun," which was followed by a dozen or more photographic books. The firm now publishes over thirty of the American Guide Series, the state guides originally prepared under the Federal Writers' Project in the 1930's.

Music publishing is not a new field of specialization in the United States. But it is obvious to even the casual observer that the popular book about music and musicians, as well as the serious musicological study, is more firmly entrenched today than it ever was, due to a large extent, of course, to the radio. Whether or not television will have a comparably deep and broad effect in popularizing the visual arts and, incidentally, the literature of these arts, remains to be seen.

At the present time other practical factors have helped certain types of arts and crafts books to a prominent position. The housing shortage, the scarcity of skilled labor, and the urge towards manual craftsmanship felt by men and women all over the country have increased books in the fields of home construction, interior decoration, furniture design and production, and many related aspects. They form an important element in the broad new stream of the "how-to-do-it" books of the American postwar world.

One generally significant observation on special publishing is the fact that the important publishing houses in special fields are not as closely concentrated in New York as are the general houses, a condition which had already developed in the course of the nineteenth century. But in contrast to the earlier existence of quite a number of small firms there has come about in certain fields a decided concentration into large, powerful concerns that are highly organized. The law publishing business, for instance, is largely concentrated in the hands of three big enterprises, the West Publishing Company in St. Paul in Minnesota—a veritable Ford enterprise—the Bancroft Whitney firm in San Francisco, and the Lawyers Cooperative Publishing Company in Rochester, New York, the latter two having several joint enterprises.

We still find in the twentieth century such specialized regional publishers, to mention but a very few, as Caxton Printers in Caldwell, Idaho, founded in 1903 to publish books on the Northwest; Bruce Publishing Company, dating back to 1891, publishing from Milwaukee both Catholic religious books and craft books; Wm. B. Eerdmans Publishing Co., since 1916 issuing a variety of books from Grand Rapids, Michigan; and Binfords & Mort of Portland, Oregon, doing regional publishing for the past twenty years.

A special publisher who has grown into a general publishing house is the firm of Prentice-Hall. In 1913 two teachers of economics at New York University, Charles W. Gerstenberg and Richard P. Ettinger, founded a company, giving the firm the maiden names of their mothers, to publish *Materials of Corporation Finance*, a case textbook they had prepared. They built up the firm supplying business men with up-to-the-minute information on taxation, labor laws, etc., in loose-leaf form. It was not until 1937 that the company entered the trade book field, and the first book of fiction was added to their list in 1945. Dr. Gerstenberg died in 1948, but Mr. Ettinger continues active as president and chairman of the board.

The production of books for the schools, which had from earliest days been a basic sector of American publishing, saw increased expansion and importance after the period reviewed in the earlier section. Most of the general publishing houses, such as Macmillan, Scribner, Harper, Appleton, had large departments, and houses specializing exclusively in textbooks increased in strength and diversity until the American Textbook Publishers' Institute, established in 1942, today has a membership of fifty-seven houses. The Institute's report on *Textbooks in Education* gives a valuable survey and includes a brief history of American textbook publishing.

Textbook publishing in the last sixty years has been affected by several rapidly developing trends, all encouraged by a new appreciation of the importance of textbooks in education. To the steady expansion of elementary schools was added, after the turn of the century, the spectacular expansion of secondary schools, the development of more special texts for colleges, and the growth of the Catholic educational program. More recently, increased attention to modern presentation of educational material and to book design has made vast changes in the field.

The 1890's began with a startling amalgamation of the textbook lists of five large houses into the American Book Company. A. S. Barnes & Co., Ivison, Blakeman, Taylor & Co., D. Appleton & Co., Van Antwerp, Bragg & Co. and Harper were the lists brought together. The cry of book trust was raised. The company prospered and expanded, but competition also increased, and in no field of publishing have new ideas found greater welcome and support. Among the important firms in contemporary textbook publishing, aside from the

American Book Company and the major general publishers with textbook departments, are Ginn, Heath, Silver Burdett, Allyn & Bacon, Scott, Foresman and Row, Peterson. Textbook publishing has been more widely scattered than other fields of publishing. Boston and Chicago rival New York as textbook publishing centers, and the names of a variety of American cities appear on textbook imprints.

Outstanding publishers in the bibliographical field are R. R. Bowker & Company, whose history has already been told in an earlier section, and the H. W. Wilson Company, both in New York. It would be difficult to overestimate the contribution made since the turn of the century by Halsey William Wilson and his associates to American bibliography. Essential to professional librarianship and to scholarship, the basic indexes published by the Wilson Company are also indispensable tools for the book trade. Probably the most widely known and used of the score or more of periodic Wilson indexes are: the *Cumulative Book Index*, with which the Wilson activities began, cataloging on a current basis all books published in English in all countries; the *Book Review Digest*, the *Reader's Guide to Periodical Literature*, and the *Abridged Reader's Guide*. An essential characteristic of the chief Wilson bibliographies is the listing not only by title and author, but by multiple subject breakdowns. Mr. Wilson, who celebrated his eightieth birthday in 1948 and is still the active president of his firm, started a supply and textbook store in 1889 while a student at the University of Minnesota. Finding the existing bibliographies insufficient for his needs as a bookseller, he went into the business of providing new ones himself, in 1898. Expanding steadily, the firm moved to White Plains, New York, in 1913, and to the Bronx, New York City, in 1917, where it now occupies three buildings. The success of the enterprise has been attributed not only to the number and precision of the listings, but also to the ingenious methods designed largely by the founder himself for the processing and organization of raw data.

From the vast stream of theological publishing of Catholic, Protestant and Jewish religions, about which alone a lengthy volume could be written, the Methodist Book Concern may be singled out as the oldest American book publishing house in continuous operation today. (Lea & Febiger of Philadelphia has direct roots back to 1785 but for the first few years they were periodical publishers only.) Founded in

1789, its early history has already been told. The important new organization of this entire publishing set-up in 1940 was the logical result of the union of the three major Methodist denominations the previous year. The merger of 1940 combined a large number of hitherto separated publishing interests and agencies, and the old name of Methodist Book Concern was changed to Methodist Publishing House. This vast program is headed by one lay director, Lovick Pierce, and one minister, Dr. Roy L. Smith.

A separate publishing unit within the Methodist publishing organization is the Abingdon-Cokesbury Press, with headquarters in Nashville, founded as a trade publishing house in 1940 "to encourage the writing of distinguished books in the broad field of evangelical Christianity." Abingdon-Cokesbury Press resulted from the merger of the older Abingdon Press, the Cokesbury Press and Stockton Press, with Pat Beaird as manager. In 1944 an active children's department was created under the editorship of Edith Patterson Meyer.

This pattern of religious book publishing for general sale as well as for denominational interest has been energetically developed by the Baptists (Judson Press and Broadman Press), the Presbyterians (Westminster Press), the Congregationalists (Pilgrim Press), the Unitarians (Beacon Press), the Lutherans (Augustana Publishing House, Concodia Publishing House and several others), the Episcopalians (Morehouse-Gorham & Co.), and the Roman Catholics through numerous special imprints such as Sheed & Ward, Bruce Publishing Company, Newman Press, as well as the old houses of P. J. Kenedy & Co. and Benziger Brothers.

University Presses

The existence and the functioning of university presses is very much an Anglo-Saxon tradition. Oxford and Cambridge, the outstanding examples of academic printing and publishing in the Old World, have no counterpart in stability and importance on the European continent, where early specialization over the entire field of human knowledge has left no room for a university press. In America, the English example was followed early. It is perhaps not quite correct to call the first printing press in Cambridge a "University Press," although by the intention of its founders and through many personal and local ties it was something very much like it. At any rate, it did establish an early tradition of printing and publishing in Cambridge, Massachusetts, a tradition which has never ceased.

The present organization known as the Harvard University Press arose from a printing office apparently established sometime in 1871 for the modest purpose of producing certain minor printing jobs for the University. In 1892 President Eliot appointed T. Bertram Williams, formerly of the Riverside Press, as Publication Agent. In 1896 circumstances made it advisable for Williams to take complete responsibility for the work of the printing office, and from then on the University embarked upon a program of more general publishing. Mr. Williams was succeeded in 1908 by Charles Chester Lane, formerly of Ginn and Company. The establishment of a course of instruction in printing in the Graduate School of Business Administration served to emphasize the need for a University Press, and in 1913 President and Fellows formally authorized the establishment of the Harvard University Press under the direction of C. C. Lane, succeeded among others by Dr. Dumas Malone, Roger Scaife, and later by Thomas J. Wilson. The gradual evolution and expansion of this organization is characteristic of the way in which the modern University Press has come into being in many places.

Two early experiments failed to mature into lasting organizations, one a university press at Cornell, first taking shape in 1869 but discontinued in 1884, the other a University Press Company at the University of Pennsylvania, started as such in 1870 and by 1890 incorporated as the University of Pennsylvania Press, which ceased existence within ten years, until its reorganization in 1921. Both universities later on saw the establishment of their presses on a sound and lasting basis.

The first university press to achieve permanence in the United States was the Johns Hopkins University Press, founded in 1878, their first book appearing in 1887. The new emphasis on graduate research, resulting largely from the acceptance of German academic concepts, called for new methods of publication.

The University of Chicago Press, it is interesting to note, was organized at the same time that the University was called to life, 1891. Donald P. Bean, now director of Stanford University Press, served as director of the University of Chicago Press from 1927 to 1942.

In 1929 he made the first comprehensive survey of university presses, which was published under the title, *American Scholarly Publishing*. Joseph A. Brandt succeeded him as head of the press, followed by W. T. Couch and Rollin D. Hemens is now its director.

Columbia University Press, the largest of American university presses in terms of annual title output, was organized in 1893. Columbia's famous president Butler was titular head of the Press from 1902 to 1946; Frederick Coykendall succeeded him and Charles G. Proffitt, his assistant since 1927, became director and active administrative officer. In 1949 and 1950 the Press made a vital contribution to the book trade and the library world by issuing the reports of the ALA's Public Library Inquiry. The Press is perhaps best known for the *Columbia Encyclopedia*, a one-volume general reference work first issued in 1935 and revised in 1950. Outstanding among university press public relations activities is Columbia's sprightly news bulletin, *The Pleasures of Publishing*, started by Donald Porter Geddes in 1934 and later edited by Fon W. Boardman.

In 1905 Princeton entered the field, adopting its present form in 1910, with Charles Scribner as an early advocate and later patron. Yale followed in 1908. As in Harvard, academic instruction in printing gave the press an added function in the university's life. Carl P. Rollins, the well-known typographer and critic of fine printing who came there in 1918, has co-operated with the Librarian of the College and with members of the faculty in offering to students interesting opportunities to observe and experiment with printing and book production methods.

The University of California Press, too, has early roots in a printing office, existing there by 1877 and nourished by the printer of the University, Joseph W. Flinn, into an important organization, with the Press established in 1893. Until his death in 1949, Samuel T. Farquhar served for many years as head of the press.

Presses have also been established (by 1949) at the Catholic University of America, at Denver, Duke, Fordham, Georgia, Illinois, Iowa State, Kansas, Kentucky, Louisiana State, Loyola, Michigan, Minnesota, Nebraska, New Mexico, New York University, North Carolina, Oklahoma, Pittsburgh, Rutgers, South Carolina, Stanford, Syracuse, Southern Methodist University in Dallas, University of Washington, and the University of Wisconsin. Each year sees some expansion in this field.

This is an impressive list. Its most important meaning is the establishment, on a sound and reasonably permanent basis, of a network of regional publishing centers, distributed widely over the entire United States. The collective program of these university presses is one of the most powerful safeguards against the threat of low standards resulting from the pressure of the mass markets, from "best sellerism" and from the automatic purchasing of books from pre-selected lists of the various book clubs.

A Report on American University Presses was prepared by Chester Kerr and published by the Association of American University Presses in 1949. "Increased attention by commercial publishers to mass markets, a position forced on them by economic circumstances," says Kerr, is one reason for "the shift to university presses of the responsibility for the publication of many 'unprofitable' or less profitable serious works of nonfiction." But, he observes, "so long as a press maintains its standards, it is going to need financial assistance and the bulk of that assistance . . . has to come from the parent institution."

The new responsibilities have caused a gradual change in management, he observes, from "a few farsighted university administrators, energetic scholars, broadminded librarians, enlightened alumni and devoted practitioners of the art of printing . . . into the hands of a new group of professionals, men and women dedicated to the aims of scholarship but also trained in the techniques of publishing."

Should a press aim at a learned or at a general audience? Kerr answers this with the assertion that it would be impossible "to explain the upward curve in the dissemination of university press books during the past decade except by crediting it to the new determination by a growing number of presses to make meaningful and available to the greatest number of citizens the best products of American scholarship."

The Older Firms Carry On

Stimulated by the competition of newcomers in the publishing field, many of the older nineteenth century firms are carrying on today with renewed vigor and energy. In fact, it can be said that practically all the important old firms are still in business today, even though many of them have undergone a thorough metamorphosis.

Two of the most substantial older houses, Harper and Appleton, were facing very serious difficulties at the end of the last century. Harper & Brothers was given a new lease on life by the banking house of Morgan, represented by George B. M. Harvey, with the Harper tradition represented by Thomas B. Wells and Henry Hoyns. In 1931 Cass Canfield became president, and he stayed in that post until 1945, when he replaced Henry Hoyns as chairman of the board. He was succeeded as president by Frank MacGregor, himself a member of the board since 1930.

Characteristic of the Harper organization today is the coexistence of a group of semi-autonomous departments, each with a large degree of independence. They are held together, as the states of the union, by an over-all "federal" management, and they share certain of the service departments. The general trade book department is under the leadership of John Fischer. Other departments include one in the combined fields of sociology, economics and politics, with Ordway Tead at the helm; college and high school texts; medicine; religion; juveniles; staple books; and, of course, *Harper's Magazine*, the sole and proud survivor of the firm's original large magazine family.

D. Appleton & Co. was also reorganized by bankers at the turn of the century, and the old house was rebuilt with a modern point of view by John W. Hiltman. A significant event in the chronicles of the firm was the merger, in 1933, with the old Century Company, which resulted in the Appleton-Century Company. W. Morgan Shuster and Dana Ferrin thus were brought into the organization. From the Century Company came their Dictionary, a hymn book department and many textbooks; from Appleton came a strong line of books on medicine and surgery, their long-established Spanish department, and a series of music albums; and in addition there were the important trade lists of both houses. The year 1948 saw another merger, when the college textbook firm of F. S. Crofts, Inc., active since 1924, was absorbed into what now became Appleton-Century-Crofts, Inc. Frederick S. Crofts, who had been connected with Century from 1905 to 1910, was made a director of the new company, while Mr. Shuster and Mr. Ferrin continued as president and vice-president, respectively. In 1950 Appleton-Century-Crofts celebrated its 125th year as a book publisher with an anniversary volume entitled *Fruit Among the Leaves*, a chronological history of the firm with samplings from a century and a quarter of publishing.

Until the 1930's the old house of G. P. Putnam's Sons was in the hands of the founder's family. At the turn of the century we find Major George Haven Putnam in command. He was born in 1844, and had entered his father's business, it will be remembered, in 1866. During his directorship five grandsons of the founder came into the firm at various times: Sydney H. and Edmund W., sons of Irving Putnam, Robert F. and George Palmer, sons of Bishop, and Major Putnam's son, Palmer Coslett. It may be added here that Herbert Putnam, the distinguished Librarian of Congress, who became Librarian Emeritus in 1939 after forty years of active service, is the fourth and youngest of the brothers.

George Palmer Putnam was especially active in the firm in the 1920's. His personal acquaintance with travelers and explorers brought such names as William Beebe, Charles Lindbergh, Admiral Byrd, and Rockwell Kent to the Putnam list. It was he who helped to arrange the first trans-Atlantic flight of Amelia Earhart, whom he later married. The year 1930 saw his separation from the publishing house, although he carried on various publishing activities on the West Coast until his death in 1950.

After Major Putnam's death in 1938 Palmer Coslett took over his cousin George Palmer's share, and two additional members were taken into the firm, Melville Minton and Earl H. Balch, who had built up since 1924 the firm of Minton, Balch & Co. This house was now merged with Putnam's, although its imprint has been retained for some publications. After Irving Putnam's death in 1931 the remaining members of the Putnam family gradually retired, and the control of the firm passed completely into the hands of Mr. Minton, who has remained president to this day, and Mr. Balch, vice-president and editor-in-chief, who resigned after a number of years. In February, 1930, a business co-ordination was brought about with the house of Coward-McCann, which had been established in 1928 by Thomas R. Coward and James McCann. The Coward-McCann list of publications has remained a separate entity. Another firm to be added to the Putnam operating group was the John Day Company.

An excellent opportunity to study the publishing activities of the house of Putnam during its hundred-year history has been offered to the public by the issue of *An American Reader*, edited by Burton Rascoe and selected from Putnam publications since 1838 to "reflect implicitly the growth and development of American ideas, the growth and development of American publishing."

At Dodd, Mead & Co., a nephew of Frank H. Dodd, Frank C., was president from 1931 to 1942, when he was elected chairman of the board. He was succeeded by Howard C. Lewis, with the company since 1913. Edward H. Dodd, Jr., vice-president and editor, represents the fourth generation of the family. Their list ranges from the books of George Bernard Shaw to Max Brand's Westerns. Dodd, Mead & Co. are also sponsors of a variety of prize contests which bring new talent to their lists.

In the twenty years following the death of Henry Holt in 1926, the firm which he founded saw many changes. Edward N. Bristol, who had joined Holt's in 1882 in its educational department, served as president for six years, becoming chairman of the board in 1932 until his retirement in 1943. His son, Herbert G. Bristol, was president from 1939 to 1945, following Richard H. Thornton, who served between the Bristols, father and son. Mr. Thornton left Holt's in 1938 to join the textbook house of Ginn. When Herbert Bristol resigned in 1945 Joseph A. Brandt was called to head the house. Mr. Brandt had been director of three university presses, at Chicago, Princeton and Oklahoma, and president of the latter university. A year later, when the controlling interest in Holt's was bought by a Texas oilman, Clint Murchison, four of the younger members of the staff, William Sloane, Keith Jennison, Helen Taylor and Norman Hood, resigned to form William Sloane Associates, as has previously been recorded. Mr. Brandt resigned as president in 1948 and returned to the university field to head the department of journalism at the University of California at Los Angeles. Edgar T. Rigg succeeded Mr. Brandt as president with Albert C. Edwards as executive vice-president. The firm has published the books of Robert Frost, four times Pulitzer Prize winner since *North of Boston* first appeared in 1914.

E. P. Dutton & Co. for long years remained in the hands of Mr. Dutton, who lived beyond the age of eighty and relinquished the reins only with his death in 1923. The publishing division of the firm then came into the capable hands of the Scottish Virginian, John Macrae. He published Samuel Butler years before the first World War. At that time the genteel tradition was still strong in America, and the general atmosphere of disillusionment and hard-boiled realism had not yet set in. Samuel Gompers' *Seventy Years of Life and Labor* was selected by John Macrae for publication in 1925. He published in this country the famous "Everyman's Library," in arrangement with J. M. Dent & Son in London. Dutton has continuously published Van Wyck Brooks for over a quarter of a century, and is known also as the publisher of Milne.

Two sons succeeded John Macrae upon his death in 1944, John, Jr. as chairman of the board until 1950, and Elliot B. Macrae as president. At that same time Nicholas Wreden, a versatile bookman, long associated with Scribner's Bookstore, joined the firm as editor and director.

Another of the old New York publishing firms which, like Dodd, Mead and Scribner, is in the hands of the third generation of the original family, is Thomas Y. Crowell Company. Thomas Y. Crowell was succeeded after his death in 1915 by his sons, J. Ogden and T. Irving Crowell. The latter was president from 1915 to 1937, when he was succeeded by his son, Robert L. Crowell. In recent years a lively and varied list has maintained the firm's place in the trade.

Houghton Mifflin, in Boston, and Little, Brown & Co., also in Boston, have come under the direction of entirely new groups of capable men. At Little, Brown & Co. Alfred R. McIntyre succeeded his father, James McIntyre, as president of the company in 1926. His frequent travels abroad are reflected on the list, where books by A. J. Cronin, C. S. Forester, E. M. Remarque and Evelyn Waugh are found alongside of such native talent as John P. Marquand and many other distinguished names. Alfred McIntyre died in 1948; he was succeeded as president by Arthur H. Thornhill. A productive alliance was formed by Little, Brown & Co. in 1925 with the Atlantic Monthly Company, which made them the publishers of books of the Atlantic Monthly Press. In 1941 a continuing fifty-year contract was signed. Little, Brown & Co. also took their share in the new mass market when they became part owners, in 1944, of the reprint firm of Grosset and Dunlap. Little, Brown has two perennial best sellers in *The Boston Cooking-School Cook Book*, Fannie Farmer's household classic, and Bartlett's *Familiar Quotations*.

The last member of the Houghton family to manage the Houghton Mifflin Company was Edward R. Houghton. He was succeeded as president in 1939 by Henry A. Laughlin. Benjamin Ticknor, a grandson of William D. Ticknor, was associated with the firm for nearly half a century; he died in 1949. Ferris Greenslet for many years was the dominating editorial influence in the firm, which has remained true to its original devotion to literary quality, without, however, sacrificing worth-while opportunities to strengthen their financial resources. Among its recent successes are Winston Churchill's brilliant war memoirs.

The only important older house which remained in the hands of the original founder until well into the twentieth century is the company started in 1881 by Frederick A. Stokes. He was assisted by two sons, Horace W. and Brett, with George Shively, formerly of Bobbs-Merrill. The firm maintained its policy of quality rather than quantity with remarkable consistency. They continued in the fine arts field, and maintained a strong children's book department under Helen Dean Fish. Frederick A. Stokes was active in the organization of the book trade, as president of the American Publishers' Association and in the organization of the National Association of Book Publishers. He was honored, in the fall of 1935, with the invitation to deliver the first of the R. R. Bowker Memorial Lectures. He died in 1939, aged 82, and was succeeded by his son, Horace W., who was president until 1941.

In that year the famous old Philadelphia firm, J. B. Lippincott Company, purchased the controlling interest in Stokes, after absorbing in the same year another imprint, that of Carrick & Evans. These steps were hailed in trade circles as a memorable gain for book publishing in the Quaker City. Lippincott celebrated its 150th anniversary in 1942. A member of the founder family, Joseph Wharton Lippincott, is chairman of the board, with Howard K. Bauernfeind as president; and, again, a fourth generation J. W. Lippincott, Jr., is active in the firm.

It is regrettable that the amount and the kind of information about each important publishing firm which it is possible to include in these pages is necessarily limited. If the available space would permit such a thing, it would be valuable and interesting to report in greater detail on the editorial and the economic policies adopted by the great American publishing firms, and on their contribution to our society and to its literary expression. The information which we can include is useful because it is not readily located elsewhere; in the earlier edition of this book this usefulness has proved itself beyond a doubt. But the wish for a more searching analysis of the contribution of each firm remains.

The house of Scribner is a case in point. The changes in the management of Charles Scribner's Sons are easily told. In 1927, three years before his death, Charles Scribner was succeeded as president by his brother, Arthur H., and five years later the third Charles came to the head of the great departmentalized business which his family had built up. His son, Charles Scribner, Jr., the fourth Charles in the firm, is now vice-president. Whitney Darrow, with the company since 1917, before that the first manager of the Princeton University Press and later one of its trustees, is executive vice-president. But what about the works that have been published in the twentieth century, the authors that have been cultivated, and the men who turned their manuscripts into books? Fortunately, the serious inquirer will find many of these questions answered in Roger Burlingame's *Of Making Many Books,* published by Scribner in 1946 in celebration of their one hundredth anniversary. Not "a merely formal history," this volume is based on the carefully preserved files of correspondence between the men at Scribner's and their many distinguished authors of bygone days. The opportunity to add to these documents of the past the correspondence with authors of the more recent generations came a few years later. Maxwell Perkins, head editor for twenty of his thirty-seven years with Scribner's, that legendary figure of American letters who has been called "the ideal editor" and "an author's best friend," died in 1947. To honor his memory, Scribner published in 1950 a volume entitled *Editor to Author, The Letters of Maxwell E. Perkins,* selected and edited by John Hall Wheelock. This book contains some of the most fascinating and lively documents of American literary life. In one of these letters Perkins writes about the editor's function: ". . . The editors I know shrink from tampering with a manuscript and do it only when it is required of them by the author, as it was by Tom [Thomas Wolfe]. When an editor gets to think differently from that, to think he knows more about a writer's book than the writer—and some do—he is dead, done for, and dangerous. When he thinks he is a discoverer because he doesn't fail to recognize talent —was a jeweler ever praised because he knew a diamond from a lump of glass?—he is a stuffed shirt, and through."

Book Distribution Methods

The main drawbacks in the American book business of the nineteenth century were the absence of an international copyright legislation and the vain struggle for a system of uniform prices. The first source of trouble, as we have seen, has been largely cured. The second one has not been solved, although some substantial progress can be reported. There is no lack of good will and some very serious efforts have been made to eliminate the evils of unfair competition, but it is difficult to say today how final the present solutions are.

The struggle for price maintenance is hard to understand without a knowledge of how books are distributed from publisher to reader. There are four general variations in the way books are sold in America to the public. They are (1) sold direct from publishers to customers; (2) sold from the publisher through the trade (wholesale and retail) to the customer; (3) sold as used books in the old and rare or second-hand market; (4) sold through the newsstands, as more recently with the paper-covered editions.

The first group includes most textbooks marketed direct to schools, colleges, and institutions, also medical, law, scientific, and technical books sold by mail or by canvassers to the various professions; or the sets of reference works of great books, or the works of one writer, sold for the publishers by canvassers; or works of popular appeal or on special subjects sold by the publishers direct by mail, or by display advertising; or book club subscriptions sold direct or through bookstores. In the case of all such types of books sold direct to consumer, the publisher guides the sales effort, plans the advertising, controls the price which the customer pays. These books distributed directly by the publisher are roughly estimated to constitute ƒ 2 2 8 Macmn. 3 2 8,

ƒ 2 1 9 Appleton — Century 2 2 2   Crofts

ƒ 2 2 0 Putnam

ƒ 2 2 2 Scribner

ƒ 3 3 3 Doubleday

ƒ 3 4 3 Simon & Schuster
                    Golden bks 3 1 6

ƒ 3 3 1 Shieed

ƒ 3 7 0 - 3 7 1 summary.

in quantity about one-half of the cloth-bound new books sold in a year.

The other half of cloth-bound new books would be those sold through bookstores and book departments in department stores, which includes also some proportion of scientific, technical, and educational books.

The greater volume of antiquarian (old and rare and secondhand) books reach their purchasers through shops found in every city at prices governed by the facts of availability and market demands.

A vast quantity of books are now being sold in paper covers at twenty-five to thirty-five cents, marketed by the publisher through chain stores and newsstands as newspapers and periodicals are sold.

Each of these four groups has been roughly estimated to exceed the hundred million mark of volumes handled per year. No fully substantiated figures exist.

There are three reasons why so large a proportion of new books are distributed through channels controlled direct by the publishers. By direct control he can maintain a desirable uniformity of prices, he can be sure his sales plan is carried out as he would wish it, and he can press for a national coverage of distribution through his own agents to all schools, by canvassers to all homes, or on newsstands in every town and hamlet.

For the field of general literature, however, which is the chief subject of this history, the only possible way to make books available to the unidentified but waiting customer is through the bookstores, and of these there is not an adequate number, as general bookstores have not been successfully maintained except in cities of 25,000 or over, or suburbs of the more substantial type.

These are some outstanding characteristics which distinguish trade book distribution in the United States from the European system. One important difference can be seen in the extraordinarily uneven geographic distribution of book outlets, another one in the great variety of channels through which books flow on their way from the publisher's warehouse into the hands of the reader.

The geographic distribution of book readers throughout the country, and the sources of supply for reading matter available to them have been the subject of careful statistical studies. Vital information about these questions was supplied by O. H. Cheney in *The Economic*

Survey of the Book Industry, first published in 1931 and reprinted with additional data in 1949. In 1938 Louis R. Wilson published his *Geography of Reading,* a study of the distribution and status of libraries in the United States. It is a volume of carefully collected information on the distribution of books through the various channels, with statistics of library expenditures for books per capita of the population in the various regions, on the distribution of rental libraries, of juvenile book departments, and the sale of encyclopedias. One thing that the maps provided by Dr. Wilson show very clearly is that the states in which most books are sold are the same ones which enjoy good library circulation. The striking thing about the picture which emerges from these studies of the 1930's is that it still shows exactly the same relationship of "strong" and "weak" regions that we have described in our section on nineteenth century book trade conditions. The "strong region" extends along the Atlantic seaboard from Maine to New Jersey, and west through Pennsylvania, and Ohio, as far "out" as Wisconsin and Illinois, leaving Minnesota, Iowa and Missouri as border territories. The other parts of the country, with the striking exceptions of California and Texas, are "weak." Nor can it be said with any assurance that the last ten years have altered this picture in its essential features.

The amazing variety of distribution channels of American trade books is another distinct feature of major importance. If one were to ask a representative of the American News Company, that mammoth wholesaler of books, who, in his opinion, buys the books today, he could point to some very staggering figures for books sold through retail channels other than regular bookstores. The Baker & Taylor Company and A. C. McClurg & Co., on the other hand, take pride in being large firms of jobbers catering to the regular book trade. They do sell to drug stores and sometimes to single persons, but the bookstores, department stores and libraries are their biggest customers.

The difficulties resulting from both the geographic conditions and from a highly competitive situation which has placed the legitimate book trade in a defensive position have long been recognized. Many efforts have been made and are still being made to create a more secure and a broader place for the role of the book in American life and to strengthen the legitimate book trade, *i.e.* the general bookstore trade.

The raising of the professional standards of regular bookstore personnel was recognized long ago as one important step. To avoid mis-understanding, I should say again that "regular bookstore" in this connection refers to a shop which deals either exclusively or primarily in books, and where owners and employees see something more than just merchandise in the books which they sell. There has been a series of experiments to provide training schools for booksellers. B. W. Huebsch, of the Viking Press, was early associated with this move-ment for a dozen years. There was first, in 1912, a lecture course under the auspices of the Booksellers' League of New York. Then there were evening lectures at various bookshops and, 1915-17, Mr. Huebsch or-ganized courses at the Y.M.C.A. Night School, and, later on, at the evening sessions of the College of the City of New York. These ex-periments came to a close in 1926, but they stimulated the trade while they lasted and caused the faithful to spread the gospel of education. A class in bookselling in Philadelphia evening high school was one of its several interesting offshoots. For five years from 1928 a three weeks' course in bookselling was conducted at the Summer School of Co-lumbia University by Frederic G. Melcher, Marion Dodd and Sarah Ball. In recent years evening courses in bookselling and publishing have been and are being offered in the School of General Studies at Columbia University. New York University has developed publishing courses and the movement has been taken up elsewhere in the country. The National Association of College Stores has held several summer training courses.

The efforts thus to strengthen the book trade from within have their counterpart in what could be described rather loosely as a co-operative public relations program of the book industry at large.

The revival of the book fair in the twentieth century is part of this program. The new book fair movement can be said to have started in 1919 with the inception, that year, of the book week idea and, the same year, with the successful Marshall Field book fair. It has been a popular, almost a casual movement, which has had no permanent identical sponsor year in and year out, and no rigid schedule. The New York *Times* National Book Fair, held in November 1936 and 1937, was the most complete affair of this kind. Later fairs have been held in large city department stores, with publishers' displays and au-thor appearances. For many years now, a very successful book fair for children only has been held at the American Museum of Natural History in New York. It is hardly necessary to point out that these fairs are quite different from their nineteenth century forerunners, since they are not aimed by the publishers at the retailers, but by the book trade as a whole at the general public.

The basic objective of the various efforts to promote book reading and book buying is to strengthen the position of the book in relationship to other media of entertainment and information. These other media are of course often used in these efforts. In the 1940's the book review pages in the daily papers were supplemented by an increasing number of Sunday sections, but by 1950 only the New York *Times,* the New York *Herald Tribune,* and the Chicago *Tribune* had separate weekly book supplements in their Sunday issues. Radio reviewing and radio dramatization of literature are well established. Television, too, is taking its share. It will surprise some readers to learn that *The Literary Market Place* for 1950 lists no less than twenty-five television programs featuring books.

Book and author luncheons, autographing parties, and many other methods for individual and collective book promotion could also be mentioned here. There seems to be growing recognition of the fact that a more highly organized, co-operative program on the part of the book industry as a whole would be vastly more effective in the long run than many individual, casual attempts here and there.

The Ohio Book Project should be mentioned in this connection as a recent example of a co-operative experiment conducted by the American Book Publishers Council in 1948 and 1949. The aim of this project, which was carried out by Joseph A. Duffy, was primarily to survey the available book outlets in the state of Ohio and to determine how these outlets could be strengthened and made more effective. Out of the experience gained through the Ohio Project, the American Book Publishers Council established, in 1950, a reading promotion program aimed at establishing close relations between the book industry and various government agencies and other organizations representing users of books on a large scale.

It is obviously impossible to attempt on these pages even the briefest enumeration of the worth-while bookstores operating throughout the country. Such an account could well be made into a book by itself. It would have to trace the continuing today of venerable old stores of the nineteenth century (which to some extent has been done on pages 243-248); it should survey in detail the experience as retailers of the great New York publishers; it should take stock of the new foundation of good individual stores in the new century, the development of such big city chains as the Doubleday bookstore chain, Womrath's in New York and Burrows in Cleveland, Brentano's branches in the various cities and Fred Harvey's chain in the West and the Southwest.

Department stores, steadily expanding their lines of merchandise, began to install books in the 1880's, Wanamaker in Philadelphia and Macy's in New York being first in the field. For many years a book department was used to attract trade to other lines by price cutting, as described elsewhere, but as time went on there came an increasing recognition of the public's appreciation of good book service. Today in most cities there is adequate bookselling in the department stores, and they account for a large percentage of American book distribution.

One encouraging feature today is the fact that not a small number of bookshops have been started on a modest scale by well-educated people with a real love of books and good taste. These "personal bookshops" have grown in importance and usefulness. Women have played a conspicuous part in this development. The personal bookshop today is found in the heart of the great cities as well as in the suburbs and in the country. It has become particularly signficant in the college town, because of the opportunity there to influence the taste and to spread the reading habit among educated young people. Marion Dodd's Hampshire Book Shop in Northampton is an excellent example. Marion Bacon's shop at Vassar and Hathaway House at Wellesley, founded by Geraldine Gordon, are among the other attractive college shops. College stores on many campuses give sometimes perfunctory but often effective support to the sale of trade books as well as the customary sale of textbooks.

A lively and interesting account of experience with a personal bookshop of thirty-five years ago is Madge Jenison's *Sunwise Turn, a Human Comedy of Bookselling*. It takes a good deal of courage and financial backing to carry such a venture beyond the critical first few years and to gain a secure foothold in the trade.

The traditional subscription method of selling books develops many book markets more effectively than can bookstores. There are today a great many kinds of book purchases by mail order and on the installment plan that come under the name of subscription selling. Practically all encyclopedia purchasing is today on the subscription basis through canvassers; a large sale of dictionaries is through this channel, as is the case with many standard sets and children's classics.

There is the highly special art of selling by direct mail through display advertising or more often by prospectuses. The method is used both by booksellers who develop records of customers' interests, and by publishers who are selling books of very specific appeal.

Again, there is the tremendous outlet for books through rental libraries, which had a great increase in the twenties and early thirties. Rental or circulating libraries are an old institution. In 1900 Seymour Eaton gave this method of book service a great fillip by starting his chain of Booklovers Libraries, which evolved into the Tabard Inn Libraries and then failed. Arthur Womrath picked up the idea and built up a successful New York chain on the pattern so many emulated. In the 1920's a rash of rental libraries started, mostly in chains which were serviced from some central point. The rental library movement leveled off in the forties, and it has been decreased by the arrival of the paperbound fiction.

Paper-covered books, on the other hand, have decidedly increased the volume of books sold through the newsstands, where books have always formed part of the stock-in-trade. One special form of the newsstand which does a particularly active book business today is the railroad bookshop, an outgrowth of modern transportation and a universal phenomenon throughout the world.

A unique American institution is the drug store. May we retell an old story? A flapper went into a bookstore and asked for lipstick, but quickly excused herself when she realized her mistake: "I'm sorry, I thought this was a drug store, I saw books in the window." The modern drug store sale of books developed originally in the 1920's as one of the ways to dispose of publishers' remainders. No publisher can accurately estimate just what printing to make of each book, and there is a constant overflow of remainders which after a period must be sold off at a price. These used to be sold wholly through catalog houses and department stores. The depression of the 1930's increased the number of books to be dumped and an extra market grew up, which now follows its own rules, has its own distributing agents, and pretty much its own public. When the vogue of the twenty-five cent books in paper covers started in earnest, the drug store became at once an important, natural outlet for the new mass product.

Of great trade importance was the development of the low-priced reprint editions of titles previously published in a regular trade edition, a custom already started at the turn of the century. Soon after 1900 there began, along with the reprinting of already published titles, the production of new books particularly for this market. The firm of Grosset & Dunlap developed upon this basis into an enterprise of first magnitude. Just before 1900 there were still in vogue certain twenty-five cent series of new copyright books in paper covers. Grosset & Dunlap began by buying up large lots of such editions and binding them in cloth at thirty-nine cents and fifty cents. Soon the firm began making direct contacts with the original publishers and printing and binding their own editions. Upon this principle Grosset & Dunlap developed into one of the largest producers of books, not only to the general trade and department stores, but also to drug stores, newsstands, five and ten cent stores, etc. Grosset & Dunlap also have their own authors, especially in the juvenile field.

This plan of fiction reprints, or "popular copyrights," was also adopted by the old firm of A. L. Burt, publishers of long lines of popular series, later absorbed by Reynal & Hitchcock and then by Doubleday. Individual publishers made sporadic experiments in starting their own reprint line, but all soon fell back on selling such rights to either Grosset or Burt, who energetically developed the market.

In the 1920's the reprinting of nonfiction was successfully launched as a supplement to the long-established practice of fiction reprinting. Doubleday began this plan with their Star Dollar Books, and the increasing success of these led to the Blue Ribbon Books, which were cooperatively issued by four large publishers under the direction of Eugene Reynal. This series was later sold out to Doubleday, who had made themselves the chief operators in that field. Their main competitor was Max Salop, who established the Harlem Book Company. He first supplied remainders to the department store and drug store market. Later on he successfully produced reprinted editions for these outlets, whose customers were often getting their first introduction to book-buying habits in this manner. Selected titles of substantial subject value, which had been issued originally in editions of from two to five thousand copies at prices such as $4.00 to $6.00, could often be marketed in printings of from ten to fifty thousand copies with all the original illustrations, at odd-penny prices of $1.49 to $2.79, etc. The odd-penny price became the earmark of a bargain reprint.

This reprinting of nonfiction had the advantage of enabling many dealers inexperienced in handling books to provide for their public a fairly good representation of general literature and of useful information. Simultaneously, reprint series of standard classics not only held their own but had an expanding sale. Everyman's Library from Dent of London, published in the United States by Dutton, Oxford's World's Classics and the Modern Library, launched with outstanding success by Random House, were the chief competitors in this field.

The steady broadening of the popular market led many to dream of producing books that would find their way to every newsstand and chain store. From Europe came the first clue to the answer for America, when the long-established paper-covered series of English novels, the Tauchnitz books, were given a new competitor in the smarter-looking Albatross Series, developed by J. Holroyd-Reece. This in turn was followed in England by Allen Lane's Penguin Series, which, beginning with a series of sixpence books for newsstands and chain stores, has extended its operation to include new titles as well as reprints, also books on arts and crafts, new translations and books for children.

A program of books for the chain stores, especially for the ten-cent counters, had already been successfully ventured in the United States in the thirties by Whitman of Racine and others. Robert de Graff, however, who had devised the first nonfiction reprints for Doubleday, evolved his plan for a twenty-five cent series of popular titles, Pocket Books, a program which would use to the utmost all that had been learned about the economical production in huge editions of paper binding with varnished covers (see page 302, 350). Large editions made possible the multiplication of outlets until 90,000 dealers were handling the books in 1950.

The series was just started when the war came and brought a paper shortage, but others had visioned the marketing possibilities of the twenty-five cent popular reprint. Avon, Dell and others followed the lead of de Graff. Penguin established an American office which sold out to Kurt Enoch and Victor Weybright as the New American Library, while Penguin's American manager, Ian Ballantine, organized Bantam Books for Grosset & Dunlap.

The development of these low-priced series has, with the book clubs, given a new turn to the American book trade, and their influence on general publishing and authorship cannot yet be determined. In both cases the authors have accepted low royalty percentages in view of large total printings, and this has started the road to lower prices on titles that can be thus marketed.

The issuance of a cheap reprint of a regularly published edition is not necessarily the cutthroat competition with the original edition that it may seem to be. By trade agreement fiction for a number of years did not go into reprint form until one year after publication, nonfiction after two years. This agreement has now broken down, but even when both editions are on sale simultaneously, they have not necessarily harmed each other. There seem to be circles here which do not touch, or which overlap only slightly.

One does not feel sure that this can be said of the book clubs, which represent yet another phase of bookselling through other than the traditional book trade channels. The book club idea was born in Germany and brought to America as an adaptation of magazine subscription and mail-order methods to the marketing of current books. After much debate, book clubs were closely defined in Germany and made to harmonize with other bookselling methods. It was specified that books sold by a club should be distinct in format and that the term "club" should be clearly defined in trade practice and to the public. In America the price comparison slant of the club advertising has kept the booksellers in varying states of critical opposition.

A book club was first projected in America in 1921, and in 1926 both the Book-of-the-Month Club and the Literary Guild got under way, followed by no less than about fifty others, some of which gained a foothold, while others failed or were absorbed very soon after their inception. Although there was from the start some misgiving among the bookstores as to the effects of the clubs, the size of the orders placed for each title selected diverted the attention of authors and publishers from the fundamental difficulties which might come up. Clubs organized for the sale of books in special fields, such as religion and history, or the Limited Editions Club, devoted to finely printed and illustrative works of world literature, have created no particular anxiety. The price competition of the Book-of-the-Month Club, with over half a million members and using printings of from 150,000 to 300,000 or more copies a month, is in the form not only of reduced prices but of premium books, one to each person who signs up for at least four books a year and a book dividend of one for each two books as purchased thereafter. The Literary Guild, now the largest club from point of view of membership, sells its books at $2.00 a volume with premiums of one book for each four purchased and two free books on joining. The Literary Guild uses department stores as well as mail order to reach subscribers, while the Book-of-the-Month Club subscriptions are taken by certain book stores as well as by book departments in department stores and, of course, by mail order. The large clubs do not buy books from the original publishers who submit titles to them, but purchase the right to print their own editions, often from the original publisher's plates. On regular monthly selections the Book-of-the-Month Club pays a royalty of 10 per cent of the price the Club charges their members and the Literary Guild offers a royalty of twelve cents a copy. In this way they get their books at a lower price than that paid by booksellers and they can therefore offer books plus premiums and dividends at price levels the dealers cannot match.

The Book-of-the-Month Club has claimed that through their extensive use of the far-flung net of U. S. Post Offices, they have brought books into a large number of communities which have no other book outlets. The readers of this volume understand readily that the absence of an evenly distributed network of general bookshops is a traditional weakness which has its roots in the social history of this country. The Book-of-the-Month Club has indeed recognized and utilized the opportunities which such a weakness presented. On the other hand it should not be forgotten that a large number of book club subscribers are located in or near centers which have adequate bookselling facilities. For these and other reasons, apprehension has grown among booksellers in recent years. The situation is aptly described by John T.

Winterich in the 1950 *Almanac* of the American Booksellers Association, which has been the mouthpiece of growing book trade resistance, in the following terms: "During the twenty years that have intervened (since 1929) the ABA and the book clubs have maintained a mutual relationship comparable to that of a dog and a cat domiciled in the same household—a state of truce which is occasionally disrupted when the pair meet suddenly around a door-jamb."

The Struggle for Price Maintenance Goes On

The reader of this volume already knows that the price-cutting evil is an old one, with roots that go back to the days when dry goods stores first discovered that books lent themselves particularly well to serve as loss leaders for their other merchandise. Even in the 1880's this unwholesome practice had reached proportions big enough to worry the legitimate book trade, whose members cast about for the means to curb the evil, without finding an adequate control. In the depression that followed the panic of 1893 chaos reigned, with the average price for fiction as low as $1.50, but customers in the East expecting and getting a 25 per cent discount. The year 1900 saw renewed efforts at price control with the founding that year of the American Booksellers Association, followed the same year by a corresponding organization of the publishers in the American Publishers Association. The stated purpose of these two organizations was to establish and to maintain a uniform level of prices.

What was the situation in Europe at the turn of the century? Although such countries as England, Germany and France enjoy the advantages of settled traditions and well-worn trade customs, the nineteenth century also had brought some very serious difficulties. There, too, price cutting threatened to disrupt the trade, and in the seventies and eighties, when conditions were particularly discouraging in America, very similar trouble was encountered in the various European countries.

Because they had the most highly developed trade and ancient traditions and because of a congenital love of order and precision, the German booksellers and publishers were the first to bring into effect a lasting system of price control. After a hard struggle the Boersenverein der deutschen Buchhändler brought, in 1888, all members of

the book trade into a close union. Membership in the organization became a vital necessity for every publisher, wholesaler and bookseller.
The breaking of the rules which governed price maintenance and discounts could lead to exclusion from the Boersenverein—equivalent
with economic ruin, because no publisher was allowed to sell to a non-
member bookseller, and no bookseller could buy from a non-member
publisher. England followed suit with its famous Net Book Agreement,
which was accepted in 1899 by the British retailers, who had been
organized locally in 1890 and nationally as The Associated Booksellers
of Great Britain and Ireland in 1895, and The Publishers' Association
of Great Britain and Ireland, organized in 1896. The Net Book Agreement provides, too, for the black-listing of any rule-breaking members
among either the publishers or the retailers associations. In 1931 members of the government, suspecting a limitation of free trade, investi-
gated the system, but reached the definite conclusion that it furthered
the public interest.

France, in the structure of its book trade, resembles America perhaps more closely than does England or Germany, in the variety of
retail outlets and the offering of books to the public in mixed and non-
chalant assortment with all kinds of other merchandise. Accordingly,
it has been difficult to enforce an all-inclusive price level. The general
book trade, however, and the majority of publishers observe the rules,
which were laid down by them in 1892. The publishers are organized
in a Syndicat des Editeurs, the retail booksellers in a Chambre Syndi-
cale des Libraires de France; Union des Syndicats des Libraires de
France. Both these associations are members of the all-embracing
Cercle de la Librairie, which was founded in 1847 and includes all
branches of the graphic arts and the book industries and trade.

It can thus be said that by 1901 an effective system of price maintenance had been put to work in three important European countries. In
America, developments took a different turn.

At that time most trade books were being sold at a discount of 20 to
25 per cent, and the figures showed that no bookseller was making any
profit on the new book business. The plan worked out between the
American Booksellers Association and the American Publishers' Association was for a new price on trade books which should be observed
by all dealers, and the American Publishers' Association cut off sup-

plies from dealers who did not observe this program of uniformity. List prices were reduced from the old level and discounts lessened. In studying the effect of this action, it should be remembered that a large part of the books sold in the country were not distributed through retail outlets, as explained above. Only the area of trade books which were sold through retail outlets were subject to the price cutting, and it was this situation that the net price agreement was intended to improve.

In the first years of the system not all books were included in the program. However, it gradually appeared advisable to have nationally uniform prices for trade books as well as for books sold direct by the publisher. Book advertising benefited from such a system because prices as announced were actual rather than artificial prices.

The fight against this new system was conducted by those department stores which had looked on books as an inducement to bring people into the store. The leader of the fight was the big department store of R. H. Macy & Co. in New York, which, when publishers refused to sell to them, bought books through agents scattered over the country. Macy's sued the Publishers' Association under the State Law of New York, but lost. Most of the department stores settled down to handling books like other merchandise, at a customary profit rather than as loss leaders. At that time, the attorney for Macy's, however, noticed the case in Federal Court which construed the Federal Anti-Trust legislation as applying to retail selling, and they succeeded in transferring their case against the publishers to the Federal Court. The case went on up to the Supreme Court and was settled against the publishers in 1914. This was a situation which had no parallel to the European book markets, where producers and retailers of books were supposed to have freedom of making arrangements to maintain prices as they chose.

Following this court decision, a new era of price cutting set in. These obviously chaotic conditions did something to educate the public to an understanding that this type of price competition was of no social or business advantage, and such legal authorities as Justice Holmes and Justice Brandeis were on record as against such business practice. However, with a verdict of $140,000 in favor of Macy, the American Publishers' Association, after meeting the payment, dissolved in 1914. Not until 1920 did the publishers organize again, when the National

Association of Book Publishers was founded, which, however, cautiously refrained from any participation in price maintenance discussions. The organization was devoted to the general promotion of the interests of the publishing trade, paying special attention to standardization of production and distribution methods. The association was reorganized in 1937 as the Book Publishers' Bureau, and again in 1946 as American Book Publishers Council.

The price maintenance efforts showed no progress. Macy continued to use books as loss leaders and to undersell bookstores and book departments which observed the retail prices set by the publishers, and other department stores finally began to follow suit. Macy's announced policy of selling goods whenever possible at 6 per cent less than elsewhere would occasionally involve two stores in a regular book price war. When another department store undersold Macy, they in turn would undersell that store, so that, for instance, volumes of the "Modern Library," published at ninety-five cents, were selling at one time for as little as eleven cents. Bookstore owners with a bitter smile admitted that they could buy stock more cheaply at these sales than from the publishers.

When Franklin D. Roosevelt became President of the United States in March, 1933, one of the suggestions of the New Deal for bettering the economic condition of the country was the National Recovery Administration. In line with the procedure established in other industries and trades, the book trade, too, was charged with the responsibility of establishing a code of fair practice. The book trade code was accepted in April, 1934. The main provision of the code contained a clause stating that the price of newly published books must not be cut within the first six months after publication date. The effects of this regulation were immediately noticed and the regular trade all over the country felt the advantages of the new stability. On May 27, 1935, while in session at their annual convention in New York, the members of the American Booksellers Association learned the distressing news that the United States Supreme Court had declared the N.R.A. codes unconstitutional. Again the book trade faced the ruins of their efforts for a healthy organization. As was to be expected, the price war was at once resumed, and in October, 1935, prices were so low that some

New York City bookshops actually did cancel their orders with publishers and sent their boys to the loss leader department stores to buy stock.

However, as it turned out, the situation was to be relieved from another angle. In hearty co-operation with retailers in other lines of business the booksellers had striven earnestly to promote the movement towards fair trade legislation. In New York State, the Feld-Crawford Fair Trade Act had been approved on May 17, 1935, following earlier experiments in California, and similar laws were passed in other states. The act was created for the purpose of protecting trademark owners, distributors and the public against injuries and uneconomic trade practices. In effect it provided protection of prices for goods of identifiable character sold in open competition, which had been purchased under contracts signed between producer and retailer. On June 25, 1935, Edmund S. McCawley, president of the American Booksellers Association, and William H. Ingersoll, former president of the famous watchmaking firm and one of the founders of the American Fair Trade League, presented to the heads of thirty large New York publishing houses a carefully prepared model contract, which was recommended for universal adoption. The contract contained the important provision that those booksellers who had failed to sign and who, after due notice, interfered with the operation of the contracts by underselling price-protected items would be held liable at law. The important test of the Feld-Crawford Fair Trade Act came for the book trade when Doubleday, Doran & Company, who had signed price-protecting contracts with the Doubleday, Doran Bookshops, Inc., brought action to restrain R. H. Macy & Co. from offering certain books at a lesser price than that fixed in these contracts.

Much to the consternation of the book trade the New York Supreme Court held that Section 2 of the Feld-Crawford Act, upon which the price-protecting contracts were based, was unconstitutional, and when, on January 7, 1936, the New York State Court of Appeals upheld the decision of the lower court, it looked once more as though all the efforts on behalf of a better organization of the book trade had been in vain. But the year 1937 brought encouraging developments. Because the United States Supreme Court had upheld Fair Trade Legislation in a strong clear-cut decision on cases appealed from the states of California and Illinois, the New York Court of Appeals, on March 9, 1937, reversed its adverse decision in the Doubleday-Macy case and upheld the Fair Trade laws in New York State. The United States Supreme Court held that Fair Trade Laws did not violate the Constitution. Congress passed the Miller-Tydings bill to the effect that the Sherman Anti-trust Laws could not be applied to the situation and that Fair Trade contracts could be maintained in interstate commerce. By 1941 forty-five states had passed Fair Trade Laws and contracts under the laws were used by practically all trade publishers. (Fair Trade Laws have not been passed by Missouri, Texas, Vermont and the District of Columbia.) However, the contracts contained a clause exempting book clubs from price maintenance on the titles selected for distribution to their subscribers, who were defined as having "bound themselves in writing to purchase not less than four monthly selections or substitutes a year."

Everyone who had followed the rapid succession of events knew that the next move would come again from the chief user of books as loss leaders, from R. H. Macy & Company. The loss leader had proved too important a business builder to be abandoned without bitter struggle. Few people realized at the time that Macy "has a gross business in all lines that is larger than the entire trade book publishing business of the United States and the firm has every incentive and every legal aid in fighting the battle to continue the loss-leader practice." (*Publishers' Weekly* editorial on May 8, 1937.)

Macy's Red Star Book Club, launched in March, 1938, was the answer. It was based on the clause in the recommended fair trade contract which exempted the book clubs from the effects of price-protecting contracts. Macy's offered, to the purchaser of at least four books, credit for one-fourth of the total amount paid, to be applied toward a fifth volume, a sum usually sufficient for a free purchase of the book. Early in 1939 Harper and Brothers, Harcourt, Brace & Co., Alfred A. Knopf, and the Beacon Book Shop brought suit against the Macy Red Star Book Club to test the question of whether or not it violated the Fair Trade Law. Macy set up a countersuit in the same proceedings against the American Booksellers Association and its officers, and against the Book Publishers' Bureau and its officers. By 1940 these suits had been postponed several times. No actual development has taken place since.

The same year, 1940, saw outstanding violations of price maintenance contracts in Baltimore, Maryland. The Remington-Putnam Book Company brought action against six other retailers, charging them with selling books at cut prices. On March 14, Judge Joseph M. Ullman ruled that copyrighted books are in fair and open competition with other commodities of the same general class and that, therefore, they are protectable under the fair trade act of Maryland. His decision was sustained, the following year, by Judge Walter J. Mitchell in the Court of Appeals. Because of certain technicalities, too involved for a detailed recital here, the situation did not clear up for a number of years. In 1944 Remington-Putnam sought an injunction against Schill's Book Shop, which was denied by the Court of Appeals in Baltimore. A wave of price cutting resulted from the dismissal of the case. In an attempt to combat this new threat to price maintenance, Remington-Putnam sued the Hutzler Bros. department store and won a temporary injunction against them. In 1945 they were granted a permanent injunction in this case.

In commenting on the general fair trade situation at that time, *Publishers' Weekly* (March 17, 1945) said: "Without these laws there could have been no such confident merchandising of new books, and, what is more, without fair trade the average price of books would be definitely higher." It also pointed out that great and unforeseen benefits from uniform prices had arisen throughout the country for the many new reprint editions at low prices. Large printings, which more than anything else made the low prices possible, have depended on a stable price situation in the new mass outlets for books.

There have been no startling new developments in recent years. However, opposition from various quarters has by no means subsided. Florida's fair trade law has twice been under attack in recent years. Misuse of special discounts to various professional groups, such as clergymen, doctors, lawyers and, particularly, college and university professors, has caused some concern among those interested in the maintenance of fair trade. Continued vigilance and generous co-operation among all groups opposed to price cutting in the book trade will still be needed in the future to safeguard the undeniable benefits of fair trade observance.

The Rare and Second-Hand Book Trade

One branch of the book trade has been and is today very little affected by the struggle that has been described in the foregoing pages. The rare and second-hand book trades follow pretty much their own rules and traditions. Not that there is any lack there of excitement, of competition, and of fluctuation of values. However, the influences which stir the rare book trade are usually quite different from those which affect current fiction, nonfiction and children's books. The rare book dealer has fewer customers than the dealer in current new books, but these customers have higher average purchasing power and it is the curtailment of the incomes of the wealthy which disturb his business. Rare book values change, but perhaps more slowly than in the general trade. New trends develop not so often in response to reviewing and to publishers' advertising as from the more slowly noticeable but more steadily effective influence of the collector and the scholar. The development of the American rare book trade and, along with it, that of book auctions, is more closely linked to the rise of the great collectors and the founding of great libraries than to the history of the general book trade. Historical and current aspects of book auctioning have been reviewed on earlier pages of this volume. There remains the need for a few facts about some of the leading personalities and firms in the rare book field. Not all these firms are necessarily dealers only in rare old volumes, such as medieval manuscripts, early printed books, Americana, books in fine bindings and beautifully illustrated, or famous for their association with distinguished persons and collections in the past, or valuable literary manuscripts and autographs. The rare book trade and the second-hand book trade touch each other and overlap. Along with the trade in exceptional values the dealers often cater to the more modest collectors, and sometimes the trade with inexpensive old books of all conceivable kinds is combined with rare book selling.

Traditional centers of the second-hand book trade are New York, Boston and Philadelphia. One of the early nineteenth century representatives of this profession in America was William Gowans, who came to New York in 1828 and stayed there until his death in 1870. Another second-hand book dealer of the pre-Civil War period was James A. Garfield, friend of Washington Irving, James Lenox, Longfellow and Poe. Joseph Sabin is perhaps better known as bibliographer and distinguished expert on American books than as a rare book dealer. He was, in fact, active not only in that capacity, but also as a book auctioneer, an importer and a publisher. He went into business for himself in 1864, and during his long and busy life was one of the driving forces back of the public library movement. He died in 1881.

A rare old character, to judge from the accounts of him, must have been John Bradburn in New York. He specialized in travel works and books about the sea. He used to visit the captains of the incoming vessels in their cabins, and there and along the waterfront he did his best business. Another old-timer, T. H. Morrell, specialized in the history of New York and the War of Independence. Purely importers of rare books from abroad were Timothy Reeve & Co., who sold to individual customers as well as to the trade. Wiley & Putnam were also active importers. One of their best customers was James Lenox.

Until November, 1934, there still lived one of the leading antiquarian book dealers of the turn of the century period, Robert H. Dodd. For many years he had been the manager of the retail and rare book department of Dodd, Mead & Company. His excellent personal and business connections placed him in a strategic position at a time when some of the great collections were being made in this country. He had a substantial share in the building up of the famous Hoe collection, and the Church collection, too, acquired much of its material from Mr. Dodd. His influence was further enhanced by his able choice of collaborators and the excellent training which he gave his men. For him worked many young people who later on, as independent dealers, have played and are playing an important part in the rare book trade. There were George H. Richmond and William Evarts Benjamin, and, particularly, James F. Drake, now succeeded by his two sons, James, Jr. and Marston, and George D. Smith, former leader in auction triumphs.

Luther S. Livingston, too, worked for a time under him. Later, when Dodd, Mead & Company concentrated upon its publishing activities, he became Mr. Dodd's partner in the new rare book firm of Dodd & Livingston. It was Luther Livingston who conceived *American Book-*

Prices Current while employed in the rare book department of Dodd, Mead. The first volume appeared in September, 1895. The volume for 1910 was the first to carry the imprint of Dodd & Livingston on the title page. After a few fruitful years of collaboration, he was honored in 1914 with the appointment as first librarian of the new Harry Elkins Widener Collection in the Harvard College Library. However, after only a few months of active service, premature death ended his career.

In 1917 Robert H. Dodd was the publisher of *American Book-Prices Current,* and he later transferred the rights to E. P. Dutton, who in turn sold these to the R. R. Bowker Company in 1929. The fiftieth anniversary volume in 1944 carried a brief history of "A Half Century of Rare Book Auctions in America," written by three later editors, Victor Hugo Paltsits, Jacob Blanck and Colton Storm. The current editor is Edward Lazare.

Several of the outstanding rare book dealers of this century have passed away within the past two decades. Charles Sessler, who died in Philadelphia in 1935 after nearly sixty years of bookselling, had among his many other important customers, the Huntington Library and the Widener Collection. Near Philadelphia, too, lived A. Edward Newton, one of the best-known collectors, who did so much to popularize and romanticize book collecting. Thomas F. Madigan, until his death in 1936, was a recognized authority in the field of autographs, as was Walter R. Benjamin, who died in 1943. A year previously, Max Harzof, head of G. A. Baker & Co. and one of the most colorful figures of the trade, had died. In 1945 Ernest Dressel North, of New York and New Jersey, died at the age of eighty-seven. His important sales included a collection of original autograph letters of the Brownings and several Shakespeare folios. Two years later Gabriel Wells, an important international figure in the handling of rare items and who for a time also owned Sotheran's London shop, died, the same year as Ernest Dawson, for more than fifty years a rare book dealer in Los Angeles. The year 1949 saw the passing of two more prominent rare booksellers, John Kidd of Cincinnati and Adolph Stager of the Cadmus Book Shop in New York. Lathrop C. Harper, grandson of one of the original Harper brothers, was a specialist in incunabula and Americana and gathered much of the material for the William L. Clements Library. At the time of his death in 1950 he was well known not only to the collectors in his fields, but to every European dealer who came to New York, as a kind and helpful friend and adviser.

And what shall I say about the inimitable Dr. A. S. W. Rosenbach? How can one describe in a few words the treasures that surprise a visitor to his shops in Philadelphia or New York; the many things that he has done, and said, and written (and written both entertainingly and convincingly, I may say) about the sanities and follies of rare books; the publication of a catalog of American children's books in his private collection and his encouragement of bibliographical studies?

The rare book trade is a separate branch of the book business, and this book aims to demonstrate its characteristic function in the overall picture—something of its structure and its regional distribution. Much as we are tempted to include here individual firms and the many colorful figures who are today giving vitality and real personal touch to the handling of old and rare and out-of-print books, we shall have to forego this pleasure.

In the old days the huge stock of Leggett's on Chambers Street in New York marked the center of the secondhand trade. Then Henry Malkan on lower Broadway rose and fell. Leggett's was succeeded by Ammon & Mackel, and today busy Thoms & Eron is near the same spot, while the name of Mendoza continues on Ann Street. P. Stammer's was the starting place of many of the lower Fourth Avenue school of secondhand booksellers, and Schulte's Book Store has set the pace in this low-priced field. Although both Mr. Stammer and Mr. Schulte have died (the former in 1946, the latter in 1950), their shops continue, and Fourth Avenue remains a vigorous center for used and out-of-print books. In the three-block area of Fourth Avenue between 8th and 13th Streets, there are now over twenty antiquarian booksellers. In fact this group has its own trade association. The two other important concentrations of the New York City rare book trade are midtown, both east and west in the 40's and 50's, and on lower Fifth Avenue. These spots are the book-hunter's paradise.

The Boston trade, on the whole, has been carried on along less expansive and less conspicuous lines than in New York, but this, Mr. Goodspeed explained, "should not be attributed to a lack of enterprise. Not more than a few drops of the golden shower which irrigated the metropolis in normal times or dazzled the streets with its plentitude in days of super-prosperity ever fell in Boston. . . . There has never been a volume trade of rare books in Boston sufficient to make profitable such a stock which, in value, might amount to half a million or more of dollars." Charles E. Goodspeed's *Yankee Bookseller* tells much that one could not have found elsewhere. Mr. Goodspeed, who died in 1950, had real sense and judgment in what he called "traffic in old books," not only in his own business, but in the way he saw the complete picture. Boston could not compete with New York, but it has nevertheless a fine tradition of dealing with rare and old volumes. There was Burnham's Bookstore, where Richard Lichtenstein entered in 1858, eleven years old, eventually to become the proprietor of the store and for many years the dean of the Boston old book trade. He was preceded in that honor in the nineties by George Emery Littlefield, specializing, on Cornhill, in Americana and genealogy, his store the center of an entire generation of collectors. On Cornhill, too, was N. J. Bartlett & Company, center for bookish Episcopal clergy, in whose shop would be found "all the volumes which Bostonians bought fifty years ago when the ambition to organize a general library of fine books was more common than it is now." Cornhill, once double-lined with old bookshops, is now marked only by Colesworthy's, of the old tradition.

Then there was the rare book department of Estes and Lauriat, that many-sided house of varied interests and activities, whose retail establishment became the Charles E. Lauriat Company. Andrew McCance's shop was on Ashburton Place. He was a close friend of P. K. Foley, high authority on American first editions, whose Hamilton Place shop had been famous of old and whose bibliography, *American Authors, 1795-1895*, was a pioneer and authoritative reference book.

It is impossible to mention in these pages the hundreds of antiquarian book stores throughout the country. Suffice it to say that New York, Philadelphia and Boston are by no means the only antiquarian book centers in America. Chicago, Los Angeles and San Francisco all have important shops, and throughout the country antiquarian books are actively handled.

January, 1948, saw the appearance of the *Antiquarian Bookman*, published by the Bowker Company under the editorship of Sol M. Malkin as the first separate trade magazine to offer weekly antiquarian news and features. A year later, after a series of informal preliminary meetings, the Antiquarian Booksellers Association of America was organized. Laurence Gomme, then of Brentano's, was elected its first president in March, 1949. The ABAA now has over two hundred members and several branches in various parts of the country.

A Note on Censorship

The acquittal of John Peter Zenger in 1734 was the first important recognition of the freedom of the press in America. Since that time the press has lived comparatively unmolested. The rights of political freedom of thought and of expression have been recognized for the book as well as for the magazine and the newspaper. But because of one particular complaint—namely, that of obscenity—authors and publishers of books, as well as many booksellers, have suffered severely. Charges of obscenity were often all the more harmful because they were indirect, and they involved a concept which is hard to define, highly subjective and rapidly changing.

Censorship of literature on the grounds of obscenity has been carefully studied and a great deal has appeared in print. An excellent, searching and exhaustive book has been written by Morris L. Ernst and William Seagle entitled *To the Pure, A Study of Obscenity and the Censor*, with a continuation in Morris Ernst and Alexander Lindey's *The Censor Marches On*. Both in his writing and through his courageous battles in the courts as attorney for publishers, Morris Ernst has perhaps done more than any other single person to combat the evil effects of unintelligent censorship.

The first Federal department to be entrusted with the fight against obscene literature was the Federal Customs. The Tariff Act, passed in 1842 and in force since then, commanded the customs to refuse admission of obscene books into the country. Since the law merely invested the Customs with the right to seize and destroy the volumes in question without further penal action to either sender or receiver, their censorship has been felt to be of a comparatively harmless kind. However, the responsibility of Customs inspectors to decide which books were obscene has led to serious errors in judgment. As late as 1933 Ernst Weyhe in New York was summoned by the Customs Authorities because a shipment of obscene pictures addressed to him had been received. It turned out that a portfolio of reproductions of Michelangelo's frescoes in the Vatican Chapel had offended the modesty of the officials.

The amazing figure of Anthony Comstock is prominently associated with the nineteenth century movement against the obscene in literature. The Comstock Acts were passed in 1868. Under Comstock's influence there was organized, in 1873, the New York Society for the Suppression of Vice, which, by a special act of the legislature of the State of New York, was given the rights of search, seizure and arrest. Other regions followed quickly, with the Western Society for the Suppression of Vice in Cincinnati, and the New England Watch and Ward Society in Boston. Also in 1873 Anthony Comstock secured the Postal Censorship laws, which granted to the Post Office the power of excluding obscene books and pictures from the mails. Earlier efforts in that direction had been vehemently and successfully combatted, for instance President Jackson's attempt in 1835 to bar antislavery literature from the mails. Now it was in the Postmaster General's discretion to decide when he should interfere.

The law of 1873 offered one loophole. It forbade the sending of obscene books through the mail. This, theoretically, kept open the possibility of distributing prospectuses by mail which allowed a bookseller to invite customers to his store to purchase the books in question. Although under the existing state regulations and through the watchfulness of the vice suppression societies this was but a slim possibility, an amendment was passed in 1888 which excluded the sending of allegedly obscene letters through the mail.

In 1881 a Boston district attorney threatened criminal prosecution for an edition of Walt Whitman's *Leaves of Grass*, first published in 1855, unless it was expurgated. The publisher withdrew the book, but a Philadelphia firm a little later issued an edition as originally written. In 1908 Boston convicted Elinor Glyn's *Three Weeks*. Later on, Sinclair Lewis' *Elmer Gantry*, Upton Sinclair's *Oil*, and Theodore Dreiser's *An American Tragedy* were the objects of criminal prosecution. Usually, however, a notification from the New England Watch and Ward Society to an informal Boston Booksellers' Committee was a sufficient means of suppression. Upon learning which titles had been objected to, the booksellers, when notified, promptly withdrew copies of these books which they may have had in stock.

In New York, D'Annunzio's *The Triumph of Death* was prosecuted in 1897, but the jury refused to convict. Dreiser's *Genius* was suppressed there in 1916. In 1923 it was published openly in New York with a jacket which announced that it had been suppressed at the instigation of the Society for the Suppression of Vice. The case is typical of the more liberal attitude found in New York courts. Of fundamental importance was the growing realization that although theoretically a book could be banned if it contained isolated obscene passages, the whole book should really be taken into consideration to arrive at a just decision.

Early in the 1930's a New York publishing house felt that the time had come for a major legal test of the increasingly liberal attitude toward so-called obscene literature. Previously, no publisher in America had dared to publish James Joyce's *Ulysses*. Copies had been smuggled into the country from Paris, where it had been published by Sylvia Beach from a bookshop she called Shakespeare & Co., and circulated with a certain amount of secrecy. Random House now purchased from Joyce the rights to an American edition and prepared to defend this important and sincere study of conscious and subconscious thinking and acting. In order to introduce their case into the courts they decided to import a copy. "The reason," wrote Bennett Cerf of Random House,[3] "that we chose to fight our case against the Government through the expedient of importing a copy and having it seized by the Customs was for the purpose of economy. Had the Government refused entry of the volume and had its claim been sustained by the courts, we would have been out only the cost of this single copy plus, of course, the advance that we had paid Mr. Joyce and legal fees. The other alternative was to set up the book in America and publish it and then wait for our tilt with the Government. This, of course, would have been a very expensive way of doing things. Once we had decided to import a copy and have it seized, it became essential that the book

[3] In a letter of May 21, 1935, written to the author of these pages in connection with the donation of the imported copy and a copy of the court proceedings to the Columbia University Library.

actually be apprehended and not slipped through in one way or another. We therefore were forced to the somewhat ludicrous procedure of having our own agent at the steamer to make sure that our property was seized by the Government." The book was seized and Random House, with Morris L. Ernst and Alexander Lindey as attorneys, brought suit against the U. S. Government. On December 6, 1933, Judge Woolsey, in the Southern District Court of New York, decided that the book was not obscene and could therefore be imported into the United States. "In *Ulysses,* in spite of its unusual frankness, I do not detect anywhere the leer of the sensualist. I hold, therefore, that it is not pornographic," wrote the judge in a memorable review of the case. Upon an appeal by the United States on August 7, 1934, the decision of the District Court was affirmed.

The Woolsey decision set an immensely valuable precedent. In and out of court it has been quoted again and again, and it has greatly aided the never-ending struggle against narrow-minded and prejudiced obscenity charges. While it is true that on the whole the higher courts have adapted increasingly enlightened and liberal attitudes in these particular matters, it is also true that hard-hitting attacks on certain books and authors considered "immoral" have continued with unremitting violence. It is also important to state that the rise of political tension, internally and externally, has brought various new elements into the censorship situation. Since the late thirties, books of opinion, expressing political, religious and social points of view, have become the object of censorship battles. On the other hand, the voluntary wartime censorship on information of potential usefulness to the enemy has come and gone without raising major problems or controversies in the book field.

A brief chronological survey of significant censorship cases in the last decade begins with the obstacles laid in the path of John Steinbeck's *The Grapes of Wrath* by certain public libraries around 1939 and 1940, on the grounds of alleged obscenity. Censorship through restriction of circulation or through non-purchase of a given title is not a new device, and it is perhaps not always as serious as other forms of suppression. But in times of heightened tension and pressure it can assume disturbing proportions. For this reason we shall find concerted defensive action on the part of the library profession in the postwar era.

Oklahoma City in August, 1940, saw a raid on Robert Wood's Progressive Bookstore, in which not only the entire stock of books but also the owner and his staff and with them a number of customers or browsers and even a carpenter fixing shelves were seized. Two types of charges were placed, one a charge of distributing literature advocating violence as a means of accomplishing political and industrial changes; the other charge was membership in the Communist Party. *Publishers' Weekly* (July 5, 1941) pointed out several alarming aspects of the case. "If the verdicts are not reversed," they wrote, "a precedent in Oklahoma and perhaps elsewhere will be established for the seizure not only of controversial literature but of other material on the same shelves, the arrest of bookshop customers present in the same shop with such material, and of booksellers offering it for sale. The point at issue is not whether the books circulated exert a good or bad influence, but whether they, rather than overt acts of illegality, constitute evidence for conviction." The case attracted considerable attention, and the Dartmouth Library asked for a list of the condemned books in order to place them on its open shelves. In 1943 all charges were dropped and the case closed.

The same year, 1940, brought attacks against the social science textbooks of Dr. Harold Rugg. They were burned in Ohio and proposed as bonfire fuel in a leading city of New York. In Ralph W. Robey's investigation of standard textbooks, sponsored by the National Association of Manufacturers, the Rugg textbooks featured heavily among those described as "un-American and derogatory to the . . . capitalist system," on the chief objection that they encouraged students to take "a critical attitude towards social conditions." As a result of these and other attacks, Dr. Rugg's books were withdrawn from active use in many communities. In the ensuing controversy liberal elements opposed such arbitrary and unenlightened censorship of textbooks by pressure groups. In his volume, *That Men May Understand*, Dr. Rugg himself gave a vigorous and adequate reply to his critics.

Official wartime censorship began soon after Pearl Harbor, on December 19, 1941, when President Roosevelt appointed Byron Price to be Director of the U. S. Office of Censorship. The basic policy of this office was to effect the withholding from publication of information potentially valuable to the axis powers, by voluntary self-censorship of authors and publishers. Between 1942 and 1945 a number of successive codes were set up and distributed which contained detailed guidance on the type of information to be withheld. These instructions were consolidated from the various requests of Government agencies and of Army, Navy and Air Force to the Office of Censorship. If a publisher was in doubt about a given manuscript, he was asked to submit it to Washington for a ruling. With one notable exception no major difficulties arose in book publishing and distribution from wartime censorshp, which everyone accepted as a necessary and vital precaution.

That one really damaging form of censorship during the war was the one imposed on the Army Library Service by the Soldier Voting Law of 1944 (Chapter XV of John Jamieson's *Books for the Army* is a detailed account of the law, its effect and amendment). Title V of this law placed certain restrictions on the dissemination of propaganda to servicemen. As originally conceived by Senator Taft, Title V would make it unlawful for Army and Navy officials to disseminate any literature or communication paid for or sponsored by the Government, which "contained political argument or political propaganda of any kind designed or calculated to affect the result of any election." It was a badly worded and ill-conceived law. As a result of senatorial protests it was changed to authorize Army and Navy to distribute periodicals for which soldiers had expressed a preference, and such books which, in the judgment of the Council on Books in Wartime, did not contain material of the prohibited type. However, the original vague definition of just what was considered objectionable remained untouched.

The official War Department interpretation of the law emphasized the sweeping character of Title V, and because of the criminal penalties involved, it admonished officers "to resolve any reasonable doubts in favor of prohibition." The provisions of this War Department letter were particularly troublesome to the Army Library Service as far as books were concerned. Except for a donation clause, the Service felt that there were really no alternatives to the strictest interpretation of the law. Nearly a hundred titles in the fields of politics, economics, history and sociology were deleted from the requisitions and also some novels, including *God's Little Acre* and *The Horse and Buggy Doctor*. Seven books of Stuart Chase disappeared from an order for the Army.

Colonel Trautman, wartime chief of the Army Library Section, first followed a policy of pointing out the follies and inconsistencies of the law whenever occasion presented itself. Later he confined himself to the strictest interpretation of the law. "Naturally, he did not overlook the possibility that the Library Section's compliance with the War Department interpretation might cause a public outcry which would lead to a revision of the law."

The Council on Books in Wartime did take effective action on June 18, 1944, by releasing a heavily publicized protest to the President and the Secretary of the Army and Navy. Senator Taft declared that the Army had misinterpreted the measure, while the War Department maintained that it was only complying with the law as written. Title V was revised and an amendment passed which removed the objectionable features of the law.

In the same year and quite apart from the realms of Army and war, an important censorship case developed in Massachusetts. It has already been pointed out how the extra-legal suppression of undesirable titles had long been practiced by intimidation through the interaction of the Watch and Ward Society, the Boston Booksellers' Board of Trade and the Police Department. Because of alleged obscenity, Lillian Smith's sincere novel of social conditions in the South, *Strange Fruit*, was unofficially banned. In a lower court trial of Abraham Isenstadt as seller and Bernard de Voto as purchaser of a copy of the book, instituted to test the legality of the ban, the judge found the book to be obscene and fined the bookseller for selling it. During the following year the Massachusetts Supreme Court sustained the ban.

As a result of protests by liberal-minded groups of authors, publishers, educators and librarians, a new bill was passed the same year, 1945. It did not alter the concept of obscenity or the criteria of evaluation, but it did change the legal procedure. Power to initiate formal action was transferred from the police to the District Attorney, and from criminal to civil procedure. Experts could now testify as to the nature of the book and the manner of its publication. Above all, the new law made the book indictable, not the bookseller, placing the burden of defensive action on publisher and author, where it more properly belonged.

The first book to be tried under the new statute was Kathleen Win-

sor's *Forever Amber*, which was acquitted in 1947 upon the intelligent
and vigorous defense of Mervin Rosenman. "The new liberal statute
fairly begged for new tactics," he wrote in the June-July, 1947 issue
of the *Authors' League Bulletin*. "Our thesis was that obscenity was
not a matter of 'depraving and corrupting' readers, nor one of 'arous-
ing lustful thoughts and lascivious desires,' nor even of 'impairment of
public morals,' " all of these constituting the criteria exclusively applied
in previous trials. Instead, he explained, "we urged that to be obscene
a book must impel the average adult—not the psychopath or the sub-
normal—to commit anti-social sexual acts." Rosenman also worked on
the "basic premise that obscenity was to a large degree determined by
the prevailing *mores* of the community." Accordingly, the defense
introduced evidence of the *mores* of Springfield and Boston in the
form of books with high sexual content available at public libraries and
bookstores, nude and semi-nude paintings and sculpture in museums
and on public buildings, pulp magazines, motion pictures and plays
currently running, etc.

The clearance of *Forever Amber* was the first instance in the twentieth century of the dismissal of an obscenity charge against a book
by a higher Massachusetts court. As such it was an important step
forward, and it inspired much hope for the future. When the ban
against Erskine Caldwell's *God's Little Acre*, which has been singled
out for persecution during much of its seventeen years of existence,
was sustained by the Massachusetts Supreme Court in August, 1950, it
was evident that such optimism had been somewhat premature. Only
the previous year a Superior Court had cleared both *God's Little Acre*
and James M. Cain's *Serenade*.

At the time, Erskine Caldwell had declared in a *Publishers' Weekly*
interview (May 14, 1949) that "censorship, in cases where obscenity
or salaciousness is not clearly defined or evident, is now a basic threat
to the freedom of the press, and to writing and reading in general.
Sooner or later it can touch everyone. . . . When the author reads
about these cases," he said, "his work is bound to be affected. He may
crawl into a hole, cutting himself down to mouse size, and try to
anticipate the various objections which may arise in different parts of
the country. Finding a solution to this problem is of extreme importance to the writer. It is perhaps the most harassing phase of American

life; he comes to feel that he must limit his interest and the scope of his ability."

In comparison with censorship conditions in Boston and Massachusetts, New York, city and state, has enjoyed a traditionally more liberal attitude of the courts. To be sure, the Watch and Ward Society of Boston has its New York counterpart in the Society to Maintain Public Decency, formerly known as the Society for the Suppression of Vice, under the aegis of Anthony Comstock's successor, John Sumner. Upon his instigation Edmund Wilson's *Memoirs of Hecate County* was confiscated in 1946 by the police, found obscene by the New York Courts, and the publisher, Doubleday, fined $1,000. The decision, which was sustained in 1948 by the United States Supreme Court in a four-to-four decision, was the first United States Supreme Court test of a state "obscene literature" statute. Also, the New York State Legislature passed the so-called McGowan Bill in February, 1947, subjecting authors to criminal prosecution for alleged indecent writing, but the bill was vetoed by Governor Dewey.

Although not directly affecting book publication or distribution in New York, the barring of *The Nation* from the approved list of school publications for three successive years from 1948 should be mentioned here. The action was taken by the Board of Supervisors of the New York City Board of Education, because of a series of articles by Paul Blanshard which dealt with the medical, educational and political influence of the Catholic Church in America. To what extent such action can influence freedom of expression became evident when the author published an extended study of the same subject as *American Freedom and Catholic Power*, and the New York *Times* refused advertising and for a time Macy's refused to stock the book.

What may be considered the most important censorship case of the postwar years occurred in Philadelphia in 1948. It is a story which begins in a rather oppressive atmosphere of arbitrary police action under elusive group pressure, but it has its happy ending on a note of sanity and reason.

On March 20, a number of vice-squad officers raided some fifty-odd book shops, department stores and newsstands, and seized over 2,000 books without a warrant. Some titles were on a list, and the members of the vice-squad had copies of this list, but they also had instructions to confiscate anything else they considered "obscene." They seized books by Erskine Caldwell and William Faulkner, James T. Farrell's *Studs Lonigan* trilogy, and a good many other titles, from such publishers as Avon, Houghton Mifflin, Knopf, Modern Library, Pocket Books, Random House and others. The action was taken by Craig Ellis, chief of the vice-squad, upon various complaints from ministers and school authorities and without reference to higher authorities. The decision as to what was "obscene" was arbitrarily made by the vice-squad without consultation with any other group. Publishers and book-sellers affected by the seizure consolidated their legal forces to fight the city's action. The final decision of Judge Curtis Bok in the Quarter Sessions Court, March 8, 1949, dismissed the Commonwealth case against the Philadelphia booksellers and cleared the nine books involved in the trial. It was a resounding victory for the progressive forces.

"It is my conclusion," said Judge Bok in his momentous decision, "that the books before me are obvious efforts to show life as it is. I cannot be convinced that the deep drives and appetites of life are very much different from what they have always been, or that censorship has ever had any effect on them except as the law's police power to preserve the peace is censorship. I believe that the consensus of preference today is for disclosure and not stealth, for frankness and not hypocrisy, and for public and not secret distribution. That in itself is a moral code.

"It is my opinion that frank disclosure cannot legally be censored, even as an exercise of the police power, unless it is sexually impure and pornographic, as I shall define these words. They furnish the only possible test for obscenity and its effects.

"These books are not, in my view, sexually impure or pornographic."

In California, in 1948, the Education Committee of the California State Senate assailed the "Building America" series of social studies, used by thousands of schools throughout the country, because of political reasons. In the same state and during the same year a Censorship Committee was set up by the Board of Supervisors of Los Angeles County in connection with a controversy over the loyalty statements required of all county employees. One of the Supervisors charged that the County Librarian, although not a communist, had "liberal thoughts that we don't like to see in the mind of the head of our library."

Alarmed by the growing number of instances of library censorship, the American Library Association in 1948 revised and strengthened its "Library Bill of Rights." A Committee on Intellectual Freedom to safeguard the rights of library users was appointed, which under the active chairmanship of David K. Berninghausen has taken a strong stand.

The American Civil Liberties Union also deserves to be mentioned for its many years of valiant struggle against attacks on the freedom of the printed word in the United States.

The American Book during World War II

The effect of World War II on the place of the American book in its own and in world society has been great. There is no better way to realize this than to imagine how the role of the book would have developed without the war. While lengthy speculation is useless, we need only try to eliminate from the last decade the war-created conditions, the new demands for books of many kinds, the unprecedented opportunities for reading and the techniques with which these opportunities were realized in the face of serious obstacles. It becomes clear at once that the war had a profound effect not only in expanding the structure of the book trade and its developing branches, but also in provoking new growth and in opening up hitherto unsuspected possibilities. It has long been the ardent desire of many people of good will that it might become possible to rouse the same enthusiasms, harness the same energies and bring about the same kind of large-scale co-operation in the enduring tasks of peacetime construction as are provoked through the emergencies of war. It is a sobering thought that the better reading habits among the adult population of the United States which the war initiated has not been as permanent in effect as was hoped.

Probably it is too early to pass final judgment on the effect of the new elements that have developed since the end of the thirties. Many of the difficulties, for instance, which the American book is encountering on its way to other nations are not permanent. The fact remains that during and immediately after the war the American book assumed an unprecedented international importance. The burning desire of a world which had come to witness the technical efficiency and the economic strength of the United States to know more of the soul of this great country than its moving pictures, magazines and radio broadcasts

had hitherto permitted, was very real. Likewise, our own government
and responsible citizens had felt increasingly the need for a new orientation of world opinion on the culture of the United States. The superior
role of the book in such a task was not always as obvious to a nation of
newspaper and magazine readers, as it was to book-reading Europeans,
for instance. Out of such circumstances grew many programs more
quickly and on a larger scale than could readily be shouldered with the
existing concepts and machinery. The important thing is that they
were recognized at all. Most of the machinery for selection, production and distribution of books for these new purposes had first to be
created in terms of existing needs. There can be little doubt that the
new role of the book in America which World War II helped so
forcefully to define, will become permanent eventually.

However much the expansion of the use of books was war-stimu-
lated, it must not be forgotten that the new era of mass markets had
dawned before the beginning of the war. The Pocket Books venture
and its numerous followers brought books, skillfully camouflaged as
semi-magazines, and distributed mainly through newsstands, to a vast
number of people who had not been in the habit of buying and reading books, and at prices which they could readily afford. The book
clubs, too, were well under way, also reaching beyond the traditional
book outlets. In addition, the mail-order catalogs broadened their attention to books, thus opening up fresh rural markets.

But the war offered new opportunities for reading. Its continuing
"hurry-up-and-wait" pattern brought unexpected leisure to innumerable men and women in and outside the armed services. Gasoline ra-
tioning tended to keep people at home, and many shortages helped to
draw attention to books. Economic factors also entered the picture.
"On the home front," wrote Joseph A. Brandt on "War and the Book
Trade" in Pierce Butler's excellent *Books and Libraries in Wartime*,
"thousands of persons who in peacetime made such meager incomes
that even a newspaper was a luxury have now, thanks to the accident
of war, been able to make respectable and even larger incomes, to the
anguish of certain reactionary groups in the country. Many of these
people thus benefited discovered for the first time the need for education. True, the education desired was purely technical, but, fortunately, about the only place one could obtain it was in books." For

many the much-needed volume of information, causing the first visit to a bookstore, became the bridge to the world of books in general.

The war itself furnished the theme for many of the new books. By the middle of the century the time lapse between an author's finished manuscript and a completed printed edition had been sharply reduced. Never before could a foreign correspondent, for instance, reach his audience so quickly and so thoroughly through a book. Books of specific instruction and more general information were not the only ones which people wanted. Beyond the demands for mere escape and entertainment were uncertainties and anxieties which gave new popularity to religious books and to volumes on social problems.

As *Time* magazine put it: "The year 1943 was to mark the second year in an epoch that all sober, responsible publishers and all carriers and custodians of United States culture had hoped for all their lives; a time when book-reading and book-buying reached outside the narrow quarters of the intellectuals and became the business of the whole vast literate population of the United States."

In 1943, also, *Fortune* magazine estimated that such mass-market publishers as Simon and Schuster and Doubleday were no longer doing business with the 750 to 1,000 booksellers which a publisher usually dealt with, plus his business with a few jobbers who would service the smaller and the near-bookshops. Instead, Simon and Schuster had found 50,000 to 60,000 outlets for their experimental simultaneous one- and two-dollar editions of Willkie's *One World*, and Doubleday 15,-000 outlets for DuMaurier's *Rebecca*.

But for the ever-present problem of shortages of material and skilled labor, here was a publisher's paradise. The legitimate book trade too had its share in the bonanza. Cultivation of the publisher's back list and the production of compact volumes helped to keep up the flow. The War Production Board watched carefully over paper supplies. By 1944 it had ruled that publishers were allowed only 75 per cent of the amount consumed in 1942. Various binders' materials, especially cloth, were also hard to procure.

The realization of limited material resources on one side and unlimited need for books on the other was one of several factors which called for the formation of a non-governmental, non-profit agency to co-ordinate the efforts of the industry in special wartime services. Such a body came into being early in 1942, when the Council on Books in Wartime was created. In addition to the publishers' organization, then known as the Book Publishers' Bureau, the original sponsors included representatives of the American Association for Adult Education, the American Booksellers Association, the American Library Association, the Authors' League of America, the National Education Association, and the American Center of the P.E.N. Club. The directors were largely drawn from the management of important publishing firms. W. W. Norton was the first chairman, and contributed substantially to the success of the enterprise. His integrity and judgment helped on many occasions to bridge difficulties and to conquer opposition from self-interested minorities. When ill health forced Norton's retirement in 1944, he was capably succeeded by Richard L. Simon.

The activities of the Council are perhaps best described in the words of its official history, which appeared in 1946: "During the four years of its life and operation [it] made available to members of the Armed Forces of the United States 108,500,000 copies of books in the Armed Services Editions, representing over 1,004 titles; supervised the publication for distribution to civilians in freed European and Asiatic countries of 3,600,000 books . . . in the Overseas Editions; arranged for three regularly scheduled radio programs and a number of special ones, totaling upward of three hundred broadcasts; issued fifty-eight carefully selected lists of books recommended for their value in orienting the American public to the war; co-operated closely with the Office of War Information, the War Department, and the Navy Department in the publication of books for the American public; played a material part in influencing the modification of legislation which, in its original form, provided for severe censorship of reading matter for the Armed Forces; was responsible for the production of seven films bringing important war books to the attention of the motion-picture theater public; arranged for speakers at many book fairs and other meetings, and initiated or co-operated in various other activities connected with the war effort."

The Armed Services Editions were initiated in the fall of 1943 in order to supply the Army Library Service with large quantities of inexpensive, expendable volumes. They had to be pocket-size, light-weight paper books which could easily be distributed not only to some 2,000 Army libraries in the United States, but also to innumerable small organizations overseas, to company dayrooms, hospitals, outposts, battle zones, searchlight and anti-aircraft battery positions, etc., wherever they happened to be located on the face of the earth. Editorial and production plans were discussed by the Council beginning in February, 1943. Innumerable problems had to find their solutions, as a result of which thirty, later forty titles to suit all tastes were selected each month by a special committee. At the height of operations over 155,000 copies each of forty titles a month were printed, on a production plan developed by Philip Van Doren Stern. Revolutionary manufacturing methods made it possible to print these books at less than six cents cost per copy.

The Armed Services Editions proved their vitality and usefulness beyond any possible doubt. They outranked all other means of distraction and entertainment in popularity, including even athletics. Lieutenant Colonel Trautman, as reported in *A History of the Council on Books in Wartime*, speaking at the annual meeting on February 1, 1945, after a tour of the European Theater, told spectacular stories of the sacrifices and risks which the boys would endure to get these books to read.

No one has tried to estimate the number or effect of the Armed Services Editions picked up by the civilian populations of both liberated and former Axis countries. A democratically minded bookseller in a small German university town asked the occupying authorities in 1945 for permission to set up a rental library of the ASE, a request which had to be refused. The bookstores in Tokyo after the war had quantities of used copies for sale at low prices. Such incidents indicate both an unforeseen role played by these messengers from overseas and the great hunger for books from America.

The Government's official answer to these demands in occupied countries was made through the Overseas Editions of the Office of War Information, plans for which matured in the course of 1944. The basic idea of OWI was the publication of paper-bound books of American origin, translated specifically for a program which would give the people of Europe a picture of what Americans were like and what they had been doing since communications had been broken off. OWI also became the purchasing agent for exports to the Continent of regular American publishers' stock. The Éditions Transatlantiques and the Overseas Editions were two parts of the same publishing plan which was carried out in New York and in London, where Harold K. Guinzburg, of Viking Press, rendered especially valuable services. The books were selected, rights procured and many other matters straightened out for the program through the active co-operation of the Council on Books in Wartime. Books were translated into French, Dutch, German and Italian. English volumes also appeared. Distribution was through regular commercial channels in each country, and retail prices were set by agreement with the local wholesalers. The subject matter of the Overseas Editions had a wide range.

The United States Armed Forces Institute (USAFI) began educational programs in 1942 for men in the armed services. These included not only contracts with various colleges for instruction in their extension divisions, but also correspondence courses and special brief study units for men in more remote regions, unable to correspond regularly or promptly. William E. Spaulding of Houghton Mifflin headed the editorial department of the Institute. According to John Jamieson's *Books for the Army*, 14,000,000 paper-bound USAFI textbooks were distributed by the Information and Education Division.

One important non-commercial channel of distribution for the Overseas Editions were the Overseas Libraries, which were developed under State Department auspices and grew into important information centers of permanent value in the postwar period. These U. S. Information libraries also saw rapid expansion and redefinition beyond the immediate war and postwar needs, and they have become significant distribution points for American ideas in books, and also in many other media of communication, all over the world.

When the Office of War Information ceased its operations, some agency was needed to facilitate the foreign distribution of American books. For this purpose leading American publishers formed the United States International Book Association, known as USIBA. It was a new development in American publishing. Its structure was that of a "big business operation, consisting of many elements belonging to publishing, jobbing, book-selling, advertising, shipping, as well as diplomacy and representation of the United States." Up to the war American publishers were hardly export-conscious, and it was estimated in

1943 that only 2 per cent of our total annual publishing business went abroad.

The establishment of USIBA in 1945 was a partial answer to the realization of the new world opportunities for the American book. By the end of its first four months, USIBA had handled $180,000 worth of business, and soon after that six American book display centers were established in Paris, Stockholm, Rome, Mexico City, Buenos Aires and Rio de Janeiro. The operations of the Paris office extended to Belgium, Holland, Switzerland and other middle European countries, while the Stockholm office covered Scandinavia.

When the Board of Directors recommended the dissolution of USIBA on December 4, 1946, on the grounds of insufficient support from its membership and the difficulty of mixing public relations with commerce, there was a good deal of disappointment not only among the firms which believed in the organization, but also in various foreign countries, where the step was felt to be a return to isolationism. The liquidation of USIBA also made it necessary for the U. S. Government to find a new method of selecting and procuring translation rights for the occupied countries, a responsibility which was assumed for a time by the *Infantry Journal*.

Various agencies, export firms and individual arrangements took USIBA's place in the commercial field. Fair arrangements in world markets with British Empire interests soon became desirable, and many problems are still awaiting their solution. The currency situation has been a distinct impediment to a large-scale distribution of American books abroad, except where ECA funds and UNESCO book coupons have bridged the gap. The CARE book program, developed for both adults' and children's needs, has also been a distinctly helpful element. But, by and large, it can be said that the full utilization of the new global opportunities for the American book cannot be realized until a broadly and generously conceived key program of all interested elements can be brought into existence and action.

Postwar Problems

As these postwar conditions came into effect, the most urgent and continuing demands from abroad were for American books of science, medicine, and technology. Books of this type are read by all peoples in the original editions. By comparison, the overseas demand for our general trade books was not nearly so great and such books were more useful abroad if printed in translations. The home market therefore remained the all-important market for the trade book and the demands here grew less while the cost of producing books, with war controls gone, rose sharply. What trade book publishing lacked was increased sales to meet the rising costs, yet such increases did not appear.

The need for a new kind of wholehearted and large-scale co-operation of all groups concerned with the future of the book in America was the main recommendation of Charles F. Bound, of the Guaranty Trust Co., in his 1949 study, *A Banker Looks at Book Publishing.* Mr. Bound points out that the Cheney Report of 1931 had already "urged the various branches of the book trade to co-operate with educational groups both to extend education and to promote reading habits during the formative school years." He discussed his conclusions with many experienced publishers, all of whom testified that this is probably the soundest long-range solution to the distribution problem which, though it is desirable, important, and in fact necessary, could not be accomplished under present conditions. Publishers face the fact that unless they are able to distribute more copies of each title published they may be forced by economic pressure to give up publishing many good books. They need to co-operate and take vigorous action. Mr. Bound believes that they will be inspired to action by the increasing threats to our way of life, for most publishers realize that good books are one of the strongest bulwarks of our democracy.

The note of concern over the future of American trade book publishing may come as a surprise to some readers. Was it not true, they will say, that the war years had given unprecedented impetus to good books, had created masses of new readers, had pushed production and distribution figures to hitherto unknown heights?

What, for instance, about the new readers created by the Armed Services Editions? The probability of their long-range effect on the reading habits of millions of young Americans was one of the arguments used by W. W. Norton as chairman of the Council of Books in Wartime to bring publishers together on the plan. Ray Trautman, observing the operation in the field of the Armed Services Editions had felt that their ". . . wide distribution may well have a lasting effect on postwar reading habits and tastes. . . . Millions of men discovered the enjoyment of reading. . . ."

It now appears that these high expectations have not been met by the actual developments. It is true that the average editions of trade books are somewhat larger now than they were before the war; also, that many people who had not been book readers at all, are now reading books in the form of inexpensive paper-bound editions. In various branches of metropolitan library systems, for instance, the Pocket Books and similar series are used most effectively in breaking down reader resistance to books, especially among adolescents, underprivileged groups, and the lesser educated. Certain titles which the general public would never have touched in their buckram-bound library editions are eagerly taken up in their gaily colored paper covers. But these meager advances do not indicate a major conversion of the nation's population towards the habitual reading of permanent literature. Nor is there any evidence of lasting economic benefit to the general book trade as a result of any vastly increased readership.

The postwar years have been called a critical period in American book publishing by many competent observers. There is an uneasy feeling that the healthy continuity and the desirable growth of book publishing are by no means assured under present programs.

It is not difficult to describe in general terms the basic economic elements of this situation. During the war the production cost of books rose by 100 per cent; since the end of the war it has receded very slightly, if at all and fresh increases of costs are threatened. Book prices on the other hand have gone up, as of 1950, only from about 20 to 35 per cent, as compared with pre-war levels. This discrepancy means that the traditional first printing of 2,000 or 3,000 copies which at the old price structure was enough to finance a title, can no longer suffice. Much larger editions, between 5,000 and 7,000 copies of a new title must now be sold if a publisher is to break even. In a good many instances such editions can be sold and the increased absorbing capacity of the reading public for trade books has to some extent helped to bridge the gap—but to some extent only.

This brings of course a difficult situation. The first novel of the promising young writer, the book that expounds the unusual or unpopular point of view, experimental and critical writing of limited appeal, all present problems to the publisher with these conditions of higher costs. Up to the war years a new novel by an unknown writer, properly presented, could be sold to perhaps 2,000 through the trade and directly to readers and several hundred to libraries—a combined sales volume sufficient to launch the author. Today, when at least 5,000 copies must be sold, the odds against it are heavy. The same holds true in the case of many books which discuss special issues and topics. "Outside of a very few broad and a few very narrow channels, there is a general drying up," observed John Jamieson in *Publishers' Weekly*, Jan. 7, 1950.

Various solutions have been sought to combat this situation. Advances to authors are kept down, royalty increments have to be tightened and the general overhead expenses have been examined rather carefully with the hope of discovering means of curtailment. There has been increased sales pressure to maintain the necessary new sales volume. Some savings have become possible in manufacturing, particularly through standardization of formats and the placing of long-term contracts for one or several seasons with one book manufacturing concern. Some of the new technological developments will also help, under certain conditions, to cut production costs. But that is not enough.

The chief compensation has been the income from subsidiary rights. Income from subsidiary rights is the money received by author and publisher through the sale of the rights to a given book or manuscript for the purposes of translation, serialization in a magazine or newspaper, or reprinting in hard covers or in one of the paper covered series, for adoption by a book club, for dramatization on the stage, over the radio or television and, last but not least, motion picture presentation.

The income from these various transactions varies from case to case and depends on the kind of contract written. The sale of motion picture rights, still an important source of income, has been less profitable since the war but still runs to large sums for suitable titles. The picture industry's loss of overseas income, or rather the tying up of substantial moneys abroad, also rising competition for the people's time and attention, have had a restraining influence on Hollywood. Book club adoptions, though lessened in totals, continue to be profitable for both author and original publisher.

Many general trade publishers have been claiming that they can show a profit on a year's varied business only through the income from subsidiary rights. This means that they must include plausible candidates for such uses in their lists. Relatively few of the books that the publisher puts on his list as adoption candidates will actually win the race, but they can color the entire list. It means that in many cases the publisher and his editors are continually influenced in their choice— they would not be human if they were not. Their need for club adoptions communicates itself very quickly to the literary agent and to the author. He, too, is continually under pressure not to write a book but to produce a marketable piece of literary property. The potentially detrimental effects of such a situation are obvious. The same trends which can hinder the valuable book of limited appeal, tend to favor the mediocre book which fits a much lower common denominator of taste.

Some readers may feel that this is an unduly pessimistic outlook. Yet, when William Miller wrote *The Book Industry*, in the Public Library Inquiry series, he found himself beset by exactly the same kind of apprehensions. He examines, for instance, the methods by which titles are chosen for the various book clubs. He points out that in 1947 Joseph Margolies, then of Brentano's, speaking at a PEN Club dinner said that among 496 titles listed as "best" or "outstanding" by 126 literary critics and others active in literary or scholarly work, he was surprised to find "only four of the seventeen (including dual selections) books-of-the-month for the year (only one Literary Guild book was named). Dorothy Canfield Fisher, at the time a Book-of-the-Month Club judge, in listing three 1947 titles in the New York *Herald Tribune*, mentioned only one of the seventeen BOMC selections; another judge, Clifton Fadiman, did not mention any."

Miller also quotes the standards announced by the People's Book Club in the Sears, Roebuck's 1948 *Spring and Summer Catalog:* "The books must be readable by every member of the family. They must be family books. . . . So if you like to read without blushing, without tearing pages out before passing the book on to the younger members of your household, we invite you . . . to read about the People's Book Club." Such criteria will be read with uneasiness by anyone familiar with the cultural directives for the production of literature and art issued in the totalitarian states. Although of course there is no evidence of deliberate totalitarian conspiracy in these parts, there is here a serious potential threat to the freedom of the written word, to the artist and the writer and a threat to the freedom of individual choice and self-enlightenment.

A Gallup poll published in February, 1950, reports: "Despite our mass education and high degree of literacy, the United States has the lowest proportion of book readers of any major democracy, judging by the results of an international survey in six nations. England ranked highest in the study, with well over half of her adult population reading some book or novel at the time the survey was conducted. Norway came next, then Canada, then Australia, and Sweden, and the United States brought up the rear, with only one adult in five reading books."

Joseph Brandt, then Director of the University of Chicago Press, writing in *Books and Libraries in Wartime*, was fearful that "unless the new voices of literature have an avenue open to them for expression, the soul of America will die. . . . The bulk of the books sold in this country," he declares, "are necessary books. They are textbooks, reference books, technical and medical books. The minority of the books sold and published are the books that enrich society, that destroy cultural lethargy. . . . I think that book publishing in this country will die absolutely when the book publishers publish only what a Gallup poll tells them in advance will succeed. . . ."

The problems which the American trade book is facing in the postwar world are not really new ones. The hereditary superiority of newspapers and magazines in the growth of American society, in the vital period of national development, has been traced thoroughly in this book. The periodical press, in the very consciousness of George Washington himself, and in the minds, instincts and intentions of innumerable subsequent leaders, was the most important instrument of intellectual communication and popular enlightenment. Inevitably this has meant that the book had to take second place, which in turn became one reason why the sound growth of a legitimate book trade organization and a stable distribution system, such as the European countries knew, could not take place.

The struggle between the legitimate book trade and new, unconventional methods of distribution, is, therefore, not a new one. But this struggle is beginning to show important proportions, and becoming clearer in its implications. We begin to see more distinctly what the alternatives are, what they mean, and what the ultimate consequences of these alternatives are apt to be.

It is probably useful if the nature of this problem is once more stated. The question is if we will continue to see the healthy future growth of a system which gives the serious book its due place, which allows the young author to say what is on his mind the way he wants to say it and reach the people to whom he wants to speak: a system that has room and continues to have room for a book which speaks to the intellectual and the minorities; a book that contains the unusual viewpoint, the experiment, the critique; a book that does not want to appeal to a low common denominator of the people's understanding— in other words continued freedom of speech in the form of the book as a very important instrument of cultural enlightenment and social growth. The question is will such books continue to be found by the readers in bookstores and libraries all over the country as the result of a free choice from a variety of offerings and in consultation with well-informed guides and advisers whose professional ambition it is not only to help their clients find what they are looking for but to guide them to new and possibly more valuable experiences. What we fear is a possible condition where mass production controls the ends, where distributor dominates producer, where the creative impulse which does not fit the prevailing taste pattern, could be suppressed or corrupted into subservience.

It is possible to say that the potential role of the book in American society is being overrated. Why, it could be argued, should a new world not create its own characteristic media of communication, seek and develop its own new and unconventional channels of distribution? Why feel bound by historical precedence in other, foreign, societies?

The answer to this objection, in the opinion of this writer, is inextricably bound up with the concept of cultural growth and cultural maturity. Nobody would deny the services that have been and are being perfomed by the vast variety of communication media that have molded American society to this time. But the question remains if the book has not a function in the cultural growth of a country that no other organ can fulfill with equal effectiveness and thoroughness. I suppose the answer to such a question is ultimately one of faith. Many

men and women in this country are united in their belief in the good
book. William Sloane, the publisher, says it in these words: "The
books which a nation publishes and reads are a major part of that nation's mind, and the most basic medium of communication between
peoples. It is essential that as many books as possible shall be good and
useful books by this criterion." Charles F. Bound, the banker, speaks
as follows: "The book is unquestionably the most important medium
of communication. In these days of crisis when the very foundations
of democracy are threatened, the book publishers have a heavy responsibility to provide the basic food to strengthen our minds and hearts
and provide nourishment to those seeking truth and knowledge. If
they cannot keep their ships afloat in the rough economic storms ahead
their ideals and their authors' ideas will go down together." Helen
Haines, friend of readers and libraries, writes thus in her *Living with
Books:* "Magazines are far more widely read than books; but not by
those who know the joys and values of reading. Magazines and newspapers—both dominant factors in American mass culture—are no more
than accessories or deterrents to reading; they do not signify that wide
ranging and rich adventure in the world of books that is real reading.
Magazines have their place, their own usefulness; but no magazine can
take the place of standard books. There are periodicals of literary
value, of scholarly, technical, or specialized importance, essential to
scholars and scientific and technical workers and to men and women
in every field. But if more Americans would read good books and
cease reading promiscuous popular magazines, we should have a higher
level of general education and intelligence."

What are the safeguards that are at hand against the dangers to the
future of the permanently valuable book? An important point to remember is the fact that a great many of the difficulties described in
these pages are confined to trade books and to their publishers. These
form, of course, a very important segment of the over-all picture, but
there are other branches. The last few decades have brought increased
concentration in special fields, new houses have been founded and special departments in general trade houses have been developed and cultivated.

The growth of the university presses, in particular, has provided a
broadly distributed network of quality publishing, regional in location

but national in view, which is becoming a bulwark against a lowering of standards. Trade publishers view these developments not with alarm but with a sense of approval. There are a number of far-sighted men in the ranks of the trade publishers who will fight valiantly to fullfill their cultural responsibilities.

The important thing for all those concerned with a healthy future of the book in America lies in the realization that such a future is by no means automatically assured. An awareness of the existing and the possible future threats and dangers is the primary weapon of every member of the present generation who believes in the vital role of the book. It is more than likely that the future will see serious attempts to create broadly co-operative movements among all those who share this belief, and such attempts are worthy of every encouragement.

APPENDIX

BIBLIOGRAPHY

THE FOLLOWING BIBLIOGRAPHY has been prepared by Janet Bogardus, of the staff of the Columbia University Libraries. It is a record of the sources used by the three contributors, collected in order to guide readers to fuller and more detailed information than that given in the text. The list was compiled from the bibliographical notes of each of the authors, which were combined into one list and supplemented with such additional titles as seemed useful and important. However, no attempt at completeness has been made, nor does the omission of a title necessarily indicate a judgment upon its value. Except in certain cases it was attempted to list the most recent editions of the books included.

KEY TO ARRANGEMENT

CULTURAL HISTORY

General Works

ADAMS, J. T. The epic of America. New ed. Boston, Little, Brown, 1933. 446 p. illus.

Another edition, Garden City Publishing Company, 1947.

BEARD, C. A. The rise of American civilization. New York, Macmillan, 1928–1942. 4 v.

v. 1, The agricultural era; v. 2, The industrial era; v. 3, America in midpassage; v. 4, The American spirit. A reissue of all four volumes appeared in 1947.

BISHOP, J. L. A history of American manufactures from 1608–1860. 3d ed., rev. and enl. Philadelphia, E. Young, 1868. 3 v. illus.

CLARK, V. S. History of manufactures in the United States, 1607–1928. 1929 ed. Washington, D. C., Carnegie Institution of Washington, 1929. 3 v. illus.

Reprint, Peter Smith, 1949.

GROLIER CLUB. One hundred influential American books printed before 1900. Catalogue and addresses. Exhibition at the Grolier Club, April eighteenth–June sixteenth, MCMXLVI. New York, Grolier Club, 1947. 139 p. illus.

PARRINGTON, V. L. Main currents in American thought; an interpretation of American literature from the beginnings to 1920. [New York, Harcourt, Brace, 1939] 3 v. in 1.

U. S. BUREAU OF THE CENSUS. A century of population growth from the first census of the United States to the twelfth, 1790–1900. Washington, Govt. print. off., 1909. 303 p. illus.

Literary History

BROOKS, VAN WYCK. The flowering of New England: 1815–1865. New and rev. ed. New York, Dutton, 1937. 550 p.

Reprinted with *New England: Indian summer, 1865–1915* under title: *Literature in New England*. Garden City, N. Y., Garden City Publishing Co., 1944. 2 v. in 1.

The Cambridge history of American literature, ed. by William P. Trent, John Erskine, Stuart P. Sherman, Carl Van Doren. New York, Putnam, 1917–1921. 4 v.

Popular edition reissued 1943. 3 v.

ELLISON, R. C. Early Alabama publications; a study in literary interests. University, Ala., Univ. of Alabama Press, 1947. 213 p.

HARTWICK, HARRY. The foreground of American fiction. New York, American Book Co. [1934] 447 p.

HOLMES, T. J. Cotton Mather; a bibliography of his works. Cambridge, Mass., Harvard Univ. Press, 1940. 3 v. illus.

——Increase Mather; a bibliography of his works. Cleveland, 1931. 2 v. illus.

——The Mather literature. Cleveland, Priv. print. for W. G. Mather, 1927. 65 p.

——The minor Mathers; a list of their works. Cambridge, Mass., Harvard Univ. Press, 1940. 218 p. illus.

JANTZ, H. S. The first century of New England verse. Worcester, Mass., American Antiquarian Society, 1944. 292 p.

——Unrecorded verse broadsides of seventeenth century New England. (*In* Papers of the Bibl. Soc. of Amer., v. 39, 1st quar., 1945, p. 1–19. illus)

MATHER, COTTON. Diary of Cotton Mather. Boston, The Society, 1911–

12. 2 pts. illus. (Collections of the Massachusetts Historical Society [ser. 7, v. 7–8])

PATTEE, F. L. First century of American literature, 1770–1870. New York, D. Appleton-Century, 1935. 613 p.

——A history of American literature since 1870. New York, Century [1915] 449 p.

——The new American literature, 1890–1930. New York, Century Co. [1930] 507 p.

QUINN, A. H. American fiction. New York, D. Appleton-Century [1936] 805 p.

SPILLER, R. E., ed. Literary history of the United States. New York, Macmillan, 1948. 3 v.

TYLER, M. C. A history of American literature. New York, Putnam, 1881. 2 v. in 1.

——A history of American literature during the Colonial period, 1607–1765. New York, Putnam, 1898. 2 v. in 1.

VAN DOREN, CARL. The American novel, 1789–1939. Rev. and enl. ed. New York, Macmillan, 1946. 406 p.

WINSOR, JUSTIN. Narrative and critical history of America. Boston, Houghton, Mifflin, 1884–89. 8 v. illus.

WRIGHT, T. G. Literary culture in early New England, 1620–1730. New Haven, Yale University Press, 1920. 322 p.

BIBLIOGRAPHY

General Works

Bibliographical essays: a tribute to Wilberforce Eames. [Cambridge, Harvard University Press] 1924. 440 p. illus.

BIBLIOGRAPHICAL SOCIETY OF AMERICA. The papers of the Bibliographical Society of America. v. 1, 1906– New York, 1906–

Bookmen's holiday; notes and studies written and gathered in tribute to Harry Miller Lydenberg. New York, New York Public Library, 1943. 573 p.

FORD, P. L. Check list of bibliographies, catalogues, reference-lists and lists of authorities of American books and subjects. Brooklyn, N. Y., 1889. 64 p.

GROWOLL, ADOLF. Book-trade bibliography in the United States in the XIXth century; to which is added A catalogue of all the books printed in the United States, with the prices and place where published, annexed.

Published by the booksellers in Boston, January, 1804. New York, Dibdin Club, 1898. LXXVII, 79 p. illus.

Reprinted 1939, Brick Row Bookshop, New York.

HARRISSE, HENRY. Bibliotheca Americana vetustissima. A description of works relating to America, published between the years 1492 and 1551. New York, G. P. Philes, 1866. 519 p.

—— ——Additions. Paris, Tross [Leipzig, Imprimerie W. Drugulin] 1872. 199 p. illus.

SABIN, JOSEPH. Bibliotheca Americana. A dictionary of books relating to America, from its discovery to the present time. Begun by Joseph Sabin, and continued by Wilberforce Eames for the Bibliographical Society of America. New York, 1868–1936. 29 v.

Publication was suspended 1892 to 1927.

STILLWELL, M. B. Incunabula and Americana, 1450–1800; a key to bibliographical study. New York, Columbia University Press, 1931. 483 p. illus.

WINSHIP, G. P. Luther S. Livingston, 1864–1914. Cambridge [Montague Press] 1915. 25 p. illus.

National Bibliography

A catalogue of books published in America, and for Sale at the Bookstore of John West. Boston, Printed by Samuel Etheridge, 1797. 36 p.

A catalogue of all books printed in the United States, with the prices and places where published annexed. Published by the book-sellers in Boston. Printed at Boston, for the booksellers, Jan. 1804. 79 p. (*Facsimile reprint in* Growoll, A. Booktrade bibliography in the U. S. 1898).

EVANS, CHARLES. American bibliography. A chronological dictionary of all books, pamphlets and periodical publications printed in the United States of America from the genesis of printing in 1639 down to and including the year 1820. Chicago, Priv. print. for the author by the Blakely Press, 1903–34. v. 1–12.

HENRY E. HUNTINGTON LIBRARY. American imprints, 1648–1797, in the Huntington Library, supplementing Evans' American bibliography; comp. by Willard O. Waters. Cambridge, Mass., Harvard Univ. Press, 1933. 95 p.

STEVENS, HENRY, SON and STILES. A century of American printing, 1701–1800; a catalogue of books and pamphlets with a few newspapers from the presses of that part of North America now called the United States. London, Stevens [1916] 166 p.

ROORBACH, O. A. Bibliotheca Americana. Catalogue of American publications,

including reprints and original works, from 1820 to 1852 inclusive. Together with a list of periodicals published in the U. S. New York, Roorbach, 1852. 652 p.

A Supplement listing publications from Oct. 1852 to May 1855, pub. 1855; an Addenda listing publications from May 1855 to Mar. 1858, pub. 1858; and v. 4 of the Bibliotheca Americana, listing publications from 1858 to Jan. 1861, pub. 1861. Continued by James Kelly's American Catalogue, 1866–71. A 4 v. reprint, including supplements, printed by Peter Smith, New York, 1939.

TRÜBNER, NIKOLAUS. Trübner's Bibliographical guide to American literature. A classified list of books published in the United States of America during the last forty years. London, Trübner, 1859. CXLIX, 554 p.

KELLY, JAMES. American catalogue of books published in the United States from Jan. 1861 to Jan. 1871. New York, Wiley, 1866–71. 2 v.

Reprinted 1938 by Peter Smith, New York.

The American catalogue of books for 1869, containing complete monthly lists of all the books published in the United States during the year 1869, with statement of size, price, place of publication and publisher's name. To which are prefixed an alphabetical and a classified index. New York, Leypoldt & Holt, 1870. 103 p.

American Catalogue. July 1, 1876–Dec. 31, 1910. New York, 1880–1911. 14 v.

Supplemented by the Annual American Catalogue, 1886–1903, 1905–06, 1908–10. Reprinted 1941 by Peter Smith, New York.

United States Catalog; books in print, 1899. Minneapolis, H. W. Wilson, 1900. 2 v.

2d ed., 1902; 3d ed., 1912; 4th ed., 1928; 5th ed., 1942; successive supplements to date. The five editions and their supplements form a comprehensive record of American publishing.

Books in print; an author-title series index to the Publishers' trade list annual, 1948– New York, Bowker, 1948–

Cumulative Book Index. v. 1, 1898– New York, H. W. Wilson, 1898–

Issued monthly; the last number of each volume covering all the publications of the year and forming the annual supplement to the United States catalog.

Publishers' Weekly, the American book trade journal. v. 1, 1872– New York, Publishers' Weekly, 1872–

Contains lists of new publications of the week.

Publishers' Trade List Annual, 1873– New York, Publishers' Weekly, 1873–

A yearly collection of publishers' catalogs.

U. S. COPYRIGHT OFFICE. Catalogue of copyright entries. 1891– Washington, Govt. Print. Off., 1891–

Selected Subject Bibliographies

ACCOUNTING BOOKS. Bentley, H. C. and Leonard, R. S. Bibliography of works on accounting by American authors. Boston, Mass., H. C. Bentley, 1934–35. 2 v.

"Introductory chapter: copyright laws and administration—their significance to bibliographers," v. 1, p. [xi]–xxi.

ALMANACS. Morrison, H. A. Preliminary check list of American almanacs, 1639–1800. Washington, Govt. Print. Off., 1907. 160 p.

ANNUALS AND GIFT-BOOKS. Faxon, F. W. Literary annuals and gift books; a bibliography with a descriptive introduction. Boston, Boston Book Co., 1912. 140 p.

——Thompson, Ralph. American literary annuals & gift books, 1825–1865. New York, H. W. Wilson, 1936. 183 p.

ARCHITECTURE. Hitchcock, H. R. American architectural books; a list of books, portfolios and pamphlets published in America before 1895 on architecture and related subjects. 2d ed. Middletown, Conn., 1939–40. 110 p.

BIBLES. Rumball-Petre, E. A. R. America's first Bibles, with a census of 555 extant Bibles. Portland, Me., Southworth-Anthoensen Press, 1940. 184 p. illus.

BROADSIDES. American Antiquarian Society. A list of early American broadsides, 1680–1800, belonging to the library of the American Antiquarian Society, Worcester, with an introduction and notes by Nathaniel Paine. Worcester, C. Hamilton, 1897. 64 p.

CATECHISMS. Eames, Wilberforce. Early New England catechisms; a bibliographical account of some catechisms published before the year 1800, for use in New England. Read in part before the American Antiquarian Society. Worcester, Mass., C. Hamilton, 1898. 111 p.

CHAPBOOKS. Weiss, H. B. American chapbooks, 1722–1842. New York, New York Public Library, 1945. 19 p.

—— ——Book about chapbooks; the people's literature of bygone times. Highland Park, N. J., The Author, 1942. 149 p.

CHILDREN'S BOOKS. Blanck, Jacob. Peter Parley to Penrod; a bibliographical description of the best-loved American juvenile books [1827–1929] New York, Bowker, 1938. 153 p.

——Kerlan, Irvin. Newbery and Caldecott awards, a bibliography of first editions, with a foreword by Frederic G. Melcher. Minneapolis, Univ. of Minnesota Press, 1949. 51 p.

——Rosenbach, A. S. W. Early American children's books. Portland, Me., Southworth Press, 1933. 354 p. illus.

COOKERY BOOKS. Gourley, J. E. Regional American cookery, 1884–1934; a list of works on the subject. New York, New York Public Library, 1936. 36 p.

——Lincoln, Waldo. Bibliography of American cookery books, 1742–1860. (*In* Proceedings of the Amer. Antiquarian Soc., n. s., v. 39, pt. 1, April, 1929. p. 85–225)

——Stark, L. M. The Whitney cookery collection. New York, New York Public Library, 1946. 26 p.

DIME NOVELS. Bragin, C., comp. Dime novels; bibliography, 1860–1928. Brooklyn, N. Y., The Compiler, 1938. 29 p. illus.

——New York Public Library. The Beadle collection of dime novels given to the library by Dr. Frank P. O'Brien. New York, 1922. 99 p. illus.

——Pearson, E. L. Dime novels; or, Following an old trail in popular literature. Boston, Little, Brown, 1929. 280 p. illus.

DRAMA. Hill, F. P. American plays printed 1714–1830; a bibliographical record. Stanford University, Calif., Stanford University Press [1934] 152 p. illus.

——Roden, R. F. Later American plays, 1831–1900; being a compilation of the titles of plays by American authors published and performed in America since 1831. New York, Dunlap Society, 1900. 132 p.

——Wegelin, Oscar. Early American plays, 1714–1830; a compilation of the titles of plays and dramatic poems written by authors born in or residing in North America previous to 1830. 2d ed., rev. New York, Literary Collector Press, 1905. 94 p. illus.

——Weingarten, J. A. Modern American playwrights, 1918–1945; a bibliography. New York, The Compiler, 1946–47. 2 pts.

DREAM BOOKS. Weiss, H. B. Oneirocritica Americana; the story of American dream books. New York, New York Public Library, 1944. 37 p.

ETIQUETTE BOOKS. Bobbitt, M. R. A bibliography of etiquette books published in America before 1900. New York, New York Public Library, 1947. 35 p.

——Schlesinger, A. M. Learning how to behave; a historical study of American etiquette books. New York, Macmillan, 1946. 95 p.

FICTION. Wegelin, Oscar. Early American fiction, 1774–1830; a compilation of the titles of works of fiction by writers born or residing in North America north of the Mexican border and printed previous to 1831. 3d ed. cor. and enl. New York, P. Smith, 1929. 37 p.

——Wright, L. H. American fiction, 1774–1850; a contribution toward a bibliography. Rev. ed. San Marino, Calif., 1948. 355 p. (Huntington Library Publications)

FIRST EDITIONS. Boutell, H. S. First editions of today and how to tell them; American, British and Irish. 3d ed. rev. and enl. by Roger Boutell. Berkeley, Calif., Univ. of California, 1949. 209 p.

——Brussel, I. R. Anglo-American first editions, 1826–1900; east to west, describing first editions of English authors whose books were published in America before their publication in England. London, Constable, 1935. 170 p. illus. (Bibliographia. no. IX)

—— ——Anglo-American first editions. Part II: West to east. 1786–1930; describing first editions of American authors whose books were published in England before their publication in America. London, Constable, 1936. 131 p. illus. (Bibliographia. no. X)

——Foley, P. K. American authors, 1795–1895; a bibliography of first and notable editions. Boston, Printed for subscribers [Publishers' Printing Co.] 1897. 350 p.

——Johnson, M. De V. Merle Johnson's American first editions. 4th ed. rev. and enl. by Jacob Blanck. New York, Bowker, 1942. 553 p.

——Stone, H. S. First editions of American authors. A manual for booklovers. Cambridge, Stone and Kimball, 1893. 223 p.

——Trade prices current of American first editions, 1936–1939 and 1937–1940. New York, Bowker, 1939–40. 2 v.

JEST BOOKS. Weiss, H. B. A brief history of American jest books. New York, New York Public Library, 1943. 19 p. illus.

LEGAL TREATISES. James, E. R. List of legal treatises printed in the British Colonies and the American States before 1801. (*In* Beale, J. H. Harvard legal essays. Cambridge, 1934. p. 159–211)

MUSIC. Sonneck, O. G. T. Bibliography of early secular American music. Rev. and enl. ed. Washington, Library of Congress, 1945. 616 p.

POETRY. New York Public Library. Early American poetry, 1610–1820. A list of works in the library. Comp. by J. C. Frank. New York, 1917. 58 p.

——Stockbridge, J. C. The Anthony memorial. A catalogue of the Harris collection of American poetry with biographical and bibliographical notes. Providence [Providence Press Co.] 1886. 320 p.

——Wegelin, Oscar. Early American poetry; a compilation of the titles of volumes of verse and broadsides by writers born or residing in North America, north of the Mexican border. 2d ed. rev. and enl. New York, P. Smith, 1930. 2 v. in 1. illus.

PRAYER BOOKS. Wright, John. Early Prayer Books for America. St. Paul, Minn., 1896. 492 p. illus.

PRIMERS. Ford, P. L. The New England primer; a history of its origin and development, with a reprint of the unique copy of the earliest known edition and many facsimile illustrations and reproductions. New York, Dodd, Mead, 1897. 354 p. illus.

——Heartman, C. F. American primers, Indian primers, Royal primers, and thirty-seven other types of non-New-England primers issued prior to 1839; a bibliographical checklist. Highland Park, N. J., Printed for H. B. Weiss, 1935. 159 p. illus.

—— ——The New-England primer issued prior to 1830; a bibliographical checklist. [3d ed.] New York, Bowker, 1934. 148 p. illus.

RAILROADS. New York Public Library. Check list of publications on American railroads before 1841; a union list of printed books and pamphlets, comp. by T. R. Thomson. New York, 1942. 250 p.

SCHOOL-BOOKS. Littlefield, G. E. Early schools and school-books of New

England. Boston, Club of Odd Volumes, 1904. 354 p. illus.

SPORTING BOOKS. Grolier Club. Early American sport. A chronological check-list of books published prior to 1860. Based on an exhibition held at the Grolier Club. Compiled by Robert W. Henderson, with an introduction by Harry T. Peters. New York, 1937. 134 p. illus.

WRITING BOOKS. Nash, Ray. Writing; some early American writing books and masters. Cambridge, Mass., Harvard College Library [n.d.] 24 p. illus.

PRINTING AND BOOKMAKING

Periodicals

American Printer. v. 1, July, 1855– New York, 1855–

Title changed: July 1885–Jan. 1897, *American Bookmaker.* Mar. 1897–Dec. 1899, *The Printer and Bookmaker.* Jan.–Feb. 1900, *The American Printer and Bookmaker.* Mar. 1900– *The American Printer.* Absorbed *The Western Printer,* Feb. 1902; *The International Printer,* Feb. 1906; *The Master Printer and Printing Trade News,* Nov. 1915.

Ars Typographica. v. 1–2, v. 3, no. 1; Spring 1918–Autumn 1934. New York, Marchbanks Press [1918–34] 3 v. in 2.

Vol. 1 (edited by F. W. Goudy) consists of 4 numbers, issued spring 1918, summer 1918, spring 1920 and autumn 1934. Vols. 2–3 (edited and published by D. C. McMurtrie) were issued quarterly July 1925–July 1926.

Bookbinding and Book Production. v. 1, Mar. 1925– New York, 1925–

From 1925 to Aug. 1936 the title was *Bookbinding Magazine; the official business paper of the industry.* In Sept. 1936 the title was changed to *Bookbinding and Book Production.*

The Dolphin; a journal of the making of books. No. 1–4, 1933–1941. New York, Limited Editions Club, 1933–1941. 4 nos. in 6.

No. 3, 1938 is "A history of the printed book."

Inland Printer; the leading trade journal of the world in the printing and allied industries. v. 1, Oct. 1883– Chicago, 1883–

PRINT: a quarterly journal of the graphic arts, 1940– Woodstock, Vt., Rudge, 1940–

Absorbed *Printing Art,* Summer 1942.

The Printer; a monthly newspaper, devoted to the interest of the "art preservative of all arts." v. 1–7, May 1858–1875. New York, Henry & Huntington, 1859–1876.

The Printers' Circular and Stationers' and Publishers' Gazette, a monthly record of events of interest to printers, publishers, stationers, lithographers, book-binders, paper-makers and kindred industries. v. 1–15, Mar. 1, 1866–1881. Philadelphia, R. S. Menamin, 1866–1881.

PRINTING ART QUARTERLY, v. 1, March 1903–1941. Cambridge, University Press, 1903–27; Chicago, Dartnell Corporation, 1927–1941.

Merged into *Print,* 1942.

General Printing History

BAUER, K. F. Aventur und Kunst; eine Cronik des Buchdruckgewerbes von der Erfindung der Beweglichen letter bis zum Gegenwart. Frankfurt a. M., Privatdruck der Bauerschen Giesserei, 1940. 437 p. illus.

MCMURTRIE, D. C. A history of printing in the United States. New York, Bowker, 1936. v. 2.

Only v. 2 pub.

MOORE, J. W. Moore's historical, biographical, and miscellaneous gatherings, in the form of disconnected notes relative to printers, printing, publishing, and editing of books, newspapers, magazines, and other literary productions, such as the early publications of New England, the United States, and the world, from the discovery of the art, or from 1420 to 1886. Concord, N. H., Printed by the Republican Press Association, 1886. 604 p.

OSWALD, J. C. A history of printing; its development through five hundred years. New York, Appleton, 1928. 403 p. illus.

Chapters XVII, XVIII, XIX deal with printing in America.

——Printing in the Americas. New York, Gregg Pub. Co. [1937] 565 p. illus.

WINSHIP, G. P. The literature of the history of printing in the United States; a survey. (*In* The Library, 4th ser., v. 3, no. 4, Mar. 1, 1923. p. [288]–303)

Colonial Printing History

BERTHOLD, ARTHUR. American colonial printing as determined by contemporary cultural forces. [1934]

Master's thesis, Univ. of Chicago, 1934. Typewritten.

HOUGHTON, H. O. Address on early printing in America, delivered before the Vermont Historical Society. Montpelier, Watchman Pub. Co., 1894. 28 p.

LEIGH, R. A. A. William Strahan and his ledgers. (*In* Trans. of the Bibl. Soc., The Library, v. 3, no. 4, March, 1923, p. 261–287)

A New England keepsake presented to all craftsmen registered at the 19th annual convention of the International Association of Printing House Craftsmen Incorporated, held at the Hotel Statler, August 14–17, 1938, Boston, Massachusetts. Printed under the auspices of the Boston Club of Printing House Craftsmen by ten New England Printers. [1938] [165] p.

SEIDENSTICKER, OSWALD. The first century of German printing in America, 1728–1830. Philadelphia, Schaefer & Koradi, 1893. 254 p. illus.

THOMAS, ISAIAH. The history of printing in America, with a biography of printers and an account of newspapers. 2d ed. Albany, J. Munsell, 1874. 2 v. illus.

——McCulloch, William. William McCulloch's additions to Thomas' History of printing. (*In* Proceedings of the Amer. Antiquarian Soc., n. s., v. 31, pt. 1, April, 1921. p. 89–247)

WINTERICH, J. T. Early American books & printing. Boston, Houghton Mifflin, 1935. 253 p. illus.

WROTH, L. C. The Colonial printer. 2d ed. rev. and enl. Portland, Me., Southworth Press, 1938. 368 p. illus.

——North America (English-speaking). (*In* Peddie, R. A. Printing, a short history of the art, 1927. p. 319–373)

19th Century Printing History

American dictionary of printing and book-making; containing a history of these arts in Europe and America, with definitions of technical terms and biographical sketches. New York, H. Lockwood, 1894. 592 p. illus.

DE VINNE, T. L. Printing in the nineteenth century. New York, Lead Mould Electrotype Foundry, 1924. 16 p. illus.

HARPEL, O. H. Poets and poetry of printerdom; a collection of original, selected and fugitive lyrics, written by persons connected with printing. Cincinnati, Harpel, 1875. 395 p. illus.

MUNSELL, CHARLES. A collection of songs of the American press, and other poems relating to the art of printing, comp. by Charles Munsell. Albany, 1868. 206 p. illus.

RINGWALT, J. L. American encyclopaedia of printing. Philadelphia, Menamin & Ringwalt, 1871. 512 p. illus.

SILVER, R. G. Problems in nineteenth century bibliography. (*In* Papers of the Bibl. Soc. of Amer., v. 43, 1st quar., 1941. p. 35–47)

Individual Colonies and States

Due to lack of space, the lists of imprints issued or sponsored by the Historical Records Survey are not included in this bibliography.

ALABAMA. Ellison, R. C. Checklist of Alabama imprints, 1807–1870. University, Ala., Univ. of Alabama Press, 1946. 151 p.

ARIZONA. McMurtrie, D. C. The beginnings of printing in Arizona. Chicago, Black Cat Press, 1937. 44 p.

ARKANSAS. Allen, A. H., ed. Arkansas imprints, 1821–1876. New York, Pub. for the Bibl. Soc. of America by R. R. Bowker, 1947. 236 p.

CALIFORNIA. Barr, Louise. Presses of northern California and their books, 1900–1933. Berkeley, Book Arts Club, Univ. of California, 1934. 276 p.

——Cowan, R. E. Bibliographical notes on early California. (*In* American Hist. Soc. Annual report, 1904. p. 267–278)

——Shinn, C. H. Early books, magazines and book-making in California

(*In* Overland Monthly, 2. ser., v. 12, Oct. 1888. p. 337–352. illus.)

——Wagner, H. R. Commercial printers of San Francisco from 1851–1880. (*In* Papers of the Bibl. Soc. of Amer., v. 33, 1939. p. 69–84)

——Wheat, C. I. The pioneer press of California. Oakland, Calif., Bio Books, 1948. 31 p. illus.

CONNECTICUT. Harlow, T. R. Early Hartford printers. Hartford, Conn., 1940. 12 p.

——Trumbull, J. H. List of books printed in Connecticut, 1709–1800. Hartford, Conn., Hartford Press, 1904. 251 p.

Supplementary lists by A. C. Bates were pub. in 1938 and 1947 by the Acorn Club, Hartford.

FLORIDA. Brigham, C. S. East Florida Gazette, 1783–1784. (*In* Proceedings of the Amer. Antiquarian Soc., n. s., v. 23, pt. 2, October, 1913)

——McMurtrie, D. C. Beginning of printing in Florida. Hattiesburg, Miss., Book Farm, 1944. 36 p.

——Wells, W. C. Two essays: one upon single vision with two eyes; the other on Dew. London, 1818.

GEORGIA. De Renne, W. J. Books relating to the history of Georgia in the library of Wymberley Jones De Renne, of Wormsloe, Isle of Hope, Chatham County, Georgia. Comp. and annotated by Oscar Wegelin. [Savannah, The Morning News] 1911. 268 p. illus.

——McMurtrie, D. C. Located Georgia imprints of the eighteenth century not in the De Renne catalogue. Savannah, Priv. print., 1934. 44 p. illus.

——[Printing in Georgia] (*In* Catalogue of the Wymberley Jones De

Renne Georgia library, Wormsloe, 1931, v. 1. p. 145-148)

ILLINOIS. McMurtrie, D. C. The first printers of Chicago, with a bibliography of the issues of the Chicago press, 1836-1850. Chicago [Cuneo Press] 1927. 42 p. illus.

Notes in supplement to "The first printers of Chicago." Chicago, Priv. print. 1931. 14 p. illus.

INDIANA. Walker, M. L. The beginnings of printing in the state of Indiana. Crawfordsville, Ind., Banta, 1934. 124 p.

KANSAS. McMurtrie, D. C. and Allen, A. H. A forgotten pioneer press of Kansas. Chicago, John Calhoun Club, 1930. 30 p. illus.

KENTUCKY. Jillson, W. R. The first printing in Kentucky. Louisville, C. T. Dearing Printing Co., 1936. 57 p. illus.

—— ——The newspapers and periodicals of Frankfort, Kentucky, 1795-1945. Frankfort, Ky., Kentucky State Hist. Soc., 1945. 82 p. illus.

—McMurtrie, D. C. and Allen, A. H. A supplementary list of Kentucky imprints, 1794-1820, additional to those recorded in American imprints inventory check lists nos. 5-6. (*In* Kentucky State Hist. Soc. Register, v. 42, 1944. p. 99-119)

LOUISIANA. McMurtrie, D. C. Early printing in New Orleans, 1764-1810. New Orleans, Searcy & Pfaff, 1929. 151 p. illus.

—— ——Louisiana imprints, 1768-1810; in supplement to the bibliography in "Early printing in New Orleans," by Douglas C. McMurtrie. Hattiesburg, Miss., Book Farm, 1942. 65 p. illus. (Heartman's Historical series, no. 62)

——Tinker, E. L. Les écrits de langue française en Louisiane au XIXe siècle; essais biographiques et bibliographiques. Paris, H. Champion, 1932. 502 p. illus.

MAINE. Griffin, Joseph. History of the press of Maine. Brunswick, The Press, [J. Griffin, 1872] 284 p. illus.

—Supplement to the History of the press of Maine, with complete indexes. Brunswick J. Griffin [1874] [289]-320 p.

——Noyes, R. W. A bibliography of Maine imprints to 1820. Stonington, Printed by Mr. and Mrs. R. W. Noyes, 1930. 132 p.

—Supplement. Stonington, Noyes, 1934. 11 p.

MARYLAND. Minick, A. R. A history of printing in Maryland, 1791-1800; with a bibliography of works printed in the State during the period. [Mimeo.] Baltimore, Enoch Pratt Free Library, 1949. 618 p.

——Reichmann, Felix. German printing in Maryland; a check list, 1768-1950. (*In* Society for the History of the Germans in Maryland. 27th report. Baltimore, Md., 1950. p. 9-70)

——Wheeler, J. T. The Maryland press, 1777-1790. Baltimore, Maryland His. Soc., 1938. 226 p. illus.

——Wroth, L. C. A history of printing in colonial Maryland, 1686-1776. Baltimore, Typothetae of Baltimore, 1922. 275 p. illus.

—— ——The St. Mary's City press; a new chronology of American printing. (*In* The Colophon, n. s., v. 1, no. 3, 1936. p. 333-357)

MASSACHUSETTS. Ford, W. C. Broadsides, ballads, &c., printed in Massachusetts, 1639-1800. [Boston] Massachusetts Hist. Soc., 1922. 483 p. illus.

——Gilmore, Barbara. A Puritan town and its imprints, Northampton,

Mass., 1786–1845. Northampton, Hampshire Bookshop, 1942. 104 p.

——Littlefield, G. E. The early Massachusetts press, 1638–1711. Boston, Club of Odd Volumes, 1907. 2 v. illus.

——McKeon, N. F. and Cowles, K. C. Amherst, Massachusetts imprints, 1825–1876. Amherst, Amherst College Library, 1946. 191 p. illus.

——Paradise, S. H. A history of printing in Andover, Mass., 1798–1931. [Andover] Andover Press, 1931. [27] p. illus.

——Pottinger, D. T. Publishing and printing, 1880–1930. (*In* Boston. Tercentenary Committee. Fifty years of Boston. [Boston, 1932] p. 521–527. illus.)

——Tapley, H. S. Salem imprints, 1768–1825; a history of the first fifty years of printing in Salem, Massachusetts, with some account of the bookshops, booksellers, bookbinders and the private libraries. Salem, Essex Institute, 1927. 512 p. illus.

MICHIGAN. McMurtrie, D. C. Early printing in Michigan, with a bibliography of the issues of the Michigan press, 1796–1850. Chicago, John Calhoun Club, 1931. 351 p. illus.

MINNESOTA. Martin, M. R. History of printing in Minnesota to 1866; accompanied by a check list of Minnesota imprints. [1931]

Columbia University, School of Library Service, Master's Essay, 1931. Typewritten.

MISSISSIPPI. McMurtrie, D. C. Bibliography of Mississippi imprints, 1798–1830. Beauvoir Community, Miss., Book Farm, 1945. 168 p. illus. (Heartman's Hist. Ser. no. 69)

—— ——Preliminary check list of Mississippi imprints, 1798–1810. Chicago, 1934. 53 p.

NEBRASKA. Writers' program, Nebraska. Printing comes to Lincoln; written and compiled by workers of the Writers program, Works Projects Administration in the state of Nebraska. Sponsored by the Ben Franklin Club of Lincoln. Lincoln, Woodruff Pt. Co., 1940. 80 p.

NEW HAMPSHIRE. Nash, Ray. Pioneer printing at Dartmouth; with a checklist of Dresden imprints by H. G. Rugg. Hanover, George T. Bailey, 1941. 40 p. illus.

——Nichols, C. L. New Hampshire printing. (*In* Proceedings of the Amer. Antiquarian Soc., n. s., v. 25, pt. 2, Oct. 1915. p. 327–330)

NEW JERSEY. Hill, F. P. Books, pamphlets, and newspapers printed at Newark, New Jersey, 1776–1900. Priv. print. [Newark, Courier-Citizen Co.] 1902. 296 p.

——Nelson, William. Check list of the issues of the press of New Jersey, 1723, 1728, 1754–1800. Paterson, Call Printing and Pub. Co., 1899. 42 p

—— ——Some New Jersey printers and printing in the eighteenth century. Worcester, Mass., American Antiquarian Society, 1911. 44 p.

NEW MEXICO. Wagner, H. R. New Mexico Spanish press. (*In* New Mexico Historical Review, v. 12, 1937. p. 1–40. illus.)

NEW YORK. Eames, Wilberforce. The first year of printing in New York, May, 1693 to April, 1694. New York, New York Public Library, 1928. 25 p.

——Follett, Frederick. History of the press in western New-York from the beginning to the middle of the nineteenth century. New York, Reprinted for C. F. Heartman, 1920. 65 p. illus.

——Hamilton, M. W. The country printer, New York state, 1785–1830. New York, Columbia Univ. Press, 1936. 360 p. illus.

——Hildeburn, C. R. A list of the issues of the press in New York, 1693–1752. Phila., Lippincott, 1889. 28 p.

—— ——Sketches of printers and printing in colonial New York. New York, Dodd, Mead, 1895. 189 p. illus.

——Hufeland, Otto. The printing press in Westchester County, 1797–1860. (*In* Westchester County Hist. Soc. Bulletin, v. XIV, 1938. p. 33–46)

——McKay, G. L. A register of artists, engravers, booksellers, bookbinders, printers & publishers in New York City, 1633–1820. New York, New York Public Library, 1942. 78 p. illus.

——McMurtrie, D. C. Bibliography of books, pamphlets and broadsides printed at Auburn, N. Y., 1810–1850. Buffalo, N. Y., Grosvenor Library, 1938. 152 p. (Grosvenor Library Bulletin, v. 20, no. 4)

—— ——Bibliography of books, pamphlets and broadsides printed at Canandaigua, New York, 1799–1850. Buffalo, N. Y., Grosvenor Library Club, 1939. 107 p. (Grosvenor Library Bulletin, v. 21, no. 4)

—— ——, ed. New York printing MDCXCIII; facsimiles in full scale of the originals of all known New York imprints of that year; with an introd. note on the typography of Bradford's early work; with a bibliographical essay on the First year of printing in New York, by Wilberforce Eames. Chicago, John Calhoun Club, 1928. 30 p. illus.

NORTH CAROLINA. McMurtrie, D. C. Eighteenth century North Carolina imprints, 1749–1800. Chapel Hill, Univ. of North Carolina Press, 1938. 198 p. illus.

——Paschal, G. W. A history of printing in North Carolina; a detailed account of the pioneer printers, 1749–1800 and of the Edwards & Broughton Company, 1871–1946, Raleigh, Edwards & Broughton, 1946. 313 p. illus.

——Weeks, S. B. The press of North Carolina in the eighteenth century. Brooklyn, N. Y., Historical Printing Club, 1891. 80 p.

NORTH AND SOUTH DAKOTA. Allen, A. H. Dakota imprints, 1858–1889. New York, Pub. for the Bibl. Soc. of Amer. by R. R. Bowker, 1947. 221 p.

OHIO. McMurtrie, D. C. Pioneer printing in Ohio. Cincinnati, Printed by students of the Printing High School, 1943. 10 p.

——Shera, J. H. An eddy in the western flow of American culture; the history of printing and publishing in Oxford, Ohio, 1827–1841. (*In* Ohio State Archaeol. and Histo. Quarterly, v. 44, 1935. p. 103–137. illus.)

——Thwaites, R. G. The Ohio Valley press before the war of 1812–1815. Worcester, Mass., Davis Press, 1909. 62 p. illus.

——Wilkie, Florence. Early printing in Ohio, 1793–1820, with a check-list of Ohio imprints for that period. [1933] 137 numbered leaves.
Columbia University, School of Library Service, Master's Essay, 1933. Typewritten.

OKLAHOMA. Foreman, C. T. Oklahoma imprints, 1835–1907. Norman, Univ. of Okla. Press, 1936. 499 p. illus.

——Hargrett, Lester. Oklahoma Imprints, 1835–1890. New York, Pub. for the Bibl. Soc. of Amer. by R. R. Bowker, 1951. 267 p.

——Silver, R. G. Bibliographical notes; a preliminary check-list of nineteenth century Oklahoma book publishers. [1944] 7 p.

Reprinted from *The Chronicles of Oklahoma*, v. 22, Nov. 1, 1944.

OREGON. Powers, Alfred. Early printing in the Oregon country. [Portland] Portland (Oregon) Club of Printing House Craftsmen [1933] [16] p. illus.

PENNSYLVANIA. Bridenbaugh, Carl. The press and the book in eighteenth century Philadelphia. (The Pennsylvania Magazine of History and Biography, v. 65, no. 1, Jan. 1941. p. 1-30)

——Brown, H. G. and Brown, M. O. A directory of the book-arts and book trade in Philadelphia to 1820 including printers and engravers. New York, New York Public Library, 1950. [131] p.

—— ——Philadelphia contributions to the book arts and book trade, 1796–1810. (*In* Papers of the Bibl. Soc. of Amer., v. 37, 4th quar., 1943. p. 275-292)

——Hildeburn, C. R. A century of printing; the issues of the press in Pennsylvania, 1685-1784. Philadelphia [Matlock & Harvey] 1885-86. 2 v.

——Metzger, Ethel. Supplement to Hildeburn's Century of printing, 1685-1775. [1930] 126 l. illus.

——Lamech, Brother, d. 1763? Chronicon ephratense; a history of the community of Seventh Day Baptists at Ephrata, Lancaster County, Penn'a. ["Lamech and Agrippa."] Tr. from the original German by J. Max Hark. Lancaster, S. H. Zahm & Co., 1880. 288 p.

——McMurtrie, D. C. The first printers of York, Pennsylvania, including the text of some of the imprints of the York press during the early days of the Revolutionary War. York, Pa., Maple press co., 1940. 48 p.

——Sachse, J. F. The German Sectarians of Pennsylvania, 1708-1800; a critical and legendary history of the Ephrata cloister and the Dunkers. Philadelphia, Printed for the author, 1899-1900. 2v. illus.

——Shoemaker, A. L. A check list of imprints of the German press of Northampton County, Pennsylvania, 1766-1905, with biographies of the printers. Easton, Pa., 1943. 162 p. illus. (Pub. of the Northampton County Hist. and Genealogical Soc., v. IV)

——Thompson, D. W. Early publications of Carlisle, Pa., 1785-1835. Carlisle, The Sentinel, 1932. 133 p.

RHODE ISLAND. Alden, J. E. Rhode Island imprints, 1727-1800. New York, Pub. for the Bibl. Soc. of Amer. by R. R. Bowker, 1949. 665 p.

——Hammett, C. E. A contribution to the bibliography and literature of Newport, R. I. Newport, 1887. 185 p. illus.

——International Typographical Union of North America. Union no. 33, Providence. Printers and printing in Providence, 1762-1907. [Providence, 1908] 212, XCVIII p.

——Rhode Island imprints; a list of books, pamphlets, newspapers and broadsides printed at Newport, Providence, Warren, Rhode Island between 1727 and 1800. [By G. P. Winship, H. M. Chapin and Rebecca Steere] Providence, The Society, 1915. 88 p. illus.

——Wroth, L. C. The first press in Providence, a study in social development. (*In* Amer. Antiquarian Soc. Proceedings, v. 51, 1942. p. 351-383)

SOUTH CAROLINA. McMurtrie, D. C. The first decade of printing in the royal province of South Carolina. London, Bibliographical Society, 1933. [425]–452 p. illus.

——Salley, A. S. The first presses of South Carolina. (*In* Bibl. Soc. of Amer. Proceedings and papers, v. 2, 1907–08. p. 28–69)

TENNESSEE. McMurtrie, D. C. Early printing in Tennessee. Chicago, Chicago Club of Printing House Craftsmen, 1933. 141 p. illus.

——Sears, J. H. Tennessee printers, 1791–1945. Kingsport, Tenn., Priv. print. by the Kingsport Press, 1945. 47 p.

TEXAS. Winkler, E. W. Check list of Texas imprints, 1846–1860. Austin, Texas State Hist. Assoc., 1949. 352 p. illus.

UTAH. McMurtrie, D. C. The beginnings of printing in Utah. Chicago, John Calhoun Club, 1931. 91 p. illus.

—— ——Notes on early printing in Utah outside of Salt Lake City. Chicago, John Calhoun Club, 1938. 9 p.

VERMONT. Cooley, E. F. Vermont imprints before 1800; an introductory essay on the history of printing in Vermont with a list of imprints, 1779–1799. Montpelier, Vermont Hist. Soc., 1937. 133 p.

VIRGINIA. McMurtrie, D. C. The beginnings of printing in Virginia. Lexington [Journalism Laboratory of Washington and Lee University] 1935. 48 p. illus.

——Norfolk copyright entries, 1837, 1851–3, 1856–7, 1858–9, 1864, 1866–71. Registers of copyrights and copies of the court records for copyrights of the Federal District Court at Norfolk, Virginia, generally referred to as the Court of the Eastern District of Virginia. Transcribed by Barbara Harris, with some notes by John Wyllie. Mimeographed for the Bibliographical Society of the University of Virginia. Charlottesville, 1947. 48 p.

——Swem, E. G. A. bibliography of Virginia. Richmond, D. Bottom, Supt. of Pub. Print., 1916–32. v. 1–4.

——Virginia State Library. A trial bibliography of colonial Virginia. Special report of the Department of Bibliography, William Clayton-Torrence, bibliographer. Richmond, D. Bottom, Supt. of Pub. Print., 1908–10. 2 v. illus. (Virginia State Library, 5th–6th annual report)

—— ——Virginia imprint series. Richmond, Virginia State Library, 1946–

Preliminary checklists for Abingdon, Fredericksburg, and Petersburg are all that have appeared so far.

WASHINGTON. McMurtrie, D. C. A record of Washington imprints, 1853–1876, and some additional Washington imprints, 1853–1876. Seattle, Univ. of Washington Press [1943] 38 p. illus.

WISCONSIN. McMurtrie, D. C. Early printing in Wisconsin. Seattle, F. McCaffrey, 1931. 220 p. illus.

WYOMING. McMurtrie, D. C. Early printing in Wyoming and the Black Hills. Hattiesburg, Miss., Book Farm, 1943. 78 p. (Heartman's Hist. Ser. no. 67)

Individual Printing Houses, Printers and Designers

ADAMS, JAMES. Hawkins, D. L. James Adams, the first printer of Delaware. (*In* Papers of the Bibl. Soc. of Amer., v. 28, 1934, pt. 1. p. 28–63)

APPLEDORE PRESS. Bullen, A. H. The Appledore Private Press, U. S. A. [1889?] 7 p.

From *The Library,* London, v. 1, 1889.

ARMITAGE, MERLE. Notes on modern printing. New York, Rudge, 1945. 71 p. illus.

——Rendezvous with the book. Brooklyn, N. Y., Priv. print., George McKibbin, 1949. 30 p. illus. (McKibbin monograph ser. no. 3)

BORRENSTEIN, DAVID A. Miller, G. J. David A. Borrenstein, a printer and publisher at Princeton, N. J., 1824–28. (*In* Papers of the Bibl. Soc. of Amer., v. 30, pt. 1, 1936. p. 1–56)

BRADFORD. Bullen, H. L. The Bradford family of printers (Number 3 in series entitled Famous American printers) (*In* American Collector, Jan. and Feb., 1926. p. 148–156, 164–170)

BRADFORD, WILLIAM. Grolier Club. Catalogue of books printed by William Bradford and other printers in the Middle Colonies. Exhibited at the Grolier Club. [New York, 1893] 100 p. illus.

——Wallace, J. W. An address delivered at the celebration of the New York Historical Society, May 20, 1863, of the two hundredth birthday of Mr. William Bradford, who introduced the art of printing into the Middle Colonies of British America, Albany, J. Munsell, 1863. 14 p.

BRADLEY, WILL. Some examples of printing and drawing, the work of Will Bradley, issued in this wise as an advertisement by the University Press, at Cambridge, U. S. A. [1898] [65] p. illus.

BURSCH, FREDERICH C. Larremore, T. A. An American typographic tragedy: the imprints of Frederich Conrad Bursch. Pt. I. Through the literary collector periods. Pt. II. Hillacre Bookhouse. (*In* Papers of the Bibl. Soc. of Amer., v. 43, 1st–2nd quar., 1949. p. 1–38, 111–172)

CAMBRIDGE PRESS. Eames, Wilberforce. The Bay Psalm Book, being a facsimile reprint of the first edition printed by Stephen Daye at Cambridge in New England in 1640; with an introduction by Wilberforce Eames. New York, Dodd, Mead, 1903. 294 p.

——Eames, Wilberforce. Bibliographic notes on Eliot's Indian Bible and on his other translations and works in the Indian language of Massachusetts. Extract from a "Bibliography of the Algonquian languages." Washington, Govt. Print. Off., 1890. 58 p. illus.

——The Oath of a free-man. With a historical study by Lawrence C. Wroth, and A note on the Stephen Daye Press by Melbert B. Cary, jr. New York, Press of the Woolly Whale, 1939. 18 p.

——Roden, R. F. The Cambridge press, 1638–1692. A history of the first printing press established in English America, together with a bibliographical list of the issues of the press. New York, Dodd, Mead, 1905. 193 p. illus.

——The University press, Cambridge. Stephen Daye and his successors, the establishment of a printing plant in what was formerly British North America, and the development of the art of printing at the University press of Cambridge, Massachusetts, 1639–1691. Cambridge, 1921. 49 p.

——Winship, G. P. The Cambridge Press, 1638–1692, a re-examination of the evidence concerning the Bay Psalm Book and the Eliot Indian

Bible, as well as other contemporary books and people. Philadelphia, Univ. of Pennsylvania Press, 1945. 385 p. illus.

CHELTENHAM PRESS. The first ten years of the Cheltenham press; being an account of various problems in printing and in advertising and of their solution. New York, Cheltenham Press, 1908. 13 p.

CLELAND, THOMAS M. The decorative work of T. M. Cleland; a record and a review, with biographical and critical introduction by Alfred E. Hamill. New York, Pynson Printers, 1929. 99 p. illus.

——Updike, D. B. Thomas Maitland Cleland. (*In* Fleuron, no. 7, 1930. p. 133–142. illus.)

COLISH, A. McPharlin, Paul. The Press of A. Colish. (*In* American Printer, v. 124, no. 4, April, 1947. p. 42–46. illus)

COLLIER, THOMAS. Fisher, S. H. The publications of Thomas Collier, printer, 1784–1808. Litchfield, Litchfield Historical Society, 1933. 98 p. illus.

COOPER, O. B. Society of Typographic Arts. The book of OZ Cooper; an appreciation of Oswald Bruce Cooper, with characteristic examples of his art in lettering, type-designing & such of his writings as reveal the Cooperian typographic Gospel. Chicago, 1949. 181 p. illus.

CUBERY, WILLIAM. Fifty years a printer. San Francisco, Cubery & Co., 1900. 19 p.

DE VINNE PRESS. Catalogue of work of the De Vinne press. Exhibited at the Grolier Club. New York, Grolier Club, 1929. 89 p. illus.

——Hopkins, F. E. The De Vinne & Marion presses; a chapter from the autobiography of Frank E. Hopkins. Meriden, Columbiad Club, 1936. 61 p. **illus.**

——Theodore Low De Vinne, printer. New York, Priv. print., De Vinne Press, 1915. 111 p. illus.

DEXTER, GREGORY. Swan, B. F. Gregory Dexter of London and New England, 1610–1700. Rochester, Leo Hart, 1949. 115 p. illus.

DWIGGINS, W. A. Mss., by WAD; being a collection of the writings of Dwiggins on various subjects, some critical, some philosophical, some whimsical. New York, Typophiles, 1947. 152 p. illus.

——WAD; the work of W. A. Dwiggins, shown by the American Institute of Graphic Arts at the gallery of the Architectural League. New York, 1937. 39 p. illus.

——Hofer, Philip. The work of W. A. Dwiggins. (*In* The Dolphin, no. 2, 1935. p. 220–230. illus.)

——Hollister, P. M. Dwiggins; a characterization. Cambridge, Mass., 1929. [16] p. illus.

FORSTER, P. JOSEPH. McMurtrie, D. C. A note on P. Joseph Forster, pioneer Alabama printer. Hattiesburg, Miss., Book Farm, 1943. 12 p. illus. (Heartman's Hist. Ser., no. 68)

FOX, JUSTUS. Nichols, C. L. Justus Fox, a German printer of the eighteenth century. Worcester, Mass., American Antiquarian Society, 1915. p. 55–69.

FRANKLIN, ANN. Chapin, H. M. Ann Franklin of Newport, printer, 1736–1763. (*In* Bibliographical essays; a tribute to Wilberforce Eames. 1924. p. 337–344)

FRANKLIN, BENJAMIN. Account books kept by Benjamin Franklin. New

York [Columbia Univ. Press] 1928–29. 2 v.

——Curtis Publishing Company. The collection of Franklin imprints in the museum of the Curtis Publishing Company, with a short-title check list of all the books, pamphlets, broadsides, &c., known to have been printed by Benjamin Franklin, comp. by William J. Campbell. Philadelphia, 1918. 333 p. illus.

——Eddy, G. S. A. work-book of the printing house of Benjamin Franklin & David Hall, 1759–1766. New York, New York Public Library, 1930. 17 p. illus.

——Ford, P. L. Franklin bibliography; a list of books written by or relating to Benjamin Franklin. Brooklyn, N. Y., 1889. 467 p.

——Franklin Institute. Meet Dr. Franklin. Philadelphia, 1943. 234 p.

——Livingston, L. S. Franklin and his press at Passy. New York, Grolier Club, 1914. 216 p. illus.

——Oswald, J. C. Benjamin Franklin, printer. [Garden City, N. Y.] Doubleday, Page, 1917. 244 p. illus.

——Van Doren, Carl. Benjamin Franklin. New York, Viking Press, 1938. 845 p. illus.

Reprint 1948, World Pub. Co.

——The writings of Benjamin Franklin; collected and ed. with a life and introduction by Albert Henry Smyth. New York, Macmillan, 1905–07. 10 v. illus.

FRANKLIN, JAMES. Chapin, H. M. James Franklin, Jr., Newport printer. (*In* American Collector, v. 2, no. 3, June 1926. p. 325–329)

GAINE, HUGH. The journals of Hugh Gaine, ed. by Paul Leicester Ford.

New York, Dodd, Mead, 1902. 2 v. illus.

GARNETT, PORTER. A documentary account of the beginnings of the Laboratory Press, Carnegie Institute of Technology. Pittsburgh, Laboratory Press, 1927, 131 p. illus.

GILLISS, WALTER. Anderson, J. A. Walter Gilliss; some notes on the man and printer. (*In* PM, an intimate journal for production managers, v. 2, no. 2, July, 1936. p. 3–48)

——Gilliss, Walter. Recollections of the Gilliss press and its work during fifty years, 1869–1919. New York, Grolier Club, 1926. 134 p. illus.

—— ——The story of a motto and a mark; being a brief sketch of a few printers' "marks" and containing the facts concerning the mark of the Gilliss press. New York, Gilliss Press, 1902. 42 p. illus.

GOODHUE, BERTRAM GROSVENOR. Book decorations by Bertram Grosvenor Goodhue. New York, Grolier Club, 1931. [82] p. illus.

——Whitaker, C. H. Bertram Grosvenor Goodhue, architect and master of many arts; the text by Hartley Burr Alexander, Ralph Adams Cram, [etc., etc.] New York, Press of the American Institute of Architects, 1925. 50, CCLXXIII p. illus.

GOUDY, FREDERIC W. Cary, M. B. A bibliography of the Village Press; including an account of the genesis of the Press by Frederic W. Goudy and a portion of the 1903 diary of Will Ransom, co-founder. New York, Press of the Woolly Whale, 1938. 205 p. illus.

——Goudy, F. W. A half century of type design and typography, 1895–1945. New York, The Typophiles,

1946. 2 v. illus. (Typophile Chapbooks, XIII–XIV)

——Lewis, Barnard. Behind the type; the life story of Frederic W. Goudy. Pittsburgh, Carnegie Institute of Technology, 1941. 113 p. illus.

——Orton, Vrest. Goudy, master of letters. Chicago, Black Cat Press, 1939. 101 p. illus.

——Spinach from many gardens; gathered by the Typophiles and fed to Frederic W. Goudy on his seventieth anniversary, 1935. [New York, 1935] [160] p. illus.

GOVERNMENT PRINTING OFFICE. Kerr, R. W. History of the Government printing office (at Washington, D. C.) with a brief record of the public printing for a century, 1789–1881. Lancaster, Pa., Inquirer Printing and Pub. Co., 1881. 196 p. illus.

——Larson, Cedric. Uncle Sam: printer, publisher and literary sponsor. (*In* The Colophon, n.g.s., v. 1, no. 1, 1939. p. [75–90])

——Schmeckebier, L. F. The Bureau of engraving and printing; its history, activities and organization. Baltimore, Johns Hopkins Press, 1929. 111 p.

—— ——The Government printing office; its history, activities and organization. Baltimore, Johns Hopkins Press, 1925. 143 p.

GRABHORN PRESS. Heller, E. R. and Magee, D. Bibliography of the Grabhorn Press, 1915–1940. San Francisco, Grabhorn Press, 1940. 193 p. illus.

HARRIS, BENJAMIN. Monaghan, Frank. Benjamin Harris, printer, bookseller, and the first American journalist. (*In* The Colophon, pt. 12, 1932. [8] p.)

HASWELL, ANTHONY. Spargo, John. Anthony Haswell, printer-patriot-ballader. Rutland, Vt., Tuttle Co., 1925. 293 p. illus.

HOLT, JOHN. Paltsits, V. H. John Holt, printer and postmaster. New York, New York Public Library, 1920. 19 p.

HUBBARD, ELBERT. Balch, D. A. Elbert Hubbard, genius of Roycroft. New York, Stokes, 1940. 320 p. illus.

——Shay, Felix. Elbert Hubbard of East Aurora. New York, W. H. Wise & Co., 1926. 553 p. illus.

IDE, SIMEON. Flanders, L. W. Simeon Ide, yeoman, freeman, pioneer printer. Rutland, Vt., Tuttle Co., 1931. 347 p. illus.

IMPERIAL PRESS. French, George. The Imperial press, a critique. Cleveland [Cleveland Printing and Pub. Co.] 1902. 32 p. illus.

LOUDON, SAMUEL. Wall, A. J. Samuel Loudon (1727–1813) merchant, printer and patriot, with some of his letters. [New York, 1922] p. 75–92. illus.

Reprinted from *Quarterly Bulletin of the New York Historical Society*, October, 1922.

MABCHBANKS PRESS. Choice books, some printed and some published, and some printed only, by the Marchbanks press. New York [193–?] [11] p.

——Emily Connor and the Marchbanks Press; a signature from "Print," September 1949. 15 p.

MARION PRESS. Larremore, T. A. The Marion Press; a survey and a checklist. Jamaica, N. Y., Queensborough Public Library, 1943. 270 p. illus.

——The Marionette, a journal of information concerning the Marion

Press. No. 1–5, Sept. 1908–July 1916. Jamaica, 1908–1916.

MEEKER, JOTHAM. McMurtrie, D. C. and Allen, H. Jotham Meeker, pioneer printer of Kansas, with a bibliography of the known issues of the Baptist Mission Press at Shawanoe, Stockbridge, and Ottawa, 1834–1854. Chicago, Eyncourt Press, 1930. 169 p. illus.

MUNSELL, JOEL. Bibliotheca Munselliana; a catalogue of the books and pamphlets issued from the press of Joel Munsell from 1828–1870. Albany, Priv. print., 1872. 191 p.

——Edelstein, D. S. Joel Munsell. New York, Columbia Univ. Press, 1950. 420 p.

—— —— Joel Munsell: printer and bibliographer. (*In* Papers of the Bibl. Soc. of Amer., v. 43, 4th quar., 1949. p. 383–396)

——Munsell, Joel. The typographical miscellany. Albany, J. Munsell, 1850. 267 p. illus.

PARKS, WILLIAM. Wroth, L. C. William Parks, printer and journalist of England and colonial America; with a list of the issues of his several presses and a facsimile of the earliest Virginia imprint known to be in existence. Richmond, William Parks Club, 1926. 70 p. illus.

RIVINGTON, JAMES. Sargent, G. H. James Rivington, Tory printer; a study of the Loyalist pamphlets of the Revolution. (*In* American Collector, v. 2, no. 3, June, 1926. p. 336–338)

ROGERS, BRUCE. American Institute of Graphic Arts. The work of Bruce Rogers, jack of all trades: master of one; a catalogue of an exhibition arranged by the American Institute of Graphic Arts and the Grolier Club of New York, with an intro- duction by D. B. Updike, a letter from John T. McCutcheon and an address by Mr. Rogers. New York, Oxford University Press, 1939. 127 p. illus.

——Haas, Irvin. Bruce Rogers: a bibliography. Mount Vernon, N. Y., Peter Pauper Press, 1936. 72 p.

——Hepburn, W. M. Notes on Bruce Rogers of Indiana. 1945. 11 p. illus.

From the *Indiana Quarterly for bookmen,* July 1945.

——[Lawrence, T. E.] Letters from T. E. Shaw to Bruce Rogers. [Mount Vernon, N. Y., William Edwin Rudge, 1933] [84] p.

—— ——More letters from T. E. Shaw to Bruce Rogers. [New York, Priv. print., 1936] [32] p.

——Pollard, A. W. Modern fine printing in England and Mr. Bruce Rogers; with a list of books and other pieces designed by Mr. Rogers. Newark, N. J., Carteret Book Club, 1916. 36 p.

——Rogers, Bruce. Paragraphs on printing; elicited [from the author] in talks with James Hendrickson on the function of the book designer. New York, Rudge, 1943. 187 p. illus.

——Rollins, C. P. B. R., America's typographical playboy. New York, Richard W. Ellis, Georgian Press, 1927. 13 p. illus.

——Barnacles from many bottoms, scraped and gathered for B. R. by the Typophiles. [New York, The Typophiles] 1935 [200] p.

——Typophiles. BR marks and remarks; the marks by Bruce Rogers, et al, the remarks by his friends. New York, The Typophiles, 1946. 149 p. (Typophile Chap Book, 15)

——Warde, Frederic. Bruce Rogers, designer of books. Cambridge, Harvard Univ. Press, 1925. 74 p. illus.

——The work of Bruce Rogers. A catalog. Introduction by D. B. Updike, a letter from John P. McCutcheon and an address by Bruce Rogers. New York, Oxford Univ. Press, 1939. 160 p. illus.

ROLLINS, CARL P. Dartmouth College. Retrospective exhibition; a half century of work and play with type. Carl Purington Rollins, Printer to Yale University. Arranged by members of the class in Graphic Arts and displayed in the Baker Library, Nov. 19th through Dec. 10th 1947. 20 p.

The Preface, by Bruce Rogers, was reprinted by the American Institute of Graphic Arts in a catalogue of an exhibition at the Grolier Club, April 27, 1949.

——Rollins, C. P. Off the dead bank; addresses, reviews and verses. New York, The Typophiles, 1949. (Chapbooks, no. 19) 139 p.

SAUER, CHRISTOPH. Mori, Gustav. Der Buchdrucker Christoph Sauer in Germantown; ein Beitrag zur Geschichte des Buchdruckes in den Vereinigten Staaten von Nordamerika. 1934. p. 224–230.

Reprinted from *Gutenberg-Jahrbuch,* 1934.

——Reichmann, Felix. Christopher Sower sr., 1694–1758, printer in Germantown. An annotated bibliography. Philadelphia, Carl Schurz Memorial Foundation, 1943. 78 p. (Carl Schurz memorial foundation. Bibliographies on German American History. no. 2)

SHORT, THOMAS. Love, W. De L. Thomas Short, the first printer of Connecticut. [Hartford, Case, Lockwood & Brainard Co.] 1901. 48 p.

SOUTHWORTH-ANTHOENSEN PRESS. Anthoensen, Fred. Types and bookmaking; containing notes on the books printed at the Southworth-Anthoensen Press. Portland, Me., Southworth-Anthoensen Press, 1943. 170 p. illus.

THOMAS, ISAIAH. The Isaiah Thomas papers—a manuscript collection in the library of the American Antiquarian Society in Worcester, Mass.

——The diary of Isaiah Thomas, 1805–1828. Ed. with an introduction and notes by Benjamin Thomas Hill. Worcester, Mass., The Society, 1909. 2 v. illus.

——Marble, A. R. From 'prentice to patron'; the life story of Isaiah Thomas. New York, D. Appleton-Century, 1935. 326 p.

——Nichols, C. L. Isaiah Thomas, printer, writer & collector; a paper read April 12, 1911, before the Club of Odd Volumes. Boston, Club of Odd Volumes, 1912. 144 p.

——Shipton, C. K. Isaiah Thomas, printer, patriot and philanthropist, 1749–1831. Rochester, N. Y., Leo Hart, 1948. 94 p. illus.

TROVILLION PRESS. Schauinger, Herman. A bibliography of Trovillion Private Press, operated by Violet & Hal W. Trovillion at the Sign of the Silver Horse. Herrin, Ill., Trovillion Private Press, 1943. 49 p. illus.

TYPOPHILES. Fulton, Deoch. The Typophiles. (*In* The New Colophon, v. 2, Part 6, June 1949. p. 143–162. illus.)

——McPharlin, Paul. The Typophiles: their sallies into book making. (*In* Publishers' Weekly, v. 146, no. 19, 23, Nov. 4, Dec. 2, 1944. p. 1855–1857, 2167–2170. illus.)

——Standard, Paul. The Typophiles of New York. (*In* Penrose Annual, v. 41, 1939. p. 32–36. illus.)

UPDIKE, D. B. Dwiggins, W. A. D. B. Updike and the Merrymount press. (*In* The Fleuron, no. 3. 1924. p. 1–8. illus.)

——Updike, D. B. In the day's work. Cambridge, Harvard Univ. Press, 1924. 69 p.

—— ——Notes on the Merrymount press & its work. Cambridge, Harvard Univ. Press, 1934. 279 p. illus.

——Updike: American printer and his Merrymount Press. [Edited by Peter Beilenson] New York, Amer. Inst. of Graphic Arts, 1947. 156 p. illus.

——Winship, G. P. Daniel Berkeley Updike and the Merrymount Press of Boston, Massachusetts, 1860, 1894, 1941. Rochester, N. Y., Leo Hart, 1947. 141 p. illus.

—— ——The Merrymount press of Boston; an account of the work of Daniel Berkeley Updike. Vienna, H. Reichner, 1929. 45 p. illus.

USTICK, STEPHEN C. Gaskill, N. B. Imprints from the press of Stephen C. Ustick, with its several locations, together with some items which were published, but not printed by him, 1794–1836. Washington, D. C. [Menasha, Wis., George Banta Pub. Co.] 1940. 93 p. illus.

WILLIAMS, WILLIAM. Williams, J. C. An Oneida County printer, William Williams, printer, publisher, editor; with a bibliography of the press at Utica, Oneida County, New York, from 1803–1838. New York, Scribner's, 1906. 211 p. illus.

ZAMORANO, DON AGUSTIN. Harding, G. L. Don Agustin V. Zamorano, statesman, soldier, craftsman, and California's first printer. Los Angeles, Zamorano Club, 1934. 308 p. illus.

ZENGER, JOHN. Heartman, C. F. Charles F. Heartman presents John Peter Zenger and his fight for the freedom of the American press. Highland Park, N. J., H. B. Weiss, 1934. 60 p. illus.

——Rutherford, Livingston. John Peter Zenger, his press, his trial, and a bibliography of Zenger imprints. New York, Dodd, Mead, 1904. 275 p. Reprinted 1941, Peter Smith, New York.

Modern Fine Printing

AMERICAN INSTITUTE OF GRAPHIC ARTS. Fifty books of the year; an [annual] exhibition of American bookmaking, selected and shown by the Amer. Inst. of Graphic Arts. 1924– New York, 1924–

The Annual of Bookmaking. 1927–1937. New York, The Colophon, 1938. [326] p. illus.

DWIGGINS, W. A. and SIEGFRIED, L. B. Extracts from an investigation into the physical properties of books as they are at present published; undertaken by the Society of Calligraphers. Boston, Pub. for the Society by W. A. Dwiggins and L. B. Siegfried, 1919. [20] p.

GALLATIN, A. E. Modern fine printing in America. New York, Priv. print., 1921. 16 p.

GRANNISS, R. S. Modern fine printing. (*In* A history of the printed book, being the third number of The Dolphin, 1938. p. 269–293)

Graphic forms; the arts as related to the book [by: Gyorgy Kepes and others]. Cambridge, Mass., Harvard Univ. Press, 1949. 128 p. illus.

HAAS, IRVIN. A bibliography of material relating to private presses. Chicago, Black Cat Press, 1937. 57 p.

——Bibliography of modern American presses. Chicago, Black Cat Press, 1935. 95 p.

JOHNSTON, PAUL. Biblio-typographica; a survey of contemporary fine printing styles. New York, Covici-Friede, 1930. 303 p. illus.

LEWIS, OSCAR. The California school of printing. (*In* The Colophon, pt. 3, August, 1930. [8] p.)

MORISON, STANLEY. Modern fine printing; an exhibit of printing issued in England, the United States of America, France, Germany, Italy, Switzerland, Czecho-Slovakia, Holland and Sweden during the twentieth century and with few exceptions since the outbreak of the war. London, E. Benn, 1925. [152] p. illus.

RANSOM, WILL. Private presses and their books. New York, Bowker, 1929. 493 p. illus.

——Selective check lists of press books; a compilation of all important & significant private presses or press books which are collected. New York, Duschnes, 1945–49. Pts. 1–10.

ROLLINS, C. P. The United States of America. (A survey of the making of books in recent years) (*In* The Dolphin, no. 1, 1933. p. 288–301. illus.)

——The United States of America (A survey of contemporary bookmaking) (*In* The Dolphin, no. 2, 1935. p. 259–268. illus.)

SIMON, OLIVER, and RODENBERG, JULIUS. Printing of to-day, an illustrated survey of post-war typography in Europe and the United States. New York, Harper, 1928. 83, [76] p. illus. "Printing in the United States by Paul Beaujon": p. 51–[70]

WARDE, B. L. B. On decorative printing in America. (*In* The Fleuron, no. 6, 1928. p. 69–93. illus.)

Who's who. (*In* Peter Piper's practical principles of plain and perfect pronunciation. Brooklyn, Mergenthaler Linotype Co., 1936. p. 77–97) This list of the contributors to the volume, with biographical information, is a valuable Who's Who of a number of the best modern American typographers, printers and illustrators.

History of Newspaper and Magazine Printing

American newspapers, 1821–1936; a union list of files available in the United States and Canada; ed. by Winifred Gregory under the auspices of the Bibl. Soc. of Amer. New York, H. W. Wilson, 1937. 791 p.

AYER, FIRM, PHILADELPHIA. N. W. Ayer and son's Directory of Newspapers and Periodicals. 1881– Philadelphia, 1881–

BEER, WILLIAM. Checklist of American periodicals, 1741–1800. Worcester, Mass., American Antiquarian Society, 1923. 18 p.

BRIGHAM, C. S. History and bibliography of American newspapers, 1690–1820. Worcester, Mass., Amer. Antiquarian Soc., 1947. 2 v.

FLANDERS, B. H. Early Georgia magazines; literary periodicals to 1865. Atlanta, Univ. of Georgia, 1944. 289 p.

HOFFMAN, F. J. The little magazine; a history and a bibliography, by F. J. Hoffman, Charles Allen and C. F. Ulrich. 2d ed. Princeton, Princeton Univ. Press, 1947. 450 p.

KOBRE, SIDNEY. The development of the Colonial newspaper. Pittsburgh, Pa., Colonial Press, 1944. 188 p.

MOTT, F. L. American journalism; a history of newspapers in the United States, through 250 years, 1690–1940. New York, Macmillan, 1941. 772 p.

——A history of American magazines. New York, Appleton, 1930–1938. v. 1–3.

3 volumes pub. so far.
Imprint of v. *2–3*: Cambridge, Mass., Harvard Univ. Press.
v. 1, 1741–1850; v. 2, 1850–1865; v. 3, 1865–1885.

NORTH, S. N. D. History and present condition of the newspaper and periodical press of the United States, with a catalogue of the publications of the census year. Washington, Govt. Print. Off., 1884. 446 p. illus.

RICHARDSON, L. N. A history of early American magazines, 1741–1789. New York, T. Nelson, 1931. 414 p.

WINSHIP, G. P. French newspapers in the United States from 1790 to 1800. (*In* Papers of the Bibl. Soc. of Amer., v. 14, pt. 2, 1920. p. 82–91)

Economics and Organization in the Printing Trade

BAKER, E. F. Displacement of men by machines; effects of technological change in commercial printing. New York, Columbia Univ. Press, 1933. 284 p. illus.

BROWN, E. C. Book and job printing in Chicago. Chicago, Univ. of Chicago Press, 1931. 363 p.

GUSTAFSON, DAVID. Who's who in printing in the United States and Canada. Published by the author, 1933–35. 3 pts. (American Printing Industry Bulletin, nos. 3–5)

STEVENS, G. A. New York typographical union, no. 6; study of a modern trade union and its predecessors. Albany, J. B. Lyon, 1913. 717 p. illus.

STEWART, ETHELBERT. A documentary history of the early organizations of printers. Indianapolis, Ind., International Typographical Union, 1907. 194 p.

UNITED TYPOTHETAE OF AMERICA. Practical apprenticeship for printers; suggestions concerning the training of apprentices for the printing crafts. Chicago, 1921. 149 p. illus.

Printing Manuals

WROTH, L. C. Corpus typographicum; a review of English and American printers' manuals. (*In* The Dolphin, no. 2, 1935. p. 157–170)

England

The English handbooks are important for an understanding of early American printing.

1683. MOXON, JOSEPH. Moxon's Mechanick Exercises; or, The doctrine of handyworks applied to the art of printing. A literal reprint in two volumes of the first edition, published in the year 1683, with preface and notes by Theo. L. De Vinne. New York, Typothetae of the City of New York, 1896. 2 v. illus.

Originally issued in 24 numbers, forming the second volume of the Mechanick Exercises.

1755. SMITH, JOHN. The printer's grammar: wherein are exhibited, examined and explained, the superficies, gradation, and properties of . . . metal types . . . and many other requisites for obtaining a more perfect knowledge of the art of printing. London, Printed for the editor and sold by W. Owen, 1755. 312 p.

1771. LUCKOMBE, PHILIP. The history and art of printing. London, Pt. by W. Adlard and J. Browne for J. Johnson, 1771. 502 p.

A reissue with new title-page of the work pub. anonymously in 1770 under title, "A concise history of the origin and progress of printing."

1808. STOWER, CHARLES. The printer's grammar; or, Introduction to the art of printing: containing a concise history of the art, with the improvements in the practice of printing, for the last fifty years. London, Print. by the editor for B. Crosby and Co., 1808. 530 p. illus.

1824. JOHNSON, JOHN. Typographia; or, The printers' instructor. London, Longman, Hurst, Rees, Orme, Brown, & Green, 1824. 2 v. illus.

1825. HANSARD, T. C. Typographia; an historical sketch of the origin and progress of the art of printing. London, Baldwin, Cradock, and Joy, 1825. 939 p. illus.

United States

1818. VAN WINKLE, C. S. Printers' guide; or, An introduction to the art of printing, including an essay on punctuation and remarks on orthography. New York, Printed and pub. by C. S. Van Winkle, 1818. 229 p.

2d ed., 1827; 3d ed., 1836.

1837. ADAMS, T. F. Typographia; a brief sketch of the origin, rise and progress of the typographic art; with practical directions for conducting every department in an office. Philadelphia, The Compiler, 1837. 372 p. illus.

2d ed., 1844; later eds., 1845, 1851, 1856.

1866. MACKELLAR, THOMAS. The American printer. Philadelphia, Mackellar, Smiths & Jordan, 1866.

Some 18 eds. of this handbook appeared by 1893.

1870. HARPEL, O. H. Harpel's typograph; or, Book of specimens containing useful information, suggestions and a collection of examples of letterpress job printing. Cincinnati, The author, 1870. 252 p. illus.

1889. BISHOP, H. G. The practical printer; a book of instruction for beginners; a book of reference for the more advanced. Albany, Bishop, 1889. 183 p. illus.

2d ed., 1891; 3d ed., 1895; 4th ed., 1903; 5th ed., 1906.

1900. DE VINNE, T. L. The practice of typography. New York, Century Co., 1900–04. 4 v. illus.

1905. AMERICAN PRINTER. American manual of typography; an exhaustive exposition of the various phases of type-composition; a text-book for the ambitious typographer; a guide and reference volume for the layout man, foreman, superintendent and employing printer. New York, Oswald Pub. Co., 1905. 104 p. illus.

Appeared originally in the *American Printer* as lessons in the American School of Typography. The preparation of the lessons was jointly the work of A. F. Mackay, G. French, F. F. Helmer, L. L. Crittenden and E. G. Gress. Mr. Gress planned the general arrangement.

1906. HITCHCOCK, F. H. The building of a book; a series of practical articles written by experts in the various departments of book making and distributing. New York, Grafton Press [1906] 375 p.

2d ed., 1929.

1907. GRESS, E. G. The American handbook of printing, containing in brief and simple style something about every department of the art and business of printing. New York, Oswald Pub. Co., 1907. 284 p. illus.

2d ed., 1909; 3d ed., 1913.

1932. STERN, P. V. An introduction to typography. New York, Harper, 1932. 214 p. illus.

1945. MYRICK, F. B. A primer in book production. New York, Bookbinding and Book Production, 1945. 95 p.

1949. MELCHER, DANIEL and LARRICK, NANCY. Printing and production handbook; how to plan, produce and use printing, advertising and direct mail. New York, McGraw Hill, 1949. 386 p. illus.

United Typothetae of America, Department of Education, has published a wide series of practical handbooks. A list of them is available under the title: Typothetae books on printing and related subjects. Typothetae Educational Bulletin, no. 5.

Printing Presses

BAKER, DANIEL. Platen printing presses; a primer of information regarding the history and mechanical construction of platen printing presses, from the original hand press to the modern job press, to which is added a chapter on automatic presses of small size. [Chicago] Pub. by the Committee on Education, United Typothetae of America, 1918. 42 p. illus.

GREEN, RALPH. The iron hand press in America; with illus. by Robert Galvin after drawings by Ralph Green. Rowayton, Conn., 1948. 39 p. illus.

HAMILTON, M. W. Adam Ramage and his presses. Portland, Me., Southworth-Anthoensen Press, 1942. 35 p. illus. (Keepsake no. 15)

HOE, ROBERT. A short history of the printing press and of the improvements in printing machinery from the time of Gutenberg up to the present day. New York, R. Hoe, 1902. 89 p. illus.

OSWALD PUBLISHING COMPANY. The American manual of presswork. New York, 1911. 155 p. illus.

2d ed., 1916.

Types and Typefounding

ANTHOENSEN, FRED. John Bell type; its loss and rediscovery; with a type-facsimile of John Bell's first type specimen, 1788. Portland, Me., Southworth-Anthoensen Press, 1939. 20 p. illus. (Keepsake no. 8)

BINNY & RONALDSON. The specimen books of Binny and Ronaldson, 1809–1812, in facsimile. [New Haven] Columbiad Club, 1936. 15, [26, 43] p.

BRUCE, DAVID. The history of typefounding in the United States; published from the unpublished manuscript dated November 1874, preserved in the Typographic Library and Museum, Jersey City, with an introduction by Douglas C. McMurtrie. New York, Priv. print., 1925. 38 p.

DWIGGINS, W. A. WAD to RR; a letter about designing type. Cambridge, Mass., Harvard College Library, Dept. of Printing and Graphic Arts, 1940. 14 p. illus.

GOUDY, F. W. The alphabet and Elements of lettering; rev. and enl., with many full-page plates and other illustrations drawn by the author. Berkeley, Univ. of California Press, 1942. 101 p. illus.

——On designing a type face. (*In* The Dolphin, no. 1, 1933. p. 3–23. illus.)

HAMILTON, F. W. Type and presses in America; a brief historical sketch of the development of type-casting and press building in the United States. Chicago, United Typothetae of America, 1918. 43 p.

LEGROS, L. A. and GRANT, J. C. Typographical printing-surfaces; the technology and mechanism of their production. New York, Longmans, Green, 1916. 732 p. illus.

MACKELLAR, SMITHS and JORDAN. 1796–1896. One hundred years. Mackellar, Smiths and Jordan Foundry,

Philadelphia, Pa. [Philadelphia, 1896] 96 p. illus.

MIDDLETON, R. H. Chicago letter founding. Chicago, Black Cat Press, 1937. 27 p.

——Making printers' typefaces. Chicago, Black Cat Press, 1938. 35, [19] p. illus.

DONNELLEY & SONS, R. R. American type designers and their work, prepared on the occasion of an exhibition at the Lakeside Press Galleries, R. R. Donnelley & Sons Company, Chicago, Ill., 1947–1948. [Chicago, 1948]

The American Institute of Graphic Arts, who brought this exhibition to New York later in 1948, issued a catalogue "American type designers and their type faces on exhibit, Sept. 29 to Oct. 30, 1948," which covers the same material.

THOMPSON, J. S. History of composing machines, a complete record of the art of composing type by machinery; also lists of patents on composing machines, American and British, chronologically arranged. Chicago, Inland Printer, 1904. 200 p.

UPDIKE, D. B. Printing types; their history, forms and use; a study in survivals. 2d ed. Cambridge, Harvard Univ. Press, 1937. 2 v. illus.

WROTH, L. C. Abel Buell of Connecticut, silversmith, type founder & engraver. [New Haven, Yale University Press] 1926. 86 p.

——The first work with American types. Cambridge, Mass., Harvard Univ. Press, 1925. 16 p. illus.

Reprinted from *Bibliographical essays; a tribute to Wilberforce Eames.*

——The origins of typefounding in North and South America. (*In* Ars typographica, v. 2, no. 4, April, 1926. p. 273–307)

Papermaking

BLAKE, MOFFITT & TOWNE. Pioneers in paper; the story of Blake, Moffitt & Towne. [San Francisco, 1930] 49 p. illus.

BLUM, ANDRÉ. On the origin of paper; tr. from the French by Harry Miller Lydenberg. New York, Bowker, 1934. 79 p. illus.

GEYER'S AMERICAN PAPER TRADE DIRECTORY, containing a complete list of all paper, fiber and wood pulp mills in the United States and Canada. v. 1, 18–? New York, 18–?

Title changed: 1885, *Geyer's Directory of the American Paper Trade.*
1886–1891, *Geyer's Reference Directory of the Booksellers and Stationers of the United States and Canada.*
1893, *Geyer's Directory of the American Paper Trade.*
1894– *Geyer's American Paper Trade Directory.*

GOOLD, WILLIAM. Early papermills of New England. Read at a meeting of the Maine Historical Society, Feb. 19, 1874. [Boston, 1875] 8 p.

HUNTER, DARD. The literature of papermaking, 1390–1800. Chillicothe, Ohio, 1925. 48 p.

——Paper making; the history and technique of an ancient craft. 2d ed. rev. and enl. New York, Knopf, 1947. 611 p. illus.

——Romance of water-marks by Dard Hunter, and a biographical sketch of the author. Cincinnati, Stratford Press, [1939?] 34 p.

HURLBUT'S PAPERMAKER GENTLEMAN. Jan. 1933–1935. South Lee, Mass., Hurlbut Paper Co., 1933–1935. v. 1–3.

JONES, H. G. Historical sketch of the Rittenhouse paper-mill. (*In* Pennsylvania Magazine of History and Biography, v. 20, 1896. p. 315-333)

LOCKWOOD's directory of the paper and allied trades. 1873- New York, 1873-

LOCKWOOD TRADE JOURNAL CO. 1690-1940, 250 years of papermaking in America. New York, 1940. 180 p. illus.

MUNSELL, J. A. A chronology of paper and papermaking. Albany, 1856. 58 p.

Five editions, under slightly varying titles, appeared by 1876.

Paper Trade Journal. v. 1, 1872- New York, Lockwood Trade Journal Co., 1872- Weekly.

The Paper World, a monthly journal of information, discussion and recital as to paper. v. 1-36, Jan. 1880-1898. Holyoke, Mass. [Paper World] 1880-1898.

STEVENSON, L. T. The background and economics of American papermaking. New York, Harper, 1940. 249 p. illus.

WEEKS, L. H. A history of paper-manufacturing in the United States, 1690-1916. New York, Lockwood Trade Journal Co., 1916. 352 p.

WEST, C. J. Bibliography of paper making and United States patents on paper making and related subjects, 1931-1933. New York, Technical Association of the Pulp and Paper Industry, 1932-34. 3 v.

——Bibliography of pulp and paper making. 1900/1928- New York, Pub. for Technical Assoc. of the Pulp and Paper Industry by Lockwood Trade Journal Co., 1928-

The first two volumes cover years 1900-1928 and 1928-1935 respectively. Issued annually from 1936.

WHEELWRIGHT, W. B. Printing papers. Chicago, Univ. of Chicago Press, 1936. 133 p. illus.

Bookbinding

ANDREWS, W. L. Bibliopegy in the United States and kindred subjects. New York, Dodd, Mead, 1902. 128 p. illus.

COLUMBIA UNIVERSITY LIBRARIES. Modern bookbinding; new design in an old craft. An international exhibition. [New York, Columbia University Library, 1935] 16 p.

DIEHL, EDITH. Bookbinding; its background and technique. New York, Rinehart, 1946. 2 v.

GROLIER CLUB. Catalogue of ornamental leather bookbindings executed in America prior to 1850. Exhibited at the Grolier Club. [New York, 1907] 106 p.

——An exhibition of some of the latest artistic bindings done at the Club bindery. New York, Grolier Club, 1906. 47 p.

HOLMES, T. J. The bookbindings of John Ratcliff and Edmund Ranger, seventeenth century Boston bookbinders. Worcester, Mass., American Antiquarian Society, 1929. 22 p. illus.

——Additional notes on Ratcliff and Ranger bindings. (*In* Proceedings of the American Antiquarian Society, October, 1929. p. 291-306. illus.)

LEHMANN-HAUPT, HELLMUT, ed. Bookbinding in America; three essays: Early American bookbinding by hand, by H. D. French; The rise of American edition binding, by J. W. Rogers; On the rebinding of old books, by Hellmut Lehmann-Haupt. Portland, Me., Southworth-Anthoensen Press, 1941. 293 p. illus.

POOR, H. W. American bookbindings in the library of Henry William Poor, described by Henri Pène du Bois.

New York, G. D. Smith, 1903. 77 p. illus.

SAUTY, ALFRED DE. Einbandkunst in den Vereinigten Staaten von Amerika. (*In* Jahrbuch der Einbandkunst. 2. Jahrg., 1928. p. 178–179. illus.)

STRANGE, E. F. American bookbindings. (*In* Modern bookbindings & their designers. (Special winter number of The Studio 1899/1900) p. 47–57. illus.)

TROW PRESS. Bib-li-op-e-gis-tic, to which is appended a glossary of some terms, used in the craft with illustrations of fine bindings. New York, Trow Press [191–] 32 p. illus.

An extensive group of articles, particularly on American library binding and on the organization of the trade is listed in Mejer's *Bibliographie der Buchbinderei-literatur*, Leipzig, Hiersemann, 1925; *Ergänzungsband*, 1924–1932.

BOOK ILLUSTRATION

General Works

American Institute of Graphic Arts. Annual exhibition, American book illustration. 1st–3d. 1926–1928; 4th. 1933; 5th. 1935.

BOLTON, THEODORE. American book illustrators; bibliographic check lists of 123 artists. New York, Bowker, 1938, 290 p.

DARTON, F. T. Modern book illustration in Great Britain and America. New York, Rudge, 1931. 144 p. illus.

DUNLAP, WILLIAM. A history of the rise and progress of the arts of design in the United States. New ed., illustrated, edited, with additions by F. W. Bayley and C. E. Goodspeed. Boston, C. E. Goodspeed & Co., 1918. 3 v.

HAMILTON, SINCLAIR. Early American book illustration (*In* Princeton University Library Chronicle, v. 6, no. 3, Apr. 1945. p. 101–126. illus)

HOWARD, H. C. Trends in the illustration of American children's books, 1770–1860. [1942] 125 l.
Columbia University, School of Library Service, Master's Essay, 1942. Typewritten.

LINTON, W. J. The history of wood-engraving in America. Boston, Estes & Lauriat, 1882. 71 p.

MAHONY, B. E., COMP. Illustrators of children's books, 1744–1945. Boston, Horn Book, 1947. 527 p. illus.

MATHER, F. J. A collection of early American illustrated books. (*In* Princeton University Library Chronicle, v. 6, no. 3, Apr. 1945. p. 99–126)

MERRILL, H. C. Wood-engraving and wood-engravers. Boston, Society of Printers, 1937.

MURRELL, WILLIAM. History of American graphic humor. New York, Whitney Museum of American Art, 1933–38. 2 v. illus.

MUSEUM OF MODERN ART. Modern painters and sculptors as illustrators. 3d ed. rev. New York, 1947. 119 p.

PITZ, H. C. A treasury of American book illustration. New York, American Studio Books and Watson-Guptill Pub., 1947. 128 p. illus.

SMITH, F. H. American illustrators. New York, Scribner, 1892. 68 p. illus.

WATSON, E. W. Forty illustrators and how they work. New York, Watson-Guptill, 1946. 318 p.

WEITENKAMPF, FRANK. American graphic art. New ed. rev. and enl. New York, Macmillan, 1924. 328 p. illus.

——Illustrated book. Cambridge, Harvard University Press, 1938. 314 p. illus.

——Trend in American book illustration. (*In* International Studio, v. 82, no. 342, Nov. 1925. p. 199–202. illus.)

WROTH, L. C. AND ADAMS, M. W. American woodcuts and engravings, 1670–1800. Providence, R. I., Associates of John Carter Brown Library, 1946. 44 p.

Individual Illustrators

ABBEY, EDWIN AUSTIN. Lucas, E. V. Edwin Austin Abbey, royal academician; the record of his life and work. New York, Scribner, 1921. 2 v. illus.

ANDERSON, ALEXANDER. Alexander Anderson; his tribute to the wood-engraving of Thomas Bewick, by Lawrance Thompson. Princeton, Princeton Univ. Press, 1940. 12 p. illus.

——Burr, F. M. Life and works of Alexander Anderson. New York, Burr Brothers, 1893. 210 p. illus.

——Early American wood engravings by Dr. Alexander Anderson and others. With an introductory preface by E. A. Duyckinck. New York, Burr & Boyd, 1877. 4 p. and 66 plates.

ANGELO, VALENTI. Haas, Irving. A bibliography of the work of Valenti Angelo. (*In* Prints, June 6, 1937. illus.)

COLE, TIMOTHY. Cole, A. P. Timothy Cole: wood-engraver. New York, Pioneer Associates, 1935. 172 p. illus.

EICHENBERG, FRITZ. A lesson in book illustration. (*In* Print, v. 2, no. 2, Summer 1941. p. 1–12. illus)

FROST, A. B. Lanier, H. W. A. B. Frost, the American sportsman's artist.

New York, Derrydale Press [1933] 154 p. illus.

HOMER, WINSLOW. Foster, A. E. Check list of illustrations by Winslow Homer in Harper's Weekly and other magazines. (*In* New York Public Library Bulletin, v. 40, no. 10, Oct. 1936. p. 842–52; [Supplementary] list, v. 44, no. 7, July 1940. p. 537–39)

——Goodrich, Lloyd. Winslow Homer. New York, Pub. for Whitney Museum of American Art by Macmillan, 1944. 241 p. illus.

——Watson, Forbes. Winslow Homer; photo research and bibliography by Aimée Crane. New York, Crown Pub., [1942] 111 p. illus.

JOHNSTON, D. C. Brigham, C. S. David Claypoole Johnston, the American Cruikshank. (*In* Proceedings of the American Antiquarian Society, v. 50, 1940. p. 98–110)

KENT, ROCKWELL. Rockwellkentiana; few words and many pictures by R. K., and, by Carl Zigrosser, a bibliography and list of prints. New York, Harcourt, Brace, 1933. 64, [86] p. illus.

——This is my own. New York, Duell, Sloan and Pearce [1940] 393 p.

Rockwell Kent. New York, American Artists Group, 1945. 64 p. (Monograph no. 2)

MARTIN, HOMER. Hamilton, Sinclair. Homer Martin as illustrator. (*In* The New Colophon, v. 1, Pt. 3, July 1948. p. 256–263. illus)

MUELLER, H. A. How I make woodcuts and wood engravings. New York, American Artists, 1945. 96 p.

NAST, THOMAS. Kouwenhoven, J. A. Th. Nast as we don't know him. (*In*

Colophon, n.g.s., v. [1] no 2, 1939. p. [37]-[48] illus)

——Paine, A. B. Th. Nast; his period and his pictures. New York, Macmillan, 1904. 583 p. illus.

PENNELL, JOSEPH. Adventures of an illustrator. Boston, Little, Brown, 1925. 372 p. illus.

——Philadelphia. Free Library. Checklist of books and contributions to books by Joseph and Elizabeth Robbins Pennell, by Victor Egbert. A Pennell exhibition in the Free Library of Philadelphia, June–August 1945. [Philadelphia, 1945] 20 p.

PYLE, HOWARD. Abbott, C. D. Howard Pyle. New York, Harper, 1925. 249 p. illus.

——Morse, W. S. and Brincklé, Gertrude. Howard Pyle. Wilmington, Del., Wilmington Society of the Fine Arts, 1921. 242 p. illus.

REMINGTON, FREDERIC. McCracken, Harold. Frederic Remington, artist of the Old West; with a bibliographical check list of Remington pictures and books. Philadelphia, Lippincott, 1947. 157 p. illus.

——Vail, R. W. G. The Frederic Remington collection. (*In* New York Public Library Bulletin, v. 33, no. 2, Feb. 1929. p. 71–75. illus.)

RUZICKA, RUDOLPH. American Institute of Graphic Arts. An exhibition of the work of Rudolph Ruzicka. New York, 1935. [16] p. illus.

——Grolier Club. Engraved and typographic work of Rudolph Ruzicka; an exhibition. New York, 1948. 36 p. illus.

WARD, LYND. Haas, Irvin. A bibliography of the work of Lynd Ward. (*In* Prints, Dec. 1936, v. 7, no. 2)

WILSON, EDWARD A. Cheever, L. O. Edward A. Wilson, book illustrator; a biographical sketch, together with a check-list of his work. Muscatine, Ia., Prairie Press, 1941. 22 p. illus.

——Kittredge, W. A. The book illustration of Edward A. Wilson and a bibliography. (*In* The Colophon, pt. 11, 1932. [14] p.)

WOODBURYS. Boleman, B. A. Deephaven and the Woodburys. (*In* The Colophon, n.g.s., v. 1, no. 3, Sept. 1939. p. [17]-[24] illus)

Engravers

BAKER, W. S. American engravers and their works. Philadelphia, Gebbie & Barrie, 1875. 184 p.

FIELDING, MANTLE. Dictionary of American painters, sculptors & engravers. New York, Struck, 1945. 433 p.

GREEN, S. A. John Foster, the earliest American engraver and the first Boston printer. Boston, Massachusetts Historical Society, 1909. 149 p. illus.

LEVIS, H. C. A bibliography of American books relating to prints and the art and history of engraving. London, Chiswick Press, 1910. 78 p.

NEW YORK PUBLIC LIBRARY. One hundred notable American engravers, 1683–1850; annotated list of prints on exhibition at the New York Public Library, 1928. [New York, 1928] 38 p. illus.

STAUFFER, D. M. American engravers upon copper and steel. New York, Grolier Club, 1907. 2 v. illus.

FIELDING, MANTLE. American engravers upon copper and steel. A supplement to David McNeely Stauffer's American engravers. Philadelphia, 1917. 365 p. illus.

GAGE, T. H. An artist index to Stauffer's "American engravers." (*In* Proceedings of the American Antiquarian Society, n.s., v. 30, 1921. p. 295–341)

WEISS, H. B. William Charles, early caricaturist, engraver and publisher of children's books; with a list of works by him in the New York Public Library and certain other collections. New York, New York Public Library, 1932. 12 p. illus.

Photomechanical Reproduction

COLUMBIA UNIVERSITY LIBRARIES. Catalogue of the Epstean Collection on the history and science of photography and its applications especially to the graphic arts [foreword by Edward Epstean; introd. by Hellmut Lehmann-Haupt] New York, Columbia Univ. Press, 1937. illus.

—Authors and short title index Epstean Collection. Corrected with additions to May 1, 1938. New York, 1938.
—Accessions May 1938–Dec. 1941, with addenda 1942. New York, 1942.

EPSTEAN, EDWARD and TENNANT, J. A. Frederic Eugene Ives, 1938. p. 226–236. illus.

Reprinted from *Journal of Applied Physics,* v. 9, April 1938.

GAMBLE, WILLIAM. The beginning of halftone. A history of the process. New York, Reprinted for the U. S. A. by E. Epstean [1927?] 22 p.

—Modern illustration processes. 2d ed. New York, Pitman, 1938. 409 p. illus.

IVES, F. E. The autobiography of an amateur inventor. [Philadelphia] Priv. print., 1928. 98 p. illus.

McCABE, L. R. The beginnings of halftone; from the note books of Stephen H. Horgan. Chicago, Inland Printer [1924] [11] p. illus.

NEWHALL, BEAUMONT. History of photography from 1839 to the present day. New York, Museum of Modern Art, 1949. 256 p. illus.

TAFT, ROBERT. Photography and the American scene; a social history, 1839–1889. New York, Macmillan, 1938. 546 p. illus.

BOOKSELLING AND PUBLISHING

Periodicals

The American Bookseller. 32 v. New York, 1876–93.
A continuation of the *American Booksellers' Guide,* 1868–75.

The American Booksellers' Guide. v. 1–7; [Nov. ? 1868]–Dec. 1, 1875. New York, American News Co. [1868]–75. 7 v. illus.
Superseded by the *American Bookseller.*

The Publishers' Weekly, the American book trade journal. v. 1, 1872– New York, 1872–

Directories

American Booktrade Directory; lists of publishers, booksellers, periodicals, trade organizations, book clubs, literary agents, etc. 1915, 1919, 1922, 1925, 1928, 1932, 1935, 1939, 1942, 1946, 1949. New York, Bowker, 1915–[49] 11 v.

The booksellers and stationers trade list: containing the names of the booksellers in the United States and Canada. Published under the auspices of the N. Y. Trade Sales Association by Miller & Hopkins. New York, May 1863. 64 p.

BURKE, W. J. and HOWE, W. D., eds. American authors and books, 1640–1940. New York, Phoenix, 1943. 858 p.

Directory of Booksellers, Newsdealers and Stationers in the United States and Canada. 5th ed. Minneapolis, H. W. Wilson, 1908. 99 leaves, 10 p.

2d ed. appeared 1903 under title: *Directory of Booksellers, Stationers, Publishers and Libraries in the United States and Canada.*

Directory of Booksellers, Stationers, and Newsdealers and Music Dealers in the United States and Canada, complete to September 1st, 1869. New York, J. H. Dingman, 1869. 317 p.

On cover: "Dingman's directory" and "Dingman's booksellers directory."

Geyer's Reference Directory of the Booksellers and Stationers of the United States and Canada. New York, 1886–91.

Appeared as a sequel to *Geyer's American Paper Trade Directory.*

Literary market place, 1940– A directory for publishers, broadcasters and advertisers. New York, Bowker, 1940–

Ed. 1–10, 1940–1950. Not issued 1941.

General and Historical

ANDREWS, W. L. The old booksellers of New York, and other papers. New York, 1895. 84 p. illus.

BERELSON, BERNARD. The Library's public; a report of the Public Library Inquiry. New York, Columbia University Press, 1949. 174 p.

BLAKE, A. V. The American bookseller's complete reference trade list, and alphabetic catalogue of books published in this country, with the publishers and authors' names and prices arranged in classes for quick and convenient reference. To which is added an article on the law of copyright. Claremont, N. H., S. Ide, 1847. 232 p.

BOYNTON, H. W. Annals of American bookselling, 1638–1850. New York, J. Wiley, 1932. 209 p.

BRADSHER, E. L. Book publishers and publishing. (*In* The Cambridge history of American literature. 1917–23. v. 4. p. 533–553)

BROTHERHEAD, WILLIAM. Forty years among the old booksellers of Philadelphia. Philadelphia, A. P. Brotherhead, 1891. 122 p.

CAVANAUGH, SISTER MARY STEPHANA. Catholic book publishing in the United States. (*In* Catholic Library World, v. 10, no. 4, Jan. 1939, p. 125–128; v. 10, no. 5, 7, Feb., Apr. 1939. p. 227–232)

DERBY, J. C. Fifty years among authors, books, and publishers. New York, Carleton, 1884. 739 p. illus.

DRUCKENMÜLLER, ALFRED. Der Buchhandel der Welt. Stuttgart, C. E. Poeshel, 1935. 272 p.

"Der Buchhandel in den Vereinigten Staaten von Amerika (USA)": p. 229–272.

DUFFUS, R. L. Books, their place in a democracy. Boston, Houghton Mifflin, 1930. 225 p.

ELLSWORTH, W. W. A golden age of authors; a publisher's recollection. Boston, Houghton Mifflin, 1919. 304 p. illus.

FISHER, D. F. Books clubs. New York, New York Public Library, 1947. 49 p. (R. R. Bowker Memorial Lectures, 11)

Appeared also as Bowker Lectures on Book Publishing, ser. 3, no. 11, 1948.

FORD, W. C. The Boston book market, 1679–1700. Boston, Club of Odd Volumes, 1917. 197 p. illus.

——Henry Knox and the London Book-Store in Boston, 1771–1774. (*In* Proceedings of the Massachusetts Historical Society, v. 61, October 1927–June, 1928, p. 225–304)

HACKETT, A. P. Fifty years of best sellers, 1895–1945. New York, Bowker, 1945. 140 p.

HALLENBECK, C. T. Book trade publicity before 1800. (*In* Papers of the Bibliographical Society of America, v. 32, 1938. p. 47–56)

HARCOURT, ALFRED. Publishing since 1900. Second of the R. R. Bowker Memorial Lectures. New York, New York Public Library, 1937. 26 p.
Also appeared as the Bowker Lecture on Book publishing, 1st ser., no. 2., 1943.

HUNGERFORD, HERBERT. How publishers win; a case record commentary. Washington, D. C., Ransdell Inc. [1931] 324 p. illus.

KRAUS, H. P. Inter-American and world book trade; problems of organiz. New York, Priv. Print., 1944. 32 p.

LITTLEFIELD, G. E. Early Boston booksellers, 1642–1711. Boston, Club of Odd Volumes, 1900. 256 p. illus.

MC CORMICK, K. D. Editors today. [New York, Typophiles, 1948] p. [131]–170 (The Bowker Lectures on Book Publishing, ser. 3 [no. 12])

MC CUTCHEON, R. P. Books and booksellers in New Orleans, 1730–1830. (*In* Louisiana Historical Quarterly, v. 20, no. 3, July 1937. p. 606–18)

MELCHER, DANIEL. Young Mr. Stone, Book Publisher. New York, Dodd, Mead, 1940. 249 p.

MILLER, MERLE. Book clubs. (*In* Harper's Magazine, v. 196, May–June 1948. p. 433–40, 511–24)

MILLER, WILLIAM. The book industry. New York, Columbia University Press, 1949. 156 p. (A Report of the Public Library Inquiry)

MOTT, F. L. Golden multitudes; the story of best sellers in the United States. New York, Macmillan, 1947. 357 p.

NICHOLS, C. L. The literary fair in the United States. (*In* Bibliographical essays; a tribute to Wilberforce Eames. 1924. p. 85–92)

SILVER, R. G. The Boston book trade, 1800–1825. New York, New York Public Library, 1949. 48 p.

STOKES, F. A. Publisher's random notes, 1880–1935. First of the R. R. Bowker Memorial Lectures. New York, New York Public Library, 1935. 45 p.
Also appeared as The Bowker Lectures on Book Publishing, 1st ser., no. 1, 1943.

SUTTON, WALTER. Cincinnati as a frontier publishing and book trade center, 1796–1830. (*In* Ohio State Archaeological and Historical Quarterly, v. 56, no. 2, April 1947. p. 117–143)

WHEELER, J. T. Booksellers and circulating libraries in colonial Maryland. [1939] 111–37 p. illus.
From Maryland Historical Magazine, v. 34, no. 2, June 1939.

WHITE, L. M. Henry William Herbert & the American publishing scene, 1831–1858. Newark, N. J., Carteret Book Club, 1943. 71 p. illus.

WILSON, L. R. The geography of reading; a study of the distribution and status of libraries in the United United States. Chicago, Amer. Library Assoc. and Univ. of Chicago Press [1938] 481 p. illus.

WINTERICH, J. T. Three lantern slides, books, the book trade and some related phenomena in America: 1876, 1901, and 1926. Urbana, Ill., Univ. of Illinois [1949] 109 p.

WOODWARD, F. E. A graphic survey of book publication, 1890–1916. Washington, Govt. Print. Off., 1917. 26 p. illus.

YARD, R. S. The publisher. Boston, Houghton Mifflin, 1913. 179 p.

Books in World War II

BUTLER, PIERCE. Books and libraries in wartime. Chicago, Univ. of Chicago Press, 1945. 159 p. illus.

COUNCIL OF BOOKS IN WARTIME. History of the Council on Books in Wartime, 1942–1946. New York, The Council, 1946. 126 p.

EDITIONS FOR THE ARMED SERVICES. Editions for the Armed Services, inc.; a history by John Jamieson together with a complete list of 1324 books, pub. for American armed forces overseas. New York, 1948. 139 p.

JAMIESON, JOHN. Books for the army; the Army Library Service in the second world war. New York, Columbia University Press, 1950.

Special Publishing

CHILDREN'S BOOKS. Seaman, L. H. Books in search of children. [New York, Typophiles] 1948. p. 33–74. (The Bowker Lectures on Book Publishing, ser. 3, [no. 10])

——Weiss, H. B. Printers and publishers of children's books in New York City, 1698–1830. New York, New York Public Library, 1948. 21 p.

LAW. Brown, G. B. The practices of law publishers as they effect law libraries. [1940]
University of Illinois Library School, Master's Thesis, 1940. Typewritten.

MAPS. Bay, Helmuth. The history and technique of map making. [New York, Typophiles, 1945] p. 103–131. (The Bowker Lectures on Book Publishing, ser. 2 no. [8])

MUSIC. Ayars, C. M. Contributions to the art of music in America by the music industries of Boston, 1640–1936. New York, H. W. Wilson, 1937. 326 p. illus.
Pt. 1, Music publishing, 17th and 18th centuries; Pt. 2, Music engraving and printing.

——Dichter, Harry and Shapiro, Elliott. Early American sheet music; its lure and its lore, 1768–1889; including a directory of early American music publishers. New York, Bowker, 1941. 287 p. illus.

——Epstein, D. J. Music publishing in Chicago prior to 1871; the firm of Cady and Root, 1858–1871 [with bibliography of publications] [1943]
Univ. of Illinois, Library School, Master's Essay, 1943. Typewritten. Pub. in Music Library Association Notes, June 1944–June 1946.

——Fisher, W. A. One hundred and fifty years of music publishing in the United States, 1783–1933. Boston, Oliver Ditson Co., 1933. 146 p. illus.

——Howe, M. A. Music publishers in New York City before 1850. A directory. New York [New York Public Library] 1917. 18 p.

——Johnson, H. E. Musical interludes in Boston, 1795–1830. New York, Columbia University Press, 1943. 366 p. illus. (Columbia Univ. Studies in Musicology, no. 5)
"Publishers," p. 223–263.

——Lynn, Thelma. The history of Wm. A. Pond & Company, publishers of the music of Stephen Foster. [1948] [72] p.
Columbia University, School of Library Service, Master's thesis, Oct. 1948. Typewritten.

——Redway, V. L. Music directory of early New York City; a file of musicians, music publishers and musical instrument-makers listed in New York directories from 1786 through 1835, together with the most important New York music publishers from 1836 through 1875. New York, New York Public Library, 1941. 102 p. illus.

SUBSCRIPTION BOOKS. Compton, F. E. Subscription books. New York, New York Public Library, 1939. (R. R. Bowker Memorial Lectures, no. 4)

Also appeared as *Bowker Lectures on Book Publishing, 1st ser., no. 4, 1943.*

TECHNICAL BOOKS. Thompson, J. S. The technical book publisher in wartimes. New York, New York Public Library, 1942. 50 p. (R. R. Bowker Memorial Lectures. 7)

Also appeared as *Bowker Lectures on Book Publishing, 2nd ser., no. 7, 1945.*

TEXTBOOKS. American Textbook Publishers Institute. Textbooks in education. New York [1949] 139 p.

——Crofts, F. S. Textbooks are not absolutely dead things. Third of the R. R. Bowker Memorial Lectures. New York, New York Public Library, 1938. 28 p.

Also appeared as *Bowker Lectures on Book Publishing, 1st ser., no. 3, 1943.*

——Pulsifer, W. E. A brief account of the educational publishing business in the United States. Atlantic City, N. J., 1921. 35 p.

UNIVERSITY PRESSES. American Council of Learned Societies Devoted to Humanistic Studies. Report on American University presses, by Chester Kerr. New Haven, Conn., Assoc. of Amer. Univ. Presses, 1949. 302 p.

——Brandt, J. A. The University of every man. [New York, Typophiles, 1948] p. [3]-30. (Bowker Lectures on Book Publishing, ser. 3. no. 9)

——Day, G. P. The function and organization of University presses. New Haven, Yale University Press, 1915. 34 p.

Individual Booksellers and Publishers

AMERICAN BAPTIST PUBLICATION SOCIETY. Stevens, D. G. The first hundred years of the American Baptist Publication Society. Philadelphia [1925] 120 p. illus.

AMERICAN NEWS COMPANY. Covering a continent; a story of newsstand distribution and sales. New York, [1930] 61 p. illus.

——Serving the reading public; America's leading distributor of books, magazines, and newspapers celebrates 80 years of growth. New York, Amer. News Co. [1944] [66] p. illus.

AMERICAN TRACT SOCIETY. Thompson, Lawrance. The printing and publishing activities of the American Tract Society from 1825 to 1850. (*In* Papers of the Bibl. Soc. of Amer., v. 35, 2nd quar., 1941. p. 81-114. illus)

APPLETON-CENTURY-CROFTS. The House of Appleton-Century. New York [1936] 48 p. illus.

——Chew, S. C. Fruit among the leaves; an anniversary anthology. New York, Appleton-Century-Crofts, 1950. 555 p. illus.

——Overton, Grant. Portrait of a publisher, and the first hundred years of the house of Appleton, 1825-1925. New York, Appleton, 1925. 95 p. illus.

BARNES, A. S., AND CO. Pratt, J. B. Century of book publishing, 1838-1938. New York, 1938. 56 p. illus.

—— ——Personal recollections, sixty years of book publishing. New York, A. S. Barnes, 1942. 67 p. illus.

——Seventy-five years of book publishing, 1838–1913. New York, 1913. 31 p. illus.

BEADLE AND ADAMS. Johannsen, Albert. The House of Beadle and Adams and its dime and nickel novels. Norman, Univ. of Oklahoma Press, 1950. 2 v. illus.

BELL, ROBERT. Illuminations for legislators and for sentimentalists. Philadelphia, 1784. 52 p.

BLAKISTON COMPANY. 1843–1943. One hundred years. Philadelphia, Blakiston Co. [1943] [37] p.

BLISS, THEODORE. Theodore Bliss, publisher and bookseller; a study of character and life in the middle period of the XIX century; ed. by Arthur Ames Bliss. [Norwalk, Ohio, American Publishers' Co.] 1911. 92 p.

BOWKER, R. R., CO. Publishers' Weekly, Jan. 18, 1947. (v. 151, no. 3) The Seventy-fifth Anniversary number. New York, Publishers' Weekly, 1947. 209–362 p.

BROOKS, EDMUND D. Grove, L. E. Of Brooks and books. Minneapolis, Univ. of Minnesota Press, 1945. 85 p. illus.

BUCKINGHAM, J. T. Buckingham, J. T. Personal memoirs and recollections of editorial life. Boston, Ticknor, Reed and Fields, 1852. 2 v. illus.

CAREY, MATHEW. Autobiographical sketches. In a series of letters addressed to a friend. Philadelphia, John Clarke, 1829. 156 p.

——Bradsher, E. L. Mathew Carey, editor, author and publisher, a study in American literary development. New York [Columbia University Press] 1912. 145 p.

——Mathew Carey, autobiography. [Brooklyn, E. L. Schwaab, 1942] 134 p. illus. (Research Classics, no. 1)

——The Mathew Carey papers. Manuscript collection in the library of the American Antiquarian Society, Worcester, Mass.

——Rowe, K. W. Mathew Carey; a study in American economic development. Baltimore, Johns Hopkins Press, 1933. 140 p. (Johns Hopkins Univ. Studies in Hist. and Pol. Science, ser. LI, no. 4)

CLARKE AND CO. McMullen, C. H. Publishing activities of Robert Clarke and Company [Cincinnati] 1858–1909 [1940]
University of Illinois, Library School, Master's thesis, 1940. Typewritten.

CLEMENS, S. L. Mark Twain in eruption; hitherto unpublished pages about men and events, by Mark Twain, ed. and with an introd. by Bernard DeVoto. New York, Harper, 1940. 402 p. illus.

——Dickinson, L. T. Marketing a best seller: Mark Twain's Innocents Abroad. (*In* Papers of the Bibl. Soc. of Amer., v. 41, 2nd quar., 1947. p. 107–122)

——Webster, S. C. Mark Twain, business man. Boston, Little, Brown, 1946. 409 p. illus.

COPELAND AND DAY. Kraus, J. W. History of Copeland and Day [Boston] 1893–1899. With a list of publications [1941]
University of Illinois, Library School, Master's thesis, 1941. Typewritten.

—— ——Messrs. Copeland & Day— publishers to the 1890's. (*In* Publishers' Weekly, v. 141, no. 12, Mar. 21, 1942. p. 1168–1171. illus)
Condensed from *A History of Copeland and Day 1893–1899; with a bibliographical*

checklist of their publications, Univ. of Illinois, Master's thesis.

CROCKER AND BREWSTER. Memorial of Uriel Crocker. Born, 13th September 1796. Died 19th July 1887. [Boston, 1891] 124 p. illus.

Contains "Books published by Crocker and Brewster."

CROWELL, THOMAS Y. Thomas Young Crowell, 1836–1915; a biographical sketch. New York, Crowell, 1926. 95 p. illus.

DERBY BROTHERS. Sutton, Walter. The Derby brothers: 19th century bookmen. (*In* University of Rochester Library Bulletin, v. 3, no. 2, Winter 1948. p. 21–29)

DODD, MEAD. Dodd, E. H. The first hundred years; a history of the House of Dodd, Mead, 1839–1939. New York, Dodd, Mead, 1939. 63 p. illus.

DOUBLEDAY, DORAN. The Country Life Press, Garden City, New York. [Garden City] 1919. 268 p. illus.

——Doran, G. H. Chronicles of Barabbas, 1884–1934. New York, Harcourt, Brace [1935] 416 p. illus.

——Doubleday, Doran & Co. (*In* Fortune, v. 13, no. 2, Feb. 1936. p. 73–77, 161–72, 178–81. illus.)

——Page, W. H. A publisher's confession. New ed. New York, 1923. 245 p.

DUTTON, E. P. & COMPANY. Seventy-five years; or, The joys and sorrows of publishing and selling books at Duttons from 1852 to 1927. New York [1927] 91 p. illus.

GINN & COMPANY. [Ginn, Edwin] Outline of the life of Edwin Ginn, including his preparation for the publishing business and the establishment of Ginn & Company. [Boston, Athenaeum Press, 1908] 24 p.

——[Lawler, T. B.] George Arthur Plimpton, 1855–1936. [Boston, D. B. Updike, Merrymount Press, 1936?] [12] p.

—— ——Seventy years of textbook publishing; a history of Ginn and Company, 1867–1937. Boston, Ginn [1938] 304 p. illus.

GOMEZ, BENJAMIN. Poore, C. G. Benjamin Gomez, bookseller. (*In* The Colophon, pt. 8, 1931. [8] p. illus.)

——Vail, R. W. G. A curtain call for Benjamin Gomez. (*In* The Colophon, pt. 9, 1932. [12] p. illus.)

GOODSPEED'S BOOKSHOP. Goodspeed, C. E. Yankee bookseller; being the reminiscences of Charles E. Goodspeed. Boston, Houghton Mifflin, 1937. 325 p. illus.

GOODRICH, S. G. Recollections of a lifetime. New York and Auburn, Miller, Orton and Mulligan, 1856. 2 v. illus.

HARPER. Abbott, Jacob. The Harper establishment; or, How the story books are made. New York, Harper [1855] 160 p. illus.

——Harper, J. H. The House of Harper. New York, 1912. 689 p. illus.

—— ——I remember. New York, 1934. 281 p. illus.

——The Harper centennial, 1817–1917; a few of the greetings and congratulations. New York [1917] 106 p. illus.

——Johnson, W. F. George Harvey, 'a passionate patriot'. Boston, Houghton Mifflin, 1929. 436 p. illus.

HEATH AND COMPANY. Forty years of service; published in commemoration of the fortieth anniversary of D. C. Heath and Company. Boston [1925] 61 p. illus.

HOLT, HENRY. Garrulities of an octogenarian editor. Boston, Houghton Mifflin, 1923. 460 p. illus.

HOUGHTON MIFFLIN. A catalogue of authors whose works are published by Houghton Mifflin and Company. Prefaced by a sketch of the firm. Boston, 1899. 205 p. illus.

——Fifty years of publishing; a history of the Educational Department of Houghton Mifflin Company. [Boston, 1930] 31 p. illus.

——Of the making of books and of the part played therein by the publishing house of Houghton Mifflin Company. [Boston, 19-?] 16 p. illus.

——A portrait catalogue of the books published by Houghton Mifflin and Company; with a sketch of the firm, brief descriptions of the various departments and some account of the origin and character of the literary enterprises undertaken. Boston, 1905-06. 267 p. illus.

——Scudder, H. E. Henry Oscar Houghton. Cambridge, Riverside Press, 1897. 160 p. illus.

JENISON, MADGE. Sunwise turn; a human comedy of bookselling. New York, Dutton [1923] 162 p.

KING, SOLOMON. Weiss, H. B. Solomon King, early New York bookseller and publisher of children's books and chapbooks. New York, New York Public Library, 1947. 16 p.

KNOPF. Alfred A. Knopf; quarter century. [1940] 52 p. illus.

Contributions by Carl Van Vechten, Carl Van Doren, Willa Cather, H. L. Mencken, Thomas Mann, Henry Seidel Canby, H. M. Lydenberg, B. W. Huebsch, Adolf Kroch, F. G. Melcher.

——The Borzoi 1925; being a sort of record of ten years' publishing. New York [1925] 351 p. illus.

——Hellman, G. T. Profile: "Publisher." (*In* New Yorker, v. 24, nos. 39-41, Nov. 20, 27, Dec. 4, 1948. p. 44-57, 36-52, 40-53)

LEA & FEBIGER. Bradley, E. S. Henry Charles Lea, a biography. Philadelphia, University of Pennsylvania Press, 1931. 391 p. illus.

——One hundred and fifty years of publishing, 1785-1935. Philadelphia, 1935. 42 p. illus.

LEYPOLDT, FREDERICK. Beswick, J. W. Work of Frederick Leypoldt, bibliographer and publisher. New York, Priv. Print., Bowker, 1942. 102 p.

LIMITED EDITIONS CLUB. 10 years and William Shakespeare: a survey of publishing activities of the Limited Editions Club, from October 1929 to October 1940. [New York, A. Colish, 1940] 82 p. illus.

LITTLE BLUE BOOKS. Haldeman-Julius, Emanuel. The first hundred million. New York, Simon & Schuster, 1928. 340 p.

LITTLE, BROWN & CO. Hillard, G. S. Memoir of James Brown, with obituary notices & tributes of respect from public bodies. Boston, Priv. print., 1856. 138 p. illus.

——One hundred years of publishing, 1837-1937. Boston [1937] 83 p. illus.

LONGMANS GREEN. The house of Longman, with a record of their bicentenary celebrations, by Harold Cox and John E. Chandler, 1724-1924. London, Longmans, 1925. 94 p. illus.

LOW FAMILY. Moss, S. A. The Low Family of New York City, publishers, 1795-1829. (*In* New York Public Library Bulletin, v. 47, no. 2, Feb. 1943. p. 87-90)

MC CLURG AND CO. Morris, J. C. The publishing activities of S. C. Griggs

and Co., 1848–1896; Jansen McClurg and Co., 1872–1886; and A. C. McClurg and Co., 1886–1900; with lists of publications. [Chicago, 1941]
University of Illinois, Library School, Master's Essay, 1941.

Mc GRAW-HILL. Addresses at a dinner tendered to James H. McGraw. Printed for distribution among his friends, January, 1927. 73 p. illus.

——McGraw-Hill Book Company, Inc. The story of forty years growth. [New York, 1949] 65 p. illus.

——Twenty-fifth anniversary, 1909–1934. New York [1934] 15 p. illus.

MACMILLAN. Morgan, Charles. House of Macmillan (1843–1943) New York, Macmillan, 1944. 247 p.

MEIN, JOHN. Alden, J. E. John Mein, publisher: an essay in bibliographic detection. (*In* Papers of the Bibl. Soc. of Amer., v. 36, 3rd quar., 1942. p. 199–214)

MERRIAM. Leavitt, R. K. Noah's ark, New England Yankees, and the endless quest; a short history of the original Webster dictionaries, with particular reference to their first hundred years. Springfield, Mass., Merriam, 1947. 106 p. illus.

——100th anniversary of the establishment of G. & C. Merriam Company, Springfield, Massachusetts, 1831–1931; publishers of the Merriam-Webster dictionaries since 1843. [Springfield, 1931] 16 p. illus.

METHODIST BOOK CONCERN. Lanahan, John. The era of frauds in the Methodist Book Concern at New York. Baltimore, Methodist Book Depository, 1896. 307 p.

——Whitlock, W. F. The story of the book concerns. Cincinnati, Jennings and Pye [1903] 204 p.

OLD CORNER BOOK STORE. Mann, D. L. A century of bookselling; the story of the Old Corner Book Store. Boston, 1928. 31 p. illus.

PUTNAM. Putnam, G. H. George Palmer Putnam, a memoir together with a record of the earlier years of the publishing house founded by him. New York, 1912. 476 p. illus.

—— ——Memories of a publisher, 1865–1915. 2d ed. New York, 1916. 494 p. illus.

—— ——Memories of my youth, 1844–65. New York, 1914. 447 p. illus.

—— ——Wide margins; a publisher's autobiography. New York, Harcourt, 1942. 351 p.

——Rascoe, Burton. American reader; a centennial collection of American writings published since 1838; selected from the publications of the house of Putnam, 1838–1938. New York, Putnam, 1938. 1026 p.

ROMAN, ANTON. Stern, M. B. Anton Roman, Argonaut of books. (*In* California Historical Society Quarterly, v. 33, no. 1, Mar. 1949. p. 1–18. illus.)

SCRIBNERS. Burlinghame, R. Of making many books; a hundred years of reading, writing and publishing. MDCCCXLVI–MDCCCCXLVI. New York, Scribners, 1946. 347 p.

——Wheelock, J. H., ed. Editor to author; the letters of Maxwell E. Perkins. New York, Scribners, 1950. 315 p. illus.

SIMON AND SCHUSTER. 20,000 per cent increase. (*In* Fortune, v. 9, no. 1, Jan. 1934. p. 48–51, 100–104. illus.)

SMITH, GEORGE D. Heartman, C. F. George D. Smith. GDS, 1870–1920. A memorial tribute to the greatest bookseller the world has ever known. Beauvoir Community, Miss., Priv. Print. as a Yuletide greeting for C. F. Heartman from the Book Farm, 1945. 31 p.

SMITH, ROSWELL. Cable, G. W. A memory of Roswell Smith. [New York, De Vinne Press, 1892] 68 p. illus.

STOKES, FREDERICK A., COMPANY. The house of Stokes 1881-1926. New York, 1926. 89 p.

STONE & KIMBALL. Kramer, Sidney. History of Stone & Kimball and Herbert S. Stone & Co., with a bibliography of their publications, 1893-1905; pref. by Frederic G. Melcher. Chicago, N. W. Forgue, 1940. 379 p. illus.

TICKNOR AND FIELDS. Fields, J. T. Biographical notes and personal sketches, with unpublished fragments and tributes from men and women of letters. Boston, Houghton Mifflin, 1882. 285 p.

—— ——Yesterdays with authors. Boston, Houghton Mifflin [1900] 419 p.

——Ticknor, Caroline. Hawthorne and his publisher. Boston, Houghton, Mifflin, 1913. 339 p. illus.

——The cost book of Ticknor and Fields and their predecessors, 1832-1858. Ed. with an introd. and notes by Warren S. Tryon and William Charvat. New York, Bibl. Soc. of Amer., 1949. 508 p. illus. (Bibl. Soc. of Amer. Monograph Ser. no. 2)

——Tryon, W. S. Book distribution in mid-nineteenth century America. Illus. by the publishing records of Ticknor and Fields, Boston. (*In* Papers of the Bibliographical Society of America, v. 41, 3rd quar., 1947. p. 210-230)

—— ——The publications of Ticknor and Fields in the South, 1840-1865. (*In* Journal of Southern History, v. 14, no. 3, Aug. 1948. p. 305-330)

—— ——Ticknor and Fields' publications in the old Northwest, 1840-1860. (*In* Mississippi Valley Historical Review, v. 34, no. 4, Mar. 1948. p. 589-610)

VAN NOSTRAND, D., CO. [Crane, E. M.] A century of book publishing, 1848-1948. New York, D. Van Nostrand [1948] 73 p. illus.

WEEMS, MASON LOCKE. Mason Locke Weems; his works and ways. Ed. by Emily Ellsworth Ford Skeel. New York, 1929. 3 v. illus.

——Wroth, L. C. Parson Weems; a biographical and critical study. Baltimore, Eichelberger Book Co., 1911. 104 p. illus.

WILEY, JOHN & SONS. The House of Wiley. 2d ed. New York, Wiley, 1948. 30 p. illus.

WILSON, H. W. Lawler, John. H. W. Wilson Co.; fifty years of bibliographic publishing. Minneapolis, Univ. of Minn. Press, 1950. 207 p. illus.

WOOD, SAMUEL. Weiss, H. B. Samuel Wood & Sons, early New York publishers of children's books. New York, New York Public Library, 1942. 18 p.

WOOD, WILLIAM, AND CO. Wood, W. C. One hundred years of publishing, 1804-1904. A brief historical account of the house of William Wood and Company. New York, 1904. 29 p. illus.

Economics

BARNETT, G. E. The printers; a study in American trade unionism. Cambridge, Mass., American Economic Association, 1909. 387 p. (American Economic Association Quarterly, 3rd ser., v. 10, no. 3, Oct. 1909)

BECHTOLD, GRACE. Book publishing. Boston, Bellman Pub. Co. [1946] 24 p. (Vocational and professional monographs, no. 63)

THE BOOM in books. (*In* Fortune, v. 28, no. 5, Nov. 1943. p. 142–145, 276. illus)

BOUND, C. F. A banker looks at book publishing. New York, Bowker, 1950. 130 p.

CHARVAT, WILLIAM. Longfellow's income from his writings, 1840–1852. (*In* Papers of the Bibl. Soc. of Amer., v. 38, 1st quar., 1944. p. 9–21)

CHENEY, O. H. Economic survey of the book industry, 1930–1931; as prepared for the National Association of Book Publishers, with 1947–1948 statistical report. New York, Bowker, 1949. 382 p.

DAVIS, ELMER. Some aspects of the economics of authorship. [New York, Typophiles, 1945] p. [3]–26. (Bowker Lectures on Book Publishing, ser. 2, [no. 5])

DOZER, D. M. The tariff on books. (*In* Mississippi Valley Historical Review, v. 36, no. 1, June 1949. p. 73–96)

KRAUS, H. P. Inter-American and world book trade; problems of organization. New York, Priv. Print., 1944. 32 p.

MC GILL, ESTHER. The book trade. (*In* Seligman, E. R. A. The economics of installment selling. 1927. v. 2. p. 374–394)

NORRIS, J. L. Pioneer marketing associations of the American book trade, 1873–1901. Chicago, 1941 28 p.

Part of thesis (PH D)—Univ. of Chicago, 1938.

ROBBINS, J. A. Fees paid authors by certain American periodicals, 1840–1850. (*In* Bibl. Soc. of Univ. of Virginia. Studies in Bibliography, II, 1949/50. p. 95–104)

SHOVE, R. H. Cheap book production in the United States, 1870–1891. Urbana, University of Illinois Library, 1937. 155 p.

WATKINS, ANN. Literature for sale. [New York, The Typophiles, 1945] p. [29]–56. (Bowker Lectures on Book Publishing, ser. 2 [no. 6]

Copyright

ALLEN, N. H. Old time music and musicians. [Andrew Law] (*In* Connecticut Quarterly, v. 3, No. 1, Jan.–March, 1897, p. 66–76.

BALL, H. G. The law of copyright and literary property. Albany, Bender, 1944. 976 p.

BOWKER, R. R. Copyright; its history and its law. Boston, Houghton Mifflin, 1912. 709 p.

CLOUTMAN, B. M. and LUCK, F. W. Law for printers and publishers. 2d ed., ed. by E. H. Hale. New York and London, Staples Press, 1949. 392 p.

CONNECTICUT STATE LIBRARY. Connecticut archives. Colleges and schools, 1661–1789. 1st series. [Documents relating to Andrew Law and John Ledyard and the copyright act] II. 147, 148, 149, 150, 151, 340.

COULTER, E. M. California copyrights, 1851–1856, with notes on certain ghost books. (*In* California Hist. Soc. Quarterly, v. 22, no. 1, Mar. 1943. p. 27–40)

DEWOLF, R. C. An outline of copyright law. Boston, J. W. Luce [1925] 330 p.

EATON, A. J. American movement for international copyright, 1837–60. (*In* Library Quarterly, v. 15, no. 2, Apr., 1945. p. 95–122)

ELLINGER, W. B. Outline of the history of copyright and its principal laws. New York, 1940. 51 l.
Prepared for the School of Library Service, Columbia University. Typewritten.

EVANS, L. H. Copyright and the public interest. New York, New York Public Library, 1949. 51 p. (R. R. Bowker Memorial Lectures, 13)

GOFF, F. R. Almost books. (*In* The New Colophon, v. 1, Pt. 2, Apr. 1948. p. 125–133)

HOWELL, H. A. Copyright law; an analysis of the law on the U. S. governing registration and protection of copyright works. 2d ed. Washington, D. C., Bur. of National Affairs, 1948. 302 p.

INTER-AMERICAN CONFERENCE OF EXPERTS ON COPYRIGHT. Proceedings, Pan American Union, June 1–22, 1946. Washington, D. C., Pan American Union, 1946. 180 p. (Congress and Conference Series, no. 51)

——Final act of the Conference, Pan American Union, June 1–22, 1946. Washington, D. C., Pan American Union, 1946. 42 p.

LADAS, S. P. International protection of literary and artistic property. New York, Macmillan, 1938. 2 v.

LEONARD, R. S. Bibliographical importance of copyright records. [1946] 8 p.
Reprinted from College and Research Libraries, Jan. 1946.

NICHOLSON, MARGARET. Manual of copyright practice for writers, publishers and agents. New York, Oxford Univ. Press, 1945. 255 p.

PAN AMERICAN UNION. Inter-American convention on the rights of the author in literary, scientific and artistic works. Washington, D. C., The Union, 1946. 28 p. (Law and Treaty Ser., no. 19)

PFORZHEIMER, W. L. Copyright and scholarship. (*In* English Institute Annual, 1940. p. 164–199)

ROBERTS, M. A. Records in the Copyright Office deposited by the United States District Courts covering the period, 1790–1870. Washington, D. C., Gov't. Print. Off., 1939. 19 p. illus.

SHOEMAKER, E. C. Noah Webster, pioneer of learning. New York, Columbia Univ. Press, 1936. 347 p. illus.

SOLBERG, THORVALD. The present international copyright situation; threats of reprisal. [Washington, D. C., 1934] 28 p.

——The United States and international copyright. New Haven, Yale University Press, 1929. 13 p.

U. S. COPYRIGHT OFFICE. Copyright enactments of the United States, 1783–1906, by Thorvald Solberg. 2d ed. rev. Washington, Govt. Print. Off., 1906. 174 p.

——Copyright law of the United States of America, being the act of March 4, 1909, as amended, together with rules for practice and procedure. Washington, D. C., Gov't. Print. Off., 1942. 76 p. (Bulletin no. 14)

WITTENBERG, PHILLIP. The protection and marketing of literary property. New York, J. Messner, Inc., [1937] 395 p.
Reprint, Boston, The Writer, Inc., 1943.

Censorship

DUNIWAY, C. A. The development of freedom of the press in Massachusetts. New York, Longmans, Green, 1906. 202 p.

ERNST, M. L. The first freedom. New York, Macmillan, 1946. 316 p.

——Sex and censorship. (*In* McDermott, J. F., ed. Sex in the arts; a symposium. New York, Harper, 1932. p. 316–328)

——and Lindley, A. The censor marches on; recent milestones in the administration of the obscenity law in the United States. New York, Doubleday, 1940. 346 p.

——and Seagle, W. To the pure. A study of obscenity and the censor. New York, Viking Press, 1928. 336 p.

RUGG, H. O. That men may understand; an American in the long armistice. New York, Doubleday, 1941. 355 p.

YOUNG, KIMBALL AND LAWRENCE, R. D. Bibliography on censorship and propaganda. Eugene, The University [1928] 133 p. (Oregon University publication. Journalism series, v. 1, no. 1)

Book Auctions

AMERICAN BOOK-PRICES CURRENT. V. 1. 1894/95– New York, Bowker, 1895–

BANGS & CO. Seventy years of book auctions in New York. [New York, 1898] [6] p.

BRIGHAM, C. S. History of book auctions in America. (*In* Bulletin of the New York Public Library, v. 39, no. 2, Feb. 1935. p. 55–90).

KEESE, W. L. John Keese, wit and litterateur. New York, D. Appleton, 1883. 96 p.

LIVINGSTON, L. S. Auction prices of books. New York, Dodd, Mead, 1905. 4 v.

MCKAY, G. H. American book auction catalogues, 1713–1934; a union list. New York, New York Public Library, 1937. 540 p. illus.

—Additions. 1946.
—Supplement, no. 2. 1948.

RODEN, R. F. Auction prices of American book-club publications. Cleveland, Rowfant Club, 1904. 70 p.

ROSENBACH, A. S. W. Books and bidders. Boston, Little, Brown, 1927. 311 p. illus.

UNITED STATES cumulative book auction records, 1940/41– New York, Want List, 1941–

INDEX